THE PANORAMA
OF THE OLD TESTAMENT

by

Thomas R. Rodgers, D.Min.

Trinity Academic Press

Trinity Academic Press

World Wide Web: trinitysem.edu - Email: contact@trinitysem.edu

All Scripture quotations taken from the King James Version of the Bible.

ISBN: 978-1-7328963-3-8

Printed in the United States of America

For whatsoever things were written aforetime were written for our learning that we through patience and comfort of the Scriptures might have hope.
Romans 15:4

TABLE OF CONTENTS

Forward

Sitting outside a beachside coffee shop in the fall of 2001 I cracked open a previous iteration of the book you now hold. I was beginning my bachelors program at *Trinity College of the Bible and Theological Seminary*, had just gotten married, and had just begun serving as a senior pastor. I was going through that time of every young man's life during which he puts away childish things, or at least, knows he should. An appreciation for a drink with more coffee than cream or sugar was emerging, and along with it a desire for a much deeper understanding of the Bible. Under the Florida sun, in the shade of a palm tree, I was transported into the world of the Old Testament. *I've never been the same!*

Often, over the years, I've told young people, church members, pastors, and seminary professors that if they want to understand the Old Testament with greater clarity, this work is the resource. It is my conviction that anyone who reads it with attention will finish with an ability to speak with familiarity about each and every book, from Genesis to Malachi. For those already fascinated with Old Testament studies, this will be a genuine page-turner. It will, likely feel far too short, and leave you wishing for more. Readers who find themselves working through the material as a matter of Christian dedication, or as part of some degree program can catch the excitement of this study as well, but they may have to do their share of work to get there. The infatuation with the Old Testament, as with the whole canon of Scripture, is what I refer to as an acceptable obsession, but it is not one that comes easily to all believers. However, for such a person, if he will walk with the Lord, and prayerfully approach these pages with a desire to understand the heart of God more deeply, he will receive far more than he invests in the journey. What you learn will stay with you for the rest of your life.

It is now almost twenty years since I sat in shade of the palms, and began that journey for myself, and as recently as four months ago I preached a message from the book of Haggai titled *Get Up and Do Something!* God's people had returned from captivity, and it was time to rebuild the temple. Yet, homes, crops, and what amounted to the Israelites' financial stability was also lying in ruin, but God spoke through Haggai and urged the people that if the House of God does not come first they will not succeed in their other endeavors. Nothing else will last. Food will be eaten, clothes will get holes, and money will be spent. If they will focus on the House of God, their efforts will have lasting impact, and the day they lay its foundation they will be blessed. That sermon was written at the beachside coffeehouse back in 2001, and I've preached it, as well as other messages inspired by *The Panorama of the Old Testament*, regularly throughout my ministry.

It should be noted that the man God used to pen the book you now hold is worthy of respect for far more than what you find here. In the words of my mother, "Tom Rodgers is a true renaissance man." It is rare to discover a topic about which he does not have insights to share. So rare in fact, I've yet to find that topic. He was a pioneer of distance education, and served as the president of the aforementioned *Trinity College & Seminary*. Under his leadership, and because of his innovation, Trinity was one of the very first online institutions of higher learning. Still, this book is the symbol of his academic contributions, and is the written work for which he will be best remembered. I was proud to call him my professor, and now I'm proud to call him my colleague and friend. Tom Rodgers is a man of integrity, humility, and wisdom. He is a more than reliable guide for your journey. Are you ready to join him?

I envy the process of learning with which you are about to engage. I wish I could experience it again for the first time. It's thrilling to be able to offer it to you. I can catch a hint of that thrill when I read it even now. Suddenly I'm transported back, twenty years, to a young man being transported back thousands more. That hunger to serve God, and ambition to know His Word that existed in my younger self is with me again, and I am invigorated for what lies ahead. Now it is your turn, and regardless of your knowledge base on the subject, there is much to be gleaned. Welcome to the world of the Old Testament!

Braxton Hunter, DMin, PhD
June 2020

I. OLD TESTAMENT STRUCTURE

-INTRODUCTION-

Welcome to the study of the Old Testament. As we examine this major portion of the Word of God, what a joy it will be to watch God develop His program for Israel and Judah from the book of Genesis through the book of Malachi. What I hope to do in this study is to share with you some truths that God has been teaching me during the past years. I believe as we look at the Old Testament it may rekindle some old fires; renew some old thoughts; and that the Holy Spirit will illuminate the pages and enlighten your mind to share these truths with those to whom you minister.

Because of the nature of the study, it will be impossible to treat every book and every truth in depth. It will be impossible to make the minds of spiritual applications for every situation in the Old Testament that we should make. We will, however, look at each book and attempt to discover where it is in the Old Testament structure; where it is in the Old Testament chronology, and why God has chosen to put it there. We will look at each book from a Biblical Theological perspective and determine the religious, social, economic, and military background in which it is placed.

I trust that as we do this together, you will begin to find new areas of truth that you can preach and teach. I will also attempt to share some things that you have possibly never heard before. As we share these things together, you will be able to make your own applications.

As you begin to teach the Old Testament, it is important to instruct people about its structure in our English Bibles. As a person begins to read from Genesis through Deuteronomy, it seems to be an easy sequence. Continuing through Joshua and Judges, we suddenly find Ruth taking place during the period of Judges, and the chronology begins to get out of sequence. Samuel and Kings are in sequence. When we read Chronicles, we are thrown back in time to a previous period of history. After Ezra, Nehemiah, and Esther, we are into the books of poetry and, once again, back in the times of David and Solomon.

Finally, the major and minor prophets take us into the era of the monarchs in the books of First and second Kings.

Lately, I have noticed that some of the study programs which stress reading through the Bible in one year will take the prophets and place them back where they belong, and are beginning to take some of the books of poetry and place them where they belong in their particular periods of history. But if the student is asked to read through the Old Testament sequentially, from Genesis to Malachi the Old Testament sequence is puzzling. If we teach the Old Testament properly, we will do so as it developed chronologically.

Study Figure 1, column 1. The first five books are known as the Law (the Pentateuch, or, the Torah). This section includes Genesis, Exodus, Leviticus, Numbers, and Deuteronomy. Following these are the 12 Historical books of Joshua, Judges, Ruth, I and II Samuel, I and II Kings, I and II Chronicles, Ezra, Nehemiah and Esther. Then, sandwiched in the middle between two groups of seventeen books, are the five books of poetry: Job, Psalms, Proverbs, Ecclesiastes, and Song of Solomon. After these, are the Major Prophets: Isaiah, Jeremiah, Lamentations (written by Jeremiah), Ezekiel, and Daniel. The last twelve Old Testament books are known as the Minor Prophets: Hosea, Joel, Amos, Obadiah, Jonah, Micah, Nahum, Habakkuk, Zephaniah, Haggai, Zechariah, and Malachi.

As we look at these thirty-nine books, we see that they fall into an orderly grouping of seventeen historical books are the books of Moses and of books of history; five experiential books are the five books of poetry; and seventeen prophetical books. The five poetic books, which deal with the individual human heart and are experiential in nature, are placed between the two groups of seventeen, at the very heart of the Old Testament.

At least thirty writers contributed to the Old Testament. Their lives were spaced out over at least one thousand years. They wrote in different places. They wrote to different people, to different nations, for different purposes. During the time of their writings, they did not dream that besides being preserved through the generations, their writings would eventually be compiled into this systematic, organized grouping which we now call the Old Testament. Can we really believe this occurred by accident? The Old Testament was designed by God and presented to us in a manner we can understand, and it becomes for us our guide for faith and practice. As Paul says in Romans 15:4: *For whatsoever things were written aforetime were written for our learning, that we through patience and comfort of the Scriptures we might have hope.*

The Old Testament will teach us what God expects of man. It will show us the various ways in which man can respond to God. It will show us how God treats nations, what God expects from nations, and how the nations in the Old Testament reacted to God. All of this will become a learning experience for us that we might better understand the One Who has created us and called us into His service.

Under these five headings (noted above), we have the history of Israel and Judah from Abram, to Malachi in 400 B.C. The history of the Jewish people from Abram through the time when Nehemiah rebuilt the walls of Jerusalem is contained in the books of law and history. The others: the five books of poetry and the seventeen major and, minor, prophets, are also part of this same historic setting with two exceptions: Malachi was written after Nehemiah and the events in Job may be during, or, precede the time of Abraham.

By the time we have read the Old Testament from Genesis through Nehemiah, we have completed the period of history from creation to 432 B.C. When we get to Esther, the books of poetry, and the major and, minor, prophets, we are entering into writings that cover the same time period as the books of history. When we put this across to the average reader, the design and of the Old Testament will be understood.

When we examine the books of law and history, we see that they were written for the purpose of presenting the historical aspects of God's program for Israel and Judah and the Gentile nations. They were written from the perspective of the historian, and in many cases were written after the fact. That is, the books were written by a later author under the inspiration of the Holy Spirit, looking back into time and recording by divine guidance God's program and purpose, and the activities of Israel and Judah during some preceding time period. When we get into the major and minor, prophets, we are reading books written by on-site observers.

As I look at these two types, I can see the books of history as having been written by historians. The historian is interested in facts and figures; he is interested in sweeping events of history and how they impacted upon the northern and southern kingdoms. When I read the prophets, I feel as though I am reading something written by an on the site reporter, as if I am watching satellite television and seeing a
Reporter, or, news commentator, standing in the Middle East giving us an on-site evaluation of what he sees, hears, and feels. The prophet was a news analyst; God's chosen man delivering a message and analyzing the responses of the people.

Is Our Old Testament Complete?

Is the Old Testament that we have God's divine Word? Does the Old Testament, contain all of God's Word as He delivered it in the Old Testament period? Are these thirty-nine books all of the books that God inspired in Old Testament times, or are there more? Are there proofs that allow us to know for certain that the thirty-nine books in our Bible are the complete Old Testament Word of God?

If there are more than thirty-nine, and if in fact some of the Apocryphal books should be in our Old Testament, then we must face several problems. For example, in Baruch 3:4, we read that God hears the prayers of the dead. Other passages would require us to accept soul sleep, purgatory, and other theological difficulties. It is necessary, to know, beyond any doubt, that our thirty-nine books contain the entire inspired Old Testament Word of God. Using logic and analysis we can discover this to be true.

The Hebrew Old Testament

Look at Luke 24:44. This is our risen Lord speaking, and he said:

And he said unto them, These are the words which I spoke unto you while I was yet with you, that all things must be fulfilled, which were written in the law of Moses, and in the prophets, and in the psalms, concerning me.

Law, prophets, writings (Psalms), the words of our risen Lord show that He recognized the three divisions which the Jews of New Testament times referred to as "Scripture." The Jews, in our Lord's time, recognized these three divisions as containing the entire body of Old Testament truth: the Law, the prophets, and the psalms (writings). This is the testimony of Flavius Josephus. Josephus was a Jewish historian, who lived from A.D. 37 to sometime after A.D. 97. He was a priest-historian. So, in the matter of analysis of Scripture, Josephus should not have made a mistake because he was skilled and trained in knowing what his people believed to be "Scripture." Quoting from, *Against Apion*, I, 8:

For we [that is, the Jews] have not an innumerable multitude of books among us, disagreeing from and contradicting one another, as the Greeks have, but only twenty-two books, which contain the records of all the past times; which are justly believed to be divine; and of them five belong to Moses, which contain his laws and the traditions of the origin of mankind till his death. The interval of time was little short of three thousand years; but as to the time from the death of Moses till the reign of Artaxerxes king of Persia,

THOMAS R. RODGERS

who reigned after Xerxes, the prophets, who were after Moses, wrote down what was done in their times in thirteen books. The remaining four books contain   hymns to God, and precepts for conduct of human life.

How can we compare our thirty-nine books with the twenty-two mentioned by Josephus? Figure 1, column 2 in the Appendix shows the original Jewish arrangement of the Old Testament. The Jew recognized the first grouping, Genesis, Exodus, Leviticus, Numbers, and Deuteronomy: five books. The second grouping, called the Prophets, as also mentioned by our Lord, contained two sections: Section one, the former prophets: Joshua, Judges and Ruth (one book), I and II Samuel (one book), I and II Kings (one book), for a total of four books. The second section known as the latter prophets, contained Isaiah, Jeremiah-Lamentations (one book), Ezekiel, and the Twelve (the minor prophets as one book), a total of four books.

In the third grouping, the Psalms or Writings, was included: Psalms, Proverbs, Job, Song of Solomon, Ecclesiastes, Esther, Daniel (who was a statesman), Ezra-Nehemiah (one book), I and II Chronicles (one book), for a total of nine books. There are nine books in the Writings, four in the Latter Prophets, four in the Former Prophets and five in the Law, for a total of twenty two books. The twenty-two books in Josephus, the twenty-two books contained in the three divisions of Law, Prophets, and Psalms, mentioned by the Lord Jesus, exactly equal the thirty nine books in our Old Testament. There is an additional proof that our thirty nine books comprise the entire Old Testament. Look at Luke 11:51 where our Lord is speaking to the religious leaders:

From the blood of Abel unto the blood of Zecharias, which   perished between the altar and the temple; verily I say unto   you, it shall be required of this generation.

The impact of our Lord's statement can hardly be underestimated. The record of the martyrdom of Zechariah is contained in II Chronicles 24:20-23. This historical event took place in 797 B.C. Therefore, our Lord has said that all of the blood, shed from the murder of Abel, just after the creation of Adam, down to the blood of Zechariah would be required of that current generation.

If we look more closely, we will see that a problem exists. Evidently, our Lord means to add impact to His message by including the blood of *all* the prophets. Yet, if we turn to Jeremiah 26:20-23, we will find that there was a prophet martyred at a later date than the death of Zechariah. Urijah was a prophet slain during the time of Jeremiah, in 600 B.C. Did our Lord not intend to include the death of Urijah?

7

If we examine the structure of the Jewish Old Testament, we will see that the first book, according to their structure, was Genesis and the last was Chronicles. Just as our first is Genesis and the last is the book of Malachi. The murder of Urijah, in the book of Jeremiah, is contained earlier in the Jewish texts than it is in ours. Therefore, our Lord's statement, *"from Abel to Zecharias,"* was not a chronological statement meaning "from Abel to 797 B.C.," it was a literary statement meaning "from the first death recorded in Genesis to the last death recorded in Chronicles," from the first book to the last book, the bloodshed by all the prophets in Scripture, Genesis to Chronicles, shall be required of this generation! In the substructure of His thought, in a very subtle way, the Lord Jesus is confirming to us that these twenty-two books, Genesis to Chronicles, which are equivalent to our thirty-nine books of Genesis to Malachi, contain the entire Word of God and can be exclusively called "Scripture."

II. CHRONOLOGY AND SCRIPTURE

How did the Old Testament individual understand when he lived? Could he say, "My name is Amos and I'm living at 767 B.C.?" Could Jeremiah have said, "My name is Jeremiah and I'm living in 600 B.C.?" They had no idea when Christ would be born. They had a hope of the Messiah, but they could not place themselves chronologically relative to our terminology of B.C. and A.D. They had to use more relevant means of identification. They said, *two years before the earthquake."* They would say: "I am here during the reign of Jotham, Ahaz, Hezekiah, and Jeroboam." They would write, as Isaiah did in Isaiah 6:1: *"In the year that King Uzziah died."* They might write, as did the author of I Kings: *"In the fourth year of Solomon's reign."* So the terminology used by Old Testament individuals, as they attempted to explain when they were present and on the scene, would be in terms of catastrophes, current events, or the reigning years of the monarchs in power.

Assyrian Chronology

As we look in the Old Testament, we can understand its Structure, relevant to sequences and chronology. Not only do we have genealogies and historical events which can be dated, there is extant evidence which allows us to measure Old Testament chronology against a secular historical sequence. This is the Assyrian Eponym List. This is a list of officials after whom the years were named. It was a custom, in the time of the Assyrians, to name a year after a king, a cup-bearer, a field marshal, a high chamberlain, a governor, and so on. Each solar year was given a different name. The man after whom the year was named was the Eponym and the year was the *eponymous* year.

Thanks to archaeology, we have a list of consecutive Eponyms dating from 892 B.C., to 648 B.C. These eponym tablets list many important events, some of which are contained in the biblical records. An example is the Eponym list which says there was a revolt in the city of Ashur, in the month of Simanu, during which time an eclipse of the sun occurred. Astronomers now know this eclipse occurred on June 15, 763 B.C. We now have an "anchor point" for dating the Old Testament. By locking into that date and looking at the Eponyms who are listed on down through the years, we learn several important things. We can secure the date of 853 B.C. for the battle of Qarqar. We know from the Assyrian records, that it involved Shalmaneser, III; that it was a battle between the Assyrians and the Syrians; and that Ahab was present at that battle. We also know that Ahab died in 853 B.C. during a battle in which he asked Jehoshaphat to join him against Syria (I Kings 22:1-35). Twelve years later there is a reference to the occasion when Jehu paid tribute to the Assyrians. The year was 841 B.C. Scripture chronology shows exactly twelve years between the death of Ahab and the ascent of Jehu to the throne. The Assyrian eponym list shows exactly twelve years between the battle of Qarqar and the time when Jehu gave tribute to the Assyrians. Also, according to Assyrian chronology, there were 152 years between the sixth year of Shalmaneser, and the time that Sennacherib invaded Jerusalem in 701 B.C. This was Hezekiah's fourteenth year as recorded in II Kings 18:13: *Now in the fourteenth year of king Hezekiah did Sennacherib king of Assyria come up against all the fenced cities of Judah, and took them.*

We now have extra-biblical evidence which will enable us to take our biblical chronology and match it against secular chronology. Dating is no longer an exercise in guesswork. We have historical proof from extant discoveries that verify and validate the chronology as the Old Testament presents it. Our Old Testament chronology is flawless and is now substantiated by historical evidences.

Old Testament Dating

The study of Old Testament chronology is paramount to our understanding of the truths contained in these thirty-nine books. Without knowledge of chronology, without good insight as to when events took place, and of the sequences and relationships between major events, we have no comprehension of the flow of history as it is contained in the Old Testament. The study of chronology is a necessary facet of theological education because only with a grasp of chronology and sequences, can we understand the flow and continuity of the Word of God. Without knowledge of when the prophets lived, without knowledge of when the invasions and dispersions and major military events took place, we have no way of knowing what many of the prophecies meant.

Knowledge of chronology becomes an important and vital apologetic for the historical accuracy of the Old Testament. Many see Old Testament prophecy as history revisited in retrospect. Many statements which we see as prophetic, the critics will say were written after the fact by men who reported previous events in a historical context. Many critics do not want to admit that God, in His sovereignty, omniscience, and omnipotence, has the power to make a prophetic statement regarding entire nations or individuals, and then bring it to pass at some time in the future. It is important to know what was said when, and what occurred when, to recognize the time gap which is necessary to add credence to the prophecy and its fulfillment. For an example of this, look at Isaiah 44:28:

> *That saith of Cyrus, He is my shepherd, and shall perform all   my pleasure: even saying to Jerusalem, Thou shalt be built;   and to the temple, thy foundation shall be laid.*

Without a knowledge of chronology, we would read this statement, possibly understand it as prophetic, or possibly not. However, by understanding when Isaiah lived, when these other events took place, and the current situation in Jerusalem and Judah, we will better understand the prophetic impact of this statement.

Isaiah records, in Isaiah 6:1, that he began his official prophetic office in the year of King Uzziah's death. We know historically, and
Chronologically, that Uzziah died in 739 B.C. This means that Isaiah, a young man at that time, began his prophetic ministry in 739 B.C. By the wildest stretch of our imaginations we cannot anticipate Isaiah having been on the scene for more than eighty years, at the most, after the year of King Uzziah's death. Acknowledging Uzziah's death in 739 B.C., if we stretch the ministry of Isaiah to eighty years (tradition records that he was martyred during the reign of Manasseh) we would end at approximately 660 B.C. as the longest possible time Isaiah could have lived as a prophet.

Using this maximum assumption of eighty years, we have to examine the biblical record and see what the situation was in Jerusalem between the years 739 and 660 B.C. We know that Jerusalem was still intact; we know the northern kingdom had been dispersed in 721 B.C.; we know that the worship system in the temple, although idolatrous at the time, was at least still in full vigor. So as Isaiah stood on the scene and made this statement contained in 44:28, the on-looker must have thought he was hallucinating because Isaiah was describing a scene that did not exist. As his listeners looked around they saw a Jerusalem with a thriving economy, and a temple with a full complement of worship systems and rituals. What could Isaiah have been talking about when he wrote in 44:28, "*Thou shalt be built*" (referring to the city), and, "*thy foundation shall be laid,*" (referring to the temple). The city was already built and the temple foundations were there to see.

Isaiah was looking with a spiritual, prophetic eye down through history, to that time in 586 B.C., at least seventy to eighty years later, after his death, when Nebuchadnezzar would breach the wall of Jerusalem during his third invasion, sack and destroy it, and burn the temple. With his spiritual eye, Isaiah saw a ravaged Jerusalem and a destroyed temple.

Then he looked beyond that to the year 539 B.C., when Cyrus gave the command that the temple should be rebuilt and that the city should be restored. In 539 B.C., this becomes a historic event which is confirmed in II Chronicles 36:23:

> *Thus saith Cyrus king of Persia, All the kingdoms of the earth hath the Lord God of heaven given me; and he hath charged me to build him an house in Jerusalem, which is in Judah.*

As we study the Old Testament, we will see that when God makes a prophecy and then brings it to pass, He always separates the prophecy and fulfillment with substantial time and includes a complexity of events so that we cannot misconstrue the fulfillment of the prophecy as coincidental. Yet, if we do not know when Isaiah lived, if we do not know the date for Isaiah 6:1, if we do not know the date in relation to the invasion of Nebuchadnezzar and the later command of Cyrus to rebuild the temple, the prophetic message and the prophetic importance of Isaiah 44:28 are meaningless and lost because we have no awareness of the gaps of time or sequences.

To understand fulfillment, and the relationship of the two, knowledge of chronology and sequences of events in the Old Testament is absolutely mandatory. Examine your current knowledge and imagine your answers to someone who asks: "When did Abram leave Ur? When was Moses born? When did Isaac die? When did Jacob stand before Pharaoh? What is the date of the Exodus? When was Saul crowned king? When did David die? When did the kingdom divide? When did Nebuchadnezzar invade Judah? When did Nehemiah rebuild the wall?" We need a key verse to know the dates of Old Testament events.

The Key Verse

The most important verse for our study of Old Testament chronology is I Kings 6:1. The author of I Kings, under the inspiration of the Holy Spirit, gives us an anchor point for our dating. Many critics believe that 480 years is another way of saying twelve generations of forty years. I do not believe this is the case. God has given us a specific number of years which we can use for an accurate dating system. Look at I Kings 6:1:

> *And it came to pass in the four hundred and eightieth year after the children of Israel were come out of the land of Egypt, in the fourth year of Solomon's reign over Israel, in the month Zif, which is the second month, that he began to build the house of the Lord.*

Several important facts are contained in this verse. (1) It is in the fourth year of Solomon's reign. (2) It is the year in which he began to build the temple. (3) It has been 480 years since the Exodus. We know from internal and external evidence, that this fourth year is 966 B.C. Because it is 966 B.C., we know that Solomon was crowned king in 970 B.C. We also know that David reigned forty years. He was Solomon's predecessor and was crowned king over Judah in 1010 B.C. Since we also know that Saul reigned for forty years (Acts 13:21), he was crowned king in 1050 B.C. Therefore, I Kings 6:1 becomes a very important anchor date for our knowledge of Old Testament chronology. Not only does it help in the years which followed Solomon's reign, it helps in the years preceding it.

Archaeology has helped us to understand the period of time during which the patriarchs lived. We often use terms such as "patriarchal age" without really knowing when that age was. Now we know from discoveries such as the Ugaritic tablets, the Ebla tablets, the Mari tablets, and many other discoveries, what the social, spiritual, religious, military, economic situation was which existed during the time of the patriarchs. You can Google these for more information.

It will be a good experience if we go through an exercise in dating which you can use with those who are interested in a deeper knowledge of the Word of God and the chronology of the Old Testament. Understanding that I Kings 6: 1, "*in the fourth year of Solomon's reign,*" was 966 B.C., and that the verse tells us it had been 480 years since the Exodus, we can add 966 and 480 to get the number 1446. Now we have a firm date for the Exodus, 1446 B.C.

Look at Exodus 12:40: "*Now the sojourning of the children of Israel, who dwelt in Egypt, was four hundred and thirty years.*" By adding 430 years to our date of 1446 for the Exodus, we discover that the time when the children of Israel began their sojourn in Egypt was 1876 B.C. This was the date when Jacob moved to Egypt. As we continue to move back in time, we turn next to Genesis 47:9:

And Jacob said unto Pharaoh, The days of the years of my pilgrimage are an hundred and thirty years: few and evil have the days of the years of my life been, and have not attained unto the days of the years of the life of my fathers in the days of their pilgrimage.

The sojourn of the children of Israel in Egypt began when Jacob stood before Pharaoh. Jacob, you recall, was called to Egypt by his son Joseph so that he could escape with his family from the famine then present in Canaan. Jacob makes the statement to Pharaoh in Genesis 47:9, that he is 130 years of age at that time. This is an important piece of information for us. If we know that Jacob stood before Pharaoh in 1876 B.C., and that he was 130 years old, we know he was born in the year 2006 B.C. By using this piece of information, we next turn to Genesis 25:26, where we read:

> *And after that came his brother out, and his hand took hold on Esau's heel; and his name was called Jacob: and Isaac was threescore years old when she bare them.*

So now we learn that when Jacob and this twin brother Esau were born, Isaac was sixty years old. Since Jacob's birth took place in 2006 B.C., Isaac was born in 2066 B.C. Back in Genesis 21:5, we learn: *"And Abraham was an hundred years old, when his son Isaac was born unto him."* Now we know that Abram was born in the year 2166 B.C. This changes our previous opinion of the type of individual Abram was when he left Ur, because archaeologists now know that in the twenty-second century B.C. Ur was a thriving metropolis. Abram, living in Ur, was not an uncultured individual but was a highly cultured, sophisticated man, accustomed to urban dwelling in one of the largest civilizations of the twenty-second century B.C. Let's add one more date to our search by turning to Genesis 12:4: *So Abram departed, as the Lord had spoken unto him; and Lot went with him: and Abram was seventy and five years old when he departed out of Haran.* This proves Abram left Haran for Canaan in the year 2091 B.C. There are many more things we can do with a chronological study.

Through the balance of this book we will look at some of the various dates as they impact on the topic. Now, possibly for the first time, you have a little better knowledge about the duration of the patriarchal period. If we assume the patriarchal period to cover the interval from the time when Abram left Haran until the time when the children of Israel entered Egypt, the span is from 2091 B.C. to 1876 B.C. However, some see the patriarchal period as extending from the time when Abram left Haran in 2091 B.C. to the death of Joseph in Genesis 50:26, in the year 1805 B.C. If we accept this latter span, we have a period of 286 years. Both are valid. See Fig. 2 in the Appendix.

III. THE CENTRAL THEME

Before considering each of the Old Testament books in detail, it is necessary to dig a little deeper. We cannot understand the Old Testament message until we have recognized its primary continuing theme. There is a crimson thread of redemption that runs throughout its pages and with the Messiah in the New Testament. The beginning of the promise and the crimson thread is Genesis 3:15 where, following Adam's sin and fall, God makes this statement:

And I will put enmity between thee and the woman, and between thy seed and her seed; it shall bruise [or crush] thy head, and thou shalt bruise his heel.

It was a declaration of war made to Satan, following the transgression of Adam, and it set the stage for the conflict between God and Satan that would follow throughout the Old Testament period. In fact, until the culmination promised through John in the book of Revelation. Because of this promised Redeemer (Messiah) the prophesied Seed of the woman, which would crush the head of Satan, Satan used every means possible to see that the prediction made in Genesis 3:15 would not come to pass.

John Milton, in his iconic poem, *Paradise Lost*, includes Satan's response after his fall. {See Isaiah 14:12 and Luke 10:18}

> *What though the field be lost?*
> *All is not lost, the unconquerable will,*
> *And study of revenge, immortal hate*
> *To wage by force or guile eternal war*
> *Irreconcilable, to our grand Foe,*
> *Who now triumphs, and in the excess of joy*
> *Sole reigning holds the tyranny of Heaven.*

With those words, fictitiously placed in the mouth of Satan, the stage is set for the battle and the conflict which will follow. God has no possibility of losing the battle, but Satan will do all in his power to try to defeat God and attempt to foil the promise made in Genesis 3:15. Throughout our study, we will see how over and over the sovereign God achieves victory and glory for Himself from every effort of Satan to destroy the Messianic line.

Adam's responsibility was to pass on the truth of God to the succeeding generations. He failed at this, and as a result the world became so wicked that God had to destroy everything which had breath. However, had God destroyed the entire world, then the promise made in Genesis 3:15 could never have been fulfilled.

Scripture tells us that *Noah found grace in the eyes of the Lord,* and through Noah and his descendents the promised line continued. It became Noah's responsibility to pass on to his sons the truth of God. Unfortunately, after several generations, the truth became diluted and mankind became idolatrous and gathered around the Tower of Babel. At that time, God confused their language and they began to establish civilizations around the earth.

Every attempt at preserving a godly line through which to bring the Savior and fulfill the plan of redemption, had so far apparently resulted in failure; man's failure, not God's. But God will not be defeated regardless of what men do. He next reached down and selected Abram as the one through whom the promised Seed of Genesis 3:15 would continue. From a promise made worldwide, which Satan had attempted to thwart, through the death of Abel, through the corruption of all mankind prior to the flood, through the rebellion of all mankind at the tower of Babel, the promise now focused on one man: Abram.

The promise was renewed through Abraham's son Isaac. It was again confirmed, not through Esau but through Jacob. It did not pass to Jacob's first-born because Satan managed to corrupt him and cause him to commit incest with Jacob's concubine. Nor did it pass to his second or third-born sons, Simeon and Levi, because Satan placed in them a spirit of murder and revenge. Through the fourth-born son, Judah, the promise continued, and down through his lineage. Finally it focused on David (II Sam. 7), and in David's descendants, culminating in the birth of Christ.

We can trace throughout the Old Testament, the crimson thread of redemption as it weaves and winds its way through history. As we study we will see how God continually thwarted the plans, guile, overt and covert actions of Satan, to destroy the Seed, as he maneuvered to make it impossible for the promise of Genesis 3:15 to be realized. But, as we shall see throughout this book, Satan failed and God caused the wrath of Satan to bring honor to His name. It will be a glorious thing to see God constantly victorious in the plan of redemption, in the program of the Messiah, and in the continuation of the promised Seed, regardless of opposition, down to that day when, as Galatians 4:4 records: *"When the fullness of time was come, God sent forth His Son,"* Who completed His victory on the cross and in His resurrection, and who is even now performing His current session in heaven making intercession.

Along with watching this warfare being waged, we will have a sub-plot to follow as we see God continue His program through His chosen people, Israel, using them as the means through which the Messiah would come. Throughout the Old Testament, we will see that God is continually pleading with His stubborn people to return to Him. The Old Testament will be an on-going saga of the failure of the children of Israel to obey the ordinances of God, until at last God has no other alternative than to disperse the ten northern tribes in 722 B.C., and finally to send the inhabitants of Judah into Babylonian Captivity in 586 B.C.

IV. A BIBLICAL CHRONOLOGY

A chronology of the Old Testament books will complete our overall picture. You may find it helpful to make a few notations in your Bible as you study. Many Bibles already contain the old James Ussher dating system and, in many instances, this is a good chronology. However, in the 17th Century Bishop Ussher did not have the benefit of the archaeological discoveries which we have, and the Eponym List which is was discovered. The dating system I have given you is used by most conservative Bible scholars.

The Day-age Theory

Rather than have one day a twenty-four hour day, the proponents of this theory believe that the day could have been a million years. Rather than having six literal twenty-four hour days, each "day" involved a period of time that could have been 6,000,000 or 60,000,000 years, or whatever seems necessary (by evolution) to complete the creation in each day, in Genesis 1.

The Revelatory Day Theory

Another position, although not widely held, is that of the revelatory day theory. This teaching suggests that, rather than a twenty-four hour day in which the actual creative activity began God gave Moses the events of creation in six days of revelation. So, on the first revelatory day, God would have said: "I am giving you this information, Moses." On the second revelatory day He gave him the next information to write; on the third day the next information, and so on. These days were not creative days, but six successive days in which God spoke to Moses about the creation of the universe.

The Gap Theory

Another widely held position is the gap theory. According to this theory, the earth was created (Gen. 1:1) and later judged (Gen. 1:2), so that what we have in Genesis 1:3 is the recreation of a previously created earth. This theory was a response to the "scientific" position that claims we are living on an earth which is millions or billions of years old. It is one way of acknowledging the possibility of the many layers of fossils in the geologic column.

The Young Earth Position

Finally, the current position, popularized by Dr. Henry Morris and displayed in the full size Ark in Kentucky, is the "biblical model", in which the earth not more than eight to ten thousand years old, created perfect ("very good") in the beginning. Then, following Adam's sin, the earth came under God's curse. According to this model, no major changes occurred in the surface of the earth until the universal flood. At that time, the fountains of the deep were broken up and the vapor canopy caved in, causing the upheavals which we can observe in the Grand Canyon and the mountain ranges. This "flood geology" explains fossils of fish in the geologic column that can be observed in the arctic regions and Antarctica because of the weight of water which covered the earth. Because of God's six literal days of creation, the vapor canopy which surrounded the earth prior to the flood, the earth was so different from what we see today, that there is no scientific method which can be used to accurately measure the age of anything on the earth today that existed prior to the flood. Carbon 14 and strontium testing are considered to be invalid.

Reading from Genesis 1:1, to the final section of Genesis chapter 50, we go from eternity past (approximately 8,000 B.C., depending on one's position), to the death of Joseph, which can be shown by tracing the chronologies in Genesis, to be 1805 B.C. The book of Exodus begins in 1876 B.C., in flashback, because Exodus 1: 1includes the names of those who came into Egypt with Jacob. Chapter 1 covers that time period from 1876 until the birth of Moses recorded in chapter 2. We read in Acts 7, that Moses was forty when he fled from Egypt. Then, he spent forty years in Midian. He was eighty years old when he led Israel out of bondage.

We can look ahead at Deuteronomy 34:7, and see that Moses died at the age of 120. This reveals that the life of Moses was divided into three periods of forty years each. Using our previous information about the date of the Exodus, we can date the birth of Moses at 1526 B.C. From Exodus 2:1, to Exodus 3:2, eighty years transpired. Then, from the night of the Passover, until the tabernacle was set up at the end of the book of Exodus, thirteen months elapsed.

Turning to Exodus 40:17, we see that by this time the children of Israel had left Egypt and gone down into Sinai; Moses made his two trips up on Mount Horeb; and the tabernacle was constructed. Verse 17 tells us that following all these events, it is only the first month of the second year. So, approximately thirteen months have elapsed between the exodus from Egypt and the end of the Exodus. You can put a date of approximately 1445 B.C. beside Exodus 40:17.

Leviticus has no chronology. One month transpired between what we examined in Exodus and the movement indicated and initiated in the book of Numbers. If you will look at Numbers 1 you will see that in verse 1, it is the first of the second month in the second year after they have come out of the land of Egypt. So, the book of Numbers begins in the second year after the exodus and covers a period of about thirty-nine years.

Exodus ended in 1445 B.C., and book of Numbers begins with that year. The death of Moses occurred in 1406 B.C. With this date, the wanderings were over, because Deuteronomy 1:3 tells us that forty years have elapsed. You can write alongside the book of Deuteronomy, and especially at 34:7, the date, 1406 B.C.

The book of Joshua began in 1406 B.C. when the leadership passed to him from Moses. From internal evidence, it appears that the vents in the book required about twenty-one years. Date the end of Joshua at 1385 B.C.

The book of Judges begins immediately after the death of Joshua. Again from internal evidence, which we will see later when we examine the book in detail, the time period lasted approximately 335 years. Those years include the book of Ruth. Judges can be dated from approximately 1385 to 1050 B.C.

The book of I Samuel begins in 1100 B.C. Although not obvious, there is a fifty year overlap between the end of Judges and the beginning of I Samuel. I Samuel covers a time span from the birth of Samuel in 1100, to the death of Saul in 1010 B.C., for a total of ninety years. II Samuel begins in 1010 and covers almost forty years of history until approximately 975 B.C.

I Kings began in 970 B.C. As an easy method of remembering, it ends with the death of Ahab, in 853 B.C. It does include a year or two following Ahab's death, but approximately 117 years are contained in the book. Using the death of Ahab as the pivotal point, II Kings takes up the history beginning in 853 B.C. and continues until 586 B.C., using the Babylonian Captivity as a memory aid for the termination of II Kings. Between these two historical events are 260 years of history. I Chronicles begins with a genealogical beginning with Adam. II Chronicles begins with King Solomon and includes forty-seven more years of history than II Kings.

Following the Babylonian captivity, Ezra writes the history of Judah from 539 B.C. to 457 B.C. for an additional eighty-two years. We have no book which covers the history of Judah from 457 to 445, so this leaves twelve years unaccounted for. Nehemiah picks up the history in 445/444 B.C. By adding these years we have 962 total years of history. This number, when subtracted from 1406 B.C., the date of the entrance into Canaan as recorded in Joshua, provides us with 444 B.C. as the date for Nehemiah and the rebuilding of the wall of Jerusalem. The dates fit like a completed jigsaw puzzle!

Following this event, Malachi records the final bit of history regarding Judah in his book which dates to approximately 400 B.C. So, the writing of the Old Testament took place beginning with Moses, 1446, to approximately 400 B.C., with the book of Malachi.

V. FOUNDING THE COVENANT NATION

The story of the covenant nation, through whom the promised Seed will come, began with Abraham. Originally, his name was Abram, and he was called by God out from Ur of the Chaldees. An examination of Genesis 11:26 shows that Abram had two brothers named Nahor and Haran. Haran was the father of Lot, Abram's nephew. Abram's other brother, Nahor, was the father of Bethuel, who became the father of Rebekah and Rebekah's brother Laban, the father of Leah and Rachel. This is the family linage that included Abram, his son Isaac, grandson Jacob, and the offspring of his two brothers Nahor and Haran. See fig. 3a in the Appendix.

The Abrahamic Covenant

Genesis, Chapters 13 through 15, contains the Abrahamic Covenant. This covenant constitutes the promise to Abram of a seed that would be too great to number and a land on which his seed would dwell. It is a promise almost too fantastic to believe, because when it was given, Abram was advanced in years and had no natural offspring through Sarai. The Scripture tells us (Gen. 15:6) that Abram believed the Lord and He counted it to him for righteousness.

We must not lose sight of the fact that Abram was a Chaldean; having been one for seventy-five years prior to the time he entered the land of Canaan. Granted, in the last few years before his entry into Canaan, God had begun to work through him and in him to condition him for service. But culturally Abram was a Chaldean.

When covenants were made in ancient Chaldea and throughout that part of the civilized world, they were affirmed and validated by the death of an animal or, depending on the importance of the covenant, a number of animals. Abram's question to God, when God presented the agreement and covenant to him regarding the seed and the land, is phrased in 15:8 where Abram asked, *"Lord God, whereby shall I know that I shall inherit it?"* In response, beginning in verse 9, God condescended to make a Chaldean covenant with the Chaldean Abram. Isn't it wonderful and marvelous how patient God is? The Creator of the universe is making a Chaldean covenant with His servant Abram, a covenant that Abram could understand.

When God began to instruct Abram to gather the animals together, Abram understood the sanctity and the importance of this covenant because of the number of animals being gathered to ratify it. In those days, when covenants were made, an animal was divided into two pieces and the two parties making the covenant walked between the divided portions of the animal. In this way, each party to the covenant was saying to the other, "If you fail to bring about your responsibility in the covenant that we have agreed on, may this very thing happen to you."

In chapter 15, God instructed Abram to divide the animals he had collected. I believe that Abram expected to walk between these divided animals *with* God. Had God and Abram walked through the divided sacrifice together, it would have been a bilateral agreement, a bilateral covenant. The fulfilling of the covenant would have been predicated on the fulfilling of the responsibility by *both* parties. But when it came time to walk through the covenant pieces, a deep sleep fell on Abram and the symbol of God, in the form of a smoking oven and torch, passed alone between the divided pieces. God passed through the divided sacrifice by Himself. In this way, it became a *unilateral* covenant. The fulfilling of the promise made to Abram to inhabit the land and to have a seed too numerous to count, was not made dependent on Abram fulfilling his responsibility to the covenant. By this unilateral covenant, made by God, passing *alone* through the divided pieces, the responsibility for its fulfillment would rest totally on God.

Ishmael and Isaac

Abram awoke from his deep sleep with the knowledge that God had confirmed the promise made to him for a seed and a land. However, Abram was now eighty-six years old and evidently believed that he needed to help God fulfill the covenant. How tragic it is when we read the promises of God, and rather than depend on Him to bring them to pass, believe that through the energy of the flesh we need to give God a hand. Archaeologists have discovered that it was the custom, when a wife was barren, for her to present her husband with a handmaiden, servant girl, or concubine, through whom the husband could have a male heir to carry on the name of the family. God's promise to Abram, in Genesis 15, was that he would have a seed and that he would have a land. But Abram, in a lapse of faith or possibly lust, became the father of Ishmael through Hagar.

Because Abram attempted to bring God's covenant to pass through the energy of the flesh, his communion with the Lord was broken by a thirteen year silence. Genesis 16:16 states that Abram was eighty six years old when Hagar gave birth to Ishmael, and Genesis 17:1 tells us that he was ninety nine years old when the Lord spoke to him again. Thirteen years elapsed between the last verse of chapter 16 and the first verse of chapter 17. Thirteen years in which Abram had time to think over his disobedience and to wonder what the final outcome would be. Finally, when Abram was ninety-nine years old, God reaffirmed to him that He and He alone would bring about the birth of the one through whom the promised seed would continue, and would generate the nation of Israel. God would accomplish it through Sarai, Abram's barren wife.

Chapter 17 describes how Abram's name was changed to Abraham. Sarai's name was changed to Sarah. Abram begged God for Ishmael
to be the son through whom God would bless him. God again reaffirmed that it would not be through Ishmael, and gave assurance again that from Sarah the son of promise would be born. Even his name was given in advance (vs. 21). The covenant that God had given to Abraham would be reaffirmed and established with Isaac. God answered Abraham's prayer with a final no!

Esau and Jacob

Genesis 23:1 tells us that Sarah lived to be 127 years of age. Abraham was 137 years old and Isaac was thirty-seven when she died. In chapter 24, when Abraham was approximately 140 years old and Isaac was forty, Abraham sent his servant to find a spouse for his son. The servant obediently traveled to visit the relatives of Abraham. As we discovered earlier, there were some relatives living in the distant country of Mesopotamia, in the city of Nahor (vs. 10.). When the servant arrived there, through a set of criteria that he had previously established, he became acquainted with Rebekah, and she returned with him to marry Isaac. Genesis 25:20 tells us that Isaac was forty years of age when he took Rebekah, the sister of Laban, to be his wife.

Genesis 25:21 says that Isaac prayed on behalf of his wife because she was barren, and the Scripture simply says, *"The Lord answered him."* and Rebekah conceived. Only when we go to verse 26, do we see that Rebekah gave birth to Esau and Jacob when Isaac was sixty years of age. Isaac prayed for twenty years. After twenty years, his consistency in prayer was rewarded and God brought His program to pass. God had previously tested the patience, stability, and faithfulness of Abraham for many years. Now in like manner, He tested the patience, stability, and faith of Isaac because he knew the promise. The covenant of the seed was confirmed through Isaac after he prayed consistently for twenty years.

The balance of Chapter 25 tells us of the differing personalities of Jacob and Esau. Esau became an outdoorsman, a skillful hunter, and we read that Isaac loved him best because he (Isaac) had a taste for game. Jacob, on the other hand, was more domesticated. He was what we call a "*homebody*." In the balance of chapter 25, we learn that Jacob used his cooking skills to entice the weary and hungry Esau. In so doing, Jacob purchased the birthright which was promised to him before his birth in vs. 23.

In chapter 27, Isaac is old and his vision failed. In concern that he would soon die, he took what he considered to be his final opportunity to extend the formal blessing to Esau as the oldest son and to Jacob as the youngest, so that they might claim their respective positions in the family. Prior to doing this, he asked that Esau would cook a savory dish for him. Instead, Jacob very stealthily prepared a savory dish and covered the exposed portions of his body with skins so that when near-sighted old Isaac reached out to touch him, he thought he was feeling Esau because Esau was a very hairy man. So, through deception, Jacob received the blessing which Isaac had planned to give to Esau. This blessing placed him above Esau in respect to his relationship with the rest of the family. Through this blessing, Jacob became the head of the family by decree of his father, Isaac. Through deception, Jacob *prevented* his father from sinning by giving the blessing to Esau.

When Esau arrived home, he was in despair because not only had Jacob purchased his birthright earlier for the bowl of stew, but had now obtained his blessing also. Esau was extremely despondent and received only the blessing ordinarily reserved for the next in line. He planned to murder his brother Jacob when the "days of mourning" were over. Rebekah heard of the plan and, because Jacob's life was in danger, she encouraged him (in 27:43) to go and stay with her brother Laban until Esau's anger subsided.

Ordinarily, we might think that all this happened when Esau and Jacob were young men. As an example of the benefits of inquiry into the Word of God through our system of chronology, let us look and see exactly how old these two were, using various Scripture verses and our dating processes. Jacob was 130 years old when he went into Egypt (see Gen. 47:9). Remembering that Jacob went to Egypt at the request of Joseph, his eleventh son, we need to look and see how old Joseph was when his father Jacob stood before Pharaoh. For this information, turn to Genesis 41:46 and see that Joseph was thirty years old when he stood before Pharaoh and was given the number two position in the kingdom. Go to Genesis 45:6 to see that just prior to Joseph's sending for his father Jacob. He addressed his brothers and explained that the famine had been in the land for two years and that five years of famine still remained. Seven good years and two bad years had gone by at the time of this statement. Since those years began when he was thirty, he was at that time, thirty-nine years old. Since he was thirty-nine when Jacob was 130, he was born when his father Jacob was ninety-one years old.

Immediately after avoiding the dangerous situation with Esau, at the urging of his mother Rebekah, Jacob had the experience at Bethel recorded in Genesis 28. There, God reconfirmed to Jacob the covenant He previously made with Abraham and Isaac. Jacob traveled on to visit Laban and stayed with him (Gen.29). When he arrived in the land where Laban lived, his eyes fell on Rachel, Laban's daughter (his distant cousin). He immediately wanted to marry her, so he and Laban struck a bargain (vs. 18). The agreement arrived at was that Jacob would serve Laban seven years to marry Rachel. The Bible says that even though he served seven years (vs.20), they seemed like just a few days because he loved her.

When the seven years were completed, he asked Laban for his daughter Rachel. On the wedding night, the young lady was ushered
into his tent in full long gowns and veil. When Jacob awakened the next morning, he had been deceived by the master deceiver. Laban had given him Leah instead of Rachel. To receive Rachel as his wife, Jacob had to agree to serve another seven years. But, rather than wait seven additional years, Laban gave him Rachel almost immediately following the celebration week of Leah's wedding.

After seven years of working for Laban, Jacob had two wives: Laban's daughters, Leah and Rachel, and the handmaiden of each. Immediately, Leah began to bear children. She gave birth to Reuben (vs.32), to Simeon (vs.33), to Levi (vs.34), and to Judah (vs.35). So, although Rachel was barren (vs.29:31), Leah gave birth to four children in rapid succession.

The important issue in chapters 29 and 30 is that in seven years, eleven male children and one daughter were born. It was a contest between Rachel, Leah, and their two handmaidens, to see who could give birth to the most children, and in doing so, please Jacob so that he would make the winner his favorite wife. In verse 20, Leah expressed the wish that now since she had given birth to six sons, hopefully, Jacob would live with her.

Throughout Leah's lifetime, Rachel was always Jacob's favorite. Leah was a faithful wife, and although Jacob had not loved her as much as he did Rachel, she did give him six sons, one of whom was Judah, the progenitor of the tribe of Judah through which the Messiah would come. In Genesis 49:31 it is interesting to notice that although Leah did not have the benefit of living with Jacob during her lifetime, when she died, and when Jacob was prepared to die, we discover that Leah had been placed in the family tomb along with Abraham and Sarah. Jacob wanted to be placed with her in the family tomb as well. Rachel, the one whom Jacob had loved the most during life, was buried in the desert on the way to Bethlehem. Leah got her wish after her death.

Finally, when the eleventh son was born (named Joseph) (30:25), Jacob said to Laban, "*Send me away so that I may go to my own country*." The seven additional years which he promised to Laban in return for Rachel were now expired and he wanted to go to his own land. If we look at Genesis 31:38, we see that he did not return to his own land after the fourteen years, but served with Laban an additional six years. During this time, he became wealthy through the multiplication of the original flocks that he was given by Laban as an inducement to stay. See fig. 3b in the Appendix.

We use this sequence to get back to the original point regarding the ages of Esau and Jacob at the time of the blessing from Isaac. If Jacob was ninety-one years old at the time of the birth of Joseph, then we must subtract fourteen years, since Joseph was the last child born just prior to Jacob's asking to be released from his bondage to Laban. Ninety-one minus fourteen is seventy seven. These two men were seventy-seven years old when Isaac asked for the savory meal so the blessing could be pronounced. Jacob was not married, he was seventy-seven years of age, living at home with his mother, and it would be another seven years before his marriage to Leah at eighty-four years of age. This puts an accurate perspective on the chronology of these two men in our study of the book of Genesis.

Joseph in Egypt

Chapter 37 begins the narrative of Joseph. We discover in verse 2, that when Joseph was seventeen years old he brought back a report about his brothers. We should observe here that Joseph was seventeen in the year 1898 B.C. The brothers he reported about were his ten older half-brothers, since Benjamin was just a baby, probably between two and seven years of age. The brothers disliked Joseph for broadcasting their sin and because he was the favorite son of Jacob. (Because of the fact Joseph was Rachel's son and she died when Benjamin was born). In verse 18, we read that they plotted against him to put him to death, but because of the pleading of Reuben, they shed no blood. They threw him in a pit and later sold him to some nomads who sold him into slavery in Egypt.

Looking back for a moment to Genesis 35, beginning in verse 33, there is a summary of the sons of Jacob. Leah gave birth to six sons. These were Reuben, Simeon, Levi, Judah, Issachar, and Zebulun. The sons of Rachel, now deceased, were Joseph and Benjamin. The sons of Bilhah, Rachel's maid, were Dan and Naphtali; the sons of Zilpah, Leah's maid, were Gad and Asher.

During this time (vs. 29), Isaac died. Verse 38 says he died at 180 years of age. Esau and Jacob were 120 years old. Isaac's death would have occurred about twelve years after Joseph disappeared. Isaac died without knowing the fate of his grandson Joseph.

Jacob was despondent. He had lost his father Isaac, and his favorite son Joseph had been missing for over a decade. He still had eleven sons at home, including the youngest, Benjamin. Little did he know that during this time, Joseph was being severely tested in Egypt. He had spent years in prison. See Psalm 105:17-20. But, God had given him special wisdom. Because he was faithful in his obedience to God, and because of his personal virtue, he had risen above his circumstances and became second only to Pharaoh in the most powerful nation on the face of the earth.

Throughout these times of suffering, depression, and imprisonment, I wonder if Joseph ever thought, "Is this worth it? I should die and end this misery" Later, he would look back and see God's hand bringing him through each of these events that seemed so disastrous at the time, until eventually he would say in Genesis 45:5: *"God did send me before you to preserve life."* God used Joseph's mistreatment, suffering, then exaltation, to preserve the Hebrew nation and the Seed of promise. What a tremendous opportunity for us to examine our lives and the situations in which we find ourselves daily, so that we, like Joseph, can look at the circumstances that surround us and see God's hand moving, shaping, and designing for our good.

Jacob and his family lived out their lives in Egypt under the protection and blessing of the Pharaoh. The last chapter of Genesis tells us that Joseph died at 110 years of age. The year was approximately 1805 B.C. He was embalmed and placed in a coffin in Egypt. It had been 361 years from the birth of Abram until the death of his Great Grandson, Joseph.

VI. DELIVERANCE FROM EGYPT

The book of Exodus begins with a synopsis of the activities which took place during the time when the children of Israel were in bondage in the land of Egypt. Chapter one records the names of those who came out of the land of Canaan into Egypt with Jacob, climaxing with the attempt of Pharaoh to kill all of their male children at birth. Because of the faithfulness of the Israelite midwives, this attempt of Pharaoh, the first of many historical efforts to annihilate the Jews, did not succeed.

The narrative of the life of Moses and his activities as the founder of the theocratic state begins in chapter two. His father and mother were named Amram and Jochebed. Jochebed was the sister of Amram's father, so Amram married his aunt. Of this union, Miriam, the older sister, was born; then Aaron, then Moses, whose birth date was 1526 B.C. After escaping the murderous plan of Pharaoh, Moses was taken into the household of the Egyptian princess, the daughter of Pharaoh and reared as an Egyptian. We know from Acts 7:22, that Moses was skilled in all of the knowledge of the Egyptians. His education, his military experience, his culture, his entire lifestyle, was totally oriented to Egypt. By the time he reached the age of forty, there was probably no greater leader, no greater potential Pharaoh in all the land than Moses.

Of special interest here is the discovery of a piece of limestone in 1995. It was in a tomb on the west side of the Nile river in Luxor. The tomb was used in (prox.) 1450 B.C. The inscription on the limestone was deciphered by a University of British Columbia Egyptologist in 2018. His conclusion was that it is an early version of the Semitic alphabet. And, it is in the order of ABC! In Exodus we read "*Moses wrote down everything the Lord had said.*" This discovery proves Moses was writing, as were others, at in 1450 B.C.

The narrative continues in Exodus 2:11. Moses went out one day and saw two men struggling together, one Egyptian and one a Hebrew. Moses murdered the Egyptian. Acts 7:23ff records the fact (little known from the book of Exodus) that in reality Moses, even at that relatively early age, believed himself to be the God-sent deliverer. However, this attempt was in the energy of the flesh and, although God had chosen him for this great task, he attempted through self-effort to bring it to pass. This never accomplishes what God has in mind. As a result, Moses had to flee from Egypt. The balance of chapter two tells us that he settled in Midian and continued his life there as a shepherd.

The narrative continues in chapter three with the description of how he met the Angel of the Lord at the burning bush. Throughout the Old Testament, the pre-incarnate Son of God will appear as the Angel of the Lord, {the Angel of the Presence.} identified as The Theophany. Yahweh tells Moses His name: "I AM that I AM." Only Yahweh has aseity. Yahweh is the active, self existent, eternal, immortal, immutable, infinitely holy Being, eternally existing as One Essence and three Persons.

Acts 7:30 provides added historical detail, telling us Moses was eighty years old. Forty years of desert life passed by the time God met Moses at the burning bush. Moses began the great task which would take the remaining forty years of his life; the triple work of deliverer, lawgiver, and founder of the Theocratic state. The time element is corroborated by Exodus 7:7, which states that Moses was eighty years old, and Aaron was eighty-three, when they stood before Pharaoh.

Forty years prior to his encounter with the Angel of the Lord and Yahweh {YHWH}at the burning bush in 1446 B.C., Moses was totally trained in the ways of the Egyptians. Acts 7:22 says he "*was mighty in words and in deeds.*" Forty years later we find him a man without self-confidence, without confidence in his abilities, a man who now claimed to be slow of speech and lacking any ability at all as a leader. I believe this follows the scriptural pattern. Forty years prior to this there was a no more logical man than Moses for God to choose to lead the children of Israel out of bondage. He was the only one, in fact, trained by the Egyptians in military strategy, philosophy, and architecture. When he met God at the burning bush, he was a broken man. You will find this to be a continuing theme throughout the Old Testament. When God acts, He reduces the numbers so that man cannot take credit. When God acts, He uses those individuals least likely to succeed so that "*no flesh should glory in His presence*" (I Cor. 1:29). When God gives the victory, He gets the honor.

It took forty years in the desert to crush Moses and to extract from him that confidence he had in himself because of his Egyptian education. It was as a shepherd, crushed, without self-confidence, stumbling in speech, that he encountered God at the burning bush with nothing in his hand except a shepherd's staff. The Lord said to him in Exodus 4:2, "*What is that in thine hand?*" He cast his rod to the ground and it became the rod of God. With this shepherd's staff, he would bring the mightiest nation in the world to its knees. God also forewarned Moses in chapter 4 that He would harden the heart of Pharaoh. Moses knew in advance (vss. 21 and 23) that Pharaoh would release the people and that eventually God would have to kill the firstborn of Egypt. When he met his people the first time (4:30), and performed signs and miracles in their presence, they bowed low and worshiped (vs.31).

In 5:21 we find the people accusing him of having made them a stench in the nostrils of Pharaoh. From the high plateau of exaltation, Moses fell into pits of depression and accused God (5:23), saying, *"Neither hast thou delivered thy people at all."* By this time, Moses also began to doubt what God would do. Following this expression of doubt by Moses, God spoke to him again (6:2) and confirmed His existence: *"I am the Lord."* (See the *"I will"* promises.). In chapter six, the sovereignty of God shines like a beacon. The doubts of Moses were dispelled; He was assured that God was going to do this because He would be faithful to the covenant He had established with Abraham, Isaac, and Jacob. After hearing these "I will" assurances from God, Moses again spoke to the people, but they still did not listen (vs. 9).

The Plagues

The contest between Jehovah and the gods of Egypt is recorded in chapters 7 through 11. Ten plagues were sent on Pharaoh's kingdom before he would finally free the Hebrews, even though his servants had warned him, *"knowest thou not yet that Egypt is destroyed?"*

Plague #1 (7:20): the Nile was turned to blood.
Plague #2 (8:7): frogs infested the land.
Plague #3 (8:17): gnats (lice) covered the land.
Plague #4 (8:24): swarms of insects.
Plague #5 (9:5): pestilence destroying the cattle.

Following plague five, a distinction was made between the cattle of the Egyptians and the cattle of the Hebrews.

Plague #6 (9:9): boils.
Plague #7 (9:23): thunder, rain, hail and fire covering the earth.
Plague #8 (10:4): locusts.
Plague #9 (10:21): darkness so thick that no light can be seen except from the dwellings of the Israelites. The tenth plague, described in chapter 11, was the death of the first born of every family in Egypt, including the slave girl behind the millstone and the firstborn of all the cattle.

Chapter 12 contains the first Passover when the people ate the sacrificed lambs while standing in readiness to depart. First, however, the blood of the slain lambs was placed on the doorposts, lintels, and the basons {thresholds} of the houses. {See Zeph. 2:14 for the same Hebrew word} The blood was in the shape of a cross: top, right, left sides, and threshold.

The Red Sea

Chapter 13 appears geographically to be a journey to a dead end; but verse 21 tells us that God was before His people in a pillar of cloud by day and a pillar of fire by night. As they came to a dead end at the Red Sea, the children of Israel began to grumble, saying (14:12), *"It had been better for us to serve the Egyptians, than that we should die in the wilderness."* We will read that this grumbling which began so early in their journey continued throughout the 40 years. On this occasion, Moses instructed them to stand back and see God operate in sovereignty and majesty as He was honored on Pharaoh (vs. 18).

In the film, *The Ten Commandments*, the Red Sea was parted, at a very narrow distance, as the Israelites went through. Remember that 600,000 men on foot, plus women and children, came out of the land of Egypt (Exod. 12:37). This was a crowd of about two million people. If they had crossed in rows of only fifteen each, they would have had 133,333 rows. If those rows of people were three feet apart, there would have been 400,000 feet (75 miles) in the column proceeding through the Red Sea. This means that by the time the tail end of the column got out of the land of Egypt and through the Red Sea, the head of the column would have been in the land of Canaan.

This was a greater miracle than we imagine. The Red Sea was probably opened up a mile wide so that the people were able to go through in a very short period of time. It was not an earthquake, or tidal wave, it was a tremendous miracle, an east wind that blew throughout the night. The Scripture says that the ground was solid. It was not muddy; it was frozen. The children of Israel walked through on dry land. But, when the chariots of Pharaoh attempted to follow them, the waters rolled back together and the pride of the Egyptian army was crushed beneath the weight of the water in the Red Sea.

In chapter 15, Moses expounds with a tremendous song of victory. Then in verse 21, Miriam begins to answer antiphonally. I think this must have been the high point of Miriam's life. She had witnessed God's majesty, His power, and His might. She sings and praises God, and she is thankful and grateful for what God has done through her brother. Yet, I am reminded of what jealousy did to Miriam only a short time later. Numbers 12 relates how she spoke out against Moses because of jealousy and God struck her with leprosy. Because of the leprosy, she was placed outside the camp for seven days.

VII. THE FIRST YEAR

Complaints, Miracles, and Water

After the great celebration of victory, the people of Israel began their journey to Canaan. After three days they ran out of water (15:22) and immediately began to grumble. God graciously provided an immediate source of water (15:25) and then led them (vs. 27) to an oasis where there were twelve springs of water and seventy date palms. They camped there and by the time they began their journey again, forty-five days had elapsed (16:1). However, they soon began to grumble and mumble again. This time, God declared that He was going to test them whether or not they will walk in His ordinances (16:2-4). The immediate cause of their complaint was the scarcity of food, but this was only the surface problem; a smokescreen behind which was bitterness toward God.

The balance of chapter 16 contains the details of the giving of the manna and instructions how it was to be gathered. Verse 35 says that the sons of Israel ate the manna for forty years. See John 6:32-35. Many have said that the manna was a natural product of the tamarisk tree which is native to that part of the Sinai. The tamarisk does drop a small droplet of honey-like substance when it is pricked. However, there are only a few districts in the area that have this kind of tamarisk plant. Besides, it gives its honey-like substance only in small amounts, and only for about three months out of the year. The entire Sinai produces less than seven hundred pounds of it annually. Manna was not a natural product of the area, but was a God-given provision. It was the means by which the children of Israel survived on "angels' food," as Psalm 78:25 described it.

Chapter 17 reports another miracle of water supply; a continuing need in a desert area - and also recounts the important battle between the Israelites and Amalakites. Joshua was the military leader for the Israelites against Amalek. Amalek and his army had chosen to come in from the flank and from the rear, attacking those people who were at the rear of the column; those who lagged behind due to age or infirmity. Because of this, God cursed the Amalakites`, saying that He would blot out the memory of Amalek from under heaven (vs. 14). Verse 16 adds that, *"the Lord will have war with Amalek from generation to generation."* Four hundred years later, He will commission an individual to exterminate them.

In chapter 18, we are introduced to Jethro, the father in Law of Moses. He carried a double name, Reuel-Jethro. He was a Kenite of the Reuel clan. He visited the Israelite encampment, taking Zipporah, the wife of Moses, and their two sons, with him. Jethro was a skilled organizer. When he saw how the responsibility for two million people rested on the shoulders of Moses, he advised him in vs. 21 to decentralize the organization, to delegate responsibility, and to place leaders over thousands and leaders over hundreds and leaders over fifties and leaders over tens. He also warned Moses that if he did not do so, *"he would surely wear out."*

In the third month (Exod. 19) Israel reached the area of Mount Sinai where God began to reveal Himself. As thunder and lightning came down, He manifested Himself to the children of Israel, not a physical presence, but as a powerful, unseen, and eternal *moral* Being. We now He is a moral Being because He gave the Ten Commandments; because we are created in the image and likeness of God, and have to manifest these moral attributes, to maintain that relationship with Him. See Isa. 33:14, 15. Since man by himself, with his fallen nature, cannot exhibit these moral qualities, he is worthy of death. Once realizing this, we must realize that either we must die, or a substitute must die in our place. The Old Testament sacrificial system was established whereby God could have fellowship with His creation. It was also a symbol of the reality of the New Covenant when Jesus Christ would die as the one-time sacrifice for all.

Chapter 20 lists the Ten Commandments. When the people began to hear God speak, they cried (vs. 19): *"let not God speak with us, lest we die."* In chapters 21 through 24, God gave further provisions necessary for fellowship. He invited Moses, Joshua, and the elders of the people up to the mountain (Exod. 24). Finally (24:18), Moses entered the cloud and spent forty days and forty nights on the mountain with God. At that time, the Lord gave him the instructions for building the tabernacle and contents (Exod. 25-31).

During that forty day period when Moses was away, the people began to sin. Chapter 32 contains the story of the construction of the golden calf. When this happened, God spoke to Moses and commanded him:

Go, get thee down; for thy people, which thou broughtest out of the land of Egypt, have corrupted themselves: They have turned aside quickly out of the way which I commanded them.

In this passage of Scripture God did not say that Satan had tempted them. He said that the people had sinned. Think of James 1:15, *"When lust hath conceived, it bringeth forth sin: and sin, when it is finished, bringeth forth death."* God was about to destroy the people for their great wickedness (32:10) but Moses leaped into the breach to intercede for them. Verse 14 tells us that God listened to Moses and honored his prayer. He gave Moses the opportunity to express his feeling about God and his feeling and love for the nation of Israel. This was Moses' testing time and he passed the test.

As Moses descended the mountain, he was confronted by Joshua who told him of the activities in the camp below. They descended together where they discovered a wild orgy was going on. People were dancing and worshiping a golden calf as the god who had brought them out of Egypt. When confronted by Moses, Aaron said that the people wanted the thing, and as they put their gold into the fire, the calf "just came out." Moses instructed the Levites to fall on everyone who was involved with the wild orgy, and they went among them with their swords, killing the offenders.

Chapter 33:6 begins a period of national repentance. The Israelites removed their ornaments and began to move out. God instructed Moses to ascend the mountain once more (chapter 34). This time, since he had destroyed the two tablets that God had written on with His own finger (31:18), Moses had to cut his own tablets and carry them up the mountain. There, God would repeat the Ten Commandments that had been shattered by Moses. We are introduced to a new set of God's attributes. Because the nation sinned, repented, and had been shown mercy, the occasion was appropriate for the revelation of this new dimension of God's character. When Moses had again ascended the mountain, the Lord God descended and met with him there. We read in (34:6-7):

And the Lord passed by before him, and proclaimed, The Lord, The Lord God, merciful and gracious, long suffering, and abundant in goodness and truth, Keeping mercy for thousands, forgiving iniquity and transgression and sin, and that will by no means clear the guilty.

When Moses heard these new attributes and His forgiveness for the sin of the people, he bowed down and worshiped.

Exodus 34:28 tells us Moses once again remained on the mountain for forty days. This time we are told that his face shone because of his contact with God. Because of the rays that literally shot out from his face, it was necessary that he put on a veil. (See II Cor. 3:13-18)

When he descended from the mountain, chapter 35 tells us that he assembled the congregation, and they took up an offering to build the tabernacle, and its contents, according to God's revealed blueprint. Chapter 40:17 records the construction was completed in the first month, in the second year, on the first day of the month. This was thirteen months since the exodus from Egypt.

VIII. ACCESS TO THE HOLIEST

--LEVITICUS--

The book of Leviticus contains no chronology. It details the means by which Israel could have access and fellowship with God. Chapter 8 contains the record of the preparation for Aaron and his sons to enter the office of high priest and the priestly offices. No sooner had this taken place, the worship system established, and the sacrifices performed, than a fire from the Lord consumed the burnt offerings (9:24). When the people saw it, *they shouted, and fell on their faces.* They knew that God was pleased with their worship and that the fire validated His acceptance of their offerings.

The fire also served as a preparatory step for their entry into the land of Canaan. Once they were exposed to the Baal worship system that was practiced there, they would be told by the inhabitants of the land that Baal was the one responsible for fire. God had given them an advance demonstration that Jehovah-God is the one responsible for this physical element.

Immediately after this demonstration, we read the account in chapter 10 of Nadab and Abihu, two sons of Aaron, who offered strange fire to the Lord. It would seem that after such an example of the power of God, and after very precise instruction from Moses as to how the ice of priest was to be administered, that they would have refrained from so foolish an act. Nevertheless, they offered strange fire. Evidently in being strange, it was not in the prescribed fashion, and, Leviticus 10:2: "*And there went out fire from the Lord, and devoured them, and they died before the Lord.*"

We do not know what kind of fire this was, but whatever its nature, it was not a fire that would consume what they were wearing, nor was it one that would burn them to ashes, for verse 5 says that men "carried them in their coats." Whether it was some kind of electrical or laser charge that would consume the life force within them and yet leave the physical body intact, we do not know. But it certainly did not consume them completely. When Aaron saw this judgment on his sons, he was moved with grief. Evidently, he began to grab his high priestly garment at the neck to "rend his garment" as was customary to demonstrate grief. Moses quickly stopped him, commanding: *"Uncover not your heads, neither rend your clothes; lest ye die"* (vs. 6).

It is important that we go back into Exodus 28:32 to see the significance of this prohibition. There it says, in describing how the garment should be constructed: *And there shall be an hole in the top of it, in the midst thereof: it shall have a binding of woven work round about the hole of it, as it were the hole of an habergeon, that it be not rent.* The high priestly garment was not to be worn, even in mourning, and Moses warned Aaron not to tear it "lest ye die." Turn to Matthew 26:64 for the encounter between Caiaphas, who was the high priest that year and Christ in their kangaroo court. Jesus had just answered the question as to whether He was the Son of God by stating (vs. 64): *Thou hast said: nevertheless I say unto you, hereafter shall ye see the Son of man sitting on the right hand of power, and coming in the clouds of heaven.*

In verse 65, *"Then the high priest rent his clothes."* When Caiaphas rent the high priestly garment, he ended the Jewish priesthood. A very few hours later, (Matt. 27:51) we read that *"the veil of the temple was rent in twain from the top to the bottom."* Between the time when Caiaphas rent the high priestly garment and the veil of the temple was rent, Jesus Christ paid the ultimate sacrifice on the cross of Calvary and became our High Priest. There is *"one mediator between God and men, the man Christ Jesus"* (I Tim. 2:5).

The book of Leviticus continues with various ordinances and rituals necessary for cleansing and fellowship with God. The book of Hebrews should be studied in its relationship to Leviticus in order to understand the various typologies and to see Christ more fully in the Old Testament in His role as the substitutionary sacrifice. Some of this wonderful typology is contained in Leviticus 23. In verse 16 the people are instructed to count fifty days after the seventh Sabbath and to present a new grain offering to the Lord. This offering was to be two loaves of bread baked with leaven as first fruits unto the Lord. If we look back earlier in the chapter to verses 9, 10, and 11, we see that the children of Israel were instructed to give a sheaf of first fruits of the harvest which would be made as in verse 13 *without leaven.*

The first fruit was a type of the Lord Jesus Christ, so there was not to be any leaven in the wave sheaf which symbolized Him. However, the offering given fifty days after the wave sheaf is identified with the day of Pentecost in the New Testament. The formation of the church fifty days after the resurrection (Acts 2) was symbolized in the wave sheaf which contained leaven. There is no evil in Christ, our resurrected Lord, but there are imperfections in the church, and there are imperfections in the believers. The two loaves are symbolic of the Gentiles and the Jews as explained in Ephesians 2:11ff.

Chapter 26 contains the "if-but" principle. As presented here, this "if-but" principle sets the stage for all of the activity from this point on. The manner in which God treats the Israelites at any given time is determined by Leviticus 26. The punishment and chastening which the Israelites received is predicated in the "if-but" principle laid down here. We should look at this chapter on a verse by verse basis. Beginning in verse 3:

*"If ye walk in my statutes, and keep my commandments, then
I will give you rain in due season, and the land shall yield her
increase, your threshing shall reach into the vintage, and the
vintage shall reach unto the sowing time: and ye shall eat your
bread to the full, and dwell in your land safety."*

God gave tremendous promises to the inhabitants of the land down through verse 13. Then we read the "but" section in verse 14: *"But if you will not hearken unto me and will not do all these commandments; and if ye shall despise my statutes, or if your Soul abhor my judgments, so that ye will not do all my commandments."*

Verse 16: *"I also will do this unto you; I will even appoint over you terror, consumption."* Verse 17: *"I will set my face against you, and ye shall be slain before your enemies."* Verse 19: *"I will break the pride of your power."* Verse 20: *"Your strength shall be spent in vain: for your land shall not yield her increase, neither shall the trees of the land yield their fruits."* Verse 22: *"I will also send wild beasts among you."* Verse 24: *Then will I also walk contrary unto you, and will punish you."* Verse 25: *"And I will bring a sword upon you."* Verse 28: *"Then I will walk contrary unto you also in fury; and I, even I, will chastise you seven times for your sins."*

Looking forward prophetically, to the time when they would be sealed up in their cities because of the siege by an enemy. Verse 29: *"And ye shall eat the flesh of your sons, and the flesh of your daughters shall ye eat."* Verse 32: *"And I will bring the land into desolation: and your enemies which dwell therein shall be astonished at it."* Verse 33: *"And I will scatter you among the heathen."* Verse 34: *"Then shall the land enjoy her Sabbaths."*

Not only does chapter 26 contain the "if-but" principle, it is also prophetic because it details the activity which will take place from the latter part of the fifteenth century B.C. down until the early part of the sixth century B.C. during the invasion of the Babylonians. The principles of chapter 26 will apply for the next eight hundred years. As the children of

Israel fail to obey God, He brought all of these calamities on them. Enemies invade; famine ravaged the land; drought caused the crops to shrivel; invading enemies and occupying forces surrounded their cities and forced the inhabitants within the cities into cannibalism.

IX. THE WILDERNESS JOURNEY

--NUMBERS--

The book of Numbers is divided into three parts. Part One goes from 1:1 to 10: 10 and describes the preparations for the march from Sinai. Part Two begins in 10:11 and continues through 21:10. This division covers the history of the wanderings. Part Three, 21:11 through chapter 36, recounts the activities that take place east of the Jordan River before the Israelites enter Canaan. As we begin to consider the land of Canaan, we need to understand the importance of the Jordan River which divides the land. The territory east of the Jordan River is referred to as the Trans-Jordan, and the land west of the Jordan River is referred to as the Cis-Jordan. {Google the recent discovery of the Bronze Age Canaanite city, En Esur}

The Tabernacle

As two million people prepared to march from Sinai to Canaan, their periods of movement and rest were regulated by the command of God through the cloud by day and the pillar of fire by night. Led by God, they would enter and reclaim the land He had promised to Abraham and to his seed. Throughout their journeying, they carried the completed tabernacle, the symbol of God's presence, among them. Its innermost object, the Ark of the Covenant, represented the throne of God. He was Israel's true king, making the nation a *Theocracy*. Israel was never to be a *Plutocracy*, where the rich ruled, or an *autocracy,* governed by one human dictator, nor a *democracy* where the crowd ruled, but a *Theocracy*, governed only by God. He commanded Moses face-to-face and Moses carried out His commands. Later, after Moses died, Joshua was instructed to seek counsel of God through Eleazer the priest. God spoke through the ephod and the breastplate of righteousness, giving the priest the instructions which Joshua was to follow in the conquest of the land.

Numbers chapter 1 tells us that an additional month had gone by since the completion of the tabernacle, and that the people were getting ready to move on from Sinai. Prior to their departure, a census was taken of all the adult males (age twenty and over). These became known as the *numbered men,* and the numbering is listed in chapter one. It is important to notice that the tribe of Levi was not included in this numbering (vs. 47) and that they did not become part of the numbered men of war. A little later (chapter 3), the Levites were appointed to their specific responsibilities. Eleazer, the son of Aaron, became high priest and chief over the tribe of Levi with full control over the activities of the sanctuary (3:32).

Chapter 4 contains important instructions concerning the Ark of the Covenant. Since no one could look upon it and live, except the High Priest just once a year, an intricate system was devised for transporting it without being observed. The priests were instructed to put a covering of skins over it and to insert poles through the rings that had been constructed at its corners. In Exodus 25:14-15, God gave specific instructions for putting the poles into the rings. They were never to be removed. They were designed to protrude from the skins. Therefore, to move it, would be a matter of collapsing the skins onto the Ark, lifting it by the poles, and bearing it along without it ever being seen.

As our study progresses, we will see later that God's rules for handling the Ark, the tabernacle, and its contents, were eventually disregarded. Even David, on one occasion, ignored these instructions and chose to move the Ark on a cart, resulting in death and tragedy. It is amazing how often we see, in the Old Testament, God being very specific about a matter, yet as time passes, the people forget, abandon, or negate His precise regulations and substitute traditions and man-made rules.

No sooner had the people begun to move toward the Promised Land, than we read (chapter 11) that they began to complain once again. In verse 6, they complained that they had no more appetite because ere was nothing to look at or eat except manna, the "angels' food" that God had given to preserve them in the wilderness. At that time, they had no idea they were going to need it for forty years. They had been out of Egypt just a little over one year and were heading toward Canaan. But already they were tired of the manna, God's divine provision. The Hebrew, "Ma'n Hu" is, "What is it?"

Moses, in distress and depression, (vs. 11), began complaining to God because he had to bear the heavy burden of shepherding such an ungrateful and recalcitrant people. "Kill me," he prayed (vs. 15). The Lord did ease his burden, but He also told the people that since they wanted meat so badly, He would give it to them in such abundance that it would come out of their nostrils. He sent them fresh meat for a full month, but while they were still chewing on it (vs. 33) He judged them by sending a severe plague.

The next chapter describes how Miriam and Aaron joined with the people in complaining against the authority of Moses. On that occasion, the Lord came down in a pillar of cloud and appeared at the doorway of the tabernacle. His words validated that Moses was His chosen spokesman (vss. 6-8). He demonstrated His anger by covering Miriam with leprosy so that she had to be exiled outside the camp for seven days (vs. 14).

By chapter 13, the children of Israel reached the borders of the land of Canaan. A map will show that they were camped in the southwest section, just south of the Mediterranean Sea and about to enter the Negev, or Southland. At that strategic location, God instructed them to send spies into the land to see that it really was as good as He had promised (vs. 19). They were also instructed to see how the people of the land lived, whether in the open, in tents, or in fortified cities. The spies traveled throughout the land for forty days and discovered that it was a land *"flowing with milk and honey,"* just as God had promised. They were able to cut such a large and heavy cluster of grapes (vs. 23) that two men carried it on a pole between them.

The produce of the land was impressive, but so were the inhabitants.When the twelve spies returned and gave their report to the congregation, they said (vss. 27-29), *"It truly is a land of milk and honey, but it is inhabited by giants."* Ten of the spies declared that a successful invasion was impossible. The natives were too large and too strong, *"and we were in our own sight as grasshoppers and so we were in their sight"* (vs. 33). Only Joshua and Caleb insisted that by obeying the Lord they could take the land.
Numbers 14:1 states, *"All of the congregation lifted up their voice, and cried; and the people wept that night."* They began to grumble again against Moses and wish they had died in Egypt. Then their complaints turned to mutiny. They determined to appoint another leader and return to Egypt (vs. 4). Joshua and Caleb tore their clothes (vs. 6) and tried desperately to stem the rebellion and convince the people that *"If the Lord delight in us, then he will bring us into this land, and give it us"* (vs. 8). For their faithfulness, they were on the verge of being stoned to death (vs. 10), when suddenly, in the midst of the turmoil, the Glory of God appeared in the tabernacle.

Imagine the scene! People running wild! Two stalwart leaders, Joshua and Caleb, about to be stoned! Then the sudden appearance of the glory of God! What a frightening time it must have been as the eyes of the rioters were suddenly riveted to the blinding glory of God who was ready to destroy them and begin a new nation with Moses. But Moses once again interceded for them, quoting the Lord's own words, *"as thou has spoken"* (vs. 17), and repeating back to Him the words He had proclaimed to Moses on the mount (vs. 18; cf. Exod. 34:6-7).

Because of Moses' intercession, God pardoned the people. Nevertheless, He said, because they have rebelled against Him ten times, they will not see the Promised Land (vss. 22-23).

In verse 29 He adds that the corpses of all their *numbered men* would die in the wilderness. That terminology excluded the tribe of Levi. They were not included among the numbered men. Those who were numbered, twenty years old and upward, who had grumbled against the Lord, would not see the land. Joshua and Caleb were also specifically excluded from the judgment. Finally, He promised, *"Your little ones, which ye said should be a prey, them will I bring in. But as for you, your carcasses, they shall fall in this wilderness"* (vss. 31-32). When we consider there were about 600,000 numbered men, and thirty-eight years, this is 14,508 days in the wilderness. This averages out to the death of forty-two or forty-three men a day, and three to four men each hour. The next thirty-eight and a half years in the wilderness was filled with a constant funeral dirge. The cries of widows and orphaned children filled the air for all those years.

As for the ten spies who brought back the bad report, they died immediately. Theirs was an instant punishment (vs. 37). Then the congregation began to mourn, saying, *"We have sinned."* They determined then to go into the land and even though Moses forbade it as further transgression of God's command, they went up recklessly, and the Amalekites and the Canaanites who lived in the hill country came down and defeated them.

Numbers 15:1 marks the beginning of the wilderness wanderings. The sinful, disobedient people, who had grumbled against God and attempted to stone to death his chosen leaders, would never see the land they had expected to inherit when they left Egypt.

X. PREPARATIONS FOR CANAAN

The book of Numbers quickly passed over the thirty-eight years in which the children of Israel were condemned to wander in the wilderness because of their lack of faith. Chapter 15 gives the regulations for performing various sacrificial offerings *"when ye be come into the land"* (vs. 2). The remainder concerned with events that took place near the end of the years of wandering.

In chapter 16, we learn about the complaints of Korah, a descendant of Levi and a member of the working priesthood with "menial" duties. His pride had gotten the best of him. Evidently, the share of duties about the tabernacle that had been designated for his family had come to seem too simple for him (cf. Num. 4:1-4, 15). He became jealous of the position of superiority that Moses and Aaron had among the children of Israel and evidently he was able to persuade men from other tribes to share his resentment (16:1). As a result, God sent swift judgment and the earth swallowed them up.

It is interesting to realize that Korah must have had descendents who were not involved in the rebellion of their ancestor. There are several Psalms ascribed to "The Sons of Korah." These Psalms have a common echo of praise for the enthroned king and a longing after the sanctuary. The descendants learned a sobering lesson from the solemn judgment on their ancestors.

As the years of wandering came to an end, the tribes became aware they would be inheriting land of Canaan. In Numbers 18:20, God spoke to Aaron and let him know that he and his descendants would not have a physical inheritance. The Lord would be their inheritance. The inheritance of the tribe of Levi was also to be the tithes paid by the other twelve tribes; that would be the remuneration for their service to the tabernacle. God did allocate designated cities throughout the land in which the Levites could dwell, but, they did not have a geographical territory to call their own as the other tribes.

Numbers 20:1 begins the fortieth year in the wilderness. At that time

Miriam died and was buried. Immediately after that, they journeyed to Mount Hor where Aaron died. Then they crossed the brook Zered. In recounting their history, Moses said (Deut. 2:14) that from Kadesh-barnea (from where the spies had been sent out) to Zered had been thirty-eight years, and at that point in time all the numbered men of war who had come out of Egypt were dead. Zered is located between Edom and Moab. Numbers 33 sums up the sequence of their travels. Verse 36 says *"they removed from Ezion-geber, and pitched in the wilderness of Zin, which is Kadesh."* From Kadesh they moved to Mount Hor at the edge of the land of Edom. There Aaron died *"In the fortieth year after the children of Israel were to come out of the land of Egypt."* This summary ties in with the account back in Numbers 20:22-29.

Moses Disobeys

Chapter 20 also contains the account of how Moses incurred the Lord's anger at the rock in Kadesh. The children of Israel were again grumbling because they were thirsty. Verse 5 says that they complained to Moses for bringing them out of Egypt to "this evil place." This was the new generation: those who came out of Egypt as children, including those who had been born in the wilderness. The adult generation that had previously drunk water from a rock (Exod. 17:6) was dead. But like their elders, this new generation was equally quick to complain.

The Lord said to Moses (vs. 8), *"Speak ye unto the rock before their eyes and it shall give forth his water."* The rock, (I Cor. 10:4), was Christ, and He had already been struck one time to yield the water. He is not to be struck again but spoken to. Moses, in anger and frustration, abandoned momentarily his intercessory role, and began to chide the children of Israel. In his anger (vs. 11) he struck the rock twice with his rod and the water gushed forth, but God said to him,

> *Because ye believed me not, to sanctify me in the eyes of the children of Israel, therefore ye shall not bring this congregation into the land which I have given them.*

What a shock this must have been to Moses. To realize that because of this sudden lapse of faith, because of a momentary sin of disbelief, anger, and frustration, he would not get to see the Promised Land. Certainly, this should teach us that no one can sin with impunity, regardless of who he is or what his station in life. We cannot sin without chastisement and judgment, because God is holy and He will always be kept holy in the sight of His people. By striking the rock twice, Moses ruined an Old Testament type of Christ. The Lord Jesus having suffered once did not suffer again Hebrews 9:12: *Neither by the blood of goats and calves, but by his own blood he entered in once into the holy place, having obtained eternal redemption for us.*

God, in His righteousness, had to follow through with His judgment on Moses, who died just before the people crossed the Jordan into the Promised Land. But isn't it wonderful how God allowed Moses to see all the land from the mountain top in the Trans-Jordan area. We can read in Matthew 17:3 that Moses did enter the Promised Land standing on the Mount of Transfiguration with the Lord Jesus.

Numbers 21:4 tells that the people became impatient because of the journey. Even though this was a new generation, they were tiring of their life in the wilderness. They began to speak out against both God and Moses (vs. 5). So God sent fiery serpents among them whose poisonous bites took many lives. God provided just one way of salvation from the poisonous bites. Moses was to make a serpent of bronze and set it up on a standard. Verse 9 says, "*It came to pass, that if a serpent had bitten any man, when he beheld the serpent of brass, he lived.*" Once again God provided a type of Christ. We read the in John 3:14-15: *As Moses lifted up the serpent in the wilderness, even so must the Son of man be lifted up: That whosoever believeth in him should not perish, but have eternal life.*

The bronze serpent, which was erected in about 1406 B.C., was around for over seven hundred years. The people kept it and as the years passed it became an integral part of their worship service. They began to treat the bronze serpent as an idol. We read in II Kings 18:4, speaking of King Hezekiah and his reforms in Judah that: *He removed the high places, and brake the images, and cut down the groves, and brake in pieces the brasen serpent that Moses had made: for unto those days the children of Israel did burn incense to it.*

Balaam

Chapters 22 through 24 detail the concern which Balak the king of Moab had when he observed the millions of Israelites moving toward his land. Balak hired Balaam the prophet to proclaim a curse against the Israelites, but God intervened and Balaam was unable to curse the Lord's people. He could only pronounce a blessing. Balak, of course, was infuriated. Of special interest is the fact that part of the blessing which Balaam prophesied upon the Israelites was a promise of the coming Messiah. In 24:17, he said, "*There shall come a Star out of Jacob, and a Sceptre shall rise out of Israel.*"

This event provided one more piece of evidence that God's plan will not be thwarted. He will speak even through an ungodly pagan prophet, because He is sovereign. He will bless whom He will bless and will curse whom He will curse. The machinations of Balaam and Balak culminated in the sin of Baal-peor. This was a low point in the history of Israel because it was in direct opposition to all that God had instructed in the previous books of the Pentateuch. He made it very clear that the children of Israel were not to involve themselves with any outside nations, nor were they to involve themselves in any illicit manner with the women of those nations. Baal-peor, as recorded in 25:1, was a fertility cult religious practice in which the children of Israel involved themselves. As a result, God's judgment fell on them.

Since Balaam could not curse the Israelites, he evidently dreamed up this enticement so that the men would involve themselves in an illicit way with the women of Moab and bring God's curse upon them. Numbers 31:16 records, after the death of Balaam, *"Behold, these caused the children of Israel, through the counsel of Balaam, to commit trespass against the Lord in the matter of Peor, and there was a plague among the congregation of the Lord."*

The description of their sin begins in 25:1:

And Israel abode in Shittim, and the people began to commit whoredom with the daughters of Moab. And they called the people unto the sacrifices of their gods: and the people did eat, and bowed down to their gods. And Israel joined himself unto Baal-peor, and the anger of the Lord was kindled against Israel. And the Lord said unto Moses, Take all the heads of the people, and hang them up before the Lord against the sun, that the fierce anger of the Lord may be turned away from Israel. And Moses said unto the judges of Israel, Slay ye everyone his men that were joined unto Baal-peor.

It seems, from a comparison of the census counts, that the Simeonites may have led in this licentious activity. Numbers 1:23 records 59,300 numbered men in the tribe of Simeon. Soon after, Numbers 26:14 records only 22,200 for Simeon. We know from Numbers 25:9 that 24,000 died in the sin of Baal-peor, so a large portion of the 24,000 may have been in the tribe of Simeon. The rest of the missing men in the comparative census may have died in some other plague, judgment, or natural causes and disease.

Final Preparations for Canaan

In Numbers 26:55, God says that the land the people will inhabit, the land of Canaan, would be divided by lot, and that each family would receive their inheritance according to the names of their tribes. By 26:64, there had been a new census, and among the numbered men there was no one (excluding the Levites) who had been present at the first numbering except Joshua, Caleb, and Moses. Verse 65 points out that this fulfilled the judgment God had pronounced at Kadesh-barnea that only Joshua and Caleb, of the numbered men, would survive the wilderness experience and enter the land.

From this time on, the activity is increasingly military in nature. With the end of the forty years in sight, they circled around the south end of the Dead Sea and began to move through the land of their near relatives, the Moabites, the Edomites, and the Ammonites. Their military activities began to result in conquered land east of the Jordan River. They defeated the Midianites, and among those slain in the battle was Balaam, They conquered two kings, Sihon and Og, who controlled major geographic areas in the Trans-Jordan, in the southern and northern areas.

When Israel established control over this Trans-Jordan area, chapter 32 records that Reuben and Gad saw the land that it was good, and they asked to have their inheritance east of the Jordan River. In addition, half the tribe of Manasseh also wanted to settle there. As a result, that area, including Gilead, became the inheritance of those two and one-half tribes. In the balance of chapter 32, we read that Moses instructed the two and one-half tribes that they could occupy the Trans-Jordan area, but they could not stay there until their fighting men had crossed into the Cis-Jordan with the remaining nine and one-half tribes and helped them to occupy the land. Only then would they be allowed to return into the Trans-Jordan and settle permanently with their families.

Chapter 33 contains Moses' written record of the route of the forty years of wandering. Verse 52 records God's command that they must drive out the inhabitants of the land and destroy their idols, images, and high places. If they are not driven out, verse 55 says, they *"shall be pricks in your eyes, and thorns in your sides."* This command includes a solemn warning. If they do not obey it, God said in verse 56, *"I shall do unto you, as I thought to do unto them."* Israel did not drive out the inhabitants. In fact, they adopted their religious practices to the extent that God later said they were worse than the Canaanites. As a result, He eventually drove out His own people from their land into dispersion and captivity.

XI. IS THE OLD TESTAMENT CREDIBLE?

Numbers 33:2 states, *"And Moses wrote their goings out according to their journeys by the commandment of the Lord."* Through the years, the Old Testament has been under attack from external critics and from internal scholars. Some of the most serious attacks against the integrity of the Old Testament have been under the guise of Christian scholarship. We are accustomed to such terms as "higher criticism," "reconstruction," or the "documentary hypothesis." Many of these theories have led many students to believe these positions were built and developed on solid exegesis and scholarship. Unfortunately, such is not the case. It is mandatory that we know for certain whether or not the Old Testament is what it claims to be. Are the works credited to Moses and the prophets just a collection of documents written by anonymous individuals, or are they, as they claim, the work of Moses and the prophets whose names are attached to their books?

Evidences for Authenticity

There are two lines of evidence which we can use to establish the credibility of the Old Testament. They are labeled "internal evidence" and "external evidence." One example of internal evidence is that the Pentateuch claims to have been written by Moses. We have just read in Numbers 33:2 that Moses recorded the journeying of the children of Israel and that he did so by the commandment of the Lord. After the battle against Amalek we read in Exodus 17:14, *"And the Lord said unto Moses, Write this for a memorial in a book."* Deuteronomy 31:22 records, *"Moses therefore wrote this song."* Deuteronomy 31:24-26:

And it came to pass, when Moses had made an end of writing the words of this law in a book, until they were finished, That Moses commanded the Levites, which bare the ark of the covenant of the Lord, saying, Take this book of the law, and put it in the side of the ark of the covenant of the Lord your God, that it may be there for a witness against thee.

All these passages provide written testimony within the Pentateuch that it was written personally by Moses. The remainder of the Old Testament provides additional testimony In Judges 3:4 we read about *"the commandments of the Lord, which he commanded their fathers by the hand of Moses."* II Kings 21:8 reminds Judah of its responsibility to *"observe to do according to all the law that my servant Moses commanded them."* And Malachi 4:4 commands, *"Remember ye the law of Moses."*

In addition, the New Testament writers, and the Lord Jesus, concur with and support the Mosaic authorship of the Pentateuch. The Pharisees questioning Jesus in Matthew 19:7 asked, *"Why did Moses then command?"* In His response (19:8) Jesus agreed, *"Moses suffered you."* Both Mark 12:19 and Luke 20:28 employ the phrase, *"Moses wrote."* In Acts 3:22 we find, *"Moses truly said"* and in Romans 10:5, *"For Moses describeth."* Many more examples could be cited. It is absolutely impossible to overcome such testimony. Especially is this true in the case of the Lord Jesus for otherwise we would have to believe either that He did not know that Moses did not write the Pentateuch, which would be a reflection on His divine omniscience; or else that He accommodated Himself to the ignorance of the people of His time, in which case we have an assault upon His integrity. I believe we can state that the one who denies Mosaic authorship of the Pentateuch denies to Christ the divine attributes that are His as the Son of God.

Evidence for the authenticity of the remainder of the Old Testament is equally clear and convincing. In Matthew 24:15, Christ mentions the historicity of Daniel. He also gives us the reality of Jonah in Matthew 12:39-40. By quoting Isaiah 42 in Matthew 12:17-21, he convinces us of the unity of the book of Isaiah. This destroys the deutero-Isaiah theory which teaches that chapters 1-39 were written by Isaiah and chapters 40-66 were the work of some pious forger or unknown author. In addition to this, the knowledge was shared by the Jews, the apostles, and later church tradition.

Preservation and Transmission

Following the completion of the Hebrew canon, the Old Testament was translated into various languages. As the years passed, the original manuscripts of Moses, the various historians, and prophets, were used and copied many times, until they eventually disappeared.

But, we can read in Jeremiah 36, an example of the meticulous care which was involved in successfully transmitting these sacred Scriptures. The prophet commanded his scribe, Baruch, to duplicate the copy of the book he had written, which the evil king Jehoiakim had cut apart destroyed in the fireplace.

Reverence for the Word of God did not diminish with the passing of the centuries. If anything, it increased with every generation. Hundreds of years later, scribes would use ingenious means to guarantee the accuracy of the scroll. Each scroll contained a count of the number of letters, the number of words, the number of lines, even such insignificant facts as the middle word or letter. When a copy was made, the letters, words, and lines would be counted and double checked against the original. If a difference existed, the entire copy would be checked until the error was located and immediately corrected. If a scroll contained more than a prescribed minimum of errors it would be destroyed.

Until a several decades ago, the oldest Hebrew manuscript dated from the ninth century A.D. There were many others dated a little later, but the present Hebrew Bible is based primarily on texts from the medieval period in the ninth century. Although most Bible scholars believed them to be accurate, there was no way to demonstrate that they had been transcribed accurately over a one thousand to fifteen hundred year time period.

Then in 1947, a discovery was made. The Dead Sea scrolls, in the caves at Qumran, were discovered by a shepherd lad. Eventually, this find would yield over 40,000 fragments representing hundreds of scrolls and including every book of the Old Testament except Esther. Many of these have been examined with great anticipation and care because some of the fragments were from scrolls that had been written 150 years before Christ. Manuscripts more than a thousand years older than any previously known were available. Careful examination and comparison of the Qumran scrolls, with existing medieval manuscripts, revealed a consistency in textual integrity which was incredible. There was very little noticeable difference between the texts written in 150 B.C. and those written in A.D. 800-900. This demonstrates accurate preservation of the text. The scroll of Isaiah shows no division between chapters 39 and 40. This scroll is on display in the Shrine of the Book in Israel. There is no gap in the scroll between chapters 39 and 40.

XII. MOSES SAYS GOODBYE

-DEUTERONOMY-

The book of Deuteronomy is a sermonic review given by Moses just prior to his death. The name Deuteronomy comes from two Greek words which were used to form the Septuagint title; *deuteros*, meaning "second," and *nomos*, meaning "law." So, the word really means "second law." This was the *second* giving of the law.

Setting for the Sermons

After the Israelites arrived in the Trans-Jordan, in the year 1406 B.C., Moses recounted to the new generation all the past events of the previous forty years. In Deuteronomy 1:1 we read: *"These be the words which Moses spake unto all Israel on this side Jordan in the wilderness, in the plain over against-the Red sea* Verse 5 gives further clarification of the locale, *"On this side Jordan, in the land of Moab, began Moses to declare this law."* This is the setting throughout the book. Deuteronomy 34:1 says, "Moses *went up from the plains of Moab unto the mountain of Nebo."* In 34:5ff - *"Moses died there in the land of Moab. And Moses was an hundred and twenty years old. And the children of Israel wept for Moses in the plains of Moab thirty days."*

As the entire host of Israelites remained on the east side or Trans-Jordan, preparations were being made for a military move across the Jordan to occupy the land in the Cis-Jordan. Almost seven hundred years before, this entire area had been promised to Abraham and his descendants. In his day *"the iniquity of the Amorites is not yet full."* (Gen. 15:16) Now it was. The period of grace had come to an end and the children of Israel were ready to occupy the land. This occupation was necessary in order to fulfill the promise to Abraham that *"I will make of thee a great nation"* (Gen. 12:2). The people who left the land of Egypt were a people, but they were not yet a nation. It takes three things to be a nation and one of these three is that there must be a people.

Next, there must be a constitution. On Mount Sinai, when God gave the Ten Commandments and the ordinances for worship, government, and daily life, the constitution was provided. So, for forty years in the wilderness they were a people with a constitution.   All that remained for national identity was the land. Once they had crossed over the Jordan and began to occupy the territory, they were a nation. Just as when the Jews occupied the land in 1948 A.D., they became a nation.

There was a second purpose for occupation. It was to be God's holy war against the inhabitants of Canaan. We read in Deuteronomy 9:4:

> *Speak not thou in thine heart, after that the Lord thy God hath cast*
> *them out from before thee, saying, For my righteousness the Lord*
> *hath brought me in to possess this land: but for the wickedness of*
> *these nations the Lord doth drive them out from before thee.*

Until the discovery of the *Ugarit* tablets in the early part of the 20th Century, we had no idea of the extent to which the religious system in the land of Canaan had corrupted itself. But because of the tablets, we can see the demonic, licentious worship system which had evolved. It was this worship system that the Israelites were warned over and over again, throughout the books of Numbers and Deuteronomy, to guard themselves against. It was because of the prevalence of this worship system in the land that the Israelites were commanded to kill every single inhabitant. If even one remained alive, that one person could corrupt the nation of Israel, and the program that they were to use to promote the true religion of Jehovah would also be corrupted.

We read a brief example of what was involved in the worship of Baal in the Baal-peor encounter related in the book of Numbers. Briefly, Baal worship was a combination of sexual activity and human sacrifice. The inhabitants of that area of the world were farmers and herdsmen. Their income and livelihood were tied to the land, whether they were Canaanites or Israelites. The most important thing to all the people was fertility. They wanted the land to be fertile, they wanted the cattle and sheep to be fertile, and they wanted their wives to be fertile. To the Canaanites, fertility was the key issue in life and their entire worship system revolved around it. As we examine the artifacts from that era, we can see that the human figures used in their idolatrous worship were designed to suggest fertility.

The word Baal means "lord" and Baalim is "lords." Baal was the god of storm and the god of fertility. One of the primary Baals was Hadad, the storm god. He was often pictured riding on a bull, one of the Canaanite symbols of fertility. One way in which the Canaanites sought to pacify Baal, was to offer their children as sacrifices. The children were to be offered without any display of emotion. If emotion was shown the sacrifice was worthless.

In the Baal temples there were both male and female cult prostitutes. These were the priests and priestesses of Baal. If a man wanted to worship Baal, he would go into the temple and join himself to a priestess. If a woman wanted to worship, she would go in and join herself to a priest. Later, in the Old Testament, these male prostitutes were called *dogs*. Through sexual relations with the priest or priestess, the worshiper was saying: "Just as fertility is taking place during this act, may Baal make my crops fertile; may Baal make my cattle fertile; may Baal make my spouse fertile." In this way, all the outward physical manifestations of fertility were worshiped.

It was because of this corrupt system that God was offended to the point of commanding the total extermination of the inhabitants of the land of Canaan. In His holy war, the Israelites were to function as the military operational invasion force. Because of this, if the Israelites had functioned with total obedience to God's commands and ordinances, they could have fought all the battles in the land of Canaan, completely occupied the land, and never lost a man in battle. Back in Numbers 31:49, following a battle in which the Israelites were completely obedient, is the report given to Moses: *"Thy servants have taken the sum of the men of war which are under our charge, and there lacketh not one man of us."*

This was God's war and He was not going to suffer the loss of any of His warriors if they fought according to His ordinances and His commandments. We will see later in the book of Joshua that this divine protection ceased. Finally, in regard to the religion of the land, Deuteronomy 11:16-17 gave the Israelites advance warning of what would happen. Moses said:

> *Take heed to yourselves, that your heart be not deceived, and ye*
> *turn aside, and serve other gods, and worship them, And then the*
> *Lord's wrath be kindled against you, and he shut up the heaven,*
> *that there be no rain, and that the land yield not her fruit, and lest*
> *ye perish quickly from off the good land which the Lord giveth you.*

Chapter 11 reaffirms the fact that it is God, the Lord Jehovah, and not Baal, who is responsible for fertility in all of creation.

PANORAMA of the OLD TESTAMENT

In addition to the sermonic and historic review reported in Deuteronomy, Moses also gave God's instructions for the occupation of the land. He announced these directives within the hearing of Joshua who, as the second in command, would use them in his conquest of the land. Deuteronomy 20 contains the Military Manual for the occupation of the land. As Moses prepared the people for what would follow, he said in verse 8: *And the officers shall speak further unto the people, and they shall say, what man is there that is fearful and fainthearted? Let him go and return unto his house, lest his brethren's heart faint as well as his heart.*

He was saying, if any of you are afraid, if any of you are cowards, go home. Do not go out to battle with us because if you get out there and decide that it is too much for you, and you want to turn and run, chances are that when others see you running they will turn aside as well. Make up your mind now. If you are going out to fight, be a man. If you are afraid to go, stay home.

Deuteronomy 20:10-14 describes the criteria for approaching the kind of city described in verse 15, which says, *"Thus shalt thou do unto all the cities which are very far off from thee, which are not of the cities of these nations."* "These nations" refers to the nations which God had instructed the Israelites to completely exterminate. But, around the peripheral areas of the land of Canaan, there were cities *"far off"* that were not specifically designated for extinction. Beginning in verse 10, God gave instructions for dealing with those cities "far off."

> *When thou comest nigh unto a city to fight against it, then pro-*
> *claim peace unto it. And it shall be, if it make thee answer of peace,*
> *and open unto thee, then it shall be, that all the people that is found*
> *therein shall be tributaries unto thee, and they shall serve thee.*
> *And if it will make no peace with thee, but will make war against*
> *thee, then thou shalt besiege it. And when the Lord thy God hath*
> *given it into thine hands, thou shalt smite every male thereof with*
> *the edge of the sword: But the women and the little ones, and the*
> *cattle, and all that is in the city, even all the spoil thereof, thou*
> *shalt take unto thyself; and thou shalt eat the spoil of thine enemies, which the Lord thy*
> *God hath given thee.*

Simply put phase one is this: When you go to a city far off, it is not designated for extinction, offer peace to it. If they come out and say, "we surrender," take them and let them serve you. If they say, "no, we will fight you," then the Lord will give you the city.

You will kill all the men, but you will take the women and children and all the cattle and keep them for yourselves. However, according to verses 16 and 17 phase two is this:

> *But of the cities of these people, which the Lord thy God doth give*
> *thee for an inheritance, thou shalt save alive nothing that breatheth:*
> *But thou shalt utterly destroy them; namely, the Hittites, and the*
> *Amorites, the Canaanites, and the Perizzites, the Hivites, and the*
> *Jebusites; as the Lord thy God hath commanded thee.*

If this seems rather extreme, the answer is in verse18: *That they teach you not to do after all their abominations, which they have done unto their gods; so should ye sin against the Lord your God.* God knew that once the people began to practice those abominations of Baalism, that their sons and daughters, their husbands and wives, would get involved in the formal worship system of the land, and that even Israelite men and women would become prostitutes in the houses of Baal. Chapter 23:17-18 has this warning:

> *There shall be no whore of the daughters of Israel, nor a Sodomite*
> *of the sons of Israel. Thou shalt not bring the hire of a whore, or the*
> *price of a dog, [a male cult prostitute] into the house of the Lord thy God for any vow: for*
> *these are abomination unto the Lord thy God.*

You will remember that shortly after the exodus, forty years prior to Deuteronomy 25, Israel encountered Amalek in battle under the leadership of Joshua. At that time God warned them that there would be battle with Amalek from generation to generation. Now, in Deuteronomy 25:17-19, Moses reminded the people once again of what happened so they would not forget their involvement with Amalek or the promise of God to eventually judge Amalek.

> *Remember what Amalek did unto thee by the way, when you were*
> *come forth out of Egypt; How he met you by the way, and smote*
> *the hindmost of thee, even all that were feeble behind thee, when*
> *thou wast faint and weary, and he feared not God. Therefore it*
> *shall be, when the Lord hath given thee rest from all thine enemies*
> *round about, in the land which the Lord thy God giveth thee for an*
> *inheritance to possess it, that thou shalt blot out the remembrance*
> *of Amalek from under heaven; thou shalt not forget it.*

Forty years after the first attack, the promised judgment against Amalek was reaffirmed. It would not be done for another 350 years.

The Song of Moses

One thing that seems to be rooted in our sinful human nature is that the younger generation forgets or ignores what the previous generation learned. We know it was Adam's job to pass on the truth of God to his descendants, and he failed. It was Noah's job to pass on the truth to his descendants, and he failed. It was the job of Abraham to pass on the knowledge of God to his descendants, and he failed. Moses likewise was instructed very plainly to pass these truths on to the sons and the sons' sons, and by this word-of-mouth method, the truth of God was to be transmitted from generation to generation (Deut.6:7; 31:12-13).

But imagine if you will, what the response was to those individuals who were five and six generations removed from Adam. When Adam tried to explain to them that he had been created by God and walked in the cool of the day with God, I am sure that wicked generation laughed and thought he was insane. When Noah tried to explain to his descendants several generations removed that he had experienced the flood; and when his sons-Shem, Ham, and Japheth- attempted to explain to their grandchildren and great-grandchildren that at one time the entire earth had been covered by water and that they had lived in the pre-flood era, I am sure they were also thought to be insane. We know how after several generations, the truth that is attempted to be passed on is mocked and scoffed at and assumed to be worthless, mythical information.

Because of this, the omniscient God told Moses that He knew what was going to happen. He described in 31:16 that soon after they were settled in the land they would play the harlot with strange gods *"and will forsake me, and break my covenant which I have made with them."* In return (vs. 17): *"I will forsake them, and I will hide my face from them."* In an attempt to prevent this, He commanded Moses to compose a song so that generations and centuries later they would remember that they had been warned about their sinful behavior. Though many things might pass away, a song or an epic poem would be learned and sung and passed down from one generation to another. It was designed to make them remember back to the time when God first gave it and its title could be *"Against Forgetfulness."* The purpose of this song (epic poem) was to remind the people that God had anticipated their failure, and that there was still hope, if they repent and turn back to Him.

The poem requires forty-three verses in chapter 32. In this marvelous piece of poetry, God reminds them that He made them drink honey from the rock and oil from the flinty rock, but that they decided to serve idols and other demons that claimed to be gods. God warned them in the song that He would heap misfortune upon them, and assured them in the end of His vengeance, and that blood would be avenged which had been shed by their enemies.

The Death of Moses

The remainder of chapter 32 contains God's instructions to Moses regarding his death, and the reason why it would occur prior to entering the land. He had failed in striking the rock the second time. In chapter 33, Moses blessed the children of Israel prior to his death, which is recorded in chapter 34. Deuteronomy 34:7 records that he lived to be 120 years old. With the death of Moses in 1406 B.C., we have completed the first five books of the Old Testament; the five books of which Moses was the author. In these books we covered the history of the world from creation through the flood, the tower of Babel, the selection of Abram, the births of Isaac, Jacob, and the sons of Jacob, the 430 years of captivity in Egypt, the birth of Moses, the plagues on Egypt, the various murmurings and rebellions of the people of Israel prior to their entering the promised land in 1406 B.C. We have seen how as a result of their grumblings and disobedience, they had to wander an extra thirty-eight years in the wilderness so that no numbered man over the age of twenty would survive to go into the Promised Land.

After the death of Moses, the new generation of people was on the east side of the Jordan River. The leader they knew for many years was dead, the baton of leadership had passed to Joshua, and the inhabitants of the land of Canaan were anticipating military activity as they looked eastward across the Jordan. They knew the Israelites had been successful in previous battles against the Midianites, and hearts were beginning to melt.

XIII. PREPARATION FOR CONQUEST

In this section, we are beginning to study a new era in the history of Israel. The wilderness wanderings were behind them. Moses was dead and Joshua was responsible to lead them into the land of Canaan, which God had earlier promised to Abraham's descendants. It has been over seven hundred years since He told Abraham that the iniquity of the Amorites was not yet full (Gen. 15:16). The seven-century period of grace had only confirmed them in their iniquity. Although God is patient, He is also holy and just, and the time of judgment for the Canaanites had come.

Many people have difficulty reconciling the vengeance of God on the Canaanites with the loving God of the New Testament. Earlier in
The previous century, this brought about a "two-god" theory: the God of the Old Testament and a God of the New Testament. But, we have discovered from the *Ugarit* tablets and other archaeological finds that they were deserving of extermination because of the effect they would have on the children of Israel if they were spared. The New Testament tells us that "*it is a fearful thing to fall into the hands of the living God*" (Heb. 10:31). The God of the Old Testament and the God of the New Testament are one. The God of the Old Testament gave the inhabitants of Canaan seven hundred years to see the error of their ways, but they waxed worse and worse, and the time had come for destruction. {Romans 1:18-28}

The Charge to Joshua

"*Moses my servant is dead,*" God announced to Joshua in chapter one, verse 2. He then gave instructions to the new leader to take the people across the Jordan, assuring them at the same time of His presence with them. Verse 5 says: *There shall not any man be able to stand before thee all the days of thy life; as I was with Moses, so I will be with thee: I will not fail thee nor forsake thee.*

The criteria for success are contained in verses 7 and 8:

> *Only be thou strong and very courageous, that thou mayest*
> *observe to do according to all the law, which Moses my servant*
> *commanded thee: turn not from it to the right hand or to the left,*

> *that thou mayest prosper withersoever thou goest. This book of the*
> *law shall not depart out of thy mouth; but thou shalt meditate*
> *therein day and night, that thou mayest observe to do according to*
> *all that is written therein: for then thou shalt make thy way*
> *prosperous, and then thou shalt have good success.*

As they were on the east side of the Jordan River, preparing to invade the Cis-Jordan, Joshua spoke to the tribes of Reuben and Gad and the half-tribe of Manasseh reminding them of the previous agreement they had made regarding the use of their fighting forces to assist the remaining nine and one-half tribes in conquering the land. Joshua said in verses 12-16:

> *And to the Reubenites and to the Gadites and to half the tribe*
> *of Manasseh, spake Joshua, saying. Remember the word which Moses the servant of the*
> *Lord commanded you, saying. The Lord your God hath given you rest, and hath given you*
> *this land. Your wives, your little ones, and your cattle, shall remain in the land which*
> *Moses gave you on this side Jordan; but ye shall pass before your brethren armed, all the*
> *mighty men of valour, and help them: Until the Lord have given your brethren rest, as he*
> *hath given you,*
> *and they also have possessed the land which the Lord your God*
> *giveth them: then ye shall return unto the land of your possession,*
> *and enjoy it, which Moses the Lord's servant gave you on this*
> *side Jordan toward the sunrising. And they answered Joshua, saying, all that thou*
> *commandest us we will do, and whithersoever thou sendest us, we will go.*

Their final remark, in verse 17, would have made me very nervous. They said: *"According as we hearkened unto Moses in all things, so will we hearken unto thee."* This is disturbing because we know that none of the tribes actually hearkened unto Moses. They continually grumbled, mumbled, and rebelled. Joshua had over 600,000 fighting men at his command ready to enter the land of Canaan and perform a military assault to occupy the territory. Numbers 26:51, where the new census was recorded, put the actual count of the numbered men at 601,730. Accusations are made by critics regarding the use of rounded numbers in Scripture. I believe Moses knew the exact number. See Numbers 11:21, where Moses says, *"The people, among whom I am, are six hundred thousand footmen."* We know from Numbers 2:32 also authored by Moses, that the numbered men at that time totaled 603,550. Numbers 11:21 is an example of Moses also using rounded numbers.

Ancient Warfare

As Joshua and his fighting men looked across the Jordan river to the Cis-Jordan they saw a land which was under the loose hegemony of Egypt. Amenhotep, III, and his royal son Amenhotep, IV, were in charge of the land militarily. The land consisted of an array of city-states. We read (Josh. 12:24) that Joshua defeated thirty-one kings. Just as today, there are mayors over cities and governors over states, the heads of the individual city-states were called kings. Although they were loosely allied to Egypt, they were usually independent of one another. Archaeologists have discovered that the typical city-state had a wall about 50 feet high and as thick 50 feet.

The Siege

The standard method of warfare in the fifteenth century B.C., and even into the middle ages 2500 years later, was known as siege warfare. An invading army had the task of breaking down the walls or battering down the gates of the city under siege. The inhabitants of the city had the task of maintaining themselves inside the city without starving to death, dying of thirst, or allowing their walls to be breached. It was usually a long stand-off. Sieges could often last two or three years. The invading forces would strip the land of all crops and food. They would pollute the area because of their numbers. Hopefully, those inside the city had enough grain stored up, and access to water. When the besieged city was able to hold out long enough, the invading army would be forced to retire to its own land. When the people inside ran out of supplies, they sometimes resorted to cannibalism. This very thing will happen later in the Old Testament to the Israelites. God had promised that if they forsook Him, they would eat their children, and that is exactly what happened. {See II Kings 6:28, 29} When things reached that point, the city eventually had to give up and allow the invading forces in. However, if the invaders could speed the operation by breaching the wall, the stand-off came to an end much more quickly.

Those inside a city would do everything possible to prevent their walls from being breached. They would pile dirt at a 45 degree angle halfway up the wall. This dirt slope was called a *glacis*, and was covered with lime. It prevented the invading forces from attacking the wall directly with their battering rams or siege towers. The inhabitants lined the tops of the walls with huge stones which could be rolled down upon the enemy as they attempted to climb the *glacis* and raise siege ladders. The inhabitants would also stand on the wall and shoot arrows and pour hot oil down on the attackers.

The invading forces had unique engines of war. Among them was the battering ram which could be carried by a man and jammed against a wall or gate. In many cases they had the battering ram suspended by ropes so they could swing it like a pendulum to get more momentum on the ram. They also had a device called the turtle. Twenty or thirty men would carry a huge shield, which looked like a turtle shell, over them. With this protection, they would attempt to tunnel under the wall to come up on the inside and take the city from within.

Joshua's Dilemma

The Israelites did not have any of these engines of war. It was not until the time of King Uzziah that they began to develop such sophisticated weapons. {See II Chronicles 26:15} The task that Joshua faced was, from a human standpoint, overwhelming. He had over 600,000 men, but no engines of war and no strategy. In addition, he was confronted with numerous, heavily fortified city-states. If it required a two to three-year siege to conquer each city, he could spend fifty years laying siege to cities and conquering them before the land could be occupied. But now, the glory and power of God became evident. This was His holy war and it was His occupation army moving into the land.

God had several strategies for victory. First, He had promised Joshua a victory, and would begin by showing the children of Israel that it was His battle. Instead of laying a long siege against Jericho, God demonstrated His power by causing the walls to fall flat. Next, He would cause a spirit of foolishness to go into the hearts of the people of Canaan so that, rather than staying inside the city they would venture out and fight Joshua on the plains. There he was quickly successful. The Lord would send swarms of hornets to drive the inhabitants from their cities out onto the plains. Finally, He would cause the kings to form confederacies so they would leave their cities to make united attacks against Joshua, enabling him to defeat several at one time. With divine intervention, the entire process of conquest was speeded up.

The spade of the archaeologist has provided supplemental information about this period. In A.D. 1887, a peasant woman was digging in the fertile soft around Amarna, Egypt, near Cairo. She unearthed almost four hundred small cuneiform tablets measuring from three inches wide to as long as nine inches, and inscribed on both sides. This was the method used in the late fifteenth century B.C. to send diplomatic correspondence back and forth from Canaan to Egypt. Thanks to the archaeologists, we know that these tablets date from about 1400 B.C. to circa 1358 B.C., and were sent to Amenhotep, III and Amenhotep, IV.

These dates encompass the time of Joshua's invasion and they mention the "Habiru," generally agreed to be the Hebrews. One tablet has this text:

Let my lord the king, the sun in heaven, take heed unto his land, for the Habiru are mighty against us. And let the king my lord stretch out his hand unto me and let him deliver me from their hands so that they may not make an end of us.

From the writings on these tablets we possibly have information of Joshua's conquest of Canaan from the viewpoint of the enemy.

XIV. THE INVASION OF JERICHO

Joshua sent two spies to view the land, especially Jericho, and they went to the house of a harlot named Rahab. If they wanted information, they could not have gone to a better place. The house of a harlot was a place where the merchants, military men, and the politicians spent time. To get inside information about a city, one could be exposed to a full complement and wide range of individuals. But, the presence of the outsiders soon became known to the inhabitants of Jericho and threats were made against them. In fear for their lives, they made an arrangement with Rahab so that if she would hide them, and tell the officials that they had fled, then her life and the lives of her family would be spared when the city was invaded. For her dwelling to be identified when the invasion began, she was told to hang a crimson cord from her window (2:18).

Rahab was an interesting woman. In verse 9 she used the sacred Hebrew word *Yahweh* for "Lord." She also identified herself, not as an idolater, but as one who actually believed in the Lord of the Hebrews. In verse 10 she described why the Canaanites were in fear of Israel. Rahab said: *We have heard how the Lord dried up the water of the Red Sea for you, when ye came out of Egypt, and what ye did unto the two kings of the Amorites, that were on the other side Jordan, Sihon and Og, whom ye utterly destroyed.* The inhabitants of Canaan were knowledgeable of what the God of the Israelites had done; but think about what event she mentioned. The Red Sea had been dried up forty years earlier, yet Rahab knew about it. The Canaanites had also been tracking the history of the Israelites since the Red Sea had been crossed. She admitted in verse 11, *"Our hearts melted because of you."* As the Canaanites looked across the river into the Trans-Jordan, they saw a large body of people. They knew that their God had dried the Red Sea up before them; they knew they had been victorious over the kings of the Trans-Jordan area; and now they were in fear of their lives anticipating the inevitable invasion.

However, Rahab was ready to help the spies in return for having her family saved because she acknowledged the God of the Israelites. When the spies told her she must tie the scarlet cord in her window, she did not wait, though she must have known she had a few days. Verse 21 says that immediately after they left, *"she bound the scarlet line in the window."*

Rahab was not a procrastinator. She made her decision quickly and did not delay in doing what she knew would save her family.

Crossing the Jordan

The previous generation of Israelites had experienced the physical power of God in His universe by witnessing the parting of the Red Sea. However, it was necessary that this new generation witness the power of God's hand in the physical universe, to give them assurance, as they entered the land of Canaan and faced the seemingly impossible odds. Chapter 3 records the new miracle which was no less magnificent than the parting of the Red Sea. At that time of year, the Jordan overflowed its banks. The snows on Mount Hermon were melting and at various locations, the Jordan would be as wide as one mile. It was possibly about a mile wide opposite Jericho. At that season, the inhabitants of Jericho and Canaan could feel secure even though an invading army was encamped across the river. The river current was swift and there was no way to make rafts large enough to take across enough fighting men to lay siege to a city. However, God was going to cause the Jordan River to "*stand up in a heap*" and the river bed to dry up.

There are four reasons for this. First, to facilitate immediate entrance into the land; and second, in order that the new generation might witness His power as the same God who brought their fathers out of Egypt. Third, Joshua's position was confirmed. He predicted the event and it came to pass. He was obviously God's divine replacement for Moses. Fourth, not only did it provide a method for crossing to facilitate military occupation; not only did it demonstrate God's power to a new generation; and not only did it validate Joshua's position as leader, but it also caused the inhabitants of Canaan to be devastated psychologically.

Imagine what it must have been like living in Canaan, feeling secure during the harvest season because the Jordan had overflowed its banks effectively barring the way of the invaders, then suddenly looking eastward and seeing the Jordan River dry up, knowing that forty years earlier it had happened at the Red Sea, and seeing the great horde of Israelites crossing the Jordan River into their territory. It must have been absolutely devastating psychologically. Since, as Rahab said, the hearts of the inhabitants melted when they heard about the Red Sea, they must have melted when they saw the Jordan River dry up. Critics have offered many explanations for the drying up of the Jordan. The most prominent is the landslide theory. Some suggest a landslide took place upstream somewhere and that Joshua took advantage of it to cross his army on a dry river bed. However, Joshua 3:13 is prophetic. Although Joshua could not have known in advance that a landslide would take place, he said, *"The waters of Jordan shall be cut off."* It had not happened yet, and it would not happen until the feet of the priests carrying the Ark stood in the water of the river.

The Israelites had all their religious objects with them. They had the tabernacle which represented the capitol of God (where the tabernacle moved, was God's capitol for His Theocratic state). They had the Ark, which was representative of God's throne (where the Ark of God was, there was His throne). The priests were carrying the Ark, and they were the ones who made intercession so that God could dwell among an unholy people. Also, Scripture is very plain when it records (vs. 15), *"Jordan overfloweth all its banks all the time of harvest."* Verse 17 says that when the priests carried the Ark of the Covenant into the river, the Jordan dried up, and Israel crossed on dry ground. The new generation saw God's power.

We examined how generations which followed great events would never believe the stories they heard from their forefathers regarding the reality of the event. God knew it would happen again. He knew that three or four generations later, their descendants would hear how God dried the Jordan River and would laugh and say, "It's impossible. It's a myth. It never happened." To prevent this, Joshua instructed men to pick up one large stone for each tribe and then stack the stones in two heaps. Verse 4:2 and following describes the piling of the stones and how, when the priests came up out of the dry riverbed, the water rushed down and covered one huge mound of stones (vs. 9). When later generations looked out into the middle of the river and saw the heap of stones under the water, they would ask, *"What mean ye by these stones?"* (vs. 6) The old men would explain how they had placed the stones there when the riverbed was dry; when God caused the waters to stand up in a heap and their ancestors crossed on dry ground and conquered the land. This would be proof that the great miracle actually occurred in the historical past. The heap of smooth stones piled at Gilgal was additional proof of the miracle (vs. 20).

Chapter 5:1 confirms that the hearts of the inhabitants of the land melted. *"Neither was there spirit in them anymore, because of the children of Israel,"* when they saw how the God of the Israelites had dried up the Jordan. The children of Israel camped at Gilgal where they kept the Passover. When they arrived at Gilgal in the Cis-Jordan area, the manna ceased and they began to eat the produce of the land, as recorded in verse 12.

Preparation for Victory

When Joshua stood by Jericho, he looked up, and verse 5:13 records that he saw a man standing with a drawn sword in his hand. Joshua asked, *"Are you for us or against us?"* The reply came, *"Nay; but as captain of the host of the Lord am I now come."* When he heard that, Joshua fell on his face. This was Christ in the Old Testament - a Theophany. The Son of God appeared in this instance as the Captain of the host of the Lord. Joshua recognized that he was being addressed by Deity, so he fell to the ground. Joshua was then given the same kind of experience that his predecessor Moses had forty years earlier at the burning bush. The inspiration of the event which Moses experienced, when he encountered God and was instructed to remove his sandals from His feet because he was on holy ground, was now given to Joshua. Joshua would never forget this experience of meeting God face-to-face. The response to Joshua's question about whose side the Man was on actually meant, "I am on My own side." The important issue to Joshua was, whose side are you on? Many still say that God is on *our* side. God is on His *own* side.

Joshua was now a man totally dedicated and prepared for his task. He had witnessed the power of God in drying the Red Sea, and the Jordan river. He knew that God had not changed in those forty years. He had the assurance from God that he would be successful and that his way would be prosperous. He was prepared spiritually after having the encounter with the Angel of the Lord and being told to remove the sandals from his feet in the same manner the Pre-Incarnate Christ had instructed Moses at the burning bush.

Israel's Preparation

The children of Israel were also ready for their task. Their spirits were high; their adrenaline was pumping; and they were eager to go up from Gilgal and tear down the walls of Jericho brick by brick. But, this was God's holy war and He was going to demonstrate to them that He did not need them to conquer the land. So, rather than ask them to perform militarily, He said, in effect, *"I do not want you to do anything. I am going to demonstrate to you that even though you are confronted with an impossible task, humanly speaking, the victory is Mine."* Jericho was a representative city. It had been around for many centuries and was still there. It was the citadel, the bastion of strength for the land of Canaan because of the strategic location adjacent to the Jordan River. This was to be a symbolic victory so the Israelites were restrained from all military activity.

Whose is the Spoil?

Prior to the invasion of Jericho, God gave specific commands regarding the "spoil" inside the city. The old cliché, "To the victor belongs the spoil," is not only true in military circles, but it is true with God as well. It was as if God said, *"This is My battle; this is My military victory. I do not need you to help Me defeat Jericho; therefore all of the spoil is Mine."*

Reading in Joshua 6:17-19:

And the city shall be accursed, even it, and all that are therein, to the Lord: And ye, in any wise keep yourselves from the accursed thing, lest ye make yourselves accursed, when ye take of the accursed thing, and make the camp of Israel a curse, and trouble it. But all the silver, and gold, and vessels of brass and iron, are consecrated unto the Lord: they shall come into the treasury of the Lord.

The word "accursed" means sanctified, or as in some translations, "under the ban." It does not mean accursed in the sense that we think of something being a curse, but it means that something is sanctified, is set apart, and belongs to God. It is His. Do not touch it. The spoil belongs to God. He is the victor in the battle of Jericho.

The Conquest

In Joshua 6:13, the Israelites were instructed to march around the city once a day for six days, and on the seventh day they were to march around the city seven times. They were also instructed to be totally silent. In verse 10, we are informed that:

Joshua had commanded the people, saying, ye shall not shout nor make any noise with your voice, neither shall any word proceed out of your mouth, until the day I bid you shout; then shall ye shout.

I suspect that Joshua had his hands full simply convincing these people to stay quiet. Their blood was boiling, they itched for military encounter and activity, but they had to humble themselves in marching around the city in total silence. I also am sure that after the third or fourth day, they began to receive some jeers and taunts from the top of the wall of Jericho. Nevertheless, the seventh day came, and after the seventh time around the city they were told to shout. When they shouted, rather than having a two to three year siege, the walls of Jericho fell flat! This was a symbolic victory demonstrating that, regardless of the fortifications put up by the inhabitants of Canaan, God could overcome all obstacles in a moment of time.

The Israelites ran into the city and began to follow God's instructions. Yet, even in the midst of all the turmoil, confusion, and the noise of battle, verse 22 records that Joshua instructed his two spies to go to Rahab's house. Despite the chaos, they kept their promise.

XV. PRIDE AND HUMILIATION

After the overwhelming victory at Jericho, *"Joshua sent men from Jericho, to Ai"* One senses that the confidence of the people was shifting from God to themselves because they said to Joshua: *Let not all the people go up, but let about two or three thousand men go up and smite Ai, and make not all the people to labour thither, for they are but few. (7:3)* In other words, "we do not need God for this little job, neither do we need all the fighting men of Israel." Their over-confident attitude is immediately apparent. Not only were they becoming overly confident in their own capability after the victory at Jericho, in which they really had no part, but they failed to consult God regarding the next battle.

Defeat at Ai

In verse 4 we read that about three thousand men went up. But, without warning the men of Ai struck down thirty-six of the men of
Israel. They fled from the city and were pursued by the men from Ai. After that defeat, the hearts of the Israelites melted as the hearts of the Canaanites had before. Because of the unexpected defeat, they lost their psychological advantage and were devastated. They were totally confused. Joshua tore his clothes and fell to the earth; but God said to him (vs. 10): *"Get thee up; wherefore liest thou thus upon thy face? Israel hath sinned, and they have also transgressed my covenant which I commanded them: for they have even taken of the accursed thing, and have also stolen, and dissembled also, and they have put it even among their own stuff. Therefore the children of Israel could not stand before their enemies.* The earlier assurance that not a man would be lost in battle had been negated. God in effect was saying. *"It is time to rise up, take these people, consecrate them, and find the individual who has sinned and brought Israel under the curse."*

This would not be an easy task. There were over 600,000 numbered men and including women and children a total of almost two million people. Even Sherlock Holmes and Scotland Yard would have difficulty finding the guilty among those two million. How was it to be done? Joshua 7:14 gives God's instructions.

> *In the morning therefore ye shall be brought according to your*
> *tribes: and it shall be, that the tribe which the Lord taketh shall*

> *come according to the families thereof, and the family which the Lord shall take shall come by households; and the household which the Lord shall take shall come man by man.*

The Lord was going to take these groups until He had filtered down to the guilty person. But again, what procedure would He use? After the death of Moses, with whom God spoke face-to-face, God revealed His will through the ephod and the breastplate of righteousness. The historical record of the construction of the ephod and the breastplate of righteousness is contained in Exodus 28:6-30. Evidently, through the stones that were on the breastplate and with the *"urim"* and *"thummim,"* God revealed His will to the priest, or to the holder of the ephod who was in His will. We know four hundred years later, in the time of David, in I Samuel 30:7-8, God responded to David through the ephod. We read:

> *David said to Abiathar the priest, Ahimelech's son, I pray thee, bring me the ephod. And Abiathar brought thither the ephod to David. And David inquired at the Lord, saying, Shall I pursue after this troop? Shall I overtake them? And he answered him, Pursue: for thou shalt surely overtake them, and without fail recover all.*

Evidently, this was the method which God prescribed. This is surmised because Moses instructed Joshua that he was to inquire through Eleazer the priest regarding the will of God in every matter.

Achan

Joshua stepped forward and announced that someone in the camp had sinned and had brought the entire camp under the judgment of God. Achan, the guilty man standing with possibly 1,999,999 other people around him, felt very secure. But, after going in and inquiring of God through the ephod, Joshua came back out and said, "The tribe of Judah is taken." The census of Numbers 26:22 revealed that there were 76,500 numbered men in Judah, so even that seemed a secure crowd in which to hide. To Achan, one in 76,500 was still good odds against discovery. As the other eleven tribes backed away, Joshua inquired again and announced that the family of the Zarhites was taken. As the other families moved back, Achan must have started getting stomach twinges and sweaty palms. Then Joshua announced that the household of Zabdi was taken. As the household of Zabdi passed by man by man, Joshua confronted Achan and asked, *"Where did you put the stuff?"*

Achan's confession (vs. 21) was a tragic one. He said, "*I saw. I coveted them, and took them.*" How my heart goes out to this man who fell and brought disgrace and shame on the tribes of Israel. I am reminded of I John 2:16, "*For all that is in the world, the lust of the flesh, and the lust of the eyes, and the pride of life, is not of the Father, but is of the world.*" And James 1:15: "*When lust hath conceived, it bringeth forth sin: and sin, when it is finished, bringeth forth death.*" Achan is a tragic example of these verses of warning.

Joshua pronounced judgment (vs. 25): "*Why has thou troubled us? The Lord shall trouble thee this day.*" Even the name Achan means trouble. They stoned him with stones and burned everything that he owned. Then they piled a huge heap of stones over the place where he died, then named the place "*the Valley of Achor,*" which means Valley of Troubling. What an epitaph to have on one's tombstone. "The Troubler of Israel!"

Cleansing Brings Victory

Following the removal of Achan and his sin from the midst of the camp, the Israelites were told to return once again to Ai, this time with God's assurance that they would defeat the inhabitants of the city. But this time God had a different plan. The battle was going to be theirs and the spoil was going to be theirs because they would partake in the military activity. If Achan had waited until they went up to Ai under God's direction, the thirty-six men would not have been lost, he would not have been executed and he would have enjoyed the spoil of the very next battle because he would have gotten it with honor, in a God-approved manner with proper priorities. He and his family could have enjoyed the blessings of the God of Israel.

In chapter 8, Joshua went up against Ai, using good military strategy. The inhabitants of Ai, thinking they were going to defeat the Israelites as before, left their city. Joshua went in from the other side, burned Ai and defeated the army. The psychological advantage was regained!

Deception by the Gibeonites

As you recall, Joshua was given a military manual which told him that he was to completely annihilate the people who occupied the land which he was to subdue. In addition, he could proclaim peace to those cities which were afar off, outside the general area in the land of occupation. Joshua chapter 9 demonstrates that, following their initial self-confidence when they first attacked Ai in the energy of the flesh without consulting God, their self-reliance had become more ingrained. We are introduced in this chapter to the inhabitants of Gibeon. If you examine a map you will see that they were located not very far away from the camp of the Israelites. By no means could they be considered a city afar off. They were inhabitants of a city destined for total annihilation because they lived in the area for   occupation.

Reading about the craftiness of the Gibeonites, leads us to believe that somehow they were aware of Joshua's military manual. Joshua 9:3ff says that when they heard what Israel did at Jericho and Ai, they acted craftily. This is the same word used in Genesis 3:1 to describe the activity of the serpent. Having heard about Jericho and Ai, the Gibeonites feared for their lives. They knew that as soon as Joshua came across the mountains with his military force, they would be annihilated. As a result, they set about to deceive Joshua and his army into making a treaty with them. They believed that the only way they could do so was to make Joshua think they lived in one of the cities afar off. With this plan of deception, they put on worn out clothes and sandals. They took bread that had been around for weeks and had become dry, crumbly, and moldy. They put worn out sacks on their donkeys, took cracked and worn out wineskins, threw dirt on themselves, and no doubt gave the appearance of having traveled for weeks or even months. As they came panting and dirty into the camp of Joshua they said (vs. 6): *"We be come from afar country: now therefore make ye a league with us."* Joshua was slightly suspicious, but in vss. 8-10:

We are thy servants. Thy servants are come because of the name
of the Lord thy God: for we have heard the fame of him, and all that
he did in Egypt. And all that he did to the two kings of the Amorites,
that were beyond Jordan. To Sihon king of Heshbon, and to Og
king of Bashan, which was at Ashtaroth.

Joshua, although suspicious, looked at the wineskins, the moldy bread, and worn out clothes and sandals. He and his leaders took counsel and decided on the basis of what they saw that the ragged strangers were right. They would make a treaty with them. But, verse 14 says, they *"asked not counsel at the mouth of the Lord."* This is the first indication of direct disobedience on the part of Joshua from the direct command given in Numbers 27:21. Joshua made peace with the Gibeonites, entered into a covenant with them to let them live, and the leaders of the congregation swore an oath. Immediately following this, Joshua set out to continue his central campaign to conquer the middle section of Canaan. It was then they discovered Gibeon was included among the cities of the central plain. Realizing what they had done, verse 18 says:

And the children of Israel smote them not, because the princes of

the congregation had sworn unto them by the Lord God of Israel.
And all the congregation murmured against the princes.

Joshua and the leaders explained that if they touched the Gibeonites, God's wrath would come down upon them because they had made a covenant in the name of the Lord. But, Joshua told the Gibeonites, "even though you deceived us and we cannot kill you, we will make you hewers of wood and drawers of water for the entire congregation." The Gibeonites readily agreed, evidently finding slavery preferable to death. In verse 24 they gave an interesting testimony as to why they had decided to practice deceit. The future effect of this plays out four Centuries later in II Samuel 21:1-14.

XVI. CONQUEST COMPLETED

When other Canaanite cities learned that the Gibeonites had become cowards and made a treaty with the occupation forces of Israel, they banded their armies together to destroy them. As a result (10:6), the Gibeonites sent emissaries to Joshua begging him to: *"Come up to us quickly, and save us, and help us: for the kings of the Amorites that dwell in the mountains are gathered together against us."*

Because of the covenant between them, Israel was bound to go to the rescue of Gibeon, but Joshua was able to lead them into battle with the Lord's gracious assurance ringing in his ears (10:8): *"Fear them not. For I have delivered them into thine hand, there shall not a man of them stand before thee."* What a tremendous promise for a military leader to receive from the Creator of the universe! A General who had received assurance like that from a sovereign God could put his cares and fears regarding his military conquests to rest. However, some military leaders would relax and slow down, knowing that the victory was certain.

Joshua did not relax and slow down. We read in chapter 10, verse 9 that he came upon the enemy quickly by marching throughout the night. Do you find that amazing? I do. I see here the interfacing of the spiritual promise and the physical activity. Joshua did not go ahead without an assurance from God. At the same time, he did not sit back and wait for God to fight the battle for him. He marched with his men through the night to come upon the enemy suddenly to attack and defeat them. This was the perfect blending of physical activity and God's promise. Joshua marched all night and engaged the enemy. In the midst of the battle, God began to drop huge hailstones on the Amorites so that, as verse 11 says, *"they were more which died with hailstones than they whom the children of Israel slew with the sword."* The conflict was too great to complete in a single day, so Joshua offered up an amazing prayer (10:12ff):

> *Then spake Joshua to the Lord in the day when the Lord delivered*
> *up the Amorites before the children of Israel, and he said in the*
> *sight of Israel, Sun, stand thou still upon Gibeon; and thou, Moon,*

in the valley of Aijalon. And the sun stood still, and the moon stayed, until the people had avenged themselves upon their enemies.

Skeptics say: "Don't you know that if the earth stood still people would be crushed because of the gravitational pull? It is only the spinning of the earth and the centrifugal force that keeps us from being crushed. Can you imagine the chaos in the universe if things should grind to a halt?" They suggest "better" explanations. For example, "possibly there was an extended period of light refraction so that the day seemed longer." Or, "possibly God gave them some kind of speeded-up activity so they got twice as much done in the same amount of time like some of the old movies that seemed to run very rapidly." "Maybe it is just poetic; it didn't really happen." It depends on how big you believe God is. The God Who spoke the heavens into existence can as easily grind them to a halt at a moment's notice and then reactivate them again. We know this is what happened because not only is Scripture correct, inspired and inerrant, but verse 14 records, *"And there was no day like that before it or after it, that the Lord hearkened unto the voice of a man: for the Lord fought for Israel."* This was not poetic and there is no scientific explanation for it. Everything stood still. God continued to demonstrate that this was His holy war, and He was in command.

Following the defeat of the central confederacy, chapter 10 lists the kings and the various locations which comprised the southern confederacy and describes how Joshua was victorious over the entire south. It was *"because the Lord God of Israel fought for Israel"* (vs. 42). Verse 43 says that the army returned to its base of operations at Gilgal. Chapter 11 describes the northern campaign and the move by Joshua and the army up into that area. In summary, verse 23 says, *"Joshua took the whole land."* Chapter 12 is a synopsis of all the victories won by Israel and ends in verse 24 with the information that thirty-one kings were defeated by Joshua.

The Distribution of the Land

Chapter 13 opens with the indication that Joshua has become too old to continue. Before his death, the land must be distributed among the remaining nine and one-half tribes. The other two and one-half tribes had already selected their land in the Trans-Jordan area. Chapter 13, verses 14 and 33, had reaffirmed the fact that the tribe of Levi would not receive a physical inheritance in the land because the Lord, the God of Israel, was their inheritance. Verses 21 through 33 are a flashback to events in the Trans-Jordan and time of Moses.

Chapter 14 begins relating events which occurred six or seven years after the entry into the land. We know this from verse 7 where Caleb said, *"Forty years old was I when Moses sent me to spy out the land,"* and verse 10 where he said, *"the Lord hath kept me alive, as he said, these forty and five years. I am this day four score and five years old."* (Remember the time period from Kadesh to the crossing of Jordan was thirty-eight years.) So, the approximate date of this chapter is 1400 B.C. Caleb at age eighty five is still claiming mountains and wanting to fight giants.

Chapters 15 through 22 detail the allotment of the land by various geographical areas among the nine and one-half tribes. The fighting men from Reuben, Gad and the half-tribe of Manasseh were mustered out to return to the Trans-Jordan following some conflict and misunderstanding about their convictions and intentions.

A Warning

Chapter 23 takes place *"a long time after that the Lord had given rest unto Israel from all their enemies round about."* Joshua by now was very old and had some serious warnings to relay concerning their associations with the inhabitants of Canaan. In verse 7, he commands that they were to have nothing to do with the Canaanite gods, not even so much as mentioning their names. If they mingled themselves with those nations, then verse 13 warned:

Know for a certainty that the Lord your God will no more drive out
any of these nations from before you; but they shall be snares and
traps unto you, and scourges in your sides, and thorns in your eyes, until ye perish from off
this good land which the Lord your God hath given you.

Joshua's Farewell

Chapter 24 presents Joshua gathering the people around him at Shechem for his final farewell. This was a revered site because it was the place where God first appeared to Abram when he entered Canaan (Gen. 12:6) and where he built his first altar in Canaan. We know that the people recognized the sacredness of the place, because Joshua 24:32 tells us that they took the bones of Joseph which they had carried up out of Egypt and buried at Shechem.

As Joshua gathered the people around him, he reminded them (vs. 12) how God had sent the hornet before the invading forces and driven out the inhabitants of the cities. He pointed out how God had given them a land they had not labored for; how they inhabited cities they had not built; how they were eating from vineyards and olive yards they had not planted. Verse 14 warns them to fear, serve the Lord alone, *"and put away the gods which your fathers served."*

Imagine! He repeated it again in verse 23: *"Now therefore put away, said he, the strange gods which are among you, and incline your heart unto the Lord God of Israel."* Even after witnessing the power of God, as He dried up the Jordan River, after witnessing His power as He drove out the inhabitants of the cities, the Israelites were still carrying idols and foreign gods with them. In verse 15 Joshua said, "Make up your minds!"

> *Choose you this day whom ye will serve; whether the gods which your fathers served that were on the other side of the flood, or the gods of the Amorites, in whose land ye dwell: but as for me and my house, we will serve the Lord.*

"Flood" is "river" and refers to the Euphrates. They had three options. They might choose to serve the ancient gods of the Chaldees as their forefathers had; or the gods of the Amorites; or they could stand with Joshua and choose to serve Jehovah. All the people responded in vs. 16, *"God forbid that we should forsake the Lord, to serve other gods."* The book of Joshua closes with the information (vs. 29) that Joshua died at 110 years. Verse 31:

> *Israel served the Lord all the days of Joshua, and all the days of the elders that outlived Joshua, and which had known all the work of the Lord, that he had done for Israel.*

Unfortunately, we will learn in Judges 2:10, that after this older generation had passed away, *"there arose another generation after them, which knew not the Lord, nor yet the works which he had done for Israel."* This is graphic proof regarding how succeeding generations look back in mockery, disrespect, and disbelief on the things that God has done for their fathers before them.

XVII. AN ERA OF BACKSLIDING

-JUDGES-

As we begin the book of Judges, we soon become aware of how quickly the people of Israel began to backslide after the death of Joshua. It began with a departure from *complete* obedience. As they settled into their new homeland, they became soft and decided there was an easier way to complete the conquest than the methods God had prescribed. After a summary of the various areas inhabited, Judges 1:28 puts the finger on the beginning of the problem by saying, *"And it came to pass, when Israel was strong, that they put the Canaanites to tribute, and did not utterly drive them out."* God had said, "Annihilate them," but the people said, "It is easier and more practical to enslave them and collect taxes from them." Already, they were starting to do what was *right in their own eyes.*

From that event onward, it was all downhill. Verse 29 says, *"Neither did Ephraim drive out the Canaanites."* Then in verse 30, *"Neither did Zebulun drive out the inhabitants."* In verse 31, *"Neither did Asher drive out the inhabitants."* Verse 33: *"Neither did Naphtali drive out the inhabitants."* Finally, in verse 34: *"And the Amorites forced the children of Dan into the mountain; for they would not suffer them to come down to the valley."* They had lost the offensive and were now being driven out by the enemy.

To make known His displeasure, the Pre-Incarnate Christ appeared before them in the form of a Theophany, as the Angel of the Lord. He denounced their disobedience and pronounced against them the prophesied judgment of Joshua 23:13. No longer would He fight for them to drive the inhabitants out, *"but they shall be as thorns in your sides, and their gods shall be a snare unto you"* (2:3).

Israel's Sin Cycle

Judges 2:10 introduces us to the new generation that *"knew not the Lord,"* and verse 11 tells us that they *"did evil in the sight of the Lord, and served Baalim."* In this chapter, we are introduced to the sin cycle that continues through the rest of Israel's national history. We are also introduced to God's various chastisements. The description of the four stages of the sin cycle begins in verse 13: *"And they forsook the Lord, and served Baal and Ashtaroth."* When

the people forsook God, they involved themselves with the idolatrous worship system of the land and God's anger was kindled against them. Phase two of the cycle is described in verse 14:

> *And the anger of the Lord was hot against Israel, and he delivered them into the hands of spoilers that spoiled them, and he sold them into the hands of their enemies round about, so that they could not any longer stand before their enemies.*

The occupation by foreign troops would last for a given period of time until eventually the people could no longer bear the oppression, but would groan and cry out in repentance. This would initiate phase

three of the cycle as described in 2:18b: *"For it repented the Lord because of their groanings by reason of them that oppressed them and vexed them."* Verse 16 summarizes phase four of the cycle: *"The Lord raised up judges, which delivered them out of the hand of those that spoiled them."* This completes the cycle of sin, oppression, repentance, and deliverance. After four cycles the people seemed to have learned their lesson, but their obedience lasted only as long as the Judge lived. Then, with the next generation, the cycle began all over again. Verse 19 sums it up:

> *And it came to pass, when the judge was dead, that they returned, and corrupted themselves more than their fathers, in following other gods to serve them, and to bow down unto them; they ceased not from their own doings, nor from their stubborn ways.*

And so it went; the cycle continued over and over and over again. It was always the same; sin, oppression, repentance, and deliverance. As we read, we want to cry out, "When will it end?" Not only did the cycle continue over and over, but it was a descending cycle. Each new generation sinned "more than their fathers." And each rallied less and less wholeheartedly behind the God-appointed Judge. As time went on, the involvement of Israel in support of the Judge became less and less, until finally, the last Judge, Samson, was bound with ropes by his people and turned over to the enemy.

There is an underlying theme running through the book of Judges. First, no flesh shall glory in God's presence. Second, when God gives victory, He brings it to pass in such a way that the human instrumentality can in no way claim that it was his effort which brought success. Examining God's choices of individuals who became Judges, we will see that they are not people one would normally expect to be champions of justice, experts in military strategy, or have the ability to rally others behind them for victory over occupation forces.

Dating the Period of the Judges

Before we go into the historical narratives of the individual Judges, we need to consider two technical aspects about the book. First of all, if we add up all of the numbers in the book of Judges, as they relate to years of rest and years of oppression, we arrive at a total of 410 years. According to our chronology based on I Kings 6:1, this is about seventy-five years too long. We learned in I Kings 6:1 that from the fourth year of Solomon's reign back to the Exodus was 480 years. If the period of the Judges was 410 years, that leaves only seventy years for the wilderness wanderings, Joshua's leadership, Saul's reign, David's reign, and Solomon's first four years. We know the wilderness wanderings were forty years, and Joshua's leadership lasted about twenty-one years. Saul and David each reigned for forty years. I Kings 6:1 records the first four years of Solomon's reign. These all total 145 years.

If we place the book of Judges using chronological parameters, we see that we can have 335 years as the period of time in Judges. This is because the Judges did not judge sequentially, but some judged simultaneously in different geographical areas. The second consideration is that the book of Judges overlaps I Samuel by a period of approximately forty-five to fifty years. Judges 13:1 begins a forty year period of oppression by the Philistines. This forty year period begins with the birth of Samson at approximately 1095 B.C. First Samuel begins with the birth of Samuel, but I Samuel 7:13 records the termination of the forty years of oppression which began in Judges 13. So, if we date the birth of Samuel at about 1100 B.C. and begin Judges 13 in 1095 B.C. with the birth of Samson and the beginning of the Philistine oppression, then the oppression comes to an end in I Samuel 7, at about the same time that Samson died in Judges 16. While Samuel was using Bethel as a central location for the small circuit of his prophetic office and function as priest and Judge, at the same time, Samson was living near the Mediterranean seacoast. He was involved in a personal vendetta against the Philistines, which God in His sovereignty was using as judgment against them.

XVIII. The BOOK OF JUDGES

Chapters 3 through 16 describe the adventures of the individual Judges as each in turn delivered Israel from an oppressor.

Othniel

Othniel's exploits begin in Judges 3:9. He was the son of Kenaz, the younger brother of Caleb. He was also Caleb's son-in-law (1: 13). He was victorious over the king of Mesopotamia and kept the land at peace for forty years.

Ehud

According to 3:12, the Israelites again became evil, and God allowed the Moabites to rise up against them. Verse 13 says that the Moabites were joined by the sons of Ammon and of Amalek. This is especially interesting in light of the earlier prediction that Israel would have war with Amalek from generation to generation. We know from   Genesis 36 that Amalek was one of the chiefs and descendants of Esau. The Moabites and Ammonites were the descendants of Lot's two sons resulting from his incest with his daughters. The three chastening rods God used were all distant relatives of Israel. For eighteen years, Israel was forced to serve the Moabites. Finally, God raised up Ehud, the left-handed man to deliver them. Ehud made a two-edged sword one cubit, (eighteen inches) long. Being left-handed, he strapped it to his right thigh.

On the pretext of carrying tribute money, he approached Eglon, the very obese king of Moab. As soon as Eglon accepted the tribute, Ehud announced that he had a private message for him, so Eglon dismissed his servants. Ehud said, *"I have a message from God for you."* Eglon stood to his feet as was customary when one expected to receive a message from deity. Then, with his left hand Ehud drew his sword and thrust it into the stomach of Eglon, pushing it so far that the fat closed over the hilt. Then he fled. By the time the dead king was discovered, Ehud had rallied the people behind him. They struck down ten thousand Moabites and the land had rest for eighty years. This is the longest period of rest recorded in Judges.

Shamgar

Only one verse (3:31) is devoted to Shamgar who, using only an ox goad, slew six hundred Philistines. An ox goad is a cattle prod, used to move stubborn animals. It is the same instrument referred to by the Lord Jesus Christ when He encountered Saul of Tarsus on the road to Damascus and said to him, *"It is hard for thee to kick against the pricks"* (Acts 9:5).

Deborah

Judge number four, Deborah, is introduced in chapter 4. She was selected by God to save the sons of Israel after they had once again turned to evil following the death of Ehud. That time God found it necessary to deliver them into the hand of Jabin, King of Canaan. His capital was Hazor and his army had nine hundred iron chariots with Sisera as Commander-in-chief. At the time Deborah was chosen, they had been under the heel of King Jabin for twenty years and were at that point in the sin cycle where they cried to the Lord for deliverance.

Deborah, who was also a prophetess (vs. 4), offered Barak the opportunity of going into battle against Sisera with God's assurance of victory, but Barak refused unless Deborah would go with him. After Sisera had gathered his chariots and his army in the valley, Deborah gave Barak the word from the Lord, *"Up; for this is the day in which the Lord hath delivered Sisera into thine hand: is not the Lord gone out before thee?"* (vs. 14) Barak and his army of ten thousand went down from Mount Tabor and won a great victory over Sisera.

For some insight into the battle, we must look at chapter 5 where we can read Deborah's poetic account of what transpired. Verses 14 and 15 name the tribes that went into the battle. Interestingly enough, they were not those best known for their military prowess, but those that were more agrarian in occupation and those who wielded the staff of office (the scribes). So this battle between Deborah and Barak, and the host of Canaanites with their nine hundred iron chariots, was not fought by military men, but by farmers. In verse 16 and following she scolded those tribes that did not join the battle. They were more interested in tending their sheep and their boats than they were in defeating the enemies of God. She went on to praise those who had *"risked their lives unto death"* (vs. 18). Verse 15 describes how they rushed into the valley. We can imagine them as they rushed down Mount Tabor armed with only pitchforks, clubs, and other crude weapons, into the valley filled with nine hundred chariots and a professionally trained, well equipped army.

To really get a grasp of their heroism, we should examine what chariot warfare was like. The Canaanites, and later the Assyrians and Babylonians equipped their chariots with sharp scythes on the axles. The horse's hooves and brow pieces were covered with sharp knife-like devices. Frequently, the chariots would pull logs 8 to 12 feet wide, covered with pitch and set aflame. The whirring scythe blades and flashing knives would cut down the opposition and the flaming logs would roll over them. It was a fearsome opponent that Barak and his army saw waiting in the valley.

Normally, the results of such a confrontation could be predicted in advance. What chance could foot soldiers, and especially farmers armed with pitchforks and clubs, have against chariots of iron with flashing scythe blades and flaming logs? But God had promised victory, and 5:15 says they *rushed* into the valley. This is the same word used in describing how David *rushed* toward Goliath. God gave them a great victory. Judges 4:16 says not a single man was left except Sisera, the commander-in-chief who fled on foot for his life. Eventually, he arrived at the tent of a woman named Jael, the wife of a Kenite. She encouraged him to enter the tent to lie down and rest. The Kenites, although neutral in their alliances, were friends of the Israelites. Sisera did not know it, but Jael had sinister plans to destroy him.

To use this narrative as a sermon, you can title it, *"The Tale of Jael's Nail."* Jael would probably have been uncomfortable with the normal weapons of war, a sword or a battle-axe, but she would feel quite at home with a tent peg and a mallet since it was the job of the women to pitch the tent. She would have a strong forearm from years of driving tent pegs and while Sisera slept, she drove the peg through his temples and pinned him to the ground.

Deborah, in her poem, rejoiced over this act just before beginning her taunt over Sisera's mother in 5:28. She painted a vivid picture of Sisera's mother looking through the lattice work (there were no glass windows in those days) waiting for the return of her overdue son and being encouraged by her friends as they sought to ease her worries by describing his expected victory and glory.

The mother of Sisera looked out a window, and cried through the lattice, why is his chariot so long in coming? Why tarry the wheels of his chariots? Her wise ladies answered her, yea, have they not sped? have they not divided the prey; to every man a damsel or two; to Sisera a prey of divers colours, a prey of divers colours of needlework on both sides, for the necks of them that take the spoil?

But Sisera lay dead, pinned to the ground in Jael's tent and Deborah summarized it in 5:31: *"So let all thine enemies perish, O Lord; but let them that love him be as the sun when he goeth forth in his might."* And the land had rest forty years.

Gideon

In Judges 6:1, the sin cycle began all over again, *"The children of Israel did evil in the sight of the Lord: and the Lord delivered them into the hand of Midian seven years."* The Midianites were like the Bedouins. They would rush across the land, burning what they could, and what they did not bum they would ravage and take. Nothing was safe. The Israelites had to hide their possessions in the dens and caves of the mountains for protection. The sin cycle had made another downward circuit. Israel had sinned and God sent in an oppressor. Verse 6 describes phase 3, *"the children of Israel cited unto the Lord."* Before delivering them, the Lord sent a prophet to remind them of the reasons they were suffering such oppression (vss. 8-10). *"Ye have not obeyed my voice."* But phase 4 was about to begin because God had chosen the one who would deliver them from the Midianites.

You could see the process of winnowing grain if you were to travel to Israel or any country where it is still gathered by hand. A high hill where the breeze blows is selected for the threshing floor. Using pitch-forks, the reapers will throw the grain high in the air where the wind can blow away the lighter chaff, as the good kernels fall back to the earth. This process has been used for thousands of years and continues today. In Judges 6, the Angel of the Lord appeared to Gideon as he was threshing grain in a most unusual place. It was *in* the winepress. Just as the threshing floor was elevated, the winepress was in a depressed spot, a dug out hole in the earth that would hold the juice when the grapes were mashed. Needless to say, one cannot expect much wind to be in a hole in the ground. But there was Gideon, fearful of the Midianites, afraid of having his grain stolen, threshing it secretly in a winepress, grain and chaff alike probably falling back down on his head.

The words of the Theophany seem strange: *"The Lord is with thee, thou mighty man of valor"* (vs. 12). At that moment, Gideon did not look like a man of valor. However, the Angel assured him that he was chosen to defeat Midian (vs. 16). Always a skeptical man, Gideon asked for a sign, and in response, his offering of bread and meat was consumed by fire from the rock. Gideon then recognized that he had seen the Lord face-to- face and built an altar.

Following the instructions by the Angel of the Lord, Gideon destroyed the Baal worship system in his city, pulling down the statues and idols. The men of the city were ready to kill him for having done this, but his father Joash defended him, saying:

> *Will ye plead for Baal? Will ye save him? He that will plead for*
> *him, let him be put to death whilst it is yet morning: if he be a god,*
> *let him plead for himself, because one hath cast down his altar.*

In verse 32: *"Therefore on that day he called him Jerubbaal, saying, let Baal plead against him, because he hath thrown down his altar."*

Gideon still lacked confidence that the Lord had actually selected him for the task of freeing Israel from the Midianites. God had revealed Himself to him, answered his request for a sign, and granted him a significant victory over the Baal worshipers. Still, he sought further reassurance by asking for the sign of the fleece. He even asked for it two times. God was patient and gave Gideon this renewed confirmation of His promised victory. Gideon rounded up an army of 32,000 men and prepared to lead them from Manasseh into the Cis-Jordan against the Midianites. When given the chance 22,000 accepted the offer to return home. "Ten thousand is still too many," the Lord said. He did not want Gideon and his army to take credit for the victory, so He set up a testing system that would eliminate most of the rest. Gideon was left with three hundred men to face and defeat an army. When the victory was won, God would get the glory!

Gideon was certainly an unlikely candidate for heroism or leadership. He had been unsure of God and himself. Over and over he asked God for a sign to reassure him. Now with only three hundred men and the Midianites encamped in the valley *"like grasshoppers for multitude,"* he heard God's instruction to go down against them. Evidently, he was still hesitant, for God said to him, *"If thou fear to go down, go thou with Purah thy servant down to the host: And thou shalt hear what they have to say"* (vss. 10-11). Gideon and his servant crawled to an outpost where guards were stationed. Just at that moment, one of the guards began to describe a dream to his companion. Can you see God's sovereign hand in all this? Just to reassure His chosen servant Gideon, He caused a man to dream; then made sure he related it to a friend just at the time Gideon was hiding in the underbrush. It was a dream designed to give Gideon confidence. Let's listen with Gideon:

> *Behold, I dreamed a dream, and, lo, a cake of barley bread tumbled into the host of*
> *Midian, and came unto a tent, and smote it that it fell, and overturned it, and his fellow*
> *answered and said, This is nothing else save the sword of Gideon the son of Joash, a man*
> *of Israel: for into his hand hath God delivered Midian, and all the host.*

When Gideon heard these words, he bowed his head and worshiped. Then, he returned to his troops and announced, *"Arise, for the Lord hath delivered into your hand the host of Midian."* The balance of chapters 7 and 8 record the victory over the Midianites and the later years and death of Gideon.

XIX. DESCENT INTO LAWLESSNESS

-JUDGES-

Chapter 9 details the activities of Abimelech, who was a son of Gideon by a concubine. Gideon fathered seventy other sons by a number of wives but Abimelech set himself up as a petty king by executing all but one of them who managed to escape. He was not one of the Judges but merely a self-appointed tyrant without a calling from God. Chapter 10 briefly mentions two more Judges. Tola, number 6, and Jair, number 7. Then it describes the eighteen year oppression when all of Israel's neighbors appear to have joined forces against them. This time God refused to deliver them until they had shown some genuine evidence of repentance. His words were scathing:

Ye have forsaken me, and served other gods: wherefore I will deliver you no more. Go and cry unto the gods which ye have chosen; let them deliver you in the time of your tribulation.

Their response was to turn to Him and because they did, He raised up Jephthah to deliver them. Jephthah's exploits, and his personal tragedy, are recorded in chapter 11 and part of chapter 12. The remainder of chapter 12 contains a list of later Judges: Ibzan, number 9; Elon, number 10; and Abdon, number 11.

Samson

Chapters 13 through 16 comprise what is probably the best-known section of the book of Judges. They contain the adventures of Samson, the last Judge of Israel. Samson's judgeship lasted for twenty years after he reached manhood, terminating with his death in approximately 1055 B.C. Samson's death occurred in the land of the Philistines when he decided to tear down the two supporting pillars which held up the building in which the Philistine lords had gathered to celebrate their victory over the God of the Israelites and the Israelite champion, Samson. The death of the Philistine lords, who were also the military leaders, corresponds to the defeat of the Philistines by Samuel in I Samuel 7. God in His sovereignty, allowed Samson to destroy the military leaders with his own death. That act helped Samuel as he rallied the people to defeat the Philistines who were left without adequate military leadership. The two events parallel and reinforce the overlap of the final years of the book of Judges with the first few chapters in I Samuel.

Archaeologists have discovered remains of Philistine temples and buildings which they erected during the twelfth century B.C. The type of construction used was such that two main pillars would support the entire building. In the excavation, they have found husks, and husks with strainers, among the various artifacts. These show that they drank strong beverages made from products with husks which required straining before drinking. These beverages were evidently part of their worship system, and we know there was drunken revelry going on when Samson was being humiliated in the Philistine temple. The proximity of the pillars to one another has been shown to be such that an individual such as Samson could lean upon them and collapse the entire structure of the building. This is exactly what took place in chapter 16 when Samson used his outstretched arm-reach to collapse the temple.

Chapters 17 and 18 are an appendix to the book. If we examine Judges from a literary perspective, we discover that chapters 1 through 16 contain the history of the period from 1385 B.C. down to approximately 1050 B.C. These are the parameters of the 335 year period of the Judges. Chapters 17 and 18 give examples of the idol worship which became prevalent as the period progressed.

The focus here is on the tribe of Dan which, having been driven from the location that God had given them, sought an alternative place to settle. Judges 18:1, records that they did not have a place to live. They had lost some of their inheritance to the Philistines, while much of their land was absorbed by Ephraim, Benjamin, and Judah.

In an effort to find a permanent inheritance and location, the Danites sent five men to spy out the entire land. Verse 7 tells us that they came to a place far north beyond the Sea of Galilee, approximately 125 miles away. The inhabitants were a quiet people and secure; there was not a ruler anywhere humiliating them; they were far from the Zidonians, and had no dealings with anyone. According to the Military Manual, these people fell into the category of "cities afar off," and it was the God-given principle that the Danites should have gone to this city and proclaimed peace to it and given the inhabitants an opportunity to surrender and to serve them. However, the evil Danites determined ahead of time that they would go in and possess the land. According to verses 27 & 28:

They came unto Laish, unto a people that were quiet and secure:
and they smote them with the edge of the sword, and burnt the city

with fire. And there was no deliverer, because it was far from Zidon.

Through this endeavor the tribe of Dan became positioned far north of the Sea of Galilee and became confirmed idol worshipers. We know they loved idols because years later, under the reign of Jeroboam I, one of the two golden calves set up in the northern kingdom was located in the territory of Dan.

An examination of the twelve tribes which will be sealed during the tribulation period, recorded in Revelation 7, reveals that the tribe of Dan is missing. Evidently, the Danites fell into such dishonor during the Old Testament period, because of their idolatry and ungodly activities that God refuses to acknowledge them, along with Ephraim, in the accounting of the tribes in Revelation chapter 7.

Appendix I is a picture of the spread of idolatry and of its corrupting influence on one tribe. Appendix II (chapters 19 through 21) presents additional insight into the corruption and moral decadence which became prevalent during the years covered by the book of Judges. It is a depressing story of sodomy and homosexuality. The period is summed up in 21:25, which closes the book by saying: *"In those days there was no king in Israel; every man did that which was right in his own eyes."*

XX. A DRAMA OF REDEMPTION

-RUTH-

We now come to a story of the village life of a pious and humble people which is a refreshing contrast to the ungodliness recorded in Judges. The book of Ruth can be called Appendix III to Judges. In fact, the Hebrew canon often included it with Judges, Verse 1 begins: *"Now it came to pass in the days when the judges ruled."*

Since we have analyzed the social, economic, military, and religious situation which prevailed during the times of the Judges, we are now able to take this little book of Ruth, presented by the Holy Spirit, and see it as a shining example of spiritual life in a dark era. It glistens like a star in the evening sky against the dark background of decadence and immorality all around them. We have a glimpse of a small community and the lives of some individuals who can be an inspiration to us.

The book of Ruth can be studied from a variety of perspectives. It is a rich book which will be a blessing to you as you teach it and to those who learn as you present it to them. You can approach the book from the perspective of history, using it to show the ancestry of the family of David and the Messiah. You can look at it from a theological perspective and examine the doctrine of redemption. You can study it from the perspective of customs and traditions and examine the levirate marriage system and the traditions which existed during that era. From a social perspective, you can see how the common people lived and how they interacted with one another. From a spiritual perspective you can see God's watch-care and direction behind the scenes, ever sovereign, ever guiding His people as they act out this narrative. From the standpoint of typology, you can see Christ, you can see the Church, and you can see the believer. From the standpoint of application, you can see yourself and those you know, in the biographies of these individuals. You can learn how to react to God in different situations, and how to see things with a spiritual eye. We can see that even when wrong decisions are made, God will still bring about His sovereign will.

For this study, we will examine the book of Ruth as literature. From this perspective, we will see six individual sections, each one complete. There are plots, sub-plots, potential bad ends and ironic twists. I want us to see it as a drama; to see the book as a stage play in four acts and six parts (Acts 1 and 4 each having 2 scenes). For the next few minutes I want you to forget where you are. Go back in time and assume you are in a theater engrossed in the drama taking place on stage.

Act I: To Moab and Back

Scene I

The scene begins with a family that had moved from Bethlehem to Moab because there was a famine in the land. We learned from Deuteronomy 28:15, 23, that when famine came on the land it was the result of sin in the nation. This is a phase in the sin cycle. A man of Bethlehem decided to leave the area and try to find sustenance somewhere else, so he went to "*sojourn*" in the land of Moab.

Elimelech left God's Promised Land to go to Moab. We might say he left the "house of bread," that is what *Bethlehem* means, and went to Moab which was the "garbage can" of the world. His name, Elimelech, meant, "God is my king," but it is rather obvious that he did not live up to it. The name of his wife was Naomi and the names of his two sons were Mahlon and Chilion. Although he went only to *"sojourn"* in the land, verse 2 tells us that he remained there. But instead of finding refuge, he found death as verse 3 tells us. Because of his lack of faith, he died in a land which was an abomination to the Israelites, for reasons the book of Judges made clear, and left a widow and two sons, without income.

Being left alone, the two sons did the next obvious thing. Each took a Moabite woman for a wife. The name of one was Orpah, which means "little dear," or "little dear one." The other was Ruth, which means "glamorous." They lived there about ten years. At the close of Scene I, there appears to be the potential for a very sad ending. Naomi, whose name meant pleasant, was now a widow. Her husband Elimelech was dead; her two sons were dead; she was dwelling in a land hated by the Israelites, with two Moabite daughters-in-law for whom she was responsible. On the positive side, we must realize something she did not; viz., that God had simply cleared the decks. He had taken the wrong-doers out of the way and was ready to act in sovereign grace.

Scene II

Scene II begins with verse 6. Naomi rose up and began the return journey to Bethlehem after she heard that the Lord had visited His people in giving them food. This demonstrates that the famine was not random chance or coincidence, but was caused by God as phase two of one of the sin cycles. Evidently, back in the land of Israel, the people were in a repentance and deliverance phase, so God had visited His people and the land to begin to produce grain again. When Naomi began the journey back to Bethlehem, both of her daughters-in-law were determined to go with her. After a little time, perhaps at a fork in the road, Naomi tried to bid the young women farewell. Verse 8ff says: *Go, return each to her mother's house: the Lord deal kindly with you, as ye have dealt with the dead, and with me. The Lord grant you that ye may find rest, each of you in the house of her husband.* At that point in time, both Orpah and Ruth insisted they would return with Naomi. But Naomi began to argue against the custom of the time. Welfare was not available, and there were no social services to care for widows, so God had provided, in Deuteronomy 25, the concept of levirate marriage. Levirate marriage provided that if a man died before he had a son to continue his name, his brother was to take the widow as his wife and father a son for his dead brother to continue the name of the deceased. This was God's way of providing adequate care for the widows of the land. It appears that Orpah and Ruth were planning to go back with Naomi and participate in the levirate marriage system, but Naomi argued against it, saying in verse 11 ff:

I am too old to have an husband. If I should have an husband also tonight, and should also bear sons; Would ye tarry for them till they were grown? Would ye stay for them from having husbands? nay, my daughters; for it grieveth me much for your sakes that the hand of the Lord is gone out against me.

After hearing her argument, Orpah kissed Naomi goodbye and returned to her people and to obscurity.

Following Ruth's statement of commitment and her vow in the name of the God of Israel (vss. 16-17), Naomi realized that she was determined to go with her, and they both came to Bethlehem where their arrival caused quite a reaction. The women of the city said, *"Is this Naomi?"* Can't you imagine the small talk? Can't you imagine the insinuations? A decade before, Naomi had left with her husband and two sons. Now she had come back ten years later, a poor destitute widow with a Moabite girl. Her husband and her two sons had died, and here they were, two widows, an Israelite and a Moabite looking like beggars.

In the eastern philosophy of that time, such circumstances were indicative of God's judgment on sin in an individual's life. On the other hand, if one were prosperous and lived a life of abundance that was the outward indication of God's blessing on a life. So when the women of the city saw the two destitute widows, they could not help but say, *"Is this*

Naomi?|In verse 20, Naomi replied, *"Do not call me Naomi call me Mara."* Mara means bitter and it is the same word that was used of the bitter waters in Exodus 15:23. Naomi was saying, *"I am bitter because God's hand has gone out against me."* She believed that God had become her enemy. *"For the Almighty hath dealt very bitterly with me."* *"I went out full,"* she continued. She had gone out with abundance, a husband and two sons. *"The Lord hath brought me home again empty: why then call ye me Naomi, seeing the Lord hath testified against me, and the Almighty hath afflicted me?"* The word *"Almighty,"* as it is used in verse 21 is the Hebrew word El Shaddai. It was the name God used for Himself when He addressed Abram, in Genesis 17, as He talked about the promise of the seed and multiplied blessing through seed too numerous to count. There seems to have been a play on words here as Naomi used this term, because God had cut off her seed. He is the Almighty, but He is not the Almighty in her case. In her mind He had afflicted her. You can see the improper response which Naomi had toward God at that point. She had been brought low through circumstances and God's hand had gone out against her for a purpose that she could not comprehend. But, she was acting improperly toward God because she mistakenly believed He was her enemy. So, rather than being pleasant, as her name implied, she became bitter.

If only Naomi could have seen the future and recognized that God had cleared the way for His sovereign grace to act in her life, her total attitude would have been different. But she had a myopic point of view. She had tunnel vision. She was hungry; she was alone with a Moabite girl; she was back in her hometown where people were speaking against her. She had lost her husband and her sons, and she was bitter. She was no longer pleasant. She had gone out full and had come back empty.

Verse 22 is a summary. It appears as if a narrator has come on the stage and says: *"So Naomi returned, and Ruth the Moabitess, her daughter-in-law, with her, and they came to Bethlehem in the beginning of barley harvest."* This was the perfect time to return. The story is just beginning and the blessing is just starting. At the end of 1:22, the curtain falls on Act I, Scene II.

Act II: Enter Boaz the Hero

Before Act II begins, it seems in verse 1 as if the Holy Spirit, as Narrator, stands before the curtain and whispers, *"Naomi had a kinsman of her husband's, a mighty man of wealth, of the family of Elimelech; and his name was Boaz."* With this introduction, the stage is set for the next act. As Act 11, Scene One begins, Ruth asked permission to go out into the harvest fields and glean after the reapers. Her desire indicates that she had knowledge of the customs of the time. The law of gleaning, designed by God as a protective measure for those unable to otherwise provide for themselves, is described in Deuteronomy 24:19:

When thou cuttest down thine harvest in thy field and hath forgot a sheaf in the field, thou shalt not go again to fetch it. It shall be for the stranger, for the fatherless, and for the widow, that the Lord thy God may bless thee in all the work of thine hand.

It was a common task for the widows in the land to follow behind the reapers and glean what remained. As Ruth went out to glean, she "happened" to come upon a portion of the field belonging to Boaz. Now we begin to see that God was working behind the scenes, guiding and directing. Of all the fields Ruth could have gleaned, she "happened" on the one belonging to Boaz. At some cross roads in Bethlehem, Ruth had a decision to make and she was sensitive enough to follow the leading of God and make the right decision. How can we ever know, or ever over-emphasize, the eternal and momentous consequences of every small decision we make? Ruth's first decision, as the three of them stood crying together on a dusty cross roads in Moab, was whether to continue on with Naomi or to turn back. She made another decision when she left her mother-in-law to go and glean. Because of a simple decision, the lineage of the Messiah was revealed.

Don't underestimate the eternal consequences of small decisions. If Ruth had made the wrong turn that morning, she would not have been in the lineage of Jesus Christ. She would not have married Boaz. She would not have been the ancestor of King David. Who would have thought, when she left the house that morning, that the field she selected would determine whether or not she would be in the ancestry of the Lord Jesus Christ, the Messiah, the Son of God?

Verse 4 reads: "*And, behold, Boaz came from Bethlehem, and said unto the reapers, The Lord be with you. And they answered him, The Lord bless thee.*" I see Boaz as a big, burly, bearded, godly businessman. I want you to think about how all of these pieces are fitting together. They "happened" to get back to Bethlehem at the beginning of the harvest. Ruth "happened" to take advantage of the law of gleaning. She wanted to glean and she was submissive. She selected the field of Boaz. Then, about the time she sat down for a little break, Boaz, the owner and her kinsman, "happened" to come from Bethlehem out to his field. He "happened" to be a godly man. And he "happened" to notice Ruth. There are too many coincidences here; we must see God's sovereign hand behind the human activity and decisions.

Boaz asked his servant in charge of the reapers, *"Whose damsel is this?"* In the vernacular of today, his words would be, *"Wow!"* The servant replied, *"It is the Moabitish damsel that came back with Naomi out of the county of Moab."* Notice that the man in charge knew all about her. I am sure the village was still talking negatively. But the servant spoke well of her as he continued (vs. 7):

> *And she said, I pray you, let me glean and gather after the reapers*
> *among the sheaves: so she came, and hath continued even from the*
> *morning until now, that she tarried a little in the house.*

Verse 8 describes an unusual event. Normally a man in that culture would not speak to a woman in public, and certainly a man in Boaz'
position would not speak to a servant girl, especially a widow gleaning among his reapers. Boaz said (vss. 8-9):

> *Hearest thou not, my daughter? Go not to glean in another field,*
> *neither go from hence, but abide here fast by my maidens: Let thine*
> *eyes be on the field that they do reap, and go thou after them: have*
> *I not charged the young men that they shall not touch thee? and*
> *when thou art athirst, go unto the vessels, and drink of that which*
> *the young men have drawn.*

Ruth's response was to fall on her face in gratitude and ask, *"Why have I found grace in thine eyes, that thou shouldest take knowledge of me, seeing I am a stranger?"* The better translation would be "foreigner," rather than stranger. The answer to Ruth's question could not have been her personal appearance. Though Boaz might have said "wow," I am sure that after working in the sun all morning, Ruth, dusty and tired, was not overly attractive. It certainly was not self-worth, because Moabites were despised and a widowed Moabite woman was not worth any consideration. It was, on the part of Boaz, unmerited favor. And so it is with us. We were dead in trespasses and sins, unable to help ourselves, but Christ, of whom Boaz was a type, extended His grace and love to us who were alienated from Him, as Boaz extended his grace and love to this foreign woman who had no reason inherent in herself to be loved.

Boaz answered her, *"It hath fully been shewed me, all that thou hast done unto thy mother in law since the death of thine husband"* (vs.11). As a leader in the community, Boaz was aware of everything that went on. He had not been listening to the murmurings and undercurrents of the women, but had been hearing with a spiritual ear. So he added (vs.12): *"The Lord recompense thy work, and a full reward be given thee of the Lord God of Israel, under whose wings thou art come to trust."* Ruth was comforted by this kindness that had been spoken to her heart, and responded, *"Though I am not like unto one of thine handmaidens."* As in the words of Jesus in John 10: 16: *"And other sheep I have, which are not of this fold: them also I must bring, and they shall hear my voice; and there shall be one fold, and one shepherd."* The typology continues to unfold.

At mealtime, Boaz invited Ruth to share the meal with his reapers and dip bread with them in the vinegar. That may not sound like a very good meal to us, but I am sure that after working all morning in the field, that bread and vinegar, (or bread and a sop as they would have called it,) had some appeal. Here I see an example of God's condescending grace. Imagine this wealthy Hebrew man condescending to eat at the table with a Moabite widow. She sat beside the reapers and he served her roasted grain. He fed her himself and Ruth even had some left after she was satisfied. I am again reminded of the Lord's grace and goodness illustrated in His feeding of the multitudes. Regardless of how much of His grace we use day by day, there is always abundance in reserve.

After Ruth left, Boaz ordered his reapers to let her glean even among the sheaves, not just the discarded husks. They were not to insult her or rebuke her. He even added, *"And let fall also some of the handfuls of grain on purpose for her."* Ruth continued working until evening, and becoming more and more excited as she saw how much good grain she was gathering. At dusk, she took home an ephah of barley and gave Naomi the leftovers she had saved.

When Naomi recognized that the day's results were unusual, she inquired about where Ruth had worked. Hearing her reply, *"The man's name with whom I wrought today is Boaz."* Naomi's reaction was the equivalent of our "Praise the Lord! (vs. 20) Ruth repeated all Boaz's words. Naomi identified him as a near kinsman and redeemer. She urged her daughter-in-law to obey his instructions: *"It is good, my daughter that thou go out with his maidens, that they meet thee not in any other field."* We also need to remember that this was a lawless era, "when every man did that which was right in his own eyes." If Ruth had been required to work outside the protection of Boaz, she could very well have been assaulted, injured, or dishonored. The harvesting required approximately seven weeks. This meant that these two widows had seven weeks of security to rely on. Chapter 2 ends with the statement that Ruth did stay close by the maids of Boaz until the end of the barley harvest and even through the wheat harvest. The curtain falls on Act II and seven weeks go by.

Act III: Ruth Seeks Redemption

When the curtain goes up on Act III Naomi begins the next step in the levirate process. I want you to notice that Naomi was the one with first option on Boaz as the kinsman-redeemer, but with a kind, loving spirit, she relinquished this right to her daughter-in-law, Ruth. *"My daughter, shall I not seek rest for thee that it may be well with thee?"* She reminded Ruth of who Boaz was, and that the harvest season was over. She knew he would be winnowing barley on the threshing floor which was a time of celebration. When the winnowing was done and they looked at the results of their harvest, they would eat, drink, and celebrate; then Boaz would go to sleep. Naomi instructed Ruth how to approach him (vss.4-5):

> *Wash thyself, therefore, and anoint thee, and put thy raiment upon*
> *thee, and get thee down to the floor; but make not thyself known*
> *unto the man, until he shall have done eating and drinking. And*
> *it shall be, when he lieth down, that thou shalt mark the place where*
> *he shall lie, and thou shalt go in, and uncover his feet, and lay thee*
> *down; and he will tell thee what thou shalt do.*

Obediently, Ruth went down to the threshing floor and did all that Naomi told her. She waited until big, kindly, burly Boaz had eaten and drunk and his heart was merry. He made a bed for himself near his heaps of grain and lay down. He was in for a surprise that night, the like of which his old bachelor's heart had never known. Verse 7 says Ruth went in at midnight, lifted up the cover and snuggled down beside him. Boaz was startled. He sat up, looked forward, and behold, there was a woman lying beside him. Imagine his surprise! "Who are you?" he asked. Ruth identified herself and added, *"Spread therefore thy skirt over thine handmaid, for thou art a near kinsman."* In spreading his garment over her he was giving the sign of acceptance. He acknowledged his role as redeemer. Notice that she requested redemption and he granted it in verses 10 and 11:

> *Blessed be thou of the Lord, my daughter: for thou hast shewed*
> *more kindness in the latter end than at the beginning, inasmuch as*
> *thou followedst not young men, whether poor or rich. And now,*
> *my daughter, fear not, I will do to thee all that thou requirest: for*
> *all the city of my people doth know that thou art a virtuous woman.*

Ruth had stayed within the prescribed family program of levirate marriage and had become obedient to Hebrew customs. I call your attention to the fact that her deportment during the past two months had been exceptional and she had acquired an excellent reputation. She was in a place where every eye was on her and every tongue was ready to spread malicious gossip about her. But she had behaved herself in such a way that her virtue and her unspotted character had become known throughout the town, and more importantly, to Boaz. But then, although he acknowledged his role as redeemer and agreed to fulfill it, he had to add in verse 12: *"And now it is true that I am thy near kinsman: howbeit there is a kinsman nearer than I."* Now, after all this, we sit back in our chairs and think, Oh, no! There's going to be a bad ending. It all looked so good, but now Boaz is not the right man after all. But, Boaz showed his godly character by adhering to the accepted social system. Lie still until morning, he instructed Ruth. Then, if he discovered that the closer relative would redeem her, *"let him do the kinsman's part."* If the other was not willing, however, *"then will I do the part of a kinsman to thee, as the Lord liveth."*

I'm sure neither got any sleep that night. Boaz was thinking, "I wonder if this other man will redeem her?" Ruth was thinking, "I could love this man. What if the other man redeems me? What does he look like? Who is he?" Here is the potential bride and groom, together throughout the night, with the possibility that another closer redeemer existed who could claim the right of redemption. Ruth lay at his feet until morning and got up before anybody could recognize her. Boaz cautioned her not to let anyone know that she had been there. This statement reveals that he was protective of her reputation. Since the prostitutes came to the threshing at harvest time, he knew that Ruth's honor would be compromised if she was seen leaving with a sack of barley.

As Ruth entered the house, Naomi asked her, literally in Hebrew, "Who are you?" What she meant was, "Are you Mrs. Boaz this morning?" Well, at that point Ruth could not say for sure, but she reported the conversation between them and gave Naomi the pledge which Boaz sent, repeating his words, *"Go not empty unto thy mother in law."* Naomi was beginning to see God demonstrate His lasting love. She had complained of coming home empty, but now she was no longer empty. Now, she knew she could rely on Boaz because we read that she instructed Ruth, *"Sit still, my daughter, until thou know how the matter will fall: for the man will not be at rest, until he has finished the thing this day."* The curtain falls on Act III, and we wait with growing suspense for it to rise again.

Act IV: Scene I

The Kinsman Redeemer

Act IV, Scene I, takes place at the city gate of Bethlehem. The gate of ancient towns was the place where political and legal decisions were made. Boaz sat down at the gate and, behold, the close relative of whom he had spoken just "happened" to pass by. This could not be a coincidence. That relative could have been in any number of places, but God drew him to the gate to confront Boaz because He was ready to bring His plan to a climax in chapter 4.

We never learn the identity of Boaz's kinsman. The Holy Spirit substitutes *"such a one"* for his name in Boaz's greeting. After asking him to sit down, Boaz stopped ten more men of the city as they passed by. They became a legal committee; because instead of written contracts, these witnesses attested to everything that transpired. Boaz states his case in verses 3 and 4:

> *Naomi, that is come again out of the country of Moab, selleth a*
> *parcel of land, which was our brother Elimelech's: And I thought*
> *to advertise thee, saying, Buy it before the inhabitants, and before*
> *the elders of my people. If thou wilt redeem it, redeem it; but if*
> *thou wilt not redeem it, then tell me, that I may know: for there is*
> *none to redeem it beside thee; and I am after thee.*

The reply of the kinsman was, *"I will redeem it."* And again we want to say, Oh, no! The love between Boaz and Ruth will not be realized because the worst thing has happened. The nearer relative has agreed to redeem the land! But Boaz had not finished yet. He went on to describe the most vital condition of the transaction. *What day thou buyest the field of the hand of Naomi, thou must buy it also of Ruth the Moabitess, the wife of the dead, to raise up the name of the dead upon his inheritance.* At that point the closer kinsman changed his mind saying, *"I cannot redeem it for myself, lest I mar mine own inheritance; redeem thou my right to thyself; for I cannot redeem it."* The final obstacle has been removed.

The rite of redemption was complicated. When a parcel of land was lost because of bankruptcy, there were certain conditions attached to the redemption of the land. Many times, the conditions for redemption were written on the inside and outside of a scroll. The scroll was sealed with seven seals and placed within the temple, or tabernacle, or within another legal depository. When someone decided to redeem the land, he went to the priest and asked to read on the outside the conditions for redemption that were duplicated on the inside of the scroll. There were three acknowledged criteria to qualify as a redeemer.

1) The redeemer must be a *relative*. That was the case for both the close redeemer of the relative for whom we have no name, and for Boaz. It was also true in the case of the Lord Jesus Christ, our Redeemer. When Adam sinned, the earth came under the curse, and the Lord Jesus became the close Relative-Redeemer to buy it back.
2) The redeemer must be *willing*. An unwilling redeemer, such as the man whose name is not given, was the same as no redeemer. Again, the Lord Jesus qualified to be our Redeemer. John 10 tells us He willingly laid down His life for His sheep. *"I lay it down of myself"* (vs. 18).
3) The redeemer must be *able* to redeem. A bankrupt redeemer was *also* the same as no redeemer. Again, the Lord Jesus qualifies because Hebrews 7:25 says of Him: *"Wherefore he is able also to save them to the uttermost that come unto God by him, seeing he ever liveth to make intercession for them."* In the same way, Boaz qualified to redeem Ruth and the inheritance of Elimelech. Again, the Lord Jesus Christ meets all the criteria to redeem us because He is a relative, He is willing, and He is able.

In Ruth 4:10, Boaz confirmed the fact that He had redeemed the land and taken Ruth to be his wife. Incidentally, it is at this point we learn that Ruth had been the wife of Mahlon. Previously, we did not know which of Naomi's sons she was married to. The city elders pronounced their blessing on the new family, and Scene I ends.

Act IV Scene II
A Happy Ending

In verse 13, Ruth became the wife of Boaz and in time, gave birth to a son. Now the women of the city came to rejoice with Naomi because she had a redeemer, saying, *"Blessed be the Lord, which hath not left thee this day without a kinsman."* Naomi had come back from Moab empty, but now the hardships were behind her. God is in control and His purpose is evident. She has progressed from being a poverty-stricken widow, to having become the grandmother of the man who would become the grandfather of King David. For the balance of the story, turn to Matthew 1:5-6. There you will learn that Ruth became the great-grandmother of King David and an ancestor of the Lord Jesus Christ.

XXI. A PRAYING MOTHER

-I SAMUEL-

An Overview

We still need to determine the starting date for the book. Alongside First Samuel 10:24, write 1050 B.C. That was when the people shouted, *"Long live the king,"* and Saul began his forty year reign, (Acts 13:21). The crowning of Saul was preceded in chapter 8 by the demand of the people for a king. Until then they were a Theocracy under the leadership of Judges. It appears that not much time went by between the demand in chapter 8, and the introduction of Saul in chapter 9, and his crowning in chapter 10 – perhaps two years at the most, so write 1052-1050 B.C. beside chapter 8. The demand for a king followed immediately after the military activity recorded in chapter 7, which is an important consideration for our dating system. The event was the Battle of Mizpeh and it marked the end of the Philistine occupation. (vss. 10 and 13):

> *The Lord thundered with a great thunder on that day upon the*
> *Philistines, and discomfited them; and they were smitten before*
> *Israel. So the Philistines were subdued, and they came no more*
> *into the coast of Israel: and the hand of the Lord was against the*
> *Philistines all the days of Samuel.*

Assuming a date of 1055 to 1050 B.C. for that battle, we can date Judges 13:1 at 1095 B.C., since it records the birth of Samson and the beginning of the forty year Philistine occupation which terminated with the Battle of Mizpeh. We still need more information in order to determine the date for the beginning of I Samuel. We find it in I Samuel 7:1, which states:

> *And the men of Kirjath-Jearim came, and fetched up the ark of the*
> *Lord, and brought it into the house of Abinadab in the hill, and*
> *sanctified Eleazar his son to keep the ark of the Lord. And it came*

to pass, while the ark abode in Kirjath-Jearim, that the time was long; for it was twenty years; and all the house of Israel lamented after the Lord.

This is a valuable piece of information, not only for our current study, but for a later study in the life of David. But for now, if we can discover the circumstances surrounding how the Ark came to be in Kirjath-Jearim for twenty years, we will have another historical event that can be used to determine the opening date for the book of First Samuel.

Introduction to the Battle at Aphek

The Philistines took possession of the Ark during the Battle at Aphek which is described in I Samuel 4. Since I will cover the actual events of this battle later, I will just summarize here by saying that the Philistines were victorious and as a result captured the Ark of the Covenant from the Israelites who had taken it with them into battle. First Samuel 5:1 records: *"And the Philistines took the Ark of God, and brought it from Ebenezer unto Ashdod."* Verse 9 tells us that during the time the Ark was in the city of the Philistines, the hand of the Lord was against the city and smote the inhabitants. Chapter 6:1 says that the Ark was in the country of the Philistines seven months. When the Philistines realized that possessing the Ark was causing their problems, they arranged for its return to Israel where, as we read, it remained in Kirjath-Jearim for twenty years. Based on this evidence, we can date the Battle of Aphek to 1075 B.C., or twenty years before the Battle of Mizpeh. The Battle of Aphek would have occurred at about the midpoint of the Philistine oppression, which takes us back to 1095 B.C. for its beginning.

We can now see that I Samuel 1:1, and the birth of Samuel, would have occurred about 1100 B.C. First Samuel 25:1 records Samuel's death and we have a fairly close date of 1012 B.C. for that chapter. Assuming that Samuel was born in 1100 B.C. and died in 1012 B.C., he would have lived eighty-eight years. That means that he was twenty-five years old at the time of the Battle at Aphek when the Philistines took possession of the Ark and between forty-five and fifty when he led the armies of Israel in the victory over the Philistines at Mizpeh, and fifty years old when he crowned Saul king. The book of I Samuel spans ninety years of Israel's history.

Our Study of I Samuel Begins

The opening portions of First Samuel give us good insight into what was going on during that era in the history of Israel. Chapter 1 introduces us to a man from the hill country of

Ephraim. His name was Elkanah and he had two wives, Hannah and Peninah. Peninah had children by Elkanah, but Hannah bore no children. But, Elkanah loved Hannah and was a godly man. Chapter one says that he went up yearly from his city to worship at Shiloh and sacrifice to the Lord of Hosts. At that time, the tabernacle and Ark were at Shiloh. The high priest was Eli and his two sons served as priests.

In the first three verses, we are introduced to Hannah, the heroine of the story and her husband, Elkanah. We are made aware that the tabernacle was in Shiloh and that Eli the high priest had two sons, Hophni and Phinehas. Then we go on to Hannah's situation. We learn that when Elkanah sacrificed, he gave portions to both his wives, but a double portion to Hannah because he loved her. The Bible says she was barren because the Lord had closed her womb. To the eastern mind, this was a terrible dilemma and a sign of the Lord's disfavor. In many parts of the world she would be looked upon as a murderess, for it was believed that she killed her husband's living seed within her own body.

We do not know why the Lord closed Hannah's womb, but we do know that everything God does is for His own glory. We also know that because she was barren for so long, her constant prayers for a son resulted in the kind of consecration which was necessary in order for her to raise Samuel and to make the promises which she did regarding his future. As Hannah went up to the tabernacle year by year, her husband's other wife taunted and ridiculed her because she was barren. Hannah wept and prayed and did not eat. Finally, in verse 11:

> *She vowed a vow, and said, O Lord of hosts, if thou wilt indeed*
> *look on the affliction of thine handmaid, and remember me,*
> *and not forget thine handmaid, but wilt give unto thine*
> *handmaid a man child, then I will give him unto the Lord*
> *all the days of his life, and there shall no razor come upon his head.*

She was in such agony as she prayed that while speaking in her heart, her lips moved as she mouthed the words although no sound came. Eli, the High Priest, looked over from the doorway of the tabernacle, and seeing her, assumed she had been drinking. *"How long wilt thou be drunken? Put away thy wine from thee,"* he scolded (vs. 14). This gives insight into Eli the High Priest. He was supposed to be a man of God with spiritual discernment. Eli was such an ungodly priest, and so spiritually undiscerning, that he could not even distinguish a godly Israelite woman praying earnestly to God, from one whom he believed was drunk with wine. But Hannah answered him respectfully and explained (vss. 15-16):

> *No, my lord, I am a woman of sorrowful spirit. I have*

*drunk neither wine nor strong drink, but have poured out
my soul before the Lord. Count not thine handmaid for a daughter
of Belial: for out of the abundance of my complaint and grief
have I spoken hitherto.*

Eli, realizing his error made a priestly reply: *"Go in peace: and the God of Israel grant thee thy petition that thou hast asked of him."* Hannah conceived and gave birth to a son and called his name Samuel. When Elkanah went up with his household to pay the yearly sacrifice, Hannah did not go but stayed home with her young son and explained (vs. 22): *"I will not go up until the child be weaned, and then I will bring him, that he may appear before the Lord, and there abide forever."* After she had weaned young Samuel, (we may assume he was about five years old), she went up to Shiloh taking with her a three year old bull and an ephah of flour..

We can increase our appreciation of what she did by looking at the situation surrounding her at that time. Assuming that Samuel was born in 1100 B.C. he was five years old in the year 1095. In Judges 13:1, we read that the Philistine oppression began. Hannah was living in an unsafe land occupied by an enemy army. There was always the fear that if they became separated they might not ever see one another again. Hannah might have rationalized that the land had been at peace when she made her vow and that God would not expect her to leave her son elsewhere during the time of turmoil.

There was yet another factor that might have given Hannah a reason for delay. Eli was an ungodly man and his two sons who served as priests were even worse. She certainly had at least some idea of the decadent and ungodly situation that existed at Shiloh and in the tabernacle of God. Gossip quickly spreads about that kind of activity. Also, she might have rationalized that she had not been aware earlier of the sinful environment at the tabernacle and could have reasoned that Samuel should not grow up in so ungodly an atmosphere. But Hannah was not putting her trust in either, Eli, Hophni, or Phinehas, but in God who had accepted her vow. She knew He would take care of Samuel in the wicked environment. Chapter one ends with the dedication of Samuel, and chapter 2:1-10 records Hannah's song of rejoicing.

I Samuel 2:12 introduces us to the sons of Eli and says that they were sons of Belial; that is, worthless men. They developed a custom that when someone was offering a sacrifice, the priest would send his servant around, while the meat was cooking, with a big three-pronged fork. He would stick his fork down into the kettle and whatever he could bring up from the pot, the priest would take for himself. They would also take the fat before it was burned. The servant would also demand that the worshiper give him the meat raw, because the priest wanted to roast it rather than having it boiled. If the worshiper insisted that the fat must be burned first according to the law, the servant threatened to take it by force. *"Wherefore, the sin of the young men was very great before the Lord."* (vs. 17) They had no respect for the offerings of the Lord and caused others to despise them also. It had been only a little over three hundred years since the law was given, yet already the priestly family and their servants were disregarding God's specific instructions. Leviticus 3 describes the preparation of various sacrificial animals with special attention to the removal of the fat, and ends in verses 16-17:

> *And the priest shall burn them upon the altar: it is the food*
> *of the offering made by fire for a sweet savour; all the fat is*
> *the Lord's. It shall be a perpetual statute for your generations*
> *throughout all your dwellings, that ye eat neither fat nor blood.*

But these wicked priests had no regard for this law. They took the fat for themselves, and we will learn later that Eli was a fat man. I believe he said to his sons, "You boys keep the fat meat coming." I Samuel 2:17: they *"Abhorred the offering of the Lord."* Verse 22: *Now Eli was very old, and heard all that his sons did unto all Israel; how they lay with the women that assembled at the door of the tabernacle of the congregation.* This is a description of sins that went even beyond licentious sexual behavior. In the Canaanite religion, the worship of Baal involved male prostitution. What the sons of Eli had done was to take the concept of male prostitution and introduce it into the tabernacle of the Lord. I believe they introduced this evil practice because they were priests of God, and if the women wanted to worship, they must do as the Baal worshipers of the land did. The women were familiar with the practice, and many would succumb to having sexual relations with the sons of Eli in a belief that it was religious. In that way, they perverted the religious system and the pure worship of Jehovah. Worst of all, they were doing it right in the tabernacle! They brought Baalism into the tabernacle of God, and the women accepted it because they saw it taking place in the Baal temples around them. (Remember God's order to kill all the Canaanites?)

One would think that Eli, as the High Priest, would do everything in his power to bring such evil and corruption to an end, to rebuke and punish his sons, possibly even to have them stoned. But he only said in verses 23 and 24: *Why do ye such things? For I hear of your evil dealings by all his people. Nay, my sons; for it is no good report that I hear: ye make the Lord's people to transgress.* Not only was Eli a pitiable character, he was a spineless milquetoast as well. Verse 25 says that the Lord desired to put his sons to death.

Because Eli would not take the situation in hand and bring it to an end, he had to be warned. In time, a man of God approached him with a prophetic message that began with a review of the Lord's historic dealings with Israel. In later times, we will see that God sent His prophets to rebuke kings. At this time he must rebuke the High Priest. Under the Theocratic system, the High Priest was the religious leader and as such he was the one to whom high respect belonged. He was answerable to God, but he had become evil like the evil kings who would come later, and God sent a prophet to rebuke him. This nameless prophet spelled out Eli's sins (vs. 29), accusing him because he *"honourest thy sons above me, to make yourselves fat with the chiefest of all the offerings of Israel."* These words indicate that Eli, as well as his sons, was implicated in the unlawful taking of the fat meat. The prophet suggested they were all a bunch of fat evil men, operating the tabernacle in ungodly fashion, for personal lust and gain, imitating the priests of Baal in the tabernacle of God. The warning of judgment is very similar to the prophecy Elijah proclaimed to Ahab centuries later. The prophet said to Eli (vss. 31-35):

Behold, the days come, that there shall not be an old man in thine house; and all the increase of thine house shall die in the flower of their age. And this shall be a sign unto thee that shall come upon thy two sons, on Hophni and Phinehas; in one day they shall die both of them. And I will raise me up a faithful priest that shall do according to that which is in mine heart and in my mind: and I will build him a sure house; and he shall walk before mine anointed forever.

Again we see the concept that no one can sin with impunity. God can and will bypass His own established organization if it becomes wicked to the point that it cannot be used. Although verse 35 is eschatological and refers eventually to our High Priest, the Lord Jesus Christ, God did bypass the organization and chose Samuel.

XXII. SAMUEL THE JUDGE

--I SAMUEL--

At the time of the visit of the unnamed prophet, several years had probably gone by since Samuel had been taken to live at Shiloh. We know from 2:19 that his mother visited him "from year to year," bringing him a new coat each time. So, when the prophet came, Samuel was probably about ten years old. Apparently, Eli paid no attention to the warnings of the unnamed prophet. In a final effort to rebuke Eli, God used young Samuel to give him a second warning.

Chapter 3 opens with God's call to Samuel. It tells us that *"the word of the Lord was precious (or rare) in those days; there was no open vision."* And no wonder when the religious system headed by Eli and his two sons was so debased and wicked. The Lord told Samuel that what He was going to do would make everyone's ears tingle. He described it in verses 12-13:

In that day I will perform against Eli all things which I have spoken concerning his house: when I begin, I will also make an end for I have told him that I will judge his house for ever for the iniquity which he knoweth: because his sons made themselves vile, and he restrained them not.

When Samuel heard God's message, he was afraid. It was a natural reaction for a ten year old boy receiving such a message to be afraid to tell Eli. But when Eli asked him what God had said, he faithfully delivered the entire message to the High Priest. When Eli heard the message, he should have fallen on his face before God. He should have taken his sons before the people and had them stoned to death. He should have repented in the dust. But what did Eli say? *"It is the Lord let him do what seemeth him good."* What a spineless jellyfish!

If this took place in the year 1090 B.C., God gave Eli fifteen years to straighten out his house. But, fifteen years went by and nothing happened. Samuel grew up and all Israel from Dan to Beersheba (this is a literary way of saying from the north to the south) *"knew that Samuel was established to be a prophet of the Lord."*

The Battle at Aphek

About fifteen years elapsed between 3:21 and 4:1, so the events of chapter 4 took place in 1075 B.C. Samuel was twenty-five years old and Israel had been under Philistine domination for about twenty years. The Philistines had assembled in battle array at Aphek, twenty miles west of Shiloh, and Israel was defeated. The elders of Israel asked one another, *"Wherefore hath the Lord smitten us today before the Philistines?"* Then they devised a plan. They would take the Ark out of Shiloh and carry it into battle. So the Ark, which represented the throne of God, was reduced, in the mentality of the people, to a mere talisman, much like a lucky rabbit's foot. When the ark arrived at the battlefront, the people thought it was going to bring them victory and even the Philistines almost lost heart when they saw it. They said (vs. 8): *Woe unto us! Who shall deliver us out of the hand of these mighty Gods? These are the Gods that smote the Egyptians with all the plagues.* Do you remember when that event happened? It was in 1446 B.C. Three hundred and seventy-five years earlier, and still it was remembered by a pagan nation.

Nevertheless, even while fearing God, the Philistines gathered their spirits and went out with determination against Israel, defeating them with a great slaughter. Thirty thousand foot soldiers fell in that battle and the Ark of God was captured, fulfilling the prophecy of First Samuel 2:32, where God said, *"Thou shalt see an enemy in my habitation."* In addition, the two sons of Eli, Hophni and Phinehas, who had carried the Ark into the battle were both killed, fulfilling the prophecy made in First Samuel 2:34, fifteen years earlier, that they would both die on the same day.

It is necessary to understand that since the Ark of God was the symbol of His strength and power, and was symbolic of His throne, that God was not defeated as the Philistines thought He was. The religion of the Philistines was polytheistic and the other surrounding nations were polytheistic also. The Ammonites, the Moabites, the Syrians, the Egyptians, all believed in more than one god. In addition to being polytheistic, they were also henotheistic. Henotheists believed that certain gods were strong in certain geographical areas and that each god was strongest in the geographical area where the nation lived that worshiped him. That is why many of the artifacts that have been discovered, including paintings on the walls of Assyrian temples, show soldiers carrying the gods of defeated nations into their cities. In fact, we can see that later on in the Old Testament. One of the kings of Judah carried the gods of another nation back to Jerusalem to worship them. Turning to II Chronicles 25:14, we read: *Now it came to pass, after that Amaziah was come from slaughter of the Edomites, that he brought the gods of the children of Seir and set them up to be his gods, and bowed down himself before them, and burned incense unto them.* Henotheism was also practiced by a king of Judah. We know the Syrians also were henotheistic because we will read later on that when the Israelites had defeated them in a battle, they said, *"Their gods are gods of the hills; therefore they were stronger than we; but let us fight against them in the plain, and surely we shall be stronger than they"* (I Kings 20:23).

Likewise, the Philistines were henotheists. When they captured the Ark they planned to carry it back to their city to strengthen their own collection of gods. But we must remember that with Jehovah the situation was quite different. It was not that He was too weak to prevent them from taking the Ark. The truth is, He allowed the Ark to be taken. Look at Psalm 78:56-64 where the psalmist is recalling historically the events which occurred in I Samuel:

Yet they tempted and provoked the most high God, and kept not his testimonies: but turned back, and dealt unfaithfully like their fathers: they were turned aside like a deceitful bow. For, they provoked him to anger with their high places, and moved him to jealousy with their graven images. When God heard this, he was wroth, and greatly abhorred Israel. So that he forsook the tabernacle of Shiloh, the tent which he placed among men; and delivered his strength [that is, His Ark] into captivity, and his glory into the enemy's hand. He gave his people over also unto the sword, and was wroth with his inheritance. The fire consumed their young men; and their maidens were not given to marriage. Their priests [Hophni and Phineas] fell by the sword; and their widows made no lamentation.

The Death of Eli

The battle at Aphek took place twenty miles west of Shiloh, and it would have spread out as the armies engaged one another and small groups of troops encountered each other in the plains and in the hills. First Samuel 4:12 says, *"And there ran a man of Benjamin out of the army, and came to Shiloh the same day with his clothes rent, and with earth upon his head."* This was not from the battle, but from his mourning the death of so many Israelites. He had rent his clothes and thrown dust on his head as he came to report to Eli, who was sitting on a stone beside the road. But the inhabitants of the city heard the news first. Then Eli heard the crying of widows and relatives and inquired what had happened. Verse 17:

The messenger answered and said, Israel is fled before the Philistines, and there hath been also a great slaughter among the people, and thy two sons also, Hophni and Phinehas, are dead, and the ark of God is taken.

Eli's mind must have flashed back fifteen years when the unnamed prophet had predicted this day and the boy Samuel confirmed it. When he heard the report, he fell backward off the stone and broke his neck, because he was old and heavy. Eli was ninety-eight years old when he fell backward and died. At the same time, the wife of Phinehas was about to give birth. When she heard that her husband and her father-in-law were dead, and that the Ark was captured, she went into labor. Although she died giving birth, she lived long enough to name her son Ichabod, which means, *"The glory of the Lord has departed from Israel."* Her last words were, *"The glory is departed from Israel; for the ark of God is taken."* {See 14:3}

Chapter 5 tells how the Ark of God was taken from the battle site over to Ashdod, which was one of the five Philistine cities by the Mediterranean seacoast. In true henotheistic fashion, they set up the Ark in the house of their god Dagon. To them, the Ark was the God of the Israelites and they would worship it also along with their fish-headed god Dagon. But God demonstrated very dramatically that He was not just another idol. When the Philistines entered their temple the next morning, they found that Dagon had fallen on his face. They set him up, but the next morning he had fallen on his face again. This time his head and the palms of his hands were cut off. The fish-head idol was humiliated and mutilated in its own temple. Following that, the hand of the Lord was heavy against the Philistines. He ravaged and smote them, and Ashdod and its territories, until finally they took counsel and said (vs. 11): *"Send away the ark of the God of Israel, and let it go again to his own place, that it slay us not, and our people."*

Of interest here is that in 3rd Century B.C. Babylonian documents, the cult of Semiramis and Tammuz, worshipped as Madonna and child, is mentioned, along with Dagon. This ancient cult began centuries earlier in ancient Babylon. (You can Google this demonic cult for more information.) Dagon was a half fish half man god worshipped by the Babylonians. The statue often had a fish shaped hat. The priests wore the fish shaped hat called a mitre. In the Pergamom Museum in Belgium, there is a stone laver with a half fish half man sprinkling holy water engraved on it. The title used for these priests was "pontiffs" meaning bridge builders. Roman emperors later used this title and increased it to *Pontificate Maximus,* meaning Great bridge builders. See Jeremiah 7:18 and 44:17-19 {five Centuries later} when the women of Judah were worshipping the Queen of Heaven: Semiramis. Ezekiel 8:14, reveals that the women in the Lord's house were weeping for her son, Tammuz. This woman with child cult has a very long history.

Chapter 6 describes the various activities that surrounded the return of the Ark to the Israelites. The Philistine priests devised a unique plan. They were superstitious people by nature, but they were not ignorant people. Notice in verses 5 and 6 how they had knowledge of the history of Israel, and knowledge of theology as well. In effect they said, *"Give glory to the God of Israel and He will ease His hand from you. Wherefore then do ye harden your hearts, as the Egyptians and Pharaoh hardened their hearts?"* So, based on their limited knowledge of theology and the history of Israel, they devised a plan to send the Ark back to Israel. God allowed them to use their cart to demonstrate that He had surrendered His power to remove it from their presence. The cattle went lowing up the hill as they pulled the Ark of God back to the Israelites.

The Battle of Mizpeh

Chapter 7 records, as we noted earlier, that men of Kirjath-Jearim took the Ark of God. Later, they placed it in a wooded area near their homes and twenty years passed. During those twenty years, from 1075 to 1055 B.C., Samuel had been active, revitalizing the people, renewing the national zeal, and preparing them spiritually to go out against the Philistines once again. Verse 4 records that they removed the Baalim and began to serve God alone. Because they did, God gave them a great victory over the Philistines. This victory, known as the Battle of Mizpeh, brought to an end the 40 years occupation that began concurrently with the announcement of the birth of Samson.

The Demand for a King

Following the great historic battle when the Israelites regained military supremacy over the Philistines, the inhabitants of Israel began to look around at the other nations. Simultaneously, we learn that even though Samuel was a godly man, his sons were ungodly. Verse 3 says they, *"turned aside after lucre, and took bribes, and perverted judgment."* Samuel cannot be held totally accountable for the fact that his sons were ungodly. It just might have been that he found himself so busy with his circuit, which revolved around Bethel, Gilgal, and Mizpeh, from his dwelling place in Ramah, that he did not spend the time with his sons that he should have. However, this is speculation. What we do know is that because of the reputation of his sons and because Israel began to look around at other nations, they decided that they were weary of their Theocratic government. They wanted a king like the nations round about them.

Their demand for a king broke the heart of Samuel. They said to him (vs. 5): *"Behold, thou art old, and thy sons walk not in thy ways: now make us a king to judge us like all the nations."* The key to their demand was *"like all the nations."* They wanted to be like everybody else. God had determined back during the wilderness wanderings, and emphasized it in the book of Deuteronomy, that they were not to be like the other nations.

But God comforted Samuel saying (vs. 7): *"They have not rejected thee, but they have rejected me, that I should not reign over them."*

Although God provided for the time when the Theocracy would become a monarchy, the Israelites were not willing to wait for His program and timing. In their haste to be like the nations around them, they insisted too early that they be given a king. And because they insisted, God granted their request. Back in Deuteronomy 17, in the year 1406 B.C., He detailed the provisions for a king, and in doing so, used the language that Israel would use three and one-half centuries later in making their demand. Verses 14 and 15 give God's earlier provision.

When thou art come unto the land which the Lord thy God giveth thee, and shalt possess it, and shalt dwell therein, and shalt say, I will set a king over me, like as all the nations that are about me; Thou shalt in any wise set him king over thee whom the Lord thy God shall choose: one from among thy brethren shalt thou set king over thee: thou mayest not set a stranger over thee, which is not thy brother.

God laid down rules and regulations in anticipation of the time when the people would ask for a king. The rules continue in 16 and 17:

> *But he shall not multiply horses to himself, nor cause the people*
> *to return to Egypt, to the end that he should multiply horses:*
> *forasmuch as the Lord hath said unto you, Ye shall henceforth*
> *return no more that way. Neither shall he multiply wives to himself that his heart turns not*
> *away: neither shall he greatly multiply to himself silver and gold.* {Compare I Kings 1:38

Interestingly, in Genesis 36:31 we know there were kings in Edom. A recent archaeological discovery, south of the Dead Sea, found evidence the Edomites were using advanced methods to mine copper in the mid eleventh century B.C. Edom was ahead of Israel with kings and copper.

Because they wanted a king like the other nations, God said, *"I will give you a king. I will give you a king who looks like a king."* Remember, we discovered in the book of Judges that the one who looks like the ideal leader may not necessarily be so. But God was going to give them a man who met their own criteria, recognizing that they did not want a spiritual man. They wanted one who could boost their personal glory. As I Samuel 8:20 records: *"That we also may be like all the nations; and that our king may judge us, and go out before us, and fight our battles."*

XXIII. INSTITUTION OF THE MONARCHY

-FIRST SAMUEL-

When the people demanded a king, Samuel gave them solemn warning regarding what they could expect. He said:

> *He will take your sons, and appoint them for himself, for his chariots, and to be his horsemen; And he will appoint him captains over thousands, and captains over fifties; and to reap his harvest, And he will take your daughters to be. cooks, and to be bakers. And he will take your fields, and your vineyards, and your olive yards, even the best of them, and give them to his servants. And he will take your menservants, and your maidservants, and your goodliest young men, and your asses, and put them to his work. He will take the tenth of your sheep: and ye shall be his servants.* (I Sam. 8:11-17)

Despite this solemn warning, the people cried even louder for a king (vs. 19), saying, *"Nay; but we will have a king over us."* So the Lord said unto Samuel (vs. 22), *"Hearken unto their voice, and make them a king."* With the establishment of the monarchy, a totally new system developed in Israel. First, there was dynastic succession. Prior to this, God raised up judges whenever Israel was ready for a deliverer. Under the monarchy, the crown would pass from father to son to grandson. Each reigning monarch expected to have a descendent in perpetuity on the throne. Second, there was centralization of power as indicated in the words of Samuel. The king would do what he wanted, when he wanted, and have the military power to back up his decisions. Third, a privileged class would begin. There would be the courtiers, relatives, and friends of the king. These people would have special privileges and the king would look to them for counsel.

Future Periods of the Monarchy

The monarchy was the most important period in Israel's history. It began with the crowning of Saul in 1050 B.C. He reigned forty years then David reigned for forty years, and I Kings 11:42 records, *"And the time that Solomon reigned in Jerusalem over all Israel was forty years."* These 120 years are the era of the united monarchy. It was the only time in Israel's history when all twelve tribes were united. The united monarchy came to an end in 931 B.C. In that year the kingdom divided. Jeroboam became king over the northern ten tribes. Rehoboam, the son of Solomon, reigned over Benjamin and Judah in the south. This period of divided monarchy lasted for 209 years, from 931 to 722 B.C., when the Assyrians invaded and dispersed the northern ten tribes.

From 722 until 586 B.C., was the era of Judah alone as a monarchy.

The Babylonian captivity began in 586 B.C. King Zedekiah was the last human monarch ever to sit on the throne of Israel or Judah. The balance of Old Testament history covers the Babylonian Captivity, the return from captivity, and the brief period known as the post-exilic community.

Saul Crowned King

The Israelites wanted a monarch like those of the other nations. In response to their demand, God granted them the most obvious man available. Saul is introduced in First Samuel 9, as a *"choice and handsome"* man. Not only was he the most handsome man in Israel, he was the tallest. From his shoulders up he towered above the people, humanly speaking, he was an ideal choice for king. When dressed in his kingly garments, he must have been a striking figure. This was the kind of person the children of Israel wanted to lead them into battle, to fight for them, and to judge them as they "went out and came in." The sovereignty of God is evident in the selection of Saul, as recorded in chapters 9 and 10. In 9:16, God said to Samuel *"Tomorrow about this time I will send thee a man."* When Samuel met Saul, he was amazed. Saul asked Samuel in verse 21: *Am not I a Benjamite, of the smallest of the tribes of Israel and my family the least of all the families of the tribe of Benjamin? Wherefore then speakest thou so to me?*

Please observe that this was a wise move politically. If someone had been chosen from the tribe of Judah, jealousy would have occurred. Instead, the most handsome and tallest man was chosen from the smallest tribe. Who could say anything but good? In chapter 10, God confirmed His selection to Saul through the instruction of Samuel. Samuel anointed him as ruler (10:1), then prophesied events to give him confidence (vss. 3-6).

Thou shalt come to the plain of Tabor, and there shall meet thee three men, one carrying three kids, and another carrying three loaves of bread, and another carrying a bottle of wine: And they will salute thee, and give thee two loaves of bread, which thou shalt receive of their hands. After that when thou art come thither to the city, that thou shalt meet a company of prophets and they shall prophesy: And the Spirit of the Lord will come upon thee, and thou shalt prophesy with them, and shalt be turned into another man.

Notice how God made the situation so complex that there was no way it could have been mere coincidence. Saul was told in advance whom he would meet and where; where they were coming from and going; what they were carrying, what they said and did. When Saul saw *"all those signs came to pass that day,"* he would know that God had been directing them. Saul would never have reason to turn his back on God, nor to doubt he was the chosen ruler. It would not have been a good move politically to leave the people out of the selection process.

Samuel called them together at Mizpeh (10:17) and began the approved and accepted elimination process. The tribe of Benjamin was first taken, then the family of Matri, and finally Saul, the son of Kish. In other nations, either the people would set up a popular hero, or a member of the warrior class would make himself king. But Israel was still a Theocracy. The people saw God's sovereign hand in the selection of their king, as He, through Samuel the prophet, made His choice clear.

During the ceremony, the people looked for Saul and could not find him. This is an indication that as a young man, Saul was shy and lacked self-confidence. Although tall and handsome, he was not yet fully aware of his capabilities, or of the reality of having been made king over God's heritage. When they found him hiding among the baggage, they lifted him (vs. 24) and shouted, *"Long live the King."*

Verse 26 says that Saul went to his house at Gibeah. Archaeologists have discovered what they believe to be the house of Saul. It was not a palace but a rustic fort. The first monarch of Israel was a tribal chieftain rather than a king who dressed in silk and costly garments.

The Ammonite Invasion

No sooner was Saul chosen than an opportunity came to prove himself. Chapter 11 begins with the invasion by Nahash the Ammonite against the inhabitants of the city of Jabesh-Gilead. The city was on the east side of the Jordan and its inhabitants were probably caught by surprise and barely had time to close their gates when the armies of Nahash laid siege against them. Not having had time to gather provisions and water to withstand a long siege, they sent a messenger under a white flag and said to Nahash, *"Make a covenant with us, and we will serve you."* Nahash replied, *"On this condition will I make a covenant with you, that I may thrust out all your right eyes, and lay it for a reproach upon all Israel."*

Naturally, the inhabitants did not look happily on that, so (vs. 3) they asked for a seven day period of grace to think it over. They would send messengers throughout Israel and if no one came to save them, they would surrender. No job description for a king had been written at that time, and Saul was plowing his field when he received the message from Jabesh-Gilead. Verses 6 and 7 record his response.

And the Spirit of God came upon Saul when he heard those tidings, and his anger was kindled greatly. And he took a yoke of oxen, and hewed them in pieces, and sent them throughout all the coasts of Israel by the hands of messengers, saying, Whosoever cometh not forth after Saul and after Samuel, so shall it be done unto his oxen. And the fear of the Lord fell on the people, and they came out with one accord.

In those early days of his reign, Saul was a humble man. By linking Samuel's name with his own, he united the political and religious aspects of the kingdom. The fighting men of Israel were numbered in Bezek, across the Jordan River from Jabesh-Gilead. Here we see the first hint of the later division, because the sons of Israel were 300,000 and the men of Judah 30,000. They informed the besieged city that by the time the sun was hot, they would have deliverance. Needless to say, the inhabitants were glad to hear this promise from their new king. The men of Jabesh-Gilead then said to Nahash (vs. 10), "*Tomorrow we will come out unto you, and ye shall do with us all that seemeth good unto you.*" But they knew that by tomorrow, their new king, with his armies, would be in hot pursuit of the Ammonites. Verse 11 says they struck down the Ammonites until the heat of the day.

Israel was proud of the first success of their new king and new regime and exclaimed to Samuel, "*Who is he that said, Shall Saul reign over us?*" They were referring to the sons of Belial described in 10:27. But Saul replied, "*There shall not a man be put to death this day; for today the Lord hath wrought salvation in Israel*" (vs.13). He was still humble and gave glory to God as he contemplated the fruits of victory from his first military encounter.

Samuel's Official Farewell

Chapter 12 begins with Samuel's review of Israel's history. He reminded them of everything God had done for them. He recalled Jacob, Moses, Aaron, Sisera, the Philistines, and the king of Moab. He reminded them how the people had served the Baals and the Ashtaroth, and how God had sent Gideon, Jephthah, and Samuel, including himself in the list of historical characters. Then he gave an account of his stewardship as judge and they exonerated him (vs. 4): "*Thou hast not defrauded us, nor oppressed us, neither hast thou taken out of any man's hand.*" But, they had begun to serve the Baals again. If you recall, the Canaanites considered Baal responsible for crop fertility, so Samuel said to them (vs. 17):

Is it not wheat harvest today? I will call unto the Lord, and he shall send thunder and rain; that ye may perceive and see that your wickedness is great, which ye have done in the sight of the Lord, in asking you a king.

This was a demonstration that they were wrong in asking for a king in advance of God's program, and it would validate the fact that God was in charge of the elements of nature responsible for fertility. Samuel called on the Lord; the Lord sent thunder and rain, and *"the people greatly feared the Lord and Samuel."*

XXIV. SAUL'S TRAGIC CHOICES

-I SAMUEL-

I Samuel 13:1 tells us that after Saul had reigned for two years he began to select an army of specialized troops. We can assume that the year was approximately 1048 to 1047 B.C. We know it was early in his reign because 14:35 says he built his first altar to the Lord. {"thirty" is not in the Hebrew text. This is a later insertion.} Based on a date of 1048 B.C., Saul's son, Jonathan, must have been twenty or twenty-one years old when Saul put him in charge of the specialized army. Saul would have been in his mid-forties, and thus approximately forty years old when he became king. Jonathan's birth would have been approximately 1070 B.C. These figures are inferences since we are not given specific dates or ages for these men, but the chronology seems to indicate their accuracy.

Saul's life was marked by four tragic sins. Three of them were the reasons why God cut off his house so that he did not become head of a royal dynasty. No descendent of Saul ever sat on the throne of Israel. The army was gathered at Gilgal anticipating the promised arrival of Samuel to offer sacrifices before they went into battle. Becoming impatient, Saul presumed to officiate at the offerings. Then Samuel arrived and asked w*hat hast thou done?"* (13:11). Samuel continued (vs. 13): *"Thou hast done foolishly, for now would the Lord have established thy kingdom upon Israel forever."* Samuel said there would be no dynastic succession in Saul's case. His son Jonathan would never wear the crown. *"But now,"* Samuel continued in verse 14,

> *"thy kingdom shall not continue: the Lord hath sought him a man after his own heart, and the Lord hath commanded him to be captain over his people, because thou hast not kept that which the Lord commanded thee."*

The year was about 1048 B.C., two years into Saul's reign. We will later learn that David was crowned king over Judah in 1010 B.C. at the age of thirty. This means he was born in 1040 B.C. So, eight years before David was born, Samuel said to Saul, *"The Lord has sought out for Himself a man after His own heart."*

Chapter 13 contains interesting information from an archaeological perspective. Remembering that it was 1048 B.C., only seven years elapsed since the battle of Mizpeh when the Philistines were defeated after their forty year occupation of the land. Verse 19 says there were no blacksmiths in the land because the Philistines had forbidden them so that the Hebrews could not make weapons. The army fought with weapons such as axes, ox goads, and pitchforks. Only Saul and Jonathan had swords as signs of their offices of king and prince.

Chapter 14 contains two important genealogies. In verse 3 we read: *"Ahiah, the son of Ahitub, Ichabod's brother, the son of Phinehas, the son of Eli, the Lord's priest in Shiloh, was wearing an ephod."* From First Samuel 22:9-12, 20, we learn that Ahiah was a short form of Ahimelech. Later we will learn that Abiathar, the son of Ahiah (or Ahimelech), served as priest for King David. The other important genealogy is in 14:49-50. Saul's sons were Jonathan, Ishui, and Melchishua, by his wife Ahinoam (vs. 50). The captain of his army was Abner, the son of Ner. In 9:1 we read that Abiel gave birth to Kish and Ner. Kish was the father of Saul and Ner was the father Abner. So, Saul and his commander-in-chief, Abner, were first cousins. In I Chronicles 8:33 we learn that Saul also had two additional sons, named Eshbaal and Ish-bosheth.

In I Samuel 14:47, there is a summary of all the battles which took place during the next twenty-two years, making a gap of twenty-two years between 14:52 and 15:1. We can date chapter 15 at 1026 B.C.

Chapter 15 narrates the second of Saul's four tragic sins. To understand it more fully, we must pick up the historical background from Deuteronomy 25:19.

> *Therefore it shall be, when the Lord thy God hath given thee rest*
> *from all thine enemies round about in the land which the Lord thy*
> *God giveth thee for an inheritance to possess it that thou shalt blot*
> *out the remembrance of Amalek from under heaven.*

This was prophetic, and the task of fulfilling it fell on the shoulders of Saul, Israel's first monarch (15:2-3). We have seen that the inhabitants of Canaan were given seven hundred years of grace. Eli had fifteen years of grace. Now the Amalekites have had four hundred years of grace since they attacked the weak and elderly Israelites after they came out of Egypt. That event was in 1446 B.C. and the year now is 1026 B.C. God has not forgotten His promise to Moses that He would blot out Amalek. God said (vs.2), *"I remember that which Amalek did to Israel,"* and in verse 3, Samuel instructed Saul, *"Go and smite Amalek, and utterly destroy all that they have, and spare them not."* Saul summoned the fighting men and numbered them. Then he *"came to a city of Amalek and laid wait in the valley"* (vs. 5). Verse 7 says that the battle raged *"from Havilah until thou comest to Shur that is over against Egypt."* Saul defeated the Amalekites and captured Agag, their king, but kept him alive. Verse 9 says:

But Saul and the people spared Agag, and the best of the sheep, and of the oxen, and of the fatlings, and the lambs and all that was good and would not utterly destroy them; but everything that was vile and refuse, that they destroyed utterly.

In direct opposition to what God had said, and in direct disobedience to His prophecy and commandment made 420 years earlier, they spared the king and whatever spoil they considered to be of value. God's chosen instrument to carry out His will failed to obey, and so His judgment fell on Saul. Following Saul's sin and failure, God spoke to Samuel and said, *"It repenteth me that I have set up Saul to be king: for he is turned back from following me."* Samuel rose early in the morning and went to meet Saul. Saul greeted him with the words, *"Blessed be thou of the Lord"* (vs. 13). This once humble man, who twenty-four years earlier had ridden himself among the baggage, had now reached the exalted plateau in his life where he blessed the priest, prophet, and judge sent by God. Samuel approached and asked, *"What meaneth then this bleating of the sheep in mine ears?"* (vs.14) Saul replied (vs. 15), *They have brought them from the Amalekites: for the people spared the best of the sheep."*

Samuel then pronounced, for the second time, God's rejection of Saul and his dynasty, while prophesying that the throne would be given to another man. Verses 17 and 18 state:

When thou wast little in thine own sight, wast thou not made the head of the tribes of Israel, and the Lord anointed thee king over Israel? And the Lord sent thee on a journey, and said, Go and utterly destroy the sinners the Amalekites, and fight against them until they be consumed. Wherefore then didst thou not obey the voice of the Lord, but didst fly upon the spoil, and didst evil in the sight of the Lord?

Saul's excuse was, *"I feared the people, and obeyed their voice."* He begged Samuel to return with him that he might be honoured *"before the elders of my people, and before Israel."* When Samuel refused and turned to leave, Saul, in desperation, grabbed Samuel's garment and tore it. Using this as an illustration, Samuel said, *"The Lord hath rent the kingdom of Israel from thee this day, and hath given it to a neighbor of thine, that is better than thou*" (vs. 28). Then he returned with Saul, but strictly as an outward show for the people. Agag was still alive and thought he was out of danger for he said, "*Surely the bitterness of death is past.*" But Samuel said to him, "*As thy sword hath made women childless, so shall thy mother be childless among women.*" Samuel cut Agag into pieces.

Verse 35 ends the narrative with a tragic epitaph:

And Samuel came no more to see Saul until the day of his death: nevertheless Samuel mourned for Saul: and the Lord repented that he had made Saul king over Israel.

XXV. THE RISE OF DAVID TO PROMINENCE

-I SAMUEL-

Approximately one year elapsed between chapters 15 and 16; then the word of the Lord came again to Samuel and instructed him to go to Jesse, the Bethlehemite, because He had selected a king from among his sons. {Ruth 4:17} Saul was fully aware, from the earlier judgments announced by Samuel, that God was raising up a king from one of the other tribes, but he did not know where or whom. Saul was becoming demented, obsessed with the fact that there was a man out there who would take his kingdom from him and keep his son Jonathan from sitting on the throne. Evidently, his hand had become very heavy on the kingdom, because in verse 2, Samuel asked, "How can I go? if Saul hears it, he will kill me." Such an act would be tantamount to treason. There was already a king on the throne whom Samuel had anointed. If he anointed someone else, Saul would surely hear about it and have him executed.

David Anointed

God gave Samuel a plan whereby the sons of Jesse would pass before him and be considered. When he looked at Eliab, the eldest, he thought, *"Surely the Lord's anointed."* Samuel's mind was just like that of the people. They also wanted a king who looked like a king. Eliab evidently had the stature and appearance of a king. But in verse 7, *The Lord said unto Samuel, Look not on his countenance, or on the height of his stature; because I have refused him: for the Lord seeth not as man seeth; for man looketh on the outward appearance, but the Lord looketh on the heart.*

Samuel began to understand very rapidly that God did not consider the way a man looked physically. It was what was inside that counted. Jesse called in the rest of his sons, and God made it clear that He had not chosen any of them. Samuel was confused. He asked, *"Are here all thy children?"* Well, he was told, there is still the youngest out tending the sheep. Samuel had him called in and when he appeared, the Lord said, *"Arise, anoint him, for this is he."* Samuel took the horn of oil and anointed him in the midst of his brothers, *"and the Spirit of the Lord came upon David from that day forward."* Psalm 78:70-72:

> *He chose David also his servant, and took him from the sheepfolds:*
> *From following the ewes great with young he brought him to feed*
> *Jacob his people, and Israel his inheritance. So he fed them according to*
> *the integrity of his heart; and guided them by the skillfulness of his hands.*

We know that David began to reign in Hebron in the year 1010 B.C. when he was thirty years old, which means he was born in 1040 B.C. We can date chapters 16 and 17 to approximately 1025-1024 B.C. Using this chronology, David was fifteen or sixteen years of age at the time he was anointed to be king over Israel. Being anointed king and becoming king were two different things. David had the right to the throne, but an ungodly man occupied it. Only God knew that Saul had fifteen more years to rule Israel as its king. David had fifteen years to live as the anointed king of Israel, but would be unable to fulfill his position until the man currently occupying the throne was slain. The next fifteen years were years of rivalry between them.

David and Goliath

We dated chapter 16 to 1026 B.C. and chapter 17 to 1025 B.C. So we see David, a young man of sixteen, anointed as king, about to become the champion of Israel. Very often, during the military activities of the time, a champion would be selected to fight the champion of an opposing army. Wars were sped up in that way; lives were spared; and political and military confrontations were brought to a rapid conclusion. However, once the champions had fought, there was no guarantee that the losing side would live up to the terms of the agreement.

This was the situation in chapter 17 as the armies of the Philistines, against whom Saul constantly fought, sent their champion Goliath to challenge a champion from Israel. Since Saul was head and shoulders taller than the rest of the people of Israel, and since he had been selected to lead the people into battle, he should have been the logical choice for Israel to send out against Goliath. In fact, he should have volunteered. But Saul wanted no part of this man. Chapter 17 says his height was six cubits and a span. Since a cubit was eighteen inches, this equaled nine feet. The span was the difference between the little finger and the thumb, which is approximately six inches. Goliath was a trained gladiator, 9 feet 6 inches tall. Clad in armor, he was a fearsome opponent.

In II Samuel 21, beginning in verse 16, we will read that there were several giants encountered later on: Ishbibenob, Saph, Lahmi, and a huge six-fingered mutant. Goliath came from "large stock" and he was the kind of champion any army would love to have. As he stood in the valley, with his armor glistening in the sunlight, the Israelites were terrified. Day after day he would go out to rebuke and humiliate the armies of Israel. His armor, which was made of scales and woven metal, weighed 125 pounds. His spearhead weighed fifteen pounds. There was not a man in Israel who would dare try to stand up to him.

The armies were about two miles apart, and the champion of the Philistines would shout across the valley that the Israelites were to choose a man who would come down to him. The terminology used in 17:8 suggested that the Philistine giant wanted a man to be sent down like a sacrifice because, humanly speaking, anyone who challenged Goliath would end up slaughtered just like a sacrifice.

David's older brothers were at the battle site because they were soldiers in Saul's army. David's job, as the youngest brother, was to take provisions to them from home and then go back and tend his father's flock in Bethlehem. The Philistine giant had been taunting the Israelites every day for forty days. On a trip to the battle zone with provisions, David learned that Saul, in desperation, had promised his daughter, riches, freedom from taxes and conscription to public service, to any man who would kill the giant opponent. When David heard this, his blood ran hot and he asked (vs. 26), *"Who is this uncircumcised Philistine, that he should defy the armies of the living God?"*

Eliab, the oldest brother, heard David speak these words. Remember, Eliab was the first one God rejected in the presence of Samuel, and because of this, he was jealous of David. Scripture says that his anger burned against David, and he asked, *"Why camest thou down hither? And with whom hast thou left those few sheep in the wilderness? I know thy pride and the naughtiness of thine heart, for thou art come down that thou mightest see the battle."* *"What have I now done?"* David asked, and he continued to speak to others who were around him. Some who heard David's words went and repeated them to Saul, who had David brought to his tent.

It is interesting to see Eliab's jealousy. He had been rejected once, had seen his younger brother as the chosen of God, and witnessed his anointing as the future king of Israel. Because of these things, his anger burned against him. Yet, David had such a sweet spirit. In many ways he was like Joseph. Joseph could have said to his brothers, "I have been waiting for this for years and now I am going to get even with you for selling me into slavery." When David did become king of Israel and Judah, he could have looked at Eliab and said, "I waited for this time. Now I can get even." But he did not.

Turn to I Chronicles 27:18 to see what happened later when David became monarch over all Israel and Judah. Chapter 26:32 informed us that David made captains over the tribes and over the different sections of the armies. Chapter 27 lists the names of the captains over the different armies and tribes. Finally, verse 18 recounts that over the tribe of Judah David selected Eliab as captain. He was in a position to rebuke Eliab for his jealousy and hatred of him back when he was a boy of around sixteen. But David, in the greatness of his forgiveness, made him captain over the tribe of Judah.

As David prepared to go to battle against Goliath, he was informed (vs. 33) that the giant had been a trained gladiator since his youth, and David, young and untrained, did not stand a chance. But David recounted his exploits as a shepherd and finally Saul said (vs. 37) *"Go, and the Lord be with thee."* David rejected the armor of Saul, picked up five smooth stones, took his shepherd's crook in his hand, along with his sling, and approached the Philistine. The Philistine cursed David by his gods. David was not a weak youth with a toy slingshot going out against a giant of the Philistines. David was a strong teenager who had already slain a lion and a bear. He knew what it was like to protect innocent sheep from the ravages of nature and wild beasts. He did not have a child's slingshot but a weapon of war, albeit not on the level of a gladiator's weapons.

A gladiator preferred the spear, the sword, and a shield in hand-to-hand combat. {See Judges 20:16} David rebuked the Philistine and assured him that God would defeat him that day. Verse 48 says David ran quickly toward the battle line. Then with one stone from his sling, David prevailed over the giant. When the Philistines saw that their champion was dead, they fled (vs. 51), reneging on their previous agreement. In verse 9 Goliath had said, "*If he be able to fight with me, and to kill me, then will we be your servants.*" Goliath was dead, but the Philistines did not honor the agreement. However, the armies of Israel, their morale renewed, pursued and slew the Philistines all the way to their own home towns, Gath and Ekron.

David and Jonathan

Chapter 18 describes the meeting of David and Jonathan. They became close friends as David began to serve in the court of Saul. We should recall now that Jonathan was approximately twenty to twenty-two years old in 1048 B.C., which means he was born about 1069 B.C. and was twenty-five to thirty years older than David. David was a teenage boy and Jonathan a middle-aged man, old enough to be his father when they became friends. Verses 3, 4:

> *Then Jonathan and David made a covenant because he loved him as his own soul. And Jonathan stripped himself of the robe that was upon him, and gave it to David, and his garments, even to his sword, and to his bow, and to his girdle.*

David prospered each time he was sent to battle. Saul set him over his men of war and it was pleasing to all the people. He soon became a national hero. The women began to sing, "*Saul hath slain his thousands, and David his ten thousands.*" Saul became angry and exclaimed, "*What can he have more but the kingdom?*" From that time on, he looked at David with suspicion. Did he suspect that David was his prophesied successor? Verse 12 says, "*And Saul was afraid of David, because the Lord was with him, and was departed from Saul.*" Chapter 18 describes Saul's first attempt to eliminate him. Although he had promised his daughter to whomever was victorious over the giant, he put an additional stipulation on the contract so that his hand would not be against David, but hopefully the Philistines would kill him. (It is interesting to read that David did the same years later when he sent Uriah into battle, so that his hand would not be against him. Instead, the hand of the enemy would be against Uriah).

David fulfilled the terms of the contract and, in fact, doubled the requirements set by Saul. Grudgingly, Saul gave Michal to David to be his wife. I am reminded of the old song, "Everything's going my way." David could certainly have sung it. He was a hero; he defeated the Philistines; the daughter of the king loved him; he married into the royal household. Everything he touched prospered, and everything Saul did went wrong. In the eyes of Saul, it was a bad omen. As a result, he became even more afraid of David. Verse 29 says, *"And Saul became David's enemy continually."*

Verse 30 records that David behaved himself more wisely than all the servants of Saul, so that his name was highly esteemed. Can this be the shepherd boy of a few years earlier? In his highest dreams and aspirations, he could never have imagined that within a very few years he would be taken from the pasture where he tended the sheep, to have a place of honor in the house of the king, and that one day he would reign on the throne of Israel. However, even though from David's point of view it appeared that everything was going his way, there was a dark, ominous side to the picture.

Chapter 19:1 tells us that Saul told Jonathan and all of his servants to put David to death. Jonathan warned David of Saul's intention, and defended David in the presence of his father. We begin now to sense the vacilating, irrational, mental state of Saul because, when he heard the voice of his son Jonathan recount the exploits of David, which were done in honor of Saul and for Saul, he relented and said David should *not* be put to death. Jonathan knew that David was the one selected to be king over Israel, and with that knowledge came the realization that he, Jonathan, would never be king of Israel. Because of the sins of his father, Jonathan knew that his friend David would wear the crown originally meant for him.

Flight from Saul

Chapter 19:8 tells us that David again fought the Philistines and was victorious. Although everyone benefited, Saul, in his petty jealousy, was angered because he was not included. He did not care that the nation prospered and was victorious over its historic enemy. His anger waxed hot against David and he attempted to kill him. However, Michal lowered David, her husband, down from a window and he escaped Saul's hand. That night David became a fugitive and will be a fugitive until the end of First Samuel. {Read Psalm 59}

XXVI. DAVID THE FUGITIVE

-I SAMUEL-

David fled from Saul confused knowing the prophet Samuel had anointed him to be king of Israel, but now was forced to flee from the man who currently occupied the throne. His first encounter after leaving his wife and home was with Ahimelech, the priest at Nob. Ahimelech had heard about the military exploits of David, and he came trembling, wondering what David wanted with him. I am sure Ahimelech knew that Saul hated David and had on occasion tried to kill him. To ease his mind, David resorted to a lie, saying (vs. 2): *"The king has commissioned me with a matter."* This lie later caused the death of Ahimelech and his entire family as we will see in chapter 22:18. David's lie, like the commitment of Joshua to the Gibeonites many centuries before, resulted in the suffering of many innocent people a short time later.

The priest helped David by giving him food and the sword of Goliath which had been kept wrapped in a cloth behind the ephod in the area where the priest lived. David then went to the most logical place, in his mind - the place where Saul would never go - that was to Achish, the king of Gath, one of the five major Philistine cities. David, I assume, believed he would not be recognized; but when he arrived at Gath, the Philistines looked at him, squinted just a little bit, and said, *"Isn't this the one about whom they sang 'Saul hath slain his thousands, and David his ten thousands?"* They knew the song celebrated David's victory over their armies.

When David realized that they recognized him, he feared Achish. In those times, a person who was insane was considered to be holy or possessed by spirits. Being superstitious, the people did not wish to harm such a one. In many of the royal courts, insane people were kept as good luck charms, or as prevention against evil spirits. David, probably realizing this, pretended to play the madman before Achish. He began to scribble and scratch on the city gates. He let saliva run out of the corner of his mouth onto his beard, and acted completely incoherent. It was the perfect disguise in the presence of the Philistines. Achish said: vss. 14-15: {Read Psalm 56.}

Lo, ye see the man is mad: wherefore then have ye brought him to me? Have I need of mad men that ye have brought this fellow to play the mad man in my presence? Shall this fellow come into my house?

Because of this deception, they drove him away and verse 22:1 says that David "*escaped to the cave Adullam.*"

Gathering Supporters

When David's brothers and his father's household learned where he was, they went down and joined him. The cave Adullam was about fifteen miles southwest of Bethlehem and approximately fifteen miles east of Gath. It was not a long journey from the city of Gath where Achish dwelt, but far enough to be safe from him and safe from King Saul as well. It was a perfect hideout. The superscription of Psalm 57, which is part of the inspired Psalm, says that it was written by David when he fled from Saul in the cave.

(vs. 1) Be merciful unto me O God, be merciful unto me: for my soul trusteth in thee: yea, in the shadow of thy wings will I make my refuge, until these calamities be overpast. (vs. 4) My soul is among lions: and I lie even among them that are set on fire, even the sons of men, whose teeth are spears and arrows, and their tongue a sharp sword. (vs. 6) They have prepared a net for my steps; my soul is bowed down: they have digged a pit before me, into the midst whereof they are fallen themselves. (vs. 7) My heart is fixed, O God, my heart is fixed: I will sing and give praise. (vs. 10) For thy mercy is great unto the heavens, and thy truth unto the clouds.

After his family joined him, chapter 22:2 goes on to say, all those who were in debt, all who were discontented, all who were in distress, gathered to him there, about four hundred men. David, in effect, became the Robin Hood of the Old Testament. All the "rabble" of the land gathered them to him. He became captain over a mob, but eventually he would make this mob of malcontents a formidable fighting force.

David went from Adullam to Mizpeh of Moab. He crossed the Jordan and said to the king of Moab, "*Let my father and my mother, I pray thee, come forth, and be with you.*" So "*they dwelt with him all the while that David was in the stronghold.*" That is, the stronghold of En-gedi west of the Dead Sea. Certainly, when Saul found out that David was organizing a small army, it would be looked upon as an attempt at a military coup. David knew his family would be in danger, so he left them with the king of Moab.

Massacre of the Priests

Before very long, Saul discovered what was happening and he accused his servants of conspiring with David. Saul was becoming paranoid about everyone and everything. At that point, Doeg the Edomite stepped forward (22:9), and reported that he happened to be present when David went up to Nob and conversed with Ahimelech the priest. His presence there was recorded in 21:7. He also reported that Ahimelech helped David by giving him, and the men with him, provisions and the sword of Goliath. Saul promptly sent for Ahimelech and asked, *"Why have ye conspired against me?"* After hearing Ahimelech's explanation, he pronounced the death sentence on him (vs. 16). *"Thou shalt surely die, Ahimelech, thou, and all thy father's house."* {Read Psalm 52}

With these words of Saul, our minds should flash back to I Samuel 2:31 where we read the curse on Eli's household. The king turned to his soldiers and commanded them to kill the priests, but they were not willing to put forth their hands against the priests of the Lord. Not so with Doeg the Edomite. He willingly killed the eighty-five priests who wore the linen ephod. Then he went to Nob and destroyed it, killing *"with the edge of the sword, both men and women, children and sucklings, and oxen, and asses, and sheep"* (vs. 19). Following this slaughter, the tabernacle and the altar were moved to Gibeon (II Chron. 1:3).

One son of Ahimelech, named Abiathar, escaped this slaughter and fled to find David. He was the sole survivor of the curse on the house of Eli. Abiathar told David all that Saul had done. David replied, no doubt in tears, *"I knew it that day, when Doeg the Edomite was there, that he would surely tell Saul: I have occasioned the death of all the persons of thy father's house"* (vs. 22). Then he invited Abiathar to stay with him. We also know from the next chapter (23:9), that Abiathar had escaped with the ephod, and evidently also the breastplate of righteousness. This man was the great-great-grandson of the wicked priest Eli.

Crises and Encouragement

Chapter 23 records the continued attempts by Saul to take the life of David. By verse 13, David's band of four hundred men had grown to six hundred. He was continually successful in escaping from Saul because *"God delivered him not into his hand."* About that time, Jonathan sought out David in the wilderness of Ziph and offered him encouragement (vs. 17). *And he said unto him, Fear not for the hand of Saul my father shall not find thee; and thou shalt be king over Israel, and I shall be next unto thee, and*

Saul my father knoweth. What spiritual insight Jonathan had! The two of them made a covenant before the Lord and Jonathan returned home.

The Ziphites reported David's hiding place to Saul, but before he could attack it, God sent a diversion. As he went after David (vs. 27), a messenger told Saul that the Philistines had made a raid on the land. Saul returned from pursuing David and went to meet the Philistines. David, having narrowly escaped, returned to his stronghold at En-gedi. {Read Psalm 54}

Saul's Life Spared

Chapter 24 opens with Saul returning from his pursuit of the Philistines and learning that David was in the wilderness of En-gedi. With three thousand of his choicest men, he went after him. Along the way, he went into a cave to rest, not knowing that David and his men already occupied it. David's men were excited urging him to take advantage of the opportunity to do away with his foe. Instead David secretly cut off the edge of Saul's robe. David's heart and conscience were so tender that even this act bothered him. In verse 6, he said, *"The Lord forbid that I should do this thing unto my master, the Lord's anointed."* This is a marked difference between a carnal and a spiritual man. The carnal man always wants to take God's program into his own hands. Or, he will not want God's program to succeed if he is not included in the process. David was a spiritual man who did not wish to intervene in any way with God's program, but would allow God to eliminate Saul in His own time. Saul, on the other hand, as a carnal man, wanted to make certain that God's program did not succeed. He attempted to kill David even though he was aware that he was God's chosen king to be his successor.

Almost one hundred years later, when Solomon discovered that God was going to take the kingdom from him and leave his descendents with only two tribes, he attempted to make certain that God's program would not succeed by attempting to take the life of the man God had chosen as his successor over the northern ten tribes. Even Solomon, who began on such a high spiritual plateau, ended his days a carnal man.

It was not so here. David had a tender heart and did not harm God's anointed. As soon as Saul left the cave, David went outside. He confronted Saul, saying: vss. 9-12:
Wherefore hearest thou men's words, saying, Behold David seeketh thy hurt? Behold this day thine eyes have seen how that the Lord had delivered thee today into mine hand in the cave: and some bade me kill thee, but mine eye spared thee, and I said, I will not put forth mine hand against my lord, for he is the Lord's anointed. Moreover, my father, see, yea,

for in that I cut off the skirt of thy robe in my hand, and kill thee not, know thou and see that there is neither evil nor transgression in mine hand, and I have not sinned against thee; yet thou huntest my soul to take it. The Lord judge between me and thee, and the Lord avenge me of thee: but mine hand shall not be upon thee." (Read Psalm 142.)

Saul, emotionally disturbed, began to cry and in his confused way, admitted his mistake (vs. 17 ff).

And he said to David, Thou art more righteous than I: for thou hast rewarded me good, whereas I have rewarded thee evil. And thou hast shewed this day how that thou hast dealt well with me: forasmuch as when the Lord had delivered me into thine hand, thou killedst me not. For if a man find his enemy, will he let him go well away? wherefore the Lord reward thee good for that thou hast done unto me this day. And now, behold I know well that thou shalt surely be king, and the kingdom of Israel shall be established in thine hand.

Why then did he not repent? Why did he not welcome David home? Because he was evil! He asked, *"Swear now therefore unto me by the Lord, that thou wilt not cut off my seed after me, and that thou wilt not destroy my name out of my father's house."* David swore and Saul returned home. David and his men returned to the stronghold. Remember that David had already sworn this same oath to Jonathan (20:15-16). By now, Saul appears unable to act rationally. He had committed his third tragic sin in the murder of the priests of Nob.

David and Nabal

The events of chapter 25 occurred only about two years before David was finally crowned king, so they can be dated to about 1012 B.C. We knew this because David lived in the country of the Philistines for a full year and four months, and he would have gone there very shortly after the events of chapters 25 and 26. By now David and his men had become professional soldiers. Their self-proclaimed job was to protect the inhabitants of the land from marauders who would raid the crops, pillage the villages, and from the philistines who occasionally sent war parties into the southern territory. In return for such protection, David and his men expected to receive food and other necessary provisions from the inhabitants of the southern area.

Chapter 25 introduces a wealthy man named Nabal and his wife Abigail. David had been protecting the southern part of the country near Carmel, which is southeast of Hebron by Ziph. It was a special time in the life of Nabal, because it was sheep-shearing day, and a time for celebration. So, David sent ten of his young men to meet Nabal and ask provisions for the army. But Nabal answered them roughly (vss. 10-11):

Who is David? And who is the son of Jesse? There be many servants now a days that break away every man from his master. Shall I then take my bread, and my water, and my flesh that I have killed for my shearers, and give it unto men, whom I know not whence they be?

The young men returned empty-handed and reported his words to David. He was enraged and cried, "*Gird ye on every man his sword.*" With four hundred of his men, he set out to get revenge.

However, one of Nabal's servants reported the incident to Abigail, Nabal's wife, testifying to the protection David had afforded them. As a result of Nabal's discourteous behavior, he concluded, "*evil is determined against our master, and against all his household: for he is such a son of Belial, that a man cannot speak to him.*" Abigail was afraid for her household, but moving swiftly, she collected generous provisions, including two hundred loaves of bread and five dressed sheep. She started out to meet David, sending some of her servants ahead and cautioning them not to tell Nabal.

Meanwhile, David was determined to kill every man in Nabal's household. "*He hath requited me evil for good,*" he said in verse 21. David was a rough man in those times, living by his wits and by his sword. Bloodshed had become his way of life, but he trusted in God. He had been forced, because of his fugitive lifestyle, to live in existence apart from the comforts of civilized life. Abigail hurried to meet him. Falling on her face she pleaded, "*Upon me, my lord, upon me let the iniquity be: Let not my lord, I pray thee, regard this man of Belial, even Nabal: for as his name is, so is he: Nabal is his name, and folly is with him.*" The name Nabal meant "fool" and he certainly lived up to his name. Then in verse 28, Abigail made a marvelous prophecy, saying, "*The Lord will certainly make my lord a sure house.*"

As a result of her intercession, David's heart was made tender and warm. He replied to her (vs. 28): "*Blessed be thy advice, and blessed be thou, which hast kept me this day from coming to shed blood, and from avenging myself with mine own hand.*" The seriousness of what he had been about to do can best be determined when we remember that just a short time before he had said to Saul (I Sam. 24:12), "*May the Lord avenge me of thee, but mine hand shall not be upon thee.*" In the heat of anger, David had temporarily forgotten that the Lord is the avenger and he was about to avenge himself. Thanks to Abigail, his temper calmed down, he abandoned his intention, and received from her hand the provisions she had brought in return for the safety he and his men had provided.

Abigail returned home to find Nabal in the midst of a feast, drunken. She waited until *"the wine was gone out of Nabal"* and then told him what she had done. When he heard of his narrow escape *"his heart died within him, and he became as a stone."* Evidently, he had a stroke and as a result, about ten days later he died. When David heard it, he exclaimed, *"Blessed be the Lord, that hath pleaded the cause of my reproach from the hand of Nabal, and hath kept his servant from evil"* (vs. 39). God did avenge both Himself and David.

Nabal was dead and David took Abigail to be his wife. Actually, she was his third wife because we learn in verse 43 that he had also taken Ahinoam of Jezreel. His first wife Michal, the daughter of Saul, had been given to Phalti, the son of Laish who was from Gallium, after David had fled from the presence of Saul.

Saul Spared Again

The Ziphites were a traitorous group of ingrates. Chapter 26 reports that once again they reported David's whereabouts to Saul; and the insane king, forgetting his earlier promise and the fact that he owed his life to David, set out after him again. David sent out spies who knew his movements and where he was encamped. Saul, with Abner, his commander-in-chief, was in the circle of the camp with his men camped around them. Like commandos, David and Abishai crawled through the underbrush down to Saul's camp. Abishai was the son of Zeruiah, David's sister. Second Samuel 2:18 tells us that Zeruiah had three sons: Joab, Abishai, and Asahel. These three were valiant warriors to whom David often turned until tragedy struck later in II Samuel 2.

Realizing that the Lord had once again put Saul within David's grasp, Abishai begged, *"Let me smite him, I pray thee, with the spear even to the earth at once, and I will not smite him the second time."* David refused, saying, *"Destroy him not: for who can stretch forth his hand against the Lord's anointed, and be guiltless?"* This is the key to David's life. He knew God would bring His program to pass in His own time. He would let God choose the means (vss. 10-11):*As the Lord liveth, the Lord shall smite him; or his day shall come to die; or he shall descend into battle, and perish. The Lord forbid that I should stretch forth mine hand against the Lord's anointed.* Then he instructed Abishai to take the spear and the cruse of water from beside Saul as he slept. They did so and escaped to a hilltop unobserved because the Lord had caused a deep sleep to fall on Saul and his men. From a safe distance, David called out to Abner, vs. 15

Art not thou a valiant man? Wherefore then hast thou not kept thy lord the king? As the Lord liveth, ye are worthy to die, because ye have not kept your master, the Lord's anointed. And now, see where the king's spear is, and the cruse of water that was at his bolster.

Awakened by the noise, Saul recognized David's voice. David addressed him directly, once more pleading his innocence of any evil intentions toward Saul his king. Saul screamed back, "*I have sinned: return, my son. I have played the fool.*" Saul abandoned his pursuit and returned to his home.

XXVII. END OF AN ERA

-I SAMUEL-

After so many years of running from Saul, David became despondent. I believe this is the best explanation of I Samuel 27:1.

And David said in his heart, I shall now perish one day by the hand of Saul: there is nothing better for me than that I should speedily escape into the land of the Philistines; and Saul shall despair of me, to seek me any more in any coast of Israel: so shall I escape out of his hand.

He was about twenty-eight years old at the time. With his army of six hundred men, he hired himself out to Achish, king of Gath, as a professional mercenary, a hired soldier of fortune, for Israel's traditional enemies, the Philistines.

Life with the Philistines

David, his men and their families, including David's two wives, lived for a time in Gath. When Saul heard of it, he abandoned his pursuit and no longer concerned himself with David. After a time, however, David requested that he and his company be assigned a city of their own based on the reason that it was not fitting for the king's servants to dwell in the royal city. Verse 6 says, *"Then Achish gave him Ziklag that day: wherefore Ziklag pertained unto the kings of Judah unto this day."* Ziklag is on the Philistine border just southeast of Gaza. Verse 7 tells us that David's mercenary activities for the Philistines lasted sixteen months. During those sixteen months, David operated as a double agent for the tribe of Judah. He would promise the king of the Philistines one thing and then do another. He benefited from the protection of the Philistines, while at the same time acting as their enemy, although they did not know it.

David's military exploits were bloody. He and his men raided the villages of the Geshurites, the Gezrites, and the Amalekites, down through the wilderness toward Egypt, killing every living soul. Periodically, he would report back to his boss, King Achish, taking him captured sheep, cattle, donkeys, camels, and clothing. Achish would ask (vs. 10), *"Whither have ye made a raid today?"* David would lie and answer, *"Against the south of Judah, and against the south of the Jerahmeelites, and against the south of the Kenites."* These three nations were traditional enemies of the Philistines. That old pirate cliché, "Dead men tell no tales," was David's philosophy at that time. He left no one alive who could report the truth back to Achish, and so Achish was pleased with his hired soldier as verse 12 says. *"And Achish believed David, saying, He hath made his people Israel utterly to abhor him; therefore he shall be my servant forever."*

About that time, the Philistine lords gathered their armies together to battle against Saul and the army of Israel. Among those leaders was Achish, who naturally planned to include David and his men in his Philistine army. His confidence in David was so great that he even promised to make him his personal bodyguard for life. The scene ended with David and his mercenaries accompanying Achish as he went to his rendezvous with the rest of the Philistine armies.

In the meantime, the Israelites were encamped by the spring in Jezreel while the Philistine armies joined one another at Aphek, which was about twenty miles west of Shiloh. When some of the Philistines recognized David and his men among Achish's personal army, the other chieftains demanded, *"What do these Hebrews here?"* Achish responded with high praise of David and his faithfulness since he had deserted to him from Saul. But, the other Philistine leaders were suspicious and angry, demanding that he be excluded from the battle. They did not trust him, and feared he would use the opportunity to be reconciled to Saul at their expense. Even these many years later, they remembered again the women of Israel had sung, *"Saul slew his thousands, and David his ten thousands."*

With apologies and regrets, Achish sent David and his men back to Ziklag after assuring him that it was only because the other chieftains demanded it. He (Achish) could not have been happier with David's faithfulness to him. (How little did he know!). Although David pretended to be hurt by his dismissal, he must have been greatly relieved to escape confronting his Israelite brothers in hand-to-hand combat. In obedience to Achish, David left the Philistine camp and returned to his headquarters. {Read Psalm 18}

Saul and the Witch of Endor

Returning to First Samuel 28:5, we learn that Saul, having moved his army to Mount Gilboa, could see, spread out in the distance, the vast number of men in the Philistine army. As a result, *"he was afraid, and his heart greatly trembled"* (vs. 5). Never had he been in more need of divine guidance, though he had long since forfeited it. When he received no answer from the Lord by any of the prescribed routes, he turned in desperation to his servants and demanded, *"Seek me a woman that hath a familiar spirit that I may go to her, and enquire of her.* "Earlier, he had banished mediums from the land (vs. 3) as the law required, but now he no longer cared where his answers came from. God or demon, it did not matter. On being informed that there was a medium living at Endor, about fifteen miles away, Saul disguised himself and made a secret journey, arriving by night to ask of her: *"Divine unto me by the familiar spirit, and bring me him up, whom I shall name unto thee."* The woman protested, fearing that this stranger might be a spy from King Saul, who had *"cut off those that have familiar spirits, and the wizards, out of the land."* It could be dangerous, even deadly, to comply with such a request. *"Wherefore then layest thou a snare for my life, to cause me to die?"* With a solemn oath, Saul promised she would come to no harm and then demanded, *"Bring me up Samuel."* The woman was surprised, and cried out in terror, when Samuel actually appeared. We know that Samuel was a man of God because he had been a prophet, a judge, and a priest in Israel. After his death, he would have been with Abraham, as Lazarus was later (Luke 16:22). It would have been impossible for a medium, a servant of Satan, to call up Samuel from the place called Paradise. God must have sent him to pronounce judgment on King Saul.

When the woman recognized Samuel and realized God was involved, she saw through Saul's disguise at once and cried out, *"Why hast thou deceived me for thou art Saul."* After again reassuring her, he asked for a description of what she had seen. She replied, *"I saw gods ascending out of the earth,"* and *"an old man cometh up; and he is covered with a mantle"* (vs. 14). Saul knew it was Samuel. He fell on his face and poured out his heart in fear and terror (vs. 15). The Philistines were massed against him; God was silent; Samuel was now his only hope. Could he expect the good counsel he had received during the early years of innocence? Never!
God was silent because He has *"departed from thee, and is become thine enemy,"* Samuel said. He reviewed the reasons   (vss. 17-18):

The Lord hath done as he spake by me: for the Lord hath rent the kingdom out of thine hand, and given it to thy neighbour, even David: Because thou obeyedst not the voice of the Lord, nor executed his fierce wrath upon Amalek, therefore hath the Lord done this thing unto thee this day.

Saul did get a word from God, but it was not a pleasant one. It was not what he wanted to hear. Samuel continued in verse 19: *Moreover the Lord will also deliver Israel with thee into the hand of the Philistines: and tomorrow shalt thou and thy sons be with me: the Lord also shall deliver the host of Israel into the hand of the Philistines.* This statement did not mean that Saul would be in the bliss of Abraham's bosom. It meant death, Sheol, the grave. He said, "You will be where I am; you will be in the grave." But Saul's life was one of many "sins of a high hand" which put him (most likely) across the great gulf from Paradise. He would still be there more than 1,000 years later when in Luke 16:22-26, our Lord said the rich man was after his death.

This encounter with the witch at Endor was Saul's fourth tragic sin. According to First Chronicles 10:13, it was an additional reason for his rejection by God. When Saul heard Samuel's words he fainted. The combination of fatigue, hunger (for he had not eaten all day or night), and terror, were too much for him. When he was revived, the woman, in pity, insisted on feeding him (vss. 21-22).

I have put my life in thy hand, Now therefore, I pray thee, hearken thou also unto the voice of thine handmaid, and let me set a morsel of bread before thee, and eat, that thou mayest have strength, when thou goest on thy way.

At the urging of his servants, Saul ate. The woman killed a fatted calf and baked bread. Like a murderer on death row, Saul ate his last meal. When he had finished, he made the long night journey back to his troops. The Philistines attacked at dawn; Saul met his doom as Samuel had predicted.

In First Samuel 30:1 the author returns to David and his departure from the Philistine army. It was a three day journey back to Ziklag and when they arrived, rather than a "Welcome Home" sign, they found the city, still smoking and burning from a raid by the Amalekites. David had been raiding Amalekite cities (27:8), and now while he was gone, they had retaliated. They took the women and children captive, along with the goods, but did not kill anyone. I draw your attention to the fact that in this regard they were more merciful than David. When he raided an Amalekite city, he killed men, women and children, leaving no one alive, with the philosophy that dead men tell no tales. David and his men were greatly distressed and wept bitterly. Then, a feeling of mutiny spread through his army and there was talk of stoning him. The people were angry and bitter, *"But David encouraged himself in the Lord his God"* (vs. 6).

The Psalms record much of David's distress in times such as this, and of how God was always his refuge and his strength. In this seeming tragedy, he turned to the Lord for wisdom to make the right decision. This event was a turning point in David's life. Calling on Abiathar the priest, and requesting the ephod which he had rescued during the slaughter at Nob, David inquired of the Lord, "*Shall I pursue after this troop? shall I overtake them?*" What a great comfort God's answer must have been to him. "*Pursue: for thou shalt surely overtake them, and without fail recover* all." With his six hundred men, he went in hot pursuit after the Amalekites. However, about two hundred of David's men became too faint to go on, so they were left behind at the brook, Besor, to watch over the baggage which was left by David's troops.

As they continued on their way, they found a fainting Egyptian in a field who had nothing to eat or drink for three days. They brought him to David, fed him, and when his spirit revived, David questioned him, learning that he was a slave to an Amalekite and had been with the raiding party, so he was able to describe the burning of Ziklag. With David's assurance of protection, he led them to where the Amalekite army was encamped. The Amalekites were reveling and celebrating the success of their invasion which had included a number of cities in addition to Ziklag. David's army attacked them by surprise and overcame them in a fierce battle. According to verses 18 and 19:

And David recovered all that the Amalekites had carried away, and David rescued his two wives. There was nothing lacking to them, neither small nor great, neither sons nor daughters, neither spoil, nor any thing that they had taken to them: David recovered all.

When they returned to the brook Besor, to the two hundred men whom they had left behind, some of David's company, described as "wicked men and men of Belial" announced that they would not divide the spoil with those who had not gone to the battle. David rebuked their greed, saying (vs. 23), "*Ye shall not do so, my brethren, with that which the Lord hath given us, who hath preserved us, and delivered the company that came against us into our hand.*" Then, in verse 24, he made an important pronouncement that became a statute and ordinance in Israel from that day forward: "*As his part is that goeth down to the battle, so shall his part be that tarrieth by the stuff: they shall part alike.*"

David was a master politician. With an eye to the future, to endear himself to the hearts of the people who dwelled in the south of Israel. This was the area of the tribe of Judah. To the elders of Judah, his old friends, he sent generous presents from the spoil he had taken from the Amalekites, with the message, "*Behold a present for you of the spoil of the Lord.*" His largest gifts went to Bethel, Ramoth, Jattir, to Hebron and a number of other cities. He also sent gifts to the cities occupied by the Jerahmeelites and the Kenites, "*and to all the places where David himself and his men were wont to haunt.*" You may be sure that the inhabitants of those places would not forget the name of David. Very shortly, this wise political move would pay off.

In chapter 31, we again return to the battle which was raging on Mount Gilboa. The fighting went heavily against the Israelites so that many were slain while others fled. As many soldiers retreated, Jonathan and his two brothers were killed while Saul was mortally wounded by an arrow. Turning to his armor-bearer he begged, *"Draw thy sword, and thrust me through therewith; lest these uncircumcised come and thrust me through, and abuse me."* The armor-bearer was afraid to do such a thing, so Saul put the hilt of the sword against the ground and fell on it. When his armor-bearer saw that he was dead, he did likewise and died. Verse 6 summarizes the situation, saying, *"So Saul died, and his three sons, and his armor-bearer, and all his men, that same day together."* The next morning, the Philistines returned to the battle field to strip the bodies of the slain of their valuables; a practice still followed by the Arabs as recently as World War II in North Africa. To their surprise and delight, they discovered a prize beyond their highest expectations -- the bodies of Saul and his sons. They cut off Saul's head, fastened his body to the wall of Beth-shan, and hung his armor in the temple of Ashtaroth.

Can it be that there is a discrepancy here? Sixty-five years earlier, following the battle of Aphek, the Philistines placed the Ark of God in the temple of Dagon. We know the Philistines worshiped the fish-headed god Dagon. But here in First Samuel 31, it says that they put his weapons in the temple of Ashtaroth. First Chronicles 10:10 adds to the confusion when it says they put his armor in the house of their gods and fastened his head in the temple of Dagon. Chronicles records the temple of Dagon; Samuel records the temple of Ashtaroth; two different pagan worship systems. Is there an answer to this? Certainly there is. Archaeologists have discovered eleventh century B.C. *dual temples.* The Philistines, who were worshipers of the fish-headed god Dagon during their conquest and henotheistic practices, had adopted the worship of Ashtaroth as well. The Bible could not be more accurate in this matter. First Samuel 31:10 mentions the temple of Ashtaroth; I Chronicles 10:10 mentions the temple of Dagon, and not until the discovery, was it known that the Philistines worshiped both Dagon and Ashtaroth.

Excavations at Ashkelon allowed scientist to extract DNA from the Philistine skeletons buried there. The DNA revealed the Philistines had European ancestry, confirming Jeremiah 47:4 and Amos 9:7 connecting them with Caphtor, modern day Crete.

When the inhabitants of Jabesh-gilead heard what the Philistines had done, the valiant men of the city walked all night and, at the risk of their lives, took the bodies of Saul and his sons down from the wall of Beth-shan, carried them back to Jabesh and burned them there.

Why would these inhabitants of Jabesh-gilead risk their lives for the bodies of dead men? Because almost forty years earlier, Saul's first military exploit was the rescue of the inhabitants of Jabesh-gilead from the invasion of Nahash the Ammonite. The first exploit was not forgotten, nor did their gratitude cool, because almost forty years later, these men risked their lives to remove the body of the man who had rescued their ancestors. With the death of Saul and his sons, his dynasty came to an end, and the ninety-year period covered by the book of I Samuel also came to an end.

XXVIII. TIME OF TRANSITION

-II SAMUEL-

David's first news of the defeat at Gilboa, and the deaths of Saul and Jonathan, came from a young Amalekite who showed him the dead king's crown and bracelet, probably stolen from his corpse. He claimed to be the one who had given the death thrust at the wounded king's request. But, the account of Saul's death in First Samuel 31, and the corresponding passage in I Chronicles 10, makes it quite evident that Saul died by his own hand. After a spontaneous expression of grief, David turned to the informer and delivered a reward he did not expect. *"How wast thou not afraid to stretch forth thine hand to destroy the Lord's anointed,"* he asked (II Sam. 1:14) and immediately had him put to death. David had refused to touch God's anointed on two occasions and he would not condone it or tolerate it at the hand of another man.

Every time I read David's tender expression of love and compassion for the man who had on several occasions attempted to kill him, I am amazed and touched by the Christ-like attitude he displayed toward his enemy (vss. 11-12). His formal lamentation, recorded in verses 19-27, is one of the great literary masterpieces of the Bible. It is a heroic poem which combines the manly virtues of honor and love.

With both King Saul and Prince Jonathan dead, David's previous political maneuvers began to work in his favor. Remember, he had sent generous gifts throughout the southland while working for King Achish. Following the Lord's instruction, David and his followers moved to Hebron. There he was met by the elders of his tribe, who anointed him king over the tribe of Judah.

Civil War

Meanwhile, up in the north across the Jordan, Abner, the son of Ner, the late Saul's commander-in-chief, had proclaimed a surviving son of Saul, named Ish-bosheth, as Israel's king in Mahanaim. Verse 9 says he: *"made him king over Gilead, and over the Ashurites, and over Jezreel, over Ephraim, over Benjamin, and over all Israel."* All of

Israel, that is, *except* the tribe of Judah. Verse 10 says that Ish-bosheth was forty years old when he became king over Israel and that he was king for two years. The tribe of Judah gave its loyalty to King David. The time that David was king in Hebron, over the tribe of Judah, was seven years and six months, five and one-half years longer than Ish-bosheth reigned in the North.

As a result of the divided loyalties, there were now two separate kingdoms in the land; eleven tribes following Ish-bosheth and one tribe following King David. David's military commander was Joab, and Ish-bosheth retained Abner, who was in reality the real power behind the throne. Although Abner had put Ish-bosheth on the throne as a convenient puppet king because he was a son of Saul, Abner was still the one in control of the eleven tribes.

Soon after, the representatives of the two armies met on opposite sides of the pool of Gibeon. General Abner suggested a contest to demonstrate which had military superiority. *"Let the young men now arise and play before us"* (vs. 14). Joab agreed, and two dozen contestants were chosen, twelve from Benjamin, Saul's tribe, and twelve from Judah. As they faced one another for hand-to-hand combat, each grabbed his opponent by the head and thrust his sword into his side. As a result of this violent conflict, all twenty-four died together. Both armies then began fighting and King David's men were victorious. David's three nephews, the sons of his sister Zeruiah, were among the fighting men. They were: Joab (the General), Abishai, and Asahel. Asahel, who is described as being unusually fleet-footed, singled out Abner to be his special target, as he and his men fled before the army of Judah. Abner evidently knew David's family, because he recognized Asahel and shouted at him to cease his pursuit and choose a lesser-known foe as his objective. He did not want to run the risk of killing Asahel, and asked, *"how then should I hold up my face to Joab thy brother?"* But, Asahel refused to be turned aside, and Abner killed him with the shaft of his spear. {2:23} Joab and Abishai continued to encourage a further pursuit of Abner. From a hilltop encampment, Abner called for a truce, crying out, *"Shall the sword devour forever?"* Joab blew a trumpet and both armies returned to their headquarters--Abner to Mahanaim and Joab to Hebron. When the casualties were totaled, Joab had lost twenty men but Abner had lost three hundred and sixty.

The law of "blood avenger" was customary in those times. Because of this system which encouraged revenge and continued bloodshed, Cities of Refuge were established (three on each side of the Jordan) where someone guilty of the accidental death of another, might flee and, under certain conditions, be protected from the blood avenger. If the manslayer could convince the elders of the City of Refuge that the death was an accident, and not premeditated murder, he could live there until the death of the current High Priest. The avenger could not follow him. After the death of the High Priest, he was free to leave the city and it was then illegal for the blood avenger to touch him. {Joshua 20}

After the skirmish by the Pool of Gibeon, the burden of duty (by custom) fell on Joab to avenge the death of his brother Asahel, and the thought began to consume him. Chapter 3 says there was a longwar (approximately one year) between the house of the deceased King Saul and the house of King David. David's armed forces kept getting stronger while those of the North under King Ish-bosheth and Abner became weaker. David's personal household was also becoming stronger. By then he had six wives with many sons.

Abner's Break with Ish-bosheth

Among the many recognized social and political customs, it was also assumed that if a man took the wife, or mistress, of a deceased monarch, he was laying claim to the throne by succession. In II Samuel 3:7, *"Saul had a concubine whose name was Rizpah, and Ish-bosheth said to Abner, Wherefore hast thou gone in unto my father's concubine?"* The significance of what Abner had done was recognized by Ish-bosheth and he was both fearful and angry. He was, as we know, only a puppet in Abner's hands, and Abner's lengthy reply confirms this (vss. 8-10).

Am I a dog's head, which against Judah do shew kindness this day unto the house of Saul thy father, and hath not delivered thee into the hand of David, that thou chargest me today with a fault concerning this woman? So do God to Abner, and more also, except, as the Lord hath sworn to David, even so I do to him; To translate the kingdom from the house of Saul, and to set up the throne of David over Israel and over Judah, from Dan even to Beersheba.

In chapter 3, verse 12, Abner began negotiating to transfer the kingdom from the control of Ish-bosheth over to King David. He offered to make a covenant with David: *"Behold, my hand shall be with thee, to bring about all Israel unto thee."* David was interested, but imposed one condition, *"Thou shalt not see my face, except thou first bring Michal Saul's daughter, when thou comest."* Ish-bosheth, admitting his own inadequacy, approved the request and while arrangements were being made to take Michal from her husband (vss. 14-16), Abner was negotiating with the elders of the northern tribes, persuading them to change their allegiance to David and make him King. Verses 17 and 18 record his argument.

Ye sought for David in times past to be king over you: Now then do it: for the Lord hath spoken of David, saying, By the hand of my servant David I will save my people Israel out of the hand of the Philistines and out of the hand of all their enemies.

He also gave special attention to persuading his own tribe Benjamin, which, because of its historical allegiance to Saul, could have persuaded the others to refuse. When he was sure of his position in representing the northern tribes, he went down to Hebron with twenty men. David received him royally, entertained him lavishly, and sent him away in peace to complete the transfer of allegiance which would put him in control of all twelve tribes.

While this summit conference was in progress, Joab, with some of his soldiers, returned. He learned what had been transpiring between the King and Abner, and was furious. Rushing in to the king, Joab cried (vss. 24-25):

What hast thou done? Behold, Abner came unto thee; why is it that thou hast sent him away, and he is quite gone? Thou knowest Abner the son of Ner, that he came to deceive thee, and to know thy going out and thy coming in, and to know all that thou doest.

Joab's Revenge

Joab, in anger, took matters into his own hands. Without King David's knowledge, he sent messengers to Abner asking that he return and meet with him. Then, he arranged for the two of them to be alone. Under the guise of friendship, Joab killed him. Verse 27 says, *"he died, for the blood of Asahel his brother."* Ironically, this act of revenge took place in Hebron, one of the Cities of Refuge. There were two reasons for Joab's action. The first was to avenge his brother's death. Second, he was afraid of losing his position as Commander of the Army. He knew that in negotiating with David, Abner would demand some concession for himself and that there was not room for two military commanders. He knew his job, his prestige, and his future, were in the balance. These factors added fuel to his desire for vengeance against Abner.

David Mourns Abner

When King David heard what had happened, he promptly issued a disclaimer for any responsibility (vs. 28ff). *"I and my kingdom are guiltless before the Lord forever from the blood of Abner the son of Ner: Let it rest on the head of Joab and on all his father's house."* Imagine the political implications! The Commander-in-Chief of the armies of Israel was murdered, assassinated, under a flag of truce, by the General of the Army of

King David. David was in danger of attack from the whole northern kingdom. He knew this and immediately ordered Joab and all the people to go into mourning for Abner. *"Rend your clothes, and gird you with sackcloth, and mourn before Abner"* (vs. 31). The King himself led the mourners in walking behind the bier during the funeral procession.

King David's behavior pleased the people just *"as whatsoever the king did pleased all the people."* Verse 37 says that *"all the people and all Israel understood that day that it was not of the king to slay Abner."* So, with this strategic move, he was successful in averting catastrophe.

Ish-bosheth is Slain

About that time, two officers of Ish-bosheth's army conspired to ingratiate themselves with King David by committing an act of treachery. They arranged, through deceit, to get into Ish-bosheth's bedroom during his daily siesta time. They murdered him, cut off his head, and traveled all night with the gruesome evidence to present to King David. Ancient monarchs considered the severed heads of their enemies to be a great prize. After being chopped off, the head would be soaked in wax or honey, then wrapped up and preserved until it could be presented to the king in exchange for a reward. We know that later in Babylonian times, heads, dangling from cords in the amphitheater, were in the decorations for Belshazzar's feast.

The two assassins of Ish-bosheth, Rechab and Baanah, approached David with their prize, saying, *"Behold the head of thine enemy, which sought thy life"* (vs. 8). David's reply was to tell them the story about the Amalekite who had brought him an account of Saul's death, two years ago, expecting a reward, and what he had done to that man, saying (vs. 10-11),

I took hold of him, and slew him. How much more, when wicked men have slain a righteous person in his own house upon his bed? Shall I not therefore now require his blood of your hand, and take you away from the earth?

He ordered the two murderers to be slain, their bodies mutilated, then hanged in public view. Then, in kindness, he buried the head of Ish-bosheth in the grave with Abner.

The Kingdom is United

Remember, we read in II Samuel 2:10 that Ish-bosheth was king for only two years. From this we know that his assassination took place in 1008 B.C., because Saul's death and David's coronation in Hebron occurred in 1010 B.C. As a result, there is a five year gap between II Samuel 4:12 and 5:1. Chapter 5 says that all the tribes of Israel came to David and, in verse 3, *"they anointed David king over Israel."* David had waited twenty-two years for this. 4 and 5 sum up his reign: *David was thirty years old when he began to reign, and he reigned forty years. In Hebron he reigned over Judah seven years and six months: and in Jerusalem he reigned thirty and three years over all Israel and Judah.* This second anointing took place in 1003 B.C. when David was thirty-seven years old.

XXIX. DAVID TAKES CHARGE

-II SAMUEL-

It had been twenty-two years since Samuel had poured the horn of oil over the head of young David as they stood in the house of his father Jesse. The intervening years had included years of military glory in Saul's court, years as an outlaw, often discouraged, and always in danger of death at the hand of Saul. Then, in 1010, there was his elevation to a throne, but only over his one tribe of Judah. But now, in II Samuel 5, in 1003, he became king over all Israel and as God's representative monarch, there was no greater man than David on the face of the earth. As head over God's chosen people, he began with precision and swiftness, to embark on several projects which would endear him to the hearts of the people and would solidify his position as king of Israel.

A New Capitol

He began immediately to seek a new and more strategic location for the capitol of his kingdom. Because of his military background, his eyes were drawn to Jerusalem, the city of the Jebusites. It was a natural location, strategically situated near the border of Judah and Benjamin, centrally located for most of his people. Its location on a hilltop was ideal from the standpoint of military defense. However, there was a problem; the city was already inhabited by the Jebusites and they held an almost impregnable position. 5:6: *And the king and his men went to Jerusalem unto the Jebusites, the inhabitants of the land; which spake unto David, saying, except thou take away the blind and the lame, thou shalt not come in hither.*

In other words, in this taunt to David, they were saying that their walls were so impregnable that even their crippled could successfully defend them. The city of Jerusalem had been inhabited by the Jebusites for at least four hundred years. To get the background of the city, we need to go back to Joshua 15:63: *As for the Jebusites, the inhabitants of Jerusalem, the children of Judah could not drive them out; but the Jebusites dwell with the children of Judah at Jerusalem unto this day.* For four hundred years the tribe of Judah had looked up at the city on its protective hill and was reminded of their earlier failure. Even during Joshua's time, lack of faith on their part had prevented them from driving out the

Jebusites as God had commanded. But, calling on his great talent as a military strategist, David sent his men up through the water tunnel to take the city from the inside. In I Chronicles 11:6-7, we are given additional insight into its capture: *And David said, whosoever smiteth the Jebusites first shall be chief and captain. So Joab the son of Zeruiah went first up, and was chief. And David dwelt in the castle; therefore they called it the city of David.*

Joab had been Commander in Chief of the army since the early years, although there is no record of an official appointment. I wonder if David's unhappiness with Joab, following the assassination of Abner, as expressed in II Samuel 3:39, could have been behind his pronouncement. It could have been an attempt to set Joab aside, hoping that some other valiant man would be the first in capturing the city of the Jebusites. But Joab was a very determined man. He captured the city, thereby maintaining and solidifying his position as Commander-in-Chief of the armies of Israel.

II Samuel 5:12 is an important verse because of the additional information it provides about the spiritual character of David. We read, *David perceived the Lord had established him king over Israel, and that he had exalted his kingdom for his people Israel's sake.* This was something Saul never realized. Saul had been a man devoid of faith. He saw the kingdom as his own, and he served only for himself and what he hoped would be his dynasty on the throne of Israel. He never saw the kingdom as belonging to God, only as belonging to himself. King David, on the other hand, knew that God had established him as king, not for his sake, but for that of His people Israel. Because of this, we can identify Saul as egocentric, that is, self-centered. David, however, was theocentric, God-centered. Everything that King David did was for God and for the advancement of His kingdom.

Philistines Defeated

Following the capture of Jerusalem, which was the first thing David did to establish his position as king, he went out to battle against the Philistines. They had come up against him when they heard he had been anointed king of Israel. Perhaps they wished to avenge his duplicity when he served Achish, or perhaps they feared him because of his military reputation and hoped to defeat him before his position was solidified. David defeated them in two separate encounters after first seeking counsel of the Lord in both cases before engaging them in battle. This endeared him to the people of Israel since the Philistines were longtime enemies and it had been the Philistines who killed Saul, their former king and his sons.

Chapter 6 records the third thing David did which demonstrated his theocentricity. As a spiritual man, versed in the Law of Moses, David knew there was no place in Jerusalem where God could be worshiped. The tabernacle and the altar were still in Gibeon. In fact, II Chronicles 1:3-4 records that they remained there until Solomon removed them to the new temple. However, the altar and tabernacle did not constitute the proper facilities for the worship of Jehovah. It was necessary to have the Ark of the Covenant, the symbol of God's throne. In Psalm 132:1-8, David recalled how he felt after becoming king and realizing that the Ark of God was not present with him. The Ark needed to be in the midst of His people.

Lord, remember David, and all his afflictions: How he sware unto the Lord, and vowed unto the mighty God of Jacob; Surely I will not come into the tabernacle of my house, nor go up into my bed; I will not give sleep to mine eyes, or slumber to mine eyelids, Until I find out a place for the Lord, an habitation for the mighty God of Jacob. Lo, we heard of it at Ephratah: we found it in the fields of the wood.

David looked for the Ark where it had been abandoned after the Philistines had returned it following its capture at the battle of Aphek in 1075 B.C. Saul had gone down and tried to use it one time, but it was never returned to its rightful place. In fact, the Ark of God, the symbol of His throne, was abandoned in the woods. Even Samuel never tried to return it; Saul never tried to return it; and David had not been able to return it because he was not in an official position to do so. But after becoming king over Israel, he defeated the Jebusites and acquired a place for worship. He defeated the Philistines and removed the possibility of invasion. Then, he went down into the woods, found the Ark of God, and brought it back up to Jerusalem with a great celebration.

Rather than following the regulations Moses had set down for transporting the Ark by means of poles through its rings, they designed and built a cart on which to return it to Jerusalem. The language of 6:4 suggests that they may have thought more of the cart than the Ark. In any case, God was displeased with the disobedience of their method of transportation, and when it began to tilt and upset the Ark, His anger burned against the man who reached out his hand to steady it. Verse 7 says, *"and God smote him there for his error, and there he died by the ark of God."*

David was very disturbed at this..In fear, he left the Ark at the nearby house of Obed-edom for the next three months. Because it was there, *"the Lord blessed Obed-edom, and all his household."* (vs. 11) David must have spent those months restudying the instructions of Moses (Numbers 4:4-6), because when he went back to resume taking the Ark to

Jerusalem, he followed the correct methods and brought it into the city with great rejoicing. The Ark of God was taken to Jerusalem by David and a special tent was made for it. Throughout David's reign, from 1010 B.C. to 970 B.C., when someone wanted to go up to the tent of meeting and sacrifice at the brazen altar, it was necessary to go to Gibeon. But after 1,000 B.C., to worship where the Ark was, that was done in Jerusalem.

In 959 B.C., following the completion of the temple in the eleventh year of his reign, Solomon took the tent of meeting, the brazen altar, and the Ark, and placed them all in the new temple. The Ark of God was placed in the holy of holies. The tent of meeting was kept in the archives of the temple.

To continue your independent study, please refer to the following Scriptures which demonstrate that during David's time the Ark was in a special tent in Jerusalem: I Chron. 15:1; 11 Chron. 1:4; II Sam. 6:17. The verses that demonstrate the tabernacle and altar were in Gibeon are: I Kings 3:4; 1 Chron. 21:29; II Chron. 1:3, 5. These verses describe how Solomon placed all these items in the new temple are: I Kings 8:4 and 11 Chron. 5:5-9.

XXX. THE DAVIDIC COVENANT

-II SAMUEL-

Because of David's faithfulness and because he had proven himself to be a theocentric, God-centered man, God is about to make some amazing promises to him. These promises are known as the Davidic Covenant. It is described in II Samuel 7. In the overall purpose of God, it is equal in its significance to the Abrahamic Covenant. The chapter begins by saying that after God had given David rest from his enemies he began to be concerned because the house of God had not been built. When he contrasted his own palace of cedar, to the tent he had prepared for housing the Ark in Jerusalem, it did not seem to be a fitting comparison. He shared his dream with Nathan, who encouraged him to fulfill it. But, God had different plans and he gave David this message, *"Shalt thou build me an house for me to dwell in whereas I have not dwelt in any house since the time that I brought up the children of Israel out of Egypt?"* (vss.5-6) Verse 11 states, *"Also the Lord telleth thee that he will make thee an house."*

The occasion for the Davidic Covenant was predicated on the fact that David wanted to build a house for God. But God "turned the tables" on David, saying, "I do not need you to build a house for me, but I will build a house for you." In verse 8, God reminded David of his humble beginnings, *"I took thee from the sheepcote, from following the sheep, to be ruler over my people, even Israel."* It does not take a great deal of imagination to understand what the job of following the sheep involves. God was reminding David of his humble roots and how He took him from the pasture, from following the sheep, to the throne of Israel. (vs. 9):

And I was with thee whithersoever thou wentest, and have cut off all thine enemies out of thy sight, and have made thee a great name like unto the name of the great men that are in the earth.

Based on His own past faithfulness to David, God made a great promise, establishing the Davidic Covenant, which had present and eschatological implications. The Davidic

Covenant consists of two parts, with each part having three Sections. Part I was fulfilled before David's death, while Part II had a later fulfillment. Section I in Part I promises to be fulfilled before David died: *"I have made thee a great name, like unto the name of the great men that are in the earth."* (vs. 9) In II Samuel 8:13 we learn that King David had a great name. Section II begins with verse 10: *"I will appoint a place for my people Israel."* He would add more land to the nation. Chapter 8 describes David's conquests over surrounding nations. Section III is in verse 11 where God said He had *"caused thee to rest from all thine enemies."* We read of this in I Chronicles 23:25.

It is important to know that the Lord did fulfill those promises to David, because they validated the Sections in Part II of the covenant which would take place after his death. Part II, Section I, begins in verse 12 where the Lord says to David:

And when thy days be fulfilled, and thou shalt sleep with thy fathers, I will set up thy seed after thee, which shall proceed out of thy bowels, and I will establish his kingdom. He shall build an house for my name, and I will establish the throne of his kingdom forever.

No monarch had ever received such a promise as this. God was promising David a seed (offspring), in perpetuity. His dynasty was to continue forever and ever. The physical proof of this was that there would always be a male heir of David to sit on the throne generation after generation. The people could look at their king and say, "there, in the descendant of David, is the physical evidence of God's promise to King David."

Sections II and III in Part II are in verse 16: *"And thine house and thy kingdom shall be established for ever before thee: thy throne shall be established forever."* David was promised three things to be realized after his death: an **eternal seed**, finally realized in the Person of the Lord Jesus Christ; an **eternal kingdom**, set aside for the present, but to be reestablished again when the Lord Jesus returns to earth; and an **eternal throne** upon which Christ Himself will sit. All these promises were conveyed by God to David through the prophet Nathan. n awe to the words of God through Nathan. Then in humility and gratitude, he sought to commune with the Lord, sitting before the Ark and saying (vs. 18ff)

Who am I, O Lord God? And what is my house, that thou hast brought me hitherto? And this was yet a small thing in thy sight, O Lord God, but thou hast spoken also of thy servant's house for a great while to come. For thy word's sake, and according to thine own heart, hast thou done all these great things.

XXXI. FURTHER VICTORIES

-II SAMUEL-

Philistines and Moabites

A major reason why God did not permit King David to fulfill his dream of building Him a temple, was that his career had been one consisting of much bloodshed. This is made clear in I Chronicles 22:8, where David is speaking. *But the word of the Lord came to me, saying, Thou hast shed blood abundantly, and hast made great wars: thou shalt not build an house unto my name, because thou hast shed much blood upon the earth.*

In II Samuel 8, we have some further evidence of this as David fights to subdue those neighboring kingdoms that still seek to cause trouble on their common borders. After a successful assault against the Philistines, he engaged in a major battle to subdue the Moabites. Here we get a little more insight into one of the customs of the day. For the most part, prisoners were not taken unless they could be profitably sold as slaves. It was not feasible to provide for their sustenance, so prisoners were usually slain after a battle. In chapter 8, David practices this custom in his military conquests.

It is interesting to remember that only a few years earlier he had entrusted his parents' safety to the king of Moab. Now, to expand his territory and secure his borders, he has engaged them in battle and defeated them. He made the captives lie down on the ground in three lines, and ordered two lines to be put to death while those in the third became his servants.

Mephibosheth

When not engaged in battle, David continued to perform those acts which drew him closer to the hearts of the people, especially those from the northern kingdom who had remained loyal to Saul and were David's former enemies. Second Samuel 9 recounts one of the things which David did to solidify his relationship with the tribe of Benjamin. The first mention of Mephibosheth occurred in II Samuel 4:4. There we learned that he was a son of Jonathan and that he was five years old when his father and grandfather were killed in battle. In the panic that followed that defeat, his nurse tried to flee with him but she dropped him. He became lame in 1010 B.C.

Chapter 9 relates how in 995 B.C., David further endeared himself to the relatives of Saul and the inhabitants of the northern kingdom through his kindness to Mephibosheth. There was a deeper motive than that, however. It was the promise and the commitment he had made to Jonathan to show kindness to his descendents, and the assurance he had given to King Saul that he would not cut off his descendents. This was an extraordinary promise because it was common practice in those days for a monarch to completely annihilate all relatives of his predecessor if he had been deposed, assassinated, or displaced by one other than his natural heir.

Mephibosheth would have been about twenty years old when David called for him. As an heir of Saul and Jonathan, he was naturally filled with fear when the king summoned him. Verse 6 says *"he fell on his face."* David had to reassure him, saying, *"Fear not."* Mephibosheth, no doubt, expected to be killed on the spot. Instead, David turned Saul's entire estate over to him, along with the lifetime services of one of Saul's former servants named Ziba. Mephibosheth was given the honor of eating continually at the king's table and being treated with all the deference accorded the king's own sons. Do not overlook the fact that this is a picture of pure grace. Mephibosheth had done nothing to earn this pardon and blessing. David's love for Jonathan, and his previous commitments to Jonathan and Saul, moved him to show this kindness, and Israel loved him for it.

Victory over Ammon and Syria

About this time, the princes of Ammon, without a probable cause, committed a serious insult to David and his emissaries. As a consequence, Joab and his brother Abishai led the army out to battle against the Ammonites, who then called upon the Syrian army for aid. Joab and Abishai defeated the Syrians and forced the Ammonites into retreat, but the Syrians called in reinforcements and drew up a great battle array against Israel. So, King David led additional soldiers into the battle. Second Samuel 10:18 records:

"The Syrians fled before Israel; and David slew the men of seven hundred chariots of the Syrians, and forty thousand horsemen. Syria, therefore, made peace with Israel and served them and feared to help the children of Ammon any more" (vs. 19).

XXXII. A TRAGIC DOWNFALL

David's sin of adultery with Bathsheba was one of passion, impulse, and emotion. However, in plotting and systematically carrying out the murder of Uriah, David committed a sin of a high hand. The severity of God's judgment upon him, appears to do with his deliberate actions of hiding his sin as much as with his original misdeed, for Nathan, when he later confronted him, said: *"thou hast killed Uriah the Hittite with the sword, and hast taken his wife to be thy wife, and hast slain him with the sword of the children of Ammon"* (II Sam. 12:9). It is as his son Solomon later wrote: *"He that covereth his sins shall not prosper: but whoso confesseth and forsaketh them shall have mercy"* (Prov. 25! & 28:13).

Not only did the systematically planned murder of Uriah bring David under the judgment of God, but by using Joab as the man who was privy to the sequence of events, he put himself in a position where Joab would always be able to control him because he knew where the "bodies were buried." He knew about the skeletons in the closet.

By sending Joab the order to place Uriah in the front line of the battle, David probably rationalized in his mind that his difficulty was Uriah's fault. He may have thought, "If only he had followed his monarch's advice to spend the night at home, the whole problem would have been solved." God does not accept human rationalizations. The prophet Nathan made it very clear that God was judging David for the murder of Uriah and for taking the dead man's wife as his own. His sin had brought disgrace on God and had made both himself and God's nation a laughing-stock for the heathen. His personal testimony was ruined. One fact overlooked in the description of Uriah's murder, is that while the fighting was in progress where Uriah had been stationed, verse 17 reports, *"and there fell some of the people of the servants of David; and Uriah the Hittite died also."* Other valiant men were sacrificed as a cover-up for the reason behind Uriah's death. So, other soldiers as well as Uriah died because of David's lust and sin.

As a final cover-up touch to his scheme, David sent a letter of consolation to Joab, saying (vs. 25), *"the sword devoureth one as well as another."* In other words, "be comforted, that is the way war goes." Then he sent for Bathsheba and made her his wife. Everything was under control with no loose ends. No one was aware of the situation except Joab. But 11:27 closes the narrative by saying, *"The thing that David had done displeased the Lord."*

Confrontation

In chapter 12, the curtain is pulled back on King David's throne room and we are allowed to see the confrontation between the prophet Nathan and the king. This was the only nation on earth where the prophet was allowed to confront a king and to rebuke him regarding his actions without losing his head. After this it will not always be so, even in Israel, but David was theocentric. Although he had allowed sin to come into his life, he still loved God and wanted to serve Him. When Nathan the prophet came to him, the king respected his words from God and was sensitive to them. This is the touchstone of David's life. He was not perfect, but neither was he stiff-necked. He did not rebel at the words of God. His heart was sensitive and when Nathan spoke to him, he listened and obeyed.

Thou Art the Man

Nathan presented David with the parable contained in verses 1-4. David passed judgment on the man described in the parable, and in doing so he had passed judgment on himself. In verse 7, Nathan pointed to him and said, *"Thou art the man."* Then he delivered God's words of judgment and future tragedies on David's family. As tragic as this judgment was, it is possible that verse 8 is even more tragic. Imagine what David could have experienced in the perfect will of God. God reminded him of everything He had done for him, and in verse 8, He says, *"And if that had been too little, I would moreover have given unto thee such and such things."* But David was not faithful in all things. He sinned, and as a result of his sin, he was judged. However, he repented and was fully restored to the will of God. David was genuinely repentant. He confessed (vs. 13), *"I have sinned against the Lord."* Not against Bathsheba and Uriah. David knew that all sin is against God. Nathan said, *"The Lord also hath put away thy sin; thou shalt not die.*{See Lev. 24:17}

Following the encounter with Nathan, David was a broken and repentant man. Nevertheless, a price must be paid. There is no miraculous deliverance from the after-effects of a sin that affects those around us or dishonors the One we profess to serve. God's words of judgment through Nathan continued (vs. 14): *"Howbeit, because by this deed thou hast given great occasion to the enemies of the Lord to blaspheme."* David would pay the price in his own household because he had destroyed the household of Uriah. The impact of what he had done would have its affect on his wives and children. David repented and God forgave and spared him, but He did not miraculously erase what everyone had seen take place.

Consequences

In addition to future judgment, God also decreed that the child that Bathsheba bore would die. After Nathan left him, the child became ill. Even though God had said *"the child shall surely die"* (vs. 14), David still sought the Lord for the child's life. He did everything he possibly could to change God's will in the matter. This is well within the program of God. David did not sit back as Eli had done and say, *"let God do what He will."* God had determined that the child would die, but David, acting 180 degrees opposite from the spineless Eli, implored the Lord to spare the baby's life. He fasted; he prayed; he lay all night on the ground. He mourned and wept and when the elders came and stood beside him, to implore him to eat, David would not because he was doing everything possible, physically and spiritually, to implore God to save his child. Then verse 18 records, *"on the seventh day, the child died."* God had not been changed.

> *And it came to pass, on the seventh day that the child died. And the servants of David feared to tell him that the child was dead; for they said, Behold, while the child was yet alive, we spake unto him, and he would not hearken unto our voice: how will he then vex himself, if we tell him that the child is dead? (12:18)*

They reasoned among themselves: "He has been mourning these seven days with praying and fasting. He will be destroyed psychologically if we tell him that his prayers have not had any effect. He would not listen to us when the child was alive. If we tell him the child has died he might harm himself." Verse 19 says that when David saw his servants whispering among themselves he knew what had happened and asked, *"Is the child dead?"* They responded, *"He is dead."* David arose; washed himself; anointed himself with oil; and changed his clothes. Then, he went to the house of the Lord to worship. After that he went home and said, "Now it's time to eat." His servants were amazed and asked him, *"What is this that thou hast done? Thou didst fast and weep for the child, while it was alive; but when the child is dead thou didst rise and eat bread."* He explained:

While the child was yet alive, I fasted and wept: for I said, who can tell whether God will be gracious to me, that the child may live? But now he is dead, wherefore should I fast? Can I bring him back again? I shall go to him, but he shall not return to me. (12:22-23)

David said, *"I shall go to him, but he shall not return to me."* This is a tremendous Old Testament statement of the future resurrection.

The Birth of Solomon

David's love for Bathsheba continued. She conceived and bore a son whom they named Solomon. Verse 24 says that *"the Lord loved him."* Sin had been forgiven and put behind them. There is no better example in all of God's Word regarding the truth of Psalm 103:10-14. David's sin with Bathsheba and the murder of Uriah were past. Bathsheba gave birth to a son who would become the greatest King to on the throne. *"And the Lord loved him."*

During all these events, the siege of Rabbah had been continuing. This was the city which was being attacked when Uriah was killed. The remainder of chapter 12 describes its finish. This conquest gives us an indication of Joab's integrity. He was a valiant man, a man of war. He knew everything David had done, and would use it to his advantage later on. Nevertheless, he was a man of integrity and knew his position in the political/military structure of the kingdom. He was now about to capture Rabbah, the capital city of the Ammonites, after a long siege. It began, you will remember, back in 11:1. So, we have an example here of how long siege warfare could take. When Joab knew the city was his, we read in verses 27-28,

And Joab sent messengers to David, and said, I have fought against Rabbah, and have taken the city of waters. Now therefore gather the rest of the people together, and encamp against the city, and take it: lest I take the city, and it be called after my name.

What Joab said, in effect was, "you go in and make the final attack." Joab had brought the city to its knees and all that remained was the triumphal entry by the victor. Joab did not want to do that lest they worship him as the hero and even name the city after him. David gathered his forces and went to Rabbah where he marched triumphantly into the city. He took the crown of gold from the head of their king and had it placed on his head which Samuel anointed many years before. King David got the glory of the victory.

XXXIII. TROUBLE IN THE FAMILY

All the events we have examined from II Samuel 11:1-12:26, are between chapters 19:19 and 20:1 in First Chronicles. Chapter 20:1-3

repeats the story of the siege and capture of Rabbah. Not only is the account of David's sin and judgment omitted from Chronicles, but all the events recorded in II Samuel 13:1-21:17, also do not appear there. Even though the author of Chronicles, under the inspiration of the Holy Spirit, saw fit to pass over these occurrences as being irrelevant to his theme, they are important to our general history and survey. We will cover them as they are recorded in II Samuel.

The Rape of Tamar

In II Samuel 13, we are introduced to some of the children of David. Back in II Samuel 3:2-3, we were given a list of the six sons born to David (each by a different wife) during his reign in Hebron. In order of birth, the first four of these were: Amnon, who would have been considered heir to the throne; Chiliab (also called Daniel, see   I Chron. 3:1), of who little is known; Absalom, and Adonijah, who both aspired to the throne of their father. Keep in mind that these young men were princes, accustomed to being catered to, having whatever they wanted, and probably proud and haughty. Later, in First Kings 1:6, in connection with Adonijah, we read that he had never been subject to parental rebuke or discipline. *"His father had not displeased him at any time in saying, why hast thou done so?"* Probably, this was David's normal pattern of parenting. In these sons, David reaped the fruit of his sin. Even though forgiven of *his* sin, he still reaped the fulfillment of God's judgment on his family, as pronounced through Nathan.

Amnon was a wicked man and, as natural heir to the throne, was probably insufferably high-handed. He was desperately enamored of his beautiful half-sister, Tamar, who was full sister to Absalom. With the connivance of his cousin Jonadab, he made plans to take her. As part of the plan, he feigned illness and loss of appetite. When his father visited him, he suggested that he could eat if *"Tamar my sister"* prepared and served his food. So it was arranged. As soon as Amnon had Tamar alone, he forced her to submit to him. Tragically, however, as soon as he had vented his lust, it turned to   hatred against her and he commanded his personal servants to throw her out and lock the door behind her. Shamed and ruined, this young Israelite princess went through all the formal motions of mourning. She put ashes on her head, rent the beautiful garment that proclaimed her a virgin of the royal family and with her hand on her head, went stumbling and crying aloud through the streets. When Absalom found her and learned what had happened, he was furious. He urged her to keep quiet and let him take care of her. *"So, Tamar remained desolate in her brother Absalom's house."* vs. 20

David's Helplessness

The story did get to David and we are told *"he was very wroth."* It is evident, however, that he made no move to punish Amnon for the crime either as father or as king. We have seen that he was unaccustomed to disciplining his children, and he was no doubt paralyzed emotionally by the memory of his own sin which Amnon could readily throw up to him. Amnon could have said: "Look what you did, Dad!" He was angry, but he was paralyzed when it came to taking action over the heinous thing that had happened in his own household. {Deuteronomy 20:29} Beginning in verse 22, the focus shifts to Absalom. Although he hated Amnon for violating his sister, he said nothing about it, either good or bad. After two years had gone by, Amnon had forgotten the matter. Absalom had not; he arranged a great sheep-shearing party and invited his father and brothers to attend. David declined, but Amnon and the rest of his brothers went along. Absalom then instructed his servants to watch for a suitable time, and kill Amnon. Thinking, perhaps, that this was a plot to seize the throne, the remaining brothers fled. Rumor sped faster, however, and by the time the news reached David, it had mushroomed into a report that all the king's sons had been slain. David promptly went into deep mourning, tearing his clothes and lying on the ground. After sowing the wind, he was beginning to reap the whirlwind. Lust, incest, rape, and murder have occurred among the members of his family.

We learned in verse 5 that Jonadab was the one who devised the scheme by which Amnon could rape his sister. In verse 32, he appears again as the two-faced individual he was. He informed the king that the rumors were false, *"for Amnon only is dead: for by the appointment of Absalom this hath been determined from the day that he forced his sister Tamar."* Having committed murder, Absalom fled to his mother's people at Geshur. But, oh, how David loved Absalom! Verse 27 says, *"David mourned for his son every day."*

The heart of the king longed to go out to Absalom, and although he was not able to, he was comforted concerning Amnon because he was dead. I believe this means that David's conscience was eased somewhat because, as long as Amnon was alive, he was overshadowed by his inability to punish him for the crime. He felt paralyzed in handling him. He knew he should be punished but did not want to go back and reopen old personal wounds. I am sure that not a day went by without David thinking about the incident between Amnon and Tamar, and berated himself for not having acted promptly at the time. But now, Amnon is dead and the matter was out of his hands and forgotten. Absalom remained in exile for three years. Then, through a series of events masterminded by Joab, and recorded in chapter 14, he was permitted to return to Jerusalem. However, two years passed before he was allowed to see his father.

An interesting sidelight about Absalom is the fact that physically he was a perfect physical specimen. In 14:25 we read that *"in all Israel there was none to be so much praised as Absalom for his beauty: from the sole of his foot even to the crown of his head there was no blemish in him."* Once a year, when he cut his hair, it was found to weigh two hundred shekels by the king's weight. The spearhead of Goliath weighed six hundred shekels which was fifteen pounds. The king's shekel may have been slightly different, but Absalom cut approximately five pounds of hair every year.

Eventually, Absalom was again allowed into his father's presence. Verse 33 says, *"he came to the king, and bowed himself on his face to the ground before the king: and the king kissed Absalom."* Unfortunately, no sooner was he back in royal favor, than he began to have aspirations toward the throne. Keep in mind, the line of normal dynastic succession. Amnon, the firstborn, was dead. We know nothing of Chiliab, who possibly did not survive to adulthood. Absalom, the third born, was next in line. David was now past middle age and Absalom had convinced himself that he could do a better job of ruling the nation. With selfish motivation, and with a superhuman effort outside the will of God, he began plotting to take the throne by force from his father, King David.

XXXIV. TREASON

Absalom was an ungodly man. Had he succeeded in establishing himself as king, it would have been a disaster for Israel. He viewed the throne as a base of power and for personal glory. He was devoid of any degree of loyalty to David, either as his father or as his king. He planned his coup carefully and only the hand of God kept him from succeeding in it. For aspiring politicians, two activities were popular: First, the person could hire professional runners to run ahead of his chariot. As they ran, they would loudly proclaim his name and his exploits. Hearing them, people would look from their doorways and windows and would soon associate his name with his face. This recognition was very helpful when it came time to muster popular support. Absalom hired fifty runners (11 Sam. 15:1). They would call out such phrases as *"Absalom is great; here comes Prince Absalom."* All heads would turn toward the handsome man with the full head of hair, riding behind the charioteer. There was probably a no more dashing figure in all of Israel. As a charismatic, popular leader of men, he was unsurpassed.

Second, a would-be leader made himself known by always being in the city gate. We have already learned that the gate was the center of political and social activity in the city. It was Lot who *"sat in the gate of Sodom"* in a place of political leadership. It was at the gate of Bethlehem that Boaz negotiated the transaction in which he gained Ruth for his wife. Likewise, it was at the gate that Absalom encountered all of those people who went in and out seeking justice from the king. Verse 2 says, *"Absalom rose up early, and stood beside the way of the gate."* Not only did Absalom promote himself during these encounters, he also poisoned their minds against King David and his advisers. He pretended to show personal interest in each person, inquiring as to where he was from and listening to his complaint. Then, he would totally agree with that person's view of his problem (vss. 3-4): *And Absalom said unto him, See, thy matters are good and right; but there is no man deputed of the king to hear thee. And Absalom said moreover, Oh that I were made judge in the land, that every man who hath any suit or cause might come unto me, and I would do him justice!*

Recognizing him as the prince, the people would attempt to prostrate themselves before him according to the custom of the day. Absalom would stop each one, kissing him as one did an equal. Verse 6 says *"And on this manner did Absalom to all Israel that came to the king for judgment."* Absalom campaigned in this way about four years. As he stood in the gate and filtered out those who were going to see the king, David eventually became insulated from the problems of the people. Verse 6 concludes, *"Absalom stole the hearts of the people."*

Finally, when Absalom knew that the time was right for action, he sought permission from King David to go on a religious pilgrimage to Hebron. Meanwhile, he had his followers so well organized that at the proper moment it could be proclaimed through the entire land, *"Absalom reigneth in Hebron."* It was not a coincidence that Absalom went to Hebron to begin his open revolt. It was the chief city of his tribe of Judah and the place where David was first inaugurated king. By going back to David's early roots, he must have expected to recruit the same support that his father had in the earlier years. To camouflage his intent, he took two hundred men from Jerusalem with him as invited guests. They were not his supporters but served to cloud his purpose. Verse 11 says, *"They went in their simplicity, and they knew not anything."* Even Ahithophel, David's closest private counselor, followed him. Verse 12: *"the conspiracy was strong; for the people increased continually with Absalom."*

Back in Jerusalem, David finally received the message: *"The hearts of the men of Israel are after Absalom."* His immediate response was that retreat would be necessary. In verse 14 he said: *Arise, and let us flee; for we shall not else escape from Absalom: make speed to depart, lest he overtake us suddenly, and bring evil upon us, and smite the city with the edge of the sword.* David was surrounded by personal bodyguards and officials who were completely loyal. They assured him, *"Behold, thy servants are ready to do whatsoever my Lord the king shall appoint."* So he and his entourage and family left, leaving behind only ten concubines.

Shortly after David had left the city, someone told him that Ahithophel his counselor was now among the conspirators with Absalom. His response was, "O *Lord, I pray thee, turn the counsel of Ahithophel into foolishness."* Shortly afterward, he was joined by Hushai, who had rent his clothes and poured dirt on his head in mourning over the King's retreat. David ordered him to return and join Absalom as a counterspy, then report their military plans back to him. He would report to David through the two loyal priests, Abiathar and Zadok: *"Behold, they have there with them their two sons, and by them ye shall send unto me everything that ye can hear"* (vs. 36).

Hushai the Double Agent

In chapter 16:15, the narrative of Absalom's invasion continues. We read that Absalom and all his followers entered Jerusalem with Ahithophel, David's former friend and counselor. Immediately Hushai, the double agent, approached him and said, *"God save the king."* Absalom was suspicious and asked, *"Is this thy kindness to thy friend? Why wentest thou not with thy friend?"* Hushai was cunning enough to be convincing. He replied (vss. 18-19):

Nay; but whom the Lord, and this people, and all the men of Israel, choose, his will I be, and with him will I abide. And again, whom should I serve? Should I not serve in the presence of his son? As I have served in thy father's presence, so will I be in thy presence.

Absalom then turned to Ahithophel and asked advice as to his next step in the *coup*. His reply was, *"Go in unto thy father's concubines, which he hath left to keep the house"* (vs. 21). This, as we have seen before, was an announcement that one claimed the position of a defeated king. *"So they spread Absalom a tent upon the top of the house; and Absalom went in unto his father's concubines in the sight of all Israel"* (vs. 22). This was his formal claim to his father's throne and it was so understood by all the people of Jerusalem. The *coup* was complete. There could be no turning back.

The advice that Ahithophel gave in II Samuel 17:1-3 was good advice for Absalom's purposes. He counseled pursuing David with an army of twelve thousand men, while the King and his supporters were exhausted after their sudden retreat. Ahithophel also promised that he would be the man to strike down the king and lead his supporters back to Jerusalem. No wonder he has been called a type of Judas! The advice *"pleased Absalom well"* (vs. 4). However, Absalom wanted a second opinion. He called Hushai, and outlined Ahithophel's strategy and asked for comments. Hushai recognized that this was good advice from Absalom's viewpoint, but very bad for David. So, as a double agent, he devised a counter-plan. But first Hushai explained why *he* believed Ahithophel's strategy would not work (vss. 8-10):

Thou knowest thy father and his men, that they be mighty men, and they be chafed in their minds, as a bear robbed of her whelps in the field: and thy father is a man of war, and will not lodge with the people. Behold, he is hid now in some pit, or in some other place: and it will come to pass, when some of them be overthrown at the first, that whosoever heareth it will say, there is a slaughter among the people that follow Absalom. And he also that is valiant, whose heart is as the heart of a lion, shall utterly melt: For all Israel knoweth that thy father is a mighty man, and they which be with him are valiant men.

Hushai presented his strategy (vss. 11-13). He said Absalom should first muster an army, *"as the sand that is by the sea for multitude"* and that Absalom personally lead it. Then they could fall upon David and his forces *"as the dew falleth on the ground"* and annihilate them all. If perchance he had taken refuge in a city, they would tear it down *"until there be not one small stone found there."* Absolom's decision is in verse 14:

Absalom and all the men of Israel said, the counsel of Hushai the Archite is better than the counsel of Ahithophel. For the Lord had appointed to defeat the good counsel of Ahithophel, to the intent that the Lord might bring evil upon Absalom.

In obedience to David's earlier instructions, we read in verse 15 that Hushai sent a complete account of the two plans to the king, passing the message through a maidservant to the two sons of the priests who had remained just outside the city to prevent being seen going in or out. They were seen, however, by a lad who promptly reported to Absalom. (vs. 18) So, they hid in the well of a friendly householder, whose wife spread grain over the opening, and sent Absalom's messengers looking for them in the opposite direction.

When the young men reached David, they passed the word from Hushai, *"Arise, and pass quickly over the water: for thus hath Ahithophel counselled against you."* Immediately that same night, David and all who were with him crossed over the Jordan into the wilderness. When Ahithophel saw that Absalom was not going to follow his advice, he knew the tragedy that would come to the side he had chosen. He saddled his donkey, hurried home, evidently to another city, set his house in order, and strangled himself. He knew he had been a traitor to David. Now he saw that God's hand was against him as well as Absalom. Suicide was his only solution.

Absalom named Amasa, a cousin of Joab, his Commander-in-Chief. As they set out in pursuit, David went to Mahanaim. At this point David's previous political savvy began to pay off. You recall that back in II Samuel 12:29-31, following the attack on Rabbah and the sons of Ammon, David did not slaughter them as he usually did. He put them to work. Now, as he fled East across the Jordan, he was met by Shobi the son of Nahash of Rabbah; Machir, son of Ammiel of Lodebar; and Barzillai, a Gileadite. The men brought need provisions that included beds, utensils, and a generous supply of food. They evidently remembered how David had spared the lives of their relatives. You will also note from II Samuel 16:1-3, that Ziba the servant of Mephibosheth had also brought supplies.

As news of Absalom's movements reached him, David saw that the time for retreat was over and it was necessary to stand and fight. He took a census of his men (who numbered in the thousands) and divided them into three companies with a third under Joab, a third under Abishai, Joab's brother, and a third under Ittai the Gittite. The old thrill of battle must have been coursing through David's veins, for he announced, "I *will surely go forth with you myself also.*" However, his people dissuaded him, saying (18:3):

Thou shalt not go forth: for if we flee away, they will not care for us: neither if half of us die, will they care for us: but now thou art worth ten thousand of us: therefore now it is better that thou succour us out of the city.

David agreed to stay behind at Mahanaim and wait by the gate for news of the battle. But, as his army passed out before him, all the people heard him command his generals, *"Deal gently for my sake with the young man, even with Absalom."*

XXXV. RESTORATION AND CONSOLIDATION

Absalom, following the advice of double agent Hushai rather than the plan of Ahithophel, set out with a large army to defeat his father. It was to be his final and fatal mistake. We read in II Samuel 18:6, that the battle was begun in the forest of Ephraim. There, the army of Israel under the leadership of Absalom was defeated as they fought against the army of their exiled king. David's army prevailed, and the slaughter was great that day, 20,000 men, as the battle was spread over the entire countryside.

As Absalom was riding on his mule, he passed under a thick oak with great tangled branches. As his head and hair became caught in the limbs of the tree, his mule kept going and left him dangling, swinging helplessly between the tree and the ground below. A soldier saw him hanging there and quickly ran and told Joab. *"Why didst thou not smite him?"* Joab demanded. *"I would have given thee ten shekels of silver, and a girdle."* The man replied, *"Though I should receive a thousand shekels of silver, yet would I not put forth mine hand against the king's son,"* (vs. 12). He reminded Joab that everyone had heard David order his commanders to *"deal gently with Absalom."* The young man probably also knew what David had done on two previous occasions, to the Amalekite who claimed to have killed King Saul, and to the two who had slain Saul's son Ish-bosheth on his bed. Even though *he* was afraid to kill Absalom, Joab had a different mentality. Wasting no further time in discussion, he took three darts (pears) and thrust them into the heart of Absalom as he dangled by his hair from the oak tree. Joab blew the trumpet announcing victory and proclaimed that the leader of the revolt had been slain. They cast Absalom into a pit and put a heap of stones over him. All of Absolom's army fled in disgrace and defeat.

David's Grief

Following the victory, a footrace ensued between Cushi, and Ahimaaz, the son of Zadok, to take the news back to King David who was waiting by the gate of Mahanaim. Ahimaaz reached the king first, but refrained from telling him that Absalom was dead, even though David specifically asked about him. When Cushi arrived with his report, he was asked the same question. *"Is the young man Absalom safe?"* He replied, *"the enemies of my lord the king, and all that rise against thee to do thee hurt, be as that young man is"* (vs. 32). His meaning was obvious. Verse 33 says, *And the king was much moved, and went up to the chamber over the gate, and wept: and as he went, thus he said, O my son Absalom, my son, my son Absalom! Would God I had died for thee, O Absalom, my son, my son!*

David's grief was totally out of proportion considering the character and revolt of Absalom, and far beyond what he had exhibited for Amnon. By this time in his life, so much tragedy had befallen him and members of his family, that he became psychologically devastated. Do you remember how he reacted when the son born of Bathsheba died? In those days, he was a man in control of himself. Now, this new tragedy has sapped that strength of character which had made him the leader he had been. He was deteriorating rapidly, physically *and* psychologically.

While he lamented, Joab was informed (19:1) how the king was weeping and mourning. Joab could not understand such depth of grief over the death of one who would have taken David's life if given the chance. The victory that David's army had enjoyed that day turned to mourning because of David's improper reaction to the death of the man who led the armies that were attempting to destroy him. As a result, the people sneaked away from the victory celebration. They crept away, verse 3: "*as people being ashamed steal away when they flee in battle.*" But David covered his face and cried loudly, "*O my son Absalom, O Absalom, my son, my son!*"
Joab delivered a stinging rebuke (vss. 5-6):

Thou hast shamed this day the faces of all thy servants, which this day have saved thy life, and the lives of thy sons and of thy daughters, and the lives of thy wives, and the lives of thy concubines, In that thou lovest thine enemies, and hatest thy friends. For thou hast declared this day, that thou regardest neither princes nor servants: for this day I perceive, that if Absalom had lived, and all we had died this day, then it had pleased thee well. Now therefore arise, go forth, and speak comfortably unto thy servants: for I swear by the Lord, if thou go not forth, there will not tarry one with thee this night: and that will be worse unto thee than all the evil that befell thee from thy youth until now.

Hearing Joab's threat, David pulled himself together and went to sit in the gate. Word of David's recovery traveled fast and all his people Joined with him in the gate and their spirits were renewed.

The Return to Jerusalem

It took time for David to regain his throne in Jerusalem. First, the tribes of Israel who had anointed Absalom sought peace and the opportunity to bring him back to his throne. Then, he offered terms of peace to his own tribe of Judah. Part of his arrangement involved the selection of Amasa, Absalom's General, to replace Joab as his Commander-in-Chief. Joab's act of slaying Absalom and his rebuke of David over Absalom were probably behind this move, but Joab was not going to take it without response and resistance.

Finally, David began the journey back across the Jordan to resume his rightful position as monarch. The activities which went on, and the obeisance of one individual (and group) after another, who had to make their peace with him as he continued his triumphal progress back to Jerusalem, are recorded in II Samuel 19:9-43.

One of the first official acts he performed when he got back to his palace was to take the ten concubines, whom he had left to keep the house, and put them under guard. These were the ones whom Absalom had raped in view of all the people in the city. David continued to provide them with sustenance, but no longer maintained a personal relationship with them. They were shut up until the day of their deaths and lived as widows.

The Revolt of Sheba

David's problems were not over. Even as he was on his way back to Jerusalem, the men of Israel and the men of Judah were arguing fiercely over which group had more right to the honor of bringing back the king (II Sam. 19:41-43). Taking advantage of this, a worthless man named Sheba attempted to lead another coup and take the crown once more from David. Although the tribe of Judah remained loyal to the king, many from Israel followed Sheba. David knew he had to act quickly. Calling in his new General, Amasa, he ordered him to muster the fighting men of Judah and be ready to go to battle within three days.

Amasa left for battle *"but he tarried longer than the set time which he had appointed him"* (II Sam. 20:5). This verse says a great deal about Amasa. He was *still* loyal to the previous opposition. He had led these men in support of Absalom. The political move David had made in giving Joab's position to Amasa was bad both tactically and strategically. It was intended to re-entrench to Judah, but it put David in serious difficulty. He needed a General who could act quickly and decisively, and Amasa was failing.

Joab, on the other hand, was a man of action. He would have had the armies of Judah ready to march within *two* days. But David did not give the job to Joab while Amasa delayed. Instead, he ordered Abishai, Joab's brother, to pursue Sheba. David realized the danger, saying, "*Now shall Sheba the son of Bichri do us more harm than did Absalom*" (vs.6). It was essential that Sheba be captured and returned for trial or else killed before he found a hiding place from which he could rally the Absolom's old supporters. At the same time, however, Joab and his hand-picked mighty men had also set out in pursuit of Sheba (vs. 8).

As Joab and his men were pursuing Sheba, they met Amasa who was finally leading his recruits for King David. This was a further indication of how much Amasa had delayed in gathering an army. Joab was in full military attire, wearing a belt with a sword in its sheath. As he went to meet Amasa, with feigned words of brotherhood (they were cousins), his sword fell out of its sheath. Amasa assumed he was disarmed and did not notice the short sword in his left hand. {the *sinister* hand} He was not alert when Joab took hold of his beard to kiss him as the short sword found its mark in his stomach. Verse 12 says, "*Amasa wallowed in blood in the midst of the highway.*"

Joab and Abishai continued to pursue Sheba, but Joab had again assumed leadership. Arriving at the city where Sheba had taken refuge, they built up a mound against it; with dirt piled at an angle to make a ramp to the top of the wall. As they were laying siege to the city, they hit the doors and walls with battering rams in order to tear them down. Inside the city, a wise woman asked to speak with Joab. Her plea, verses 18-19, was an eloquent one. She began by telling Joab that her city, Abel, was noted for its wise people.

They were wont to speak in old time, saying, they shall surely ask counsel at Abel, and so they ended the matter. I am one of them that are peaceable and faithful in Israel. Thou seekest to destroy a city and a mother in Israel. Why wilt thou swallow up the inheritance of the Lord?

Joab assured her that he had no desire to destroy the city, but he had to have Sheba because he was traitor to the king. The woman then quickly persuaded the people to cut off Sheba's head and throw it over the wall to Joab. As soon as he had received it, he blew the trumpet and the army returned to David in triumph. Verse 23 records that Joab was once again head of the army. He had regained and secured his position as the military leader. David, having survived two rebellions, was again safely reigning over Israel from his throne.

David's Last Battle

Chapter 21 contains the record of the famine which occurred as a result of Saul's earlier attempt to exterminate the Gibeonites and the retaliation that was demanded. As a consequence of this, David retrieved the bones of Saul and Jonathan from the hands of the men of Jabesh-gilead, who had so heroically rescued them from the Philistines. Together with the victims of the Gibeonite revenge, he buried them in the tomb of Kish, Saul's father.

Then, once again, David was forced to fight against the Philistines. At this time it became apparent that he was growing old because he became weary during the heat of the battle. One of the Philistine giants was close to killing him, and he had to be rescued by Abishai. This prompted his men to say, *"Thou shalt go no more out with us to battle, that thou quench not the light of Israel."*

David's Song of Thanksgiving

Chapter 22 records David's magnificent song of praise to the Lord for His lifetime of goodness. Verses 2-51 of this chapter are paralleled in Psalm 18:2-50. Chapter 23, which is labeled his last words and which continue his praise, confirm for us that he was the inspired writer of many of the Psalms. Look at the first four verses.

Now these be the last words of David. David the son of Jesse said, and the man who was raised up on high, the anointed of the God of Jacob, and the sweet psalmist of Israel, said, The Spirit of the Lord spake by me, and his word was in my tongue. The God of Israel said the Rock of Israel spoke to me; He that ruleth over men must be just, ruling in the fear of God. And he shall be as the light of the morning, when the sun riseth, even a morning without clouds; as the tender grass springing out of the earth by clear shining after rain.

Not only do these words confirm the fact that God spoke through David, they also give us God's criteria for successful leadership. The balance of chapter 23, contains a recount of some of the historic activities of the valiant men under David. It is a salute to these ancient heroes as their names and deeds are recorded for posterity.

XXXVI. PREPARATION FOR THE TEMPLE

The information in II Samuel 24 is not dated but occurred rather late in David's life. It is paralleled in I Chronicles 21, and much of its significance is related to the building of the future temple which was in the mind and heart of David. We read in II Samuel 24:1 that *"the anger of the Lord was kindled against Israel, and he moved David against them to say, go, number Israel and Judah."* First Chronicles 21:1 gives further insight into this incident when it indicates that it was Satan who prompted David to number the people of Israel and Judah. Rather than a conflict in Scripture, this event was a case of God permitting Satan to test David. David was getting old and evidently losing some of the confidence which he had in God as the leader of the armies of Israel. As a result, he began to think his strength came from the numbers in his reserve and standing armies rather than from God.

David's order to number the men displeased God, and surprisingly, it displeased Joab as well. In this instance, Joab seems to have shown more spiritual insight into the purposes of God than David. He made a vigorous attempt to persuade the king to countermand his order, even becoming eloquent in his protest, as recorded in verse 3:

And Joab said unto the king, Now the Lord thy God add unto the people, how many soever they be, an hundredfold, and that the eyes of my lord the king may see it: but why doth my lord the king delight in this thing?

Joab urged, do not worry about numbers or quantity. The Lord will give you as many people as you need when you need them. He might have added a reminder of the Lord's promise that the people would be as the stars of heaven and the sand on the seashore. But David was king and his supreme authority prevailed over Joab's resistance. The census-taking project was a long task and Verse 8 says it took nine months and twenty days. Joab and his team made a wide circuit throughout the land making sure to obey the king's order. Then they came back and gave the count to David.

David's Repentance

It appears that as soon as Joab placed the figures before him, David knew that he had done wrong. *"I have sinned greatly in that I have done,"* he cried out to the Lord (vs. 10). *"Take away the iniquity of thy servant, for I have done very foolishly."* The next morning the Lord's response came to him through Gad, the prophet: *"I offer thee three things; choose thee one of them, that I may do it unto thee."* This is evidence that God's forgiveness does not preclude the need for restitution, or the need for a public display of His displeasure. All the people in the land witnessed the fact that David had begun to put his confidence in numbers rather than in God. The faith of every inhabitant was affected by David's lack of faith. God had been offended and His position in Israel had been diminished. **God** said to David, you have three alternatives from which to choose. Either God will send you seven years of famine. Or, if you prefer you will flee for three months before your enemies while they pursue you. Or, God can send three days of plague into the land. Which do you choose? Notice that none of these penalties would fall on David alone. As King over God's people, his sin caused them all to suffer.

The Plague

David's choice demonstrated that he was a man of godly understanding: *"let us fall now into the hand of the Lord for his mercies are great, and let me not fall into the hand of man"* (vs. 14). So God sent a plague over the land, during which time 70,000 men died from the far north to the far south. What a terrible thing! David's lack of faith and his sin resulted in the death of 70,000 people. It was as if God said, David, you have put your faith in numbers and quantity. I will show you how with the stroke of My hand, I can remove numbers from you. Your victories do not depend on numbers. I can give them or I can take them away. David was permitted to see the Angel of the Lord as He prepared to smite Jerusalem with the plague, standing with drawn sword over the threshing floor of Araunah the Jebusite (Ornan in II Chronicles 21). Again he cried out in repentance (vs. 17);

And David spake unto the Lord when he saw the angel that smote the people, and said, Lo, I have sinned, and I have done wickedly; but these sheep, what have they done? Let thine hand, I pray thee, be against me, and against my father's house.

But David's house could not be cut off because of the Davidic Covenant. So the people must be smitten instead. But David's prayer was heard. Again, Gad came to him with the word of the Lord, saying, *"Go up, rear an altar unto the Lord in the threshing floor of Araunah the Jebusite."* Quickly David obeyed the Lord's command and went up to the threshing floor. He bought his threshing floor, his oxen for sacrifice, and his tools for the firewood. The last verse of 11 Samuel says (24:25):

And David built there an altar unto the Lord, and offered burnt

*offerings and peace offerings. So the Lord was entreated for the
land, and the plaque was stayed from Israel.*

For the full significance of this, go to I Chronicles 22:1: *"Then David said, This is the
house of the Lord God, and this is the altar of the burnt offering for Israel."* God had made
known His choice of the site where His temple and His altar were to be placed. This is now
the *Dome of the Rock*, and the site of the Muslim holy place, the *El-Aqsa* mosque. In 1967
General Moshe Dyan gave it to the Arabs. It has been a Muslim owned site since that time.

It is evident that the events of II Samuel covered less than forty years, the length of
David's reign. He ascended the throne at its beginning, in 1010 B.C. and he was still alive
when the book ended. The gap between the end of 11 Samuel and the beginning of I Kings
is covered in I Chronicles 22-29. Here we have recorded the preparations David made for
the temple which Solomon was to build. As soon as God had showed him where the
temple was to be built, he began to amass the necessary building materials and to instruct
Solomon in the details of the work. {22:7, 8}

*And David said to Solomon, My son, as for me, it was in my mind to build an house unto
the name of the Lord my God: But the word of the Lord came to me saying, Thou hast shed
blood abundantly, and hast made great wars: thou shalt not build an house unto my name,
because thou hast shed much blood upon the earth in my sight.*

It is here that we learn why it was that back in II Samuel 7, when David had desired to
build a house for God, the Lord had said, *"No, you will not build Me a house. "* God
explained that the honor of building the temple would go to David's son (22:9, 10):

*Who shall be a man of rest, and I will give him rest from all his enemies round about; for
his name shall be Solomon, and I will give peace and quietness unto Israel in his days. He
shall build an house for my name; and he shall be my son, and I will be his father, and I
will establish the throne of his kingdom over Israel for ever.*

This is a further confirmation of the Davidic Covenant announced in II Samuel 7. It
indicates that Solomon was the selected son to carry on the lineage of David which would
continue through the time of the Messiah. Solomon would become the lamp unto David.
And Solomon, not a man of blood, would be the one who would build the temple of God in
Jerusalem. First Kings credits Solomon with building the temple of God, but we read in I
Chronicles, that David made great preparations for its construction. In 22:14, he said,

I have prepared for the house of the Lord an hundred thousand talents of gold, and a thousand talents of silver, and of brass and iron without weight, for it is in abundance: timber also and stone have I prepared.

In addition to that, he had selected workmen: stonecutters, masons, carpenters, and all manner of skillful people. He commanded Solomon to arise and build. He also commanded all the leaders of Israel to help his son Solomon in this great work.

Chapter 28 records how David assembled all the officials of Israel; the princes of the various tribes, and stood to his feet to confirm the building program that God had given to him for his son Solomon. Beginning in Verse 11, he turned over to Solomon all the plans for the building which were precise in every detail. First Chronicles 28:19 is an amazing verse, indicating that David had received the temple plan directly from God,

"The Lord made me understand in writing by his hand upon me, even all the works of this pattern. According to all that I shew thee, after the pattern of the tabernacle, and the pattern of all the instruments thereof, even so shall ye make it. And look that thou make them after their pattern, which was showed thee in the mount."

God did not depend on human instrumentality. He gave in writing the pattern by which He wanted those items built.

XXXVII. THE KINGDOM OF SOLOMON

-1 KINGS-

First Kings opens with the kingdom in transition. David had become advanced in age and was bedridden. Although Solomon had been chosen as his successor, as we realize from I Chronicles 22-29, he had not been officially anointed. As a result, for a brief period, the power structure in the kingdom was loose and weakened due to King David's incapacity and the uncertainty regarding his successor.

Adonijah Seeks the Throne

Adonijah stepped into this vacuum. I Kings 1:5 records that he *"exalted himself, saying, I will be king."* As David's oldest surviving son, he was undoubtedly laying claim to his natural right. Then, to gain attention, he did what Absalom had done, "he prepared him chariots and horsemen, and fifty men to run before him." With some surprise we read (vs. 7), that he was able to recruit Joab and Abiathar the priest, David's old friend from Nob, who was also one of the spies who worked with Zadok at the time of Absalom's rebellion. However, Zadok the priest, Nathan the prophet, and some other of David's oldest supporters and his band of mighty men, remained loyal to the king.

Next, Adonijah prepared a great feast to which he invited all of his supporters, his brothers, and the leading men of Judah. The men loyal to David were not invited and obviously neither was Solomon.

While this political rally was going on, Nathan asked, *"Hast thou not heard that Adonijah doth reign, and David our lord knoweth it not?"* (vs. 11) Old and in bed, David no longer had a grasp on events in the kingdom. Nathan suggested that Bathsheba inform the king what was happening, and remind him of his promise that her son Solomon would be his successor. Following her announcement, Nathan would go in and confirm her story. Nathan and Bathsheba had a scenario prepared to act out before the king. Bathsheba went into David's bedchamber and told him all that Adonijah was doing. She pointed out that all the king's sons, except Solomon, had been invited, and that even Joab and Abiathar were among them. She reminded him of his promise concerning Solomon, and then pointed (vss. 20-21).

And thou, my lord, 0 king, the eyes of all Israel are upon thee, that thou shouldest tell them who shall sit on the throne of my lord the king after him. Otherwise it shall come to pass, when my lord the king shall sleep with his fathers, that I and my son Solomon shall be counted offenders.

While she was speaking, Nathan entered and confirmed her report, diplomatically prefacing his words with a question: "*Hast thou said, Adonijah shall reign after me, and he shall sit upon my throne?*" (vs 24). Then he described Adonijah's activities just as Bathsheba had done, including the fact that he, Zadok, and Solomon, had not been invited. He concluded, "*Is this thing done by my lord the king, and thou hast not shewed it unto thy servant, who should sit on the throne of my lord the king after him?*" (vs. 27) In verse 28 we see a glimpse of the David of old. The news had aroused him to decisive action. Then, calling Bathsheba back into his presence, he renewed the vow he had made to her (vs. 30): *Even as I sware unto thee by the Lord God of Israel, saying, Assuredly Solomon thy son shall reign after me, and he shall sit upon my throne in my stead, even so will I certainly do this day.*

King David was once again in control of his kingdom. He ordered Nathan and Zadok to get Solomon and have him ride on the king's own mule to Gihon where he would be anointed as king. They would then blow the trumpet and shout, "God save King Solomon." They would then return to Jerusalem and place Solomon on the throne. All the men around David responded with a hearty "Amen." The old David was back in action again. {Notice that King David had a mule. He had not multiplied horses as his son would. I Kings 4:26}

Solomon Anointed

Beginning in verse 38, Nathan and Zadok followed the king's instructions. Solomon was anointed and the populace responded with a spontaneous and noisy celebration that included both shouting and musical instruments. The noise was heard all the way to Enrogel where Adonijah's inauguration party was going on. Joab was the first to be concerned at the sound. Abiathar's son Jonathan soon arrived with the complete story (vss. 43-46):

Verily our lord king David hath made Solomon king And. hath sent him with Zadok the priest, and Nathan the prophet and they have caused him to tide upon the king's mule; and have anointed him king in Gihon; and they are come up from thence rejoicing, so that the city rang again. This is the noise that ye have heard. And also Solomon sitteth on the throne of the kingdom.

He also described the approval of the king's servants who had said, *"God make the name of Solomon better than thy name, and make his throne greater than thy throne."*

That was the end of Adonijah's victory party. His guests left quickly and in fear, knowing they had been accessories to the crime of treason. Adonijah was afraid also, as well he might be, and ran to clutch the horns of the altar for protection. When Solomon heard that, he sent a message of forgiveness. *"If he will shew himself a worthy man, there shall not a hair of him fall to the earth: but if wickedness shall be found in him, he shall die"* (vs. 52). Adonijah quickly went and prostrated himself before Solomon, his half-brother, who said briefly: *"Go to thine house."*

I Kings Chapter 2 we read King David's final instructions to Solomon, his successor. He was asking Solomon to take care of some of the *"dirty laundry"* he was leaving behind. He reminded Solomon of Joab's misdeeds and instructed him that he *"let not his hoarhead go down to the grave in peace.* He recalled the insults of Shimei who threw dirt and rocks at him when he fled from Absalom. David had sworn personally not to harm him but said that Solomon must find a way to bring *"his hoarhead down to the grave with blood."* David also remembered Barzillai, to whom he owed gratitude for succor and great kindness. Most of all, he reminded Solomon that the prosperity and success of his future on the throne depended on his walking in the ways of the Lord God, *"to keep his statutes, and his commandments, and his judgments, and his testimonies, as it is written in the law of Moses"* (vs. 3). When all these instructions had been given *"David slept with his fathers"*

Verse 11 is a summary of David's forty year reign. He reigned seven years in Hebron (1010 B.C. to 1003 B.C.) and thirty-three years in Jerusalem, as king over Israel and Judah (1003 to 970 B.C.). In the year 970 B.C. "sat Solomon upon the throne of David his father and his kingdom was established greatly." (vs. 12)

Adonijah

Soon after his father's death, Adonijah did a very foolish thing. He asked Bathsheba to intercede with King Solomon to give him the Shunammite girl who had served King David in his old age. We have previously seen the significance attached to the act of taking a woman from a previous king's harem. Solomon saw this request as an attempt by Adonijah to overthrow him and gain the throne. It gave Solomon sufficient reason to have Adonijah slain. It was a touchy situation, however, because Adonijah was the natural heir to the throne and he had a substantial following. Solomon could not trust just anyone to carry out the order. He selected Benaiah, the head of David's old personal bodyguard and probably the most trusted military man in the kingdom with the responsibility of executing Adonijah. Verse 25 says, "He *fell upon him that he died."*

In verse 27, the king dealt with Abiathar, the priest who had joined the defection to Adonijah, by dismissing him from the priesthood, *"that he might fulfill the word of the Lord, which he spake concerning the house of Eli in Shiloh."* Abiathar was the last active priest who was a member of the family under the curse in I Samuel 2:31. Although he had joined the opposition to Solomon, his faithfulness to David in the past saved his life; and Solomon would not kill a priest of the Lord. He appointed Zadok to replace him.

Joab

Joab knew that he would be next and fled to the horns of the altar.
(A 2019 excavation at Tel Shiloh, the early location of the tabernacle, uncovered what appeared to be the corner of an altar.)
Solomon sent Benaiah to execute him also. When Joab refused to leave the altar, but insisted he would die there. Solomon said, *"So be it."* He recounted Joab's crimes in justification, and pronounced that his blood would not be on the head of David and his descendants. After Joab was dead, he commissioned Benaiah to the position of Commander-in-Chief, previously held by Joab.

Shimei

Next, the king sent for Shimei and made an arrangement under which he might live, but be under the watchful eyes of Solomon's servants. The arrangement stated that he was never to set foot outside Jerusalem. After three years, Shirnei broke the agreement by leaving town, and once again Solomon sent Benaiah, the assassin to carry out his sentence of execution. With that final execution, *"the kingdom was established in the hand of Solomon"* (vs.46). David's last orders had been carried out, and the final opposition to Solomon's monarchy was eliminated.

Before proceeding to chapter 3, where we begin to get further insight into the personality, life, and kingdom of Solomon, it is necessary to make a final comment regarding King David. When he died in 970 B.C., he left behind for his successor Solomon a united monarchy. The twelve tribes had finally been welded into a cohesive unit. Although occasionally, there were attempts to rend one tribe from another and to divide the twelve tribes, when David died, the twelve tribes were supportive of King Solomon. This unification was something Saul was never able to achieve. Saul was never able to weld the twelve tribes into a cohesive unit, and it took David the time of his entire monarchy to do so. We know this because even late in his reign, during the rebellion of Sheba, there was a division among the tribes.

It was a common practice in those days to make political alliances with surrounding nations by intermarriage among the royal families. This went on prior to the time of Solomon and it continued on down through history into the twentieth century among many of the European monarchies. It was a form of protection. If the monarchies of different nations were intermarried, it would be logical that there would not be military activity or conflict between them. God had specifically commanded that Israel was not to join in this practice. But Solomon, in an attempt to expand his kingdom and protect himself, not completely trusting in God to protect Israel from invasion by other nations, especially the powerful nations which surrounded him, began to marry for the purpose of political and military expediency. I Kings 11:1-2:

> *But King Solomon loved many strange women, together with the daughter of Pharaoh, women of the Moabites, Ammonites, Edomites, Zidonians, and Hittites; Of the nations concerning which the Lord said unto the children of Israel, Ye shall not go in to them, neither shall they come in unto you: for surely they will turn away your heart after their gods.*

This involvement of Solomon in political marriages began his downfall. I Kings 3:1 records his marriage to the daughter of the Pharaoh of Egypt. He brought her to the city of Jerusalem, and kept her there until he finished building the house of the Lord and his house in 946 B.C. {II Chronicles 8:1} Following David's death, the people began to drift away religiously because in verse 2 we read, *"The people sacrificed in high places."* Verse 3 adds that *"Solomon loved the Lord only he sacrificed and burnt incense in high places."* We begin to see as early as I Kings 3 that Solomon is going to be a divided man.

Solomon's Wisdom

Early in his reign, Solomon went up to Gibeon to sacrifice on the altar. {I Chronicles 21:29} God appeared to him and said, *"Ask what I shall give thee."* (3: 5) In verse 9, Solomon made his request, *"Give thy servant an understanding heart to judge thy people."* The request so pleased God that He not only granted it, but added, *"I have also given thee that which thou hast not asked, both riches, and honor; so that there shall not be any among the kings like unto thee all thy days"* (vs. 13).

God promised to make Solomon the greatest king who ever lived. There was a stipulation, however. Verse 14 reads: *"If thou wilt walk in my ways, to keep my statutes and my commandments, as thy father David did walk, then I will lengthen thy days."* Solomon was beginning to experience the *"if--but"* relationship which God had earlier given to the entire nation of Israel. The continuance of Solomon's dynasty over all of Israel would be predicated on Solomon's obedience. Remember the specifics of the Davidic Covenant, when God told David He would raise up one after him to be His son, and He would be a father to him? However, the stipulation was, *"If he commit iniquity, I will chasten him."* Solomon would become the first of David's descendents whom God had to chastise for sin. The same relationship would continue on down through the Messianic line from Solomon to Rehoboam and down through time to the last king, Zedekiah. Each descendent of David who sat on the throne would be chastised for his sins in accordance with the conditions given in the Davidic Covenant.

Solomon's God-given wisdom was immediately put to the test. He was approached by two women who both claimed to be the mother of the living infant after the other had died during the night. I Kings 3:28 says that when the Israelites heard of the judgment that Solomon handed down in the case *"they feared the king: for they saw that the wisdom of God was in him, to do judgment."*

Building the Temple

Chapters 5 through 7 record Solomon's work of building the temple. Chapter 6:1 is the pivotal verse on which we based our chronology, because it dates the beginning of the construction to Solomon's fourth year (966 B.C.). Verse 30 says it took seven years to complete the temple, so the completion date was 959 B.C. Chapter 7:1 is an interesting verse. Solomon, who had taken seven years to complete God's house, spent thirteen years to complete his own house. We again detect that Solomon was a divided man. His loyalties were divided; his attention to the monarchy was divided; his attention to spiritual things was becoming more and more divided. Chapter 9:10 tells us he spent a total of twenty years building the Lord's house and his own house. That date was 946 B.C. When these two building projects were completed, he had been reigning for twenty-four years. He was forty years on the throne.

Chapter 8 contains the details of the dedication of the temple. At that time, the Ark of the Covenant was placed in the Holy of Holies. It was 487 years old, and the items which had once been placed inside it had been lost except for the two tablets of stone which Moses had placed there. Verse 10 tells us that the *Shekinah* glory filled the house of the Lord. This was an indication that God was pleased with the work which Solomon had done in accordance with the pattern given by his father David. {Exodus 40:34, 35}

The formal prayer of dedication, which was given by Solomon, begins in verse 22. It is a beautiful example of prayer which can be followed by believers today. Read Solomon's prayer and study how you can implement his structure into your personal prayer life.

XXXVIII. A FOOLISH WISE MAN

As we look at the latter half of Solomon's reign, we stand in awe at the tragedy of lost potential. As it was with David, so it was with Solomon. He forfeited many of the blessings which God would have bestowed on him. I Kings 4:29-34 describes his wisdom and potential.

And God gave Solomon wisdom and understanding. And Solomon's wisdom excelled the wisdom of all the children of the east country, and all the wisdom of Egypt for he was wiser than all men and his fame was in all nations round about. And he spake three thousand proverbs: and his songs were a thousand and five. And he spake of trees, from the cedar tree even unto the hyssop. He spake also of beasts and of fowl and of creeping things and of fishes. And there came of all people to hear the wisdom of Solomon, from all kings of the earth, which had heard of his wisdom.

Solomon predated Aristotle by six centuries. Although Aristotle categorized flora and fauna in his time, Solomon had done it six hundred years earlier as shown by the description of his prolific writing on a myriad of subjects.

God Meets With Solomon

I Kings 9:1-2 seems to indicate a turning point in Solomon's life.

And it came to pass, when Solomon had finished the building of the house of the Lord, and the king's house, and all Solomon's desire which he was pleased to do, That the Lord appeared to Solomon the second time, as he had appeared unto him at Gibeon.

God knew that Solomon's heart was drifting toward apostasy. Over twenty-four years had passed and He found it necessary to meet with Solomon again. At this second appearance, God strengthened the restrictions of the earlier "*if-but*" requirement, saying in verses 3-5, *I have heard thy prayer and thy supplication. I have hallowed this house, if thou wilt walk before me, as David thy father walked then I will establish the throne of thy kingdom upon Israel forever.* This was the "if" clause. The "but" occurs in verses 6-9.

But if ye shall at all turn away from following me then will I cut off Israel out of the land which I have given them; and this house will I cast out of my sight. Everyone that passeth by it shall be astonished
and shall say, Why hath the Lord done thus unto this land, and to this house? And they shall answer, because they forsook the Lord their God, who brought forth their fathers out of the land of Egypt.

"This house" was the temple which Solomon had built and dedicated. God was giving him a solemn prophecy of what would happen. The earlier appearance at Gibeon had simply promised blessing if Solomon was obedient. Now, God reiterated that promise, but added a stern warning that if he did not obey, God would cut off Israel and would destroy the temple.

The first promise was predicated on obedience. No warning was necessary at that time. Had Solomon been a man of an upright heart and continuing fidelity to God, the warning of such future consequences would not have been necessary. Solomon had arrived at that place in his life because he was beginning to do all *"which he was pleased to do."* He was accumulating hundreds of wives and they were beginning to steal away his heart from fidelity to the Lord. God predicted judgment if Solomon would not obey.

God's words to Solomon constituted two separate and distinct prophecies. The first was fulfilled when Israel was cut off from the land in 722 B.C.; the second, when the temple was destroyed in 586 B.C. This chapter is not history, it is prophecy. We know that the events of this chapter took place in 946 B.C. God, the Sovereign of time and history, foretold that Israel would be cut off and the temple would be destroyed.

When we read this pronouncement by God, our minds should think back to II Samuel 7 and to the earlier promise to David regarding the seed that would be in existence forever. How can we equate the threat of Israel being cut off from the land, with the promise to David that his seed, throne, and kingdom would be established forever? It sounds paradoxical. If Solomon were to fail, how could God cut off Israel from the land and still maintain the integrity of the Davidic Covenant?

It is necessary now to move ahead sixteen years after this prophecy. When Solomon died, the kingdom was divided. His son, Rehoboam, will become king in the South over Judah and Benjamin. Jeroboam (no relation to Solomon), will become king over the ten tribes of the northern kingdom. To fulfill the threat made to Solomon when he did not obey, God divided the kingdom after his death. By dividing the kingdom and maintaining the integrity of the Davidic covenant through the Southern kingdom, God was able to cut off Israel from the land in 722 B.C. because Israel was the Northern kingdom. The Northern kingdom had no relationship to the Messianic line.

Chapter 10 provides some indications of the wealth that Solomon had accumulated in fulfillment of the earlier promise made by God when He first appeared to him at Gibeon. The Queen of Sheba had heard of his kingdom. Recent archaeological discoveries have unearthed many of her personal items in Yemen, 1,400 to the South. She made the long journey to see Solomon's wealth and hear his wisdom. After she arrived in Jerusalem, and saw the splendor, wealth, and the opulence of the kingdom of Solomon, she had to exclaim, *"The half was not told me."* (vs. 7)

Chapter 10:14 says that Solomon took in 666 talents of gold in a year. That is about 83,000 pounds. If you have a calculator handy you can look at the current price of gold, which on this day is about $1,400.00 per ounce, and see that 83,000 pounds of gold {1,328,000 ounces}was a huge fortune. Archaeologists have discovered that in the tenth century B.C., in some of the areas where Solomon had His mines, large nuggets could be found on the surface of the ground. Following the removal of all the surface gold, they had to begin to dig, but they could still find gold just beneath the surface. However, as they used up that supply, the mines had to go deeper down into the earth to maintain the amount of gold required.

Solomon's Idolatry

In chapter 11, we discover that in his later years, Solomon began to worship the idols which his wives had brought in from their respective lands. Verse 3 says he had seven hundred wives. These were his princesses. In addition to these, he had three hundred concubines. These foreign women turned his heart away from the Lord. *"His wives turned away his heart after other gods: and his heart was not perfect with the Lord his God, as was the heart of David his father"* (vs. 4). This verse summarizes the lives of David and Solomon. David's heart was with God; Solomon's heart was partly with God and partly with the other gods. As David left behind a united monarchy because he was a united man, Solomon left behind a divided monarchy because he was a divided man. In his later years, he succumbed to the requests of his wives to go and worship with them. They were involved in detestable Baal practices and abominable activities in the worship of Moloch. It is difficult to imagine that Solomon would involve himself in these abominations.

We also see in this verse that David was a measuring rod for all the kings who would follow. David was a man after God's own heart. He was a theocentric man. From his time onward, kings would be measured against David in regard to their performance on the throne, spiritually and politically.

Verse 7 indicates that Solomon built *"An high place for Chemosh, the abomination of Moab, in the hill that is before Jerusalem, and for Molech, the abomination of the children of Ammon."* These detestable idols on the hill east of Jerusalem were used for human sacrifices. Others suffer when God's man sins, and Solomon is not excluded from the tragedy of this phenomenon. The high places that he built in the latter years of his reign to please his wives and to worship himself would corrupt the spirituality of the people of Israel for the next three hundred years. Solomon did not sin alone. He was responsible for spiritual apostasy during the next three centuries.

How could it be that the man who wrote so many proverbs and wise sayings, who received a special gift of wisdom from God, who was promised all the riches of the world, who was greater in riches and power and wisdom than any other man who ever lived, fall prey to idol worship and demonic activity? Simply this: Those worship systems that Solomon was involved in were sexually oriented and Solomon was a womanizer. That was his Achilles' heel. Hosea confronted this later when he said in 4:11-12, *"Whoredom and wine and new wine take away the heart. The spirit of whoredoms hath caused them to err."* Whoredom, or harlotry, the Baal sexually focused worship cult became the tragedy of Solomon's life.

As the beautiful sensuous women to whom he was married asked him to involve himself with them in their worship systems, I am certain when he first began, he thought, "God will understand. I will do it only once." But as he became more and more involved, verse 8 says, *"And likewise did he for all his strange wives, which burnt incense and sacrificed unto their gods."* For the last few years of his reign he was useless as a king, he was useless to God, and he was consumed with his wives and their sensual worship systems."

And the Lord was angry with Solomon" (vs. 9), the third time He spoke to him, and this time His words were judgment. (11-13):

I will surely rend the kingdom from thee, and will give it to thy servant. Notwithstanding in thy days I will not do it for David thy father's sake: but I will rend it out of the hand of thy son. Howbeit I will not rend away all the kingdom; but will give one tube to thy son for David my servant's sake, and for Jerusalem's sake.

The wheels were set in motion for the division of the kingdom, and the destruction of Israel, so God could bring to pass the prophecy He had made earlier when He visited Solomon the second time. Immediately following the third visitation, in keeping with His promise in the Davidic Covenant, God began to send the chastening rods of other nations upon Solomon. Verse 14 says He raised up an adversary to Solomon, Hadad the Edomite. From that point in time forward, Solomon had no rest from his enemies.

At the same time that he was being oppressed by nations from outside the land, verse 26 tells us that "*Jeroboam the son of Nebat lifted up his hand against the king.*" Jeroboam, a revolutionary, was valiant and industrious. When Solomon realized this, he appointed him over all the forced labor in the house of Joseph, the descendants of Ephraim and Manasseh. As Jeroboam was leaving the city one day, he met Ahijah the prophet, who had clothed himself with a new garment. He removed the new cloak and ripped it into twelve pieces and said to Jeroboam, "*Take thee ten pieces: for thus saith the Lord, the God of Israel, Behold I will rend the kingdom out of the hand of Solomon, and will give ten tribes to thee.*" God also said that it would take place under Rehoboam's, reign, not Solomon's reign. In addition, He gave Jeroboam a promise similar to that which He had made earlier to Solomon, that He would be with him and build him an enduring house as He had for David "*if thou wilt hearken unto all that I command thee*" (vs. 38). Finally He added, "*And I will afflict the seed of David, but not for ever*" (vs.39).

We learned as we studied the life of Saul, that he was a very carnal man. One indication of this was that although he knew David had been chosen of God to be king of Israel, he sought to put him to death because he was determined to circumvent God's plan. One would think that Solomon, being such a wise man, would have learned from Saul's failed attempt. Recognizing God's sovereignty, he should have repented, confessed his sins, destroyed his idols and high places, and cast himself on the Lord's mercy; at the same time being submissive to God's judgment as David had in the matter of Bathsheba's baby. But Solomon's heart was not like David's. Instead, just as Saul had tried to kill God's anointed, so Solomon tried to kill the man whom God had appointed to take the ten tribes away from him and his descendents. Verse 40 says, "*Solomon sought therefore to kill Jeroboam.*" We see from this verse how far adrift Solomon had become spiritually. Jeroboam fled from his presence and took refuge with Shishak, king of Egypt, where he remained until the death of Solomon. The chapter ends. (vss. 41-43):

And the rest of the acts of Solomon, and all that he did, and his wisdom, are they not written in the book of the acts of Solomon? And the time that Solomon reigned in Jerusalem over all Israel was forty years. And Solomon slept with his fathers, and was buried in the city of David his father. And Rehoboam his son reigned in his stead.

David and Solomon Compared

Comparing David and his son Solomon is an easy task. David was a king in every sense of the word, a monarch after God's own heart. Solomon, by contrast, was an indulged and sometimes slothful son. Solomon became a man of ease. He could enjoy the good life because he never had to work for anything. David's life was one of struggle. He had to fight while in exile from Saul. He had to shed blood to maintain the integrity of his kingdom and against enemies from within his family, e.g., Absalom; and from outside his family. He was accustomed to fighting for everything he had. Solomon, on the other hand, was born with a silver spoon in his mouth and lived a life of relative ease. David had fought with his bare hands; he had killed a lion and a bear, fought and killed the giant; he had fought with the sword, often against overwhelming odds. Solomon probably never picked up a sword in his life. David knew what it was like not to know where his next meal was coming from. Solomon had never experienced hard times. David had sinned on several occasions, but his heart was tender. He repented and when he was broken, he returned to God. Solomon appears to have been on a continual downhill slide into spiritual oblivion. He did not repent and turn back to God, and he left behind a divided kingdom.

From the human side, the division was caused by Solomon's heavy taxes on the people and the meeting between Rehoboam and Jeroboam, the new leader of the Northern Kingdom. But, there was both a divine and human side to the division. In 931 B.C., the kingdom was divided. The legal heir to the throne, Rehoboam, the son of Solomon, reigned over the southern kingdom, afterward called Judah, was Judah and the smaller tube of Benjamin. Jeroboam would be king over the northern ten tribes, afterward called Israel. For the next two hundred and nine years there would be two nations, Judah and Israel; separate politically, religiously, and militarily.

XXXIX. HEBREW POETRY

When Solomon died in 931 B.C., the eighty year monarchy ended. The two primary contributors to the poetry and wisdom literature of Israel had passed from the scene. Therefore, before continuing with the reign of Rehoboam at the division of the kingdom, we will consider the books of Job, Psalms, Proverbs, Ecclesiastics, and the Song of Solomon of Solomon. David was the primary contributor to the Psalms, and Solomon wrote many Proverbs, as well as being the author of Ecclesiastes and Song of Solomon.

In ancient times, the wise men wrestled with two basic questions: One, the basic problems of life; namely, pain, suffering, and why evil seems to prosper, (or why those individuals involved in evil-doing seem to prosper). And two, the concept of how to live out a life with skill. It may be said that the problems people face today have not changed since 1000 B.C. If you ask individuals on the street today what they are concerned with, may answer, "What is the purpose of life? Why is there pain and suffering? Why is it that I see evil people prospering while I live right and never seem to succeed?" In the books of Proverbs, Ecclesiastes, and Job, these questions can be satisfied. In the book of Psalms, and in the Song of Solomon, we find expressions of poetry in its highest form following the ancient Hebrew motif.

In the book of Psalms, we become aware of God as a Person. As we study the Psalms, we will see God in His glory. We will see Him as a divine Person, intensely interested in every single individual. The book of Psalms, as we have it in our Old Testament consists of one hundred fifty individual psalms. As we examine the one hundred fifty psalms which make up the *Psalter. These* are divided into five separate books. Each one ends with a similar benediction.

"Blessed be the Lord God of Israel from everlasting to everlasting. Amen and amen." (Psalm 41:13)

"And blessed be his glorious name forever. And let the whole earth be filled   with his glory. Amen and amen." (Psalm 72:19)

"Blessed be the Lord for evermore. Amen and Amen."

(Psalm 89:52)

"Blessed be the Lord God of Israel from everlasting to everlasting. and let all the People say, Amen, Praise ye the Lord."   (Psalm 106:48)

Psalm 150 is the final benediction to the fifth book of Psalms, and as such is a total benediction for the Psalter. *"Praise ye the Lord. Praise God in his sanctuary: praise him in the firmament of his power."* (vs. 1) Verses 2 through 5 all begin with the word "praise, " then verse 6 concludes, " *Let everything that hath breath praise the Lord. Praise ye the Lord."*

Authorship and Dating

We know that at least seventy-three psalms were written by David. He was the primary contributor to the *Psalter*. But, as we look at the *Psalter*, we can see that it extends over quite a long period of time. As a collection, it was put together by priests after the return from Exile, so the total *Psalter* as we now have it, was organized after 536 B.C. The collection itself is actually more recent than the dates of the individual Psalms that make up the collection.

For example, turn to Psalm 90 which has the superscription *"A prayer of Moses the man of God."* Most scholars believe that the superscriptions are part of the inspired text. They are contained in the oldest manuscripts we have. We know that in the Hebrew text, A what we have as verse one in our English book of Psalms, is verse two in the Hebrew Psalms. The superscriptions on the individual psalms in our text are verse one in the Hebrew. In Psalm 90, *"A prayer of Moses the man of God,"* is verse one in the Hebrew text. We know that Psalm 90 was written prior to 1406 B.C., the date of Moses' death. So, we have at least one psalm dating back into the fifteenth century B. C. For another example on the time span of the *Psalter*. Look at Psalm 126. The superscription is "A song of degrees," so that does not help with the date. However, when we read the Psalm, we see when the historical event was celebrated.

When the Lord turned again the captivity of Zion we were like
them that dream. Then was our mouth filled with laughter, and our tongue with singing.
Turn again our captivity, O Lord, as the streams in the south.

The historical setting is the return from Babylonian captivity in 536 B.C. Israel returned to their land under the leadership of Zerubbabel.

By looking at the dates of Psalm 90 and Psalm 126, we can conclude that the book of Psalms spans at least nine hundred years.

Hebrew Poetic Style

If we read the Old Testament in the original Hebrew, we would discover that about fifty per cent of it is written in poetic form. Many translations available today have the poetic sections indented so that they may be more easily recognized. In the King James and the dual column Bibles, it is almost impossible to see the sections that are poetic in nature. Poetry in Hebrew is not the same as poetry in English. God used poetry when he spoke to man, and man often used poetry when he responded to God. Man's deepest emotions can be stirred and brought out poetically. God's deepest emotions and God's revelation can be delivered effectively in poetic form.

We usually think of poetry as rhyme involving sounds. Although Hebrew poetry often has rhyme it is more often a play on words which is not distinguishable in the English translation. It is a rhyming of ideas called parallelism. The type of poetry which rhymes sounds is termed assonance. Assonance, or pleasant rhyming of sounds, is the type of poetry most familiar to us. The Hebrew poets matched ideas rather than sounds. They would write a line then shadow it with another line.

Have you ever looked across a calm lake at houses and woods, and seen a perfect reflection in the water upside down? Hebrew poetry is like that. Wordsworth said it in this manner: *"The swan upon St. Mary's lake floats double": (swan and reflection; swan/shadow)*

That is how Hebrew poetry floats. Idea and shadow; Idea and Reflection; It is exciting to go through Psalms and discover the various types of parallelism. Many books are available which deal with poetry in the Psalms and the Old Testament text in general. For this study, we will limit our examination to four basic types of parallelism, three of which are found primarily in Psalms. The first type is synonymous parallelism; that is, two lines or two ideas which say the same thing. Look at Psalm 2:1-4. There we will see line and shadow, a very normal type. The poet will make a statement and then repeat it in almost the same way.

Verse 1: *Why do the heathen rage*, (one way) *and the people imagine a vain thing?* (another way)

Verse 2:   *The kings of the earth set themselves,* (one way) *and the rulers take counsel together,* (another way)

Verse 3:   *Let us break their bands asunder,* (one way) *and cast away their cords from us.* (another way)

Verse 4:   *He that sitteth in the heavens shall laugh:* (one way) *the Lord shall have them in derision.* (another way)

So it goes throughout the Psalm. You will also find this type of parallelism the Major and Minor Prophets.

A second type is emblematic parallelism. The poet will make a point and then picture it, or vice versa. See Psalm 23.

Verse 1: *The Lord is my shepherd; (picture) I shall not want (point)*
 Verse 2a: *He maketh me to lie down in green pastures;* (picture)
Verse 2b: *He leadeth me beside the still waters.* (picture)
Verse 3a: *He restoreth my soul*: (point)

This is the pattern in every Psalm where emblematic parallelism is used: Psalm 42:1 is a perfect example: *As the hart panteth after the water brooks,* (picture) *so panteth my soul after thee, O God.* (point)
It is a beautiful system of illustration. Discover other examples of emblematic parallelism for yourself as you study the other Psalms.

The next type is *synthetic parallelism*. This is when the poet takes an idea and expands upon it. It is as if we took a collapsed telescope and pulled out one section, then another, and another, so that it just keeps on expanding. This type is a little more difficult to discover, but Psalm one is an excellent example. Look at verses 1 and 2.

Blessed is the man that walketh not in the counsel of the ungodly,
(This is similar to a collapsed telescope: pull on it.); *nor standeth in the way of sinners.* (keep pulling.); *nor sitteth in the seat of the scornful.*(Pull it more.); *But his delight is in the law of the Lord.*
(Stretch it.); *and in his law doth he meditate day and night.*

The fourth type of parallelism is not common in the book of Psalms, but is used frequently in Proverbs from 10:1 through Chapter 31. It is antithetical parallelism. The writer states a thesis, then gives an antithesis. Look at Proverbs 10:1: *A wise son maketh a glad father.* (thesis) *but a foolish son is the heaviness of his mother.* (antithesis).

This form, using *but* as a pivot continues through Proverbs.

The Subjects in Psalms

When David had the Ark of the Covenant returned to Jerusalem, he also developed a formal worship service around it. First Chronicles 16:4 outlines the system he developed: *"And he appointed certain of the Levites to minister before the ark of the Lord."* He had Levites made into a Levitical choir using psalms and musical instruments as a full complement to worship. Then, he divided the choir into three groups, one *"to record,"* another *"to thank,"* and a third *"to praise."* We can do the same today with choirs, and the psalms, if we see how David utilized them. We will examine these three words he used to describe the three types of subject matter in his psalms.

Remembrance

He instructed the first group of Levites *"to record."* A better rendering of this word is *"to remind."* David was using specific Psalms to *remind* God. Psalm 70 has this word in the superscription. *"To the chief musician: A Psalm of David to bring to remembrance."* These Psalms are usually a petition or a lament. There are two categories of lament Psalms. First, the *communal* lament, where the entire nation petitions and laments (Psalms 44, 74, 79, 80 and 83 are examples). Then there are *individual, personal*, lament Psalms. These are found frequently throughout the Psalter. The key to the lament Psalm is usually in the opening line. It will begin, *"O God,"* or *"O Shepherd of Israel."* It identifies the Psalm just as the opening line identifies most writing. For example, *"Dear..."* begins a personal letter. *"Whereas the party of the first part"* begins a legal document.

To a second group of Levites, David said: *"Your job is to thank God."* The second group was to sing Psalms of thanksgiving. To the third group David said: *"Your job is to praise God."* The word literally means to *rave* about God. When God specifically meets a need, people are to praise Him. The Levites were to praise God for His attributes and for what He had done. Throughout the book of Psalms, you will see the various ways that God is praised in the different forms of Hebrew poetry.

The three *Subject* Psalms David designed for them to be used in worship are: to *invoke*, (or remind God) to *thank* God, and to *praise* God. As the Levites and the congregation gathered around the Ark, David would raise his hand and one group would sing reminders. He would raise it to another group and they would sing thanksgiving. Again he would raise it to the third and they would sing praises. In this way, God was honored and worshiped publicly.

When we master the *Psalter*, we can implement the Psalms in our personal lives. We can *remind* God, *thank* God, and *praise* God, with the inspired Psalms contained in His Word. As we do, our prayer lives will take on a dramatic new dimension. We can also implement the Psalms in the public worship service to *remind* and *thank* and *praise* God. The congregation will be lifted to new heights of worship as we return to God His inspired Word.

Psalm Construction

The Greek word *poema* means *"to do,"* or *"to make,"* and is the word from which we derive our word poem or poetry. Under the guidance of the Holy Spirit, the psalmist would create beautiful masterpieces. It was Spurgeon who said, *"The Holy Spirit thus deigned to speak to men in forms which were attractive to the attention and helpful to the memory. He is often plain or elegant in his manner, but He does not disdain to be quaint or formal if thereby his design of instruction can be more surely reached."*

Acrostic Psalms

One type of construction is the acrostic. Psalm 119 is an example of this format. It was written so each of the eight stanzas begins with the next letter of the alphabet. The first eight verses begin with aleph, the Hebrew equivalent of our letter A. It is a difficult concept to see since our English Bibles are not translated this way. What follows shows how the first eight verses would appear in the original Hebrew text.

A blessing is on them that are undefiled in the way, and walk in the law of Jehovah.
A blessing is on them that keep his testimonies, and that seek him with the whole heart.
Also on them that do no wickedness; but walk in his ways.
A law hast thou given unto us that we should keep thy precepts diligently.
Ah, Lord, that my ways were made so direct that I might keep thy statutes.
And then shall I not be confounded for I have respect unto all thy commandments.

As for me, I will thank thee with an unfeigned heart when I shall have learned thy righteous judgments.
An eye will I have unto thy ceremonies. O forsake me not utterly.
Psalm 25 is another example. With minor changes, each of the 22 verses begins with the next letter of the Hebrew alphabet.

And so it goes throughout the Hebrew alphabet. Many Bibles begin each stanza with its beginning letter in the Hebrew alphabet, so that the acrostic can be seen by the reader. Under the guidance of the Holy Spirit, the psalmists created beautiful pieces of writing like a weaver would create fine embroidery; with balance and symmetry.

Psalm 44 is an example of a different structure. In the original, it consists of twenty-six lines and looks like an inverted ziggurat. The Babylonian ziggurats were graduated stepped pyramids in design. The lower platform might be 200 x 200 feet, the next 160 x 160, the third 120 x 120, the next 80 x 80. Psalm 44 is a stepped design turned upside down. In the original, verses 1-8, comprise a ten line *confidence* section. Verses 9-16 are an eight line *lament*. Verses 17-22 are a six line *protest*. Verses 23-26 are a four line *petition*.

Psalm 44 is also an example of a *reminder* or *lament* Psalm because it contains all four of the sections that comprise the perfect lament: a *confidence* section, a *lament* section, a *protest* section and a *petition* section. I encourage you to study this Psalm so you can recognize these sections when you see them in other Psalms. You will not find another Psalm which is such a perfect example of the lament psalm, consisting of all four sections. However, you will find, throughout the *Psalter*, many that contain two or three of the sections, and possibly others with four, but in a different sequence.

Another interesting fact about Psalm 44 is that it shows us how people in that time drew encouragement from the past. Internal evidence indicates that it was written prior to 600 B.C. because the dates of Nebuchadnezzar's three invasions were 605, 597, and 586 B.C. Psalm 44 was written when Judah still had a standing army. When they needed encouragement for their battles, they remembered the exploits of Joshua, looking to God's victories through him and calling on God to give them the same kind of triumph. They used the Word of God in much the same way as we do today.

XL. TWO SPECIAL CATEGORIES

Messianic Psalms

Our study of Psalms would not be complete without consideration of *the Messianic Psalms*. These are Psalms concerned with the Messiah. They were given to the psalmist by the Lord Jesus Christ in His pre-incarnate eternal state. As the Lord Jesus looked down throughout the corridors of time from eternity past, He poured out His heart in anticipation of the sufferings and sorrows that He knew He would endure. In these Psalms, we have a glimpse of what He knowingly faced for us. Many *Messianic Psalms* were written by David between 1010 and 970 B.C., one thousand years before the crucifixion and resurrection of the Lord Jesus Christ. There are three types of *Messianic Psalms*.

Messianic Psalms

In a *Messianic Psalm* there is some feature in the life of the psalmist that is intended by the Holy Spirit to be a picture or type of the coming Messiah. Some particular feature or aspect of his life; some characteristic of the individual; or something he does or experiences, is a type of the Messiah. In the *Messianic Psalm*, not all in the psalmist's life, activities, or circumstances mentioned, are Messianic. Otherwise, in many instances we would end up with heresy. Only some feature of the Psalm is the type. Psalm 69 is a lament, or reminder, Psalm. Verse 5 demonstrates that the entire Psalm is not Messianic. It reads, *"O God, thou knowest my foolishness; and my sins are not hid from thee."* This cannot refer to Messiah because He was sinless. {John 14:30} In verse 7 we read, *"Because for thy sake I have borne reproach; shame hath covered my face."* With this statement David's experience becomes a type of the Messiah. He continues in verse 8, *"I am become a stranger unto my brethren, and an alien unto my mother's children."* Notice the synonymous parallelism in these two verses. Again, David's experience made him a type of Christ, who in His lifetime became a stranger and an alien because His relatives believed He was "beside himself." {Mark 3:21}

Continuing in Psalm 69, verse 9 says, *"For the zeal of thine house hath eaten me up."* As a theocentric individual, David was so consumed with the worship of Jehovah that he spent hours and days in worship at the Ark in Jerusalem and at the tabernacle and brazen altar in Gibeon. In this Psalm he said, *"I am just consumed with God, I am consumed with worshiping God."* A thousand years later, when the Apostle John saw the Lord Jesus in His zeal for the temple, he wrote in John 2:17, *"And his disciples remembered that it was written, The zeal of thine house hath eaten me up."* They linked the Lord Jesus to His ancestor David and in this Psalm.

Prophetic Messianic Psalms

In Psalm 69:12, David's experience is a type of Christ: *"They that sit in the gate speak against me; and I was the song of the drunkards."* Look at verses 19 and 20:

Thou has known my reproach, and my shame, and my Dishonor. Reproach hath broken my heart; and I am full of heaviness; and I looked for some to take pity, but there was none; and for comforters, but I found none.

As the Lord Jesus Christ was on the cross one thousand years later, looking at the faces staring up at Him, He saw them shooting out the lip, wagging their heads, mocking Him and saying, *"Thou Son of God come down from the cross and save thyself."* As the psalmist said, He found no pity in any of the eyes or faces looking up at Him in sullen pride and arrogance.

Again, in verse 21, the psalmist says, *"They gave me also gall for my meat; and in my thirst they gave me vinegar to drink."* We have no evidence that this happened to David. Therefore, when he uses this kind of vocabulary, he steps beyond the category of a *Typical Messianic Psalm*, and moves into the category of a *Typical-Prophetic Messianic Psalm*. Up to this point, history has been in play in David's life. He experienced the rebuke of his friends when he fled from Saul, and was abused by Shimei when he fled from Absalom. When he was across the Jordan after Absalom had invaded Jerusalem, I am certain he was the song of the drunkards, and even later during the rebellion of Sheba. So, in those portions of the Psalm, David was experiencing things that the Lord Jesus would later experience.

David never experienced the gall and the vinegar. In a *Typical-Prophetic Messianic Psalm*, history is not the only fact. In the *Typical-Prophetic Messianic Psalm*, the psalmist's vocabulary goes beyond his personal experiences and he begins to express ideas and occurrences which he never encountered or experienced himself. I do not know what the psalmist thought as he wrote such words under the inspiration of the Holy Spirit. He may have believed it was figurative language. But the figurative language and what may sometimes have even appeared to be *hyperbole* was literally fulfilled in the Lord Jesus Christ. So the definition for a *Typical-Prophetic Messianic Psalm* is history *plus* inspired foresight, with the psalmist going beyond himself and his own experience.

Much of the center of thought in the Messianic Psalms has to do with the sufferings of the Lord Jesus. Which of us can really know the sufferings of crucifixion? We do know it was an agony beyond compare. The Roman cross was short and the victim of crucifixion was rarely more than two feet above the ground. While the victim remained alive, wild dogs would come in from the desert and chew on his legs. The victim could live for two or three days in agony.

During crucifixion, the victim was first placed on the cross which was on the ground. Nails were driven through the hands at the juncture of the wrist, and then through the feet to secure him in that position. The cross was then raised and dropped into a previously dug hole. When it struck the bottom of the hole, the impact would usually pull loose the shoulder joints and ligaments, as the entire body weight pulled against the wrists with the force of the cross being dropped. In this distended position, diaphragmatic action was immediately reduced. Breathing became shallow and as the victim sank lower, he began to suffocate. In order to breathe, and to relieve the pain in his hands, he would push himself back up with his feet. But, this action caused the pain in his feet to be so excruciating, that he would again sag to relieve it. As this agonizing cycle continued, the victim began to take on grotesque zigzag, letter Z position, with the body skewed to one side and the knees pointed out in the opposite direction. As death began to creep slowly on, a semi *rigor mortis* began.

Because of the loss of diaphragmatic action, and the fact that the bones were pulled out of joint, the victim began to not only suffocate, but also to become extremely thirsty. Add to that the fact that he was impaled naked and helpless for all to see. It was a pain, agony, and humiliation beyond compare. The Lord Jesus suffered with a crown of thorns and a mutilated back as He bore our sins on the cross. In the Garden of Eden, God said nature would bring forth thorns as a result of Adam's fall. When the soldiers made the crown of thorns and pressed it on the head of the Savior, the thorny diadem had significance. He was bearing the curse for all creation.

Scripture is very plain when it says, *"It pleased the Lord to bruise him"* (Isa. 53:10). Because He was a lamb slain from before the foundation of the world, in anticipation of His agony to be endured for our sakes, Christ opened His heart to the psalmist as he penned in Psalm 22:1, "*My God, my God, why hast thou forsaken me? Why art thou so far from helping me?*" David was in desperate trouble when he penned this, and the Messiah would be in more desperate trouble when He used those words as He was on the cross. Also,

Verse 7: *All they that see me laugh me to scorn: they shoot out the lip, they shake the head.*

Verse 14: *I am poured out like water, and all my bones are out of joint: and my heart is like wax.*

As the Lord Jesus looked down while suspended on the cross with all of His ribs visible, His breathing becoming shallow, He said, "*my bones are out of joint.*" Verse 16: "*They pierced my hands and my feet.*" There is no historical record that David ever had his hands and feet pierced. As he penned this, he must have wondered what he was writing; but a thousand years later the Lord Jesus literally experienced this. The prophecy continues in verse 18: "*They part my garments among them, and cast lots for my vesture.*" In no way can this be historical. It is prophecy as Christ Himself inspired David to write what He would later experience when He paid the ultimate penalty for sin on Calvary's cross.

Completely Prophetic Messianic Psalms

The third type of Messianic Psalm is one which is completely prophetic. Psalm 110 is an example of this type. The Lord Jesus quoted from it to prove that He was the Messiah. In Matthew 22:41ff, we read,

While the Pharisees were gathered together, Jesus asked them, Saying, What think ye of Christ? Whose son is he? They say unto him, the son of David. He saith unto them, how then doth David in the spirit call him Lord, saying, the Lord said unto my Lord, Sit thou on my right hand, till I make thine enemies thy footstool? If David then call him Lord, how is he his son?

His enemies were so confounded they did not challenge Him from that time forward. Our Lord used Psalm 110:1: "*The Lord said unto my Lord, Sit thou at my right hand, until I make thine enemies thy footstool.*" As king of Israel, David was number one, answerable only to God. This is the crux of the question. How did David have a Lord between himself and God? David was writing in Psalm 110:1: "*The Lord said unto my Liege.*" David tells of his greater Lord, the Messiah, but He will be his future Son. As we look back with the benefit of the New Testament, we know exactly how this happened. Psalm 110 is a

Completely Prophetic Messianic Psalm. It contains no history, no historical counterpart, no typology or picture. In Psalm 110, only David's greater Counterpart, Messiah, risen and ruling, is in view.

Imprecatory Psalms

One type of psalm remains to be considered: the *Imprecatory Psalm.* This type demonstrates righteous indignation. In these, the psalmist says such things as "*Break out their teeth. Destroy them. Defeat them. Wreak vengeance on them.*" There are at least eighteen of these psalms, containing 368 verses, of which only about seventy-five include anything that can be called in imprecation. They have long been a subject of discussion, because in them the psalmist, under the inspiration of the Holy Spirit, calls down violence, vengeance, wrath, and revenge on the recipient of the imprecation.

The proper view of the Imprecatory Psalms rests on a variety of elements that we must take into consideration. First, these expressions contain the longing of an Old Testament saint for the vindication of God's righteousness. For example, David was a man of piety. He was God's anointed. Yet his enemies lived in ease, honor, and luxury, in Saul's court. Is it any wonder that David longed for a reversal of conditions that would answer all doubt concerning God's righteousness, and assure him of the reality of his anointing and future position as king?

Second, these were utterances of zeal for the kingdom of God. David was acutely conscious of the sanctity of his own anointed office. His whole life centered on serving God as king over His people. Yet at that time Saul was also anointed. David's greatest respect for this holy office prevented him from ever touching Saul. Yet because David was God's representative, his enemies were no longer his but God's. David might ask for these people a fate in keeping with their current condition.

Third, the utterances in the Imprecatory Psalms are the Old Testament expression of God's hatred of sin. David's thoughts were not chiefly against Saul, or even Absalom, but rather against the sycophants and political intriguers who urged them on: Doeg, Cush, Ahithophel, and others. It was impossible for David to differentiate between Satan and the sinner. Doctrines such as *soteriology, demonology, angelology*, were not developed in his time. These Psalms present God's attitude toward sin, and the impenitent and persistent sinner.

Fourth, as a preface to our later consideration of the book of Job, we must remember that these were more simplistic times and the eastern mind looked at a person as being either under God's curse or God's blessing. From this viewpoint, one who prospered was evidently a recipient of God's blessing. And one who was suffering, was evidently under God's curse because of some sin in his life. When David, or anyone else, observed evil men prospering, they would call for God's judgment to fall on them as a vindication of God's righteousness. It was part of David's concept of *Lord let thy name be hallowed in the earth*. It is the concept of the prayer which the Lord gave His disciples, "*Thy kingdom come thy will be done.*"

As David looked around and saw mankind in a rebellious state against God, and saw evil in the world, he knew it slandered the name of God. Even though such men were wicked, they were part of God's creation. David saw God's name being maligned, and God's character maligned, because His creation was in a state of disobedience. So he prayed: "Call down judgment on them! Vindicate Your position! Destroy the evil doers so that others will see it and know that God is in heaven and He punishes evil."

XLI. THE BOOK OF PROVERBS

The book of Proverbs offers the keys to life. Quite simply, it is a book of practical advice on how to live wisely. It holds up samples of life and asks, *"Is this wisdom or is this folly?"* It offers an example, a little cameo, scenario, or characteristic of personality, and asks, *"What is this?"* "What are the qualities of a good wife?" "What are the dangers of loose living?" Job, and also Solomon in Ecclesiastes, each ask questions such as: *"why?"* and *"how?"* The authors in Proverbs ask *"what?"*

Because of the complex nature of this book, we need to look carefully at its structure and authorship. The following list is an outline that includes both authors and compilers.

I.   Title, Introduction, and Motto (1:1-7)
11.   A Father's Praise of Wisdom (1:8 - 9:18)
III.   Proverbs of Solomon (10:1 - 22:16)
IV.   Words of Wise Men (22:17 - 24:22)
V.   Further Wise Words (24:23 - 24:34)
VI.   Hezekiah's Collection (25:1 - 29:27)
VII.   The Words of Agur (30:1-33)
VIII. The Words of King Lemuel (31:1-9)
IX.   Example of Wifely Excellence (31:10-21)

As in the book of Psalms, Proverbs was collected over several centuries. The Proverbs which Solomon wrote can be dated between 970 and 931 B.C. The collection authorized by Hezekiah must have been put together in the late eighth century B.C. With the names of these two kings, it is obvious that the material was put together over a period of at least two centuries.

The book of Proverbs is a king's handbook, or a leader's manual. It is applicable to us, as born-again believers, not only for present wise living, but as those who will reign with Christ in His future kingdom. So, for both our present and our future, we need to be versed in the skills of leadership. The book of Proverbs will teach us *how* to become astute leaders, able to discern between complex issues. It is easy today to find ourselves in the quandary of *situation ethics,* the doctrine of flexible morality, and *subjective morality,* when each person decides what is right and wrong. Knowledge of the book of Proverbs will dissolve the gray areas.

Proverbs is ideally suited to daily reading because it contains thirty-one chapters. As a result of this structure, you can begin to study it on any day of the month. If you start on the fourteenth, then begin reading Proverbs 14. You will have a chapter for every day of a thirty-one day month. For a month with thirty days, just read through chapter 30, and begin the next day with chapter 1. You should systematically read the book of Proverbs every month. Based on what God's Word says, you will experience a dramatic change in your life. Many Christian leaders make it their practice to read through this book every month. As it becomes engrained in your thought processes, you will develop a keen spirit of discernment. You will recognize the scoffer, the friend, the fool, the wise man, the sluggard. You will learn, "*What is wisdom? What is folly?* You will learn, as chapter 1 suggests, *"to know"* (vs. 2), *"to receive"* (vs. 3), *"to give"* (vs. 4), *"to understand"* (vs. 6). As you wrestle with these maxims and pithy little sayings, you will develop keen mental acumen. Your logic will be more factual and you will develop a spirit of discernment and deduction.

Proverbs 1:2 says, *"To know wisdom."* The word in Hebrew is *hokmah*, and although it means "wisdom," at the root of the word it means "to have a skill." Most of us are victims of our environment. If we lost our computers and smart phones, then were asked what we could do only a few would have an income producing skill.

In Old Testament times it was necessary for everyone to have a skill to be productive. This is demonstrated in Exodus 28. The man upon whom God put a spirit of wisdom, or *hokmah*, could go into the field and gather ripe flax and spin it into linen thread. He would set up his warp and woof for weaving and make cloth. With that he could make a properly fitting garment for Aaron, the high priest. He knew how to take roots and berries to make colored dyes for the cloth. One man could do the job from beginning to end and he must have found great satisfaction in it. The Bible says he had a spirit of wisdom: *hokmah*.

How does this relate to us in this Century? We must learn how to become skillful at living well. The eastern philosopher, the authors of Proverbs, the wise men of the Old Testament, saw life as a garment. Each day another thread is woven into it. Depending on the person's relationship to God, and level of spirituality, it may be a
beautiful garment when it is completed, or a garment with blank spots and defects. If only we could see our lives as God sees them from the viewpoint of eternity! He sees the results of the trials, temptations, tribulations, chastisements of closed and open doors, and

temporary tragedies. He recognizes how they are woven together for the perfection of the individual. The temptations, tribulations, and tragedies that come into our lives, enable God to knock off the rough edges on this piece of coal and turn out a diamond fit for the Master's use. But, when the chisel is striking and the diamond cutter is working, it can be difficult to endure.

In one sense, we are like an insect walking across the canvas of a famous masterpiece. It senses only the ups and downs, the ridges and rough edges of the oils, as the artist brushed them on the canvas. It can never get back far enough to see that the rough spots, taken together, created a painting which is inspiring to behold: *hokmah*. This is the skill of living out your life day by day, weaving thread after thread into the fabric of life, so that when it is over you can look at the whole and see a completed and beautiful fabric woven day by day consistently in accordance with God's perfect will. The wisdom literature, and especially Proverbs, gives us the skills we need to live our daily lives with *hokmah*.

"And instruction." (1:2) This word is better translated "discipline." Discipline is the inner requirement for receiving instruction. Discipline has become a negative word. No one wants to receive discipline. It is often missing in schools and even in our homes. People do not realize that they are free only if they are disciplined. As we discipline ourselves to purity and to God's standard of life, old habit patterns are dissolved. As the maxims of Proverbs become part of our daily life, personality, and thought processes, we become truly free. The book of Proverbs gives the reader both *hokmah* (wisdom) and discipline.

We live in a time of instant gratification. What we want, we want now. We no longer save for future gratification because plastic money makes everything and anything available immediately. Many today want spirituality and knowledge of God's Word in the same instant manner. But God has not designed His Word or His wisdom to be received in this way. Proverbs 2 presents eight steps to the wisdom of God. As we begin to practice these steps, we discipline ourselves to become skilled in the art of living.

1) Proverbs 2:1: *"If thou wilt receive my words."* There must be a desire on the part of the recipient to receive what God has to say.
2) *"And hide my commandments with thee."* You hide them as one would hide treasure. You hide them so no one can take them.
3) Verse 2: *"incline thine ear unto wisdom."* You have to hear what is going on. You must be ready and willing to hear, not stiff-necked, not haughty or proud, but ready to hear.

4) *"Apply thine heart to understanding."* You must be willing to say, "Lord, here I am. My heart is open and pure because my sins are confessed and I am ready to learn what You want to teach me."

5) Verse 3: *"if thou criest after knowledge."* This indicates that the search for knowledge is not a casual one. The *need* must be there. A cry must be made: "O God, give me the knowledge of Your Word."

6) At the same time you cry for knowledge, you must cry also for discernment. Verse 3: *"and liftest up thy voice for understanding."* The cry must be loud and audible. These desires come from the heart and are necessary to convince God that you are sincere. Just as we are instructed not to cast our pearls before swine, so God is not going to send His wisdom to those who are not sincere about receiving it.

7) *"If thou seekest her as silver"* (vs. 4). This is a physical seeking. This is how to search the Word of God; as diligently as you would search for silver.

8) Finally, in verse 4: using *synonymous* parallelism, *"and searchest for her as for hid treasures."* Will you search the Word of God that way? Will you give your riches and all you have and risk your life to find the wisdom of God? This is what God demands. He said, *"And ye shall seek me, and find me, when ye shall search for me with all your heart"* (Jer. 29:13).

A few subjects for study are: Chatting: 10:19; Eating: 15:16,17; Cheating: 20:14; Faithful Messengers: 25:13; Unfaithful Messengers: 10:26 & 26:6; Unfaithful People: 25:19; A Foolish Companion: 25:20; The Boomerang Effect: 26:27; Honoring a Fool: 26:1 & 8; Self Praise: 27:1; Contending with a Fool: 29:9; The Danger of Flattery: 29:5; A Good Name: 22:1.

XLII. THE BOOK OF JOB

Because the five books we are studying are called poetry, does not mean they are the products of human imagination. They describe real people who had real experiences; they grappled with profound problems. They concerned themselves with the experiences of the godly in the vicissitudes of the painful life which was theirs "*under the sun.*" In the book of Job, we see the death of the self-life of Job through the fires of affliction and the new vision himself as God sees him. The self-life, with its self-goodness, self-reason, self-religion, self-esteem, and self-everything, is laid bare so all can see. The man who at first was said to be the most "righteous" man on earth (Job 1:8) is found at last on his face before God, saying, "*I abhor myself in dust and ashes*" Job 42:6).

Date and Setting

Most conservative scholars believe that the book of Job is at least as old as the time of Abraham. Since the book contains no reference to
the established worship system in effect from the time of Moses, it is assumed that the events occurred during the patriarchal period or earlier. Its setting is in the land of Uz. We are not certain where that was located, although many believe that it was in Arabia. It could be anywhere and everyone who reads the book can associate with it.

Many scholars, including Clarence Larkin, in his classic book, *Dispensational Truth* {Chapter 32} believe that Job was involved in the construction of the Great Pyramid at Giza. (See Isaiah 19:19, 20) and the descriptions in Job 38:4-6, as compared to the incredible dimensions in the Great Pyramid. *Google* will give you research and information about Job and the Great Pyramid.

In Job 1:1, we are introduced to Job, a man blameless and upright. He feared God and eschewed evil. He had seven sons and three daughters, and was very wealthy. In material possessions he lacked for nothing. After introducing us to Job and his various religious practices, the Holy Spirit pulls back the curtain of heaven and allows us to listen to a conversation which takes place between God and Satan. In reply to God's question as to where he has been, Satan responds that he has been walking around throughout the earth in (vs. 7). God responded and threw down the gauntlet of challenge: *"Hast thou considered my servant Job, that there is none like him in the earth?"*

Satan's response represents the greatest calumny against God that had ever been delivered. Its gist was that a person who served and loved God was interested only in His rewards. According to Satan, no one would love God just because of who He is. If you were not so good to him, Satan intimated to God, Job would curse you to your face. To prove him wrong, God threw down the gauntlet: *"All that he hath is in thy power; only upon himself put not forth thine hand."*

Satan departed and tragedy began to fall upon Job like a trip hammer in rapid staccato blows. The Sabians attacked (vs. 15), fire fell (vs. 16), the Chaldeans raided (vs. 17), the house was blown down and killed all his children (vs. 18). Each report came on the heels of the preceding one. In a few minutes time, Job learned of the loss of all he valued: possessions, crops, animals, servants, and children. Still, he did not curse God or shake his fist at Him. Instead, he tore his robe, shaved his head, and fell to the ground. His statement in verse 21 is the answer to the most profound issue of human existence. *"Naked came I out of my mother's womb, and naked shall I return thither: the Lord gave, and the Lord hath taken away; blessed be the name of the Lord.*

We will find that much of the content of the book of Job revolved around the concept of *theodicy*. Theodicy comes from two Greek words, t*heos*-God, and *dike*-justice. Or, how can we vindicate the justice of God in relation to evil? How can we justify God's holiness and the existence of evil? It is the continuing theme in the book.

Job had lost all his possessions but still had his health. Chapter 2 pulls back the curtain once again and we are now listening to another meeting. God pointed out that Job *"holdeth fast his integrity, although thou movedst me against him, to destroy him without cause"* (vs. 3). "No wonder," is Satan's reply, "You have not touched him physically." *"Put forth thine hand now, and touch his bone and his flesh, and he will curse thee to thy face"* (vs. 5). Again, God gave Satan a limited power: *"Behold, he is in thine hand, but save his life"* (vs. 6).

Satan then inflicted Job with boils from the soles of his feet to the crown of his head. Many believe that that this was leprosy. Job sat out on an ash heap and scraped himself with a potsherd (a piece of broken pottery), the only thing available to scrape the scabs from his body. By this time, even his wife had experienced too much, and said, *"Dost thou still retain thine integrity? Curse God, and die."* Later on we will find Job beginning to question and challenge God, and to vacillate between despair and trust. But, at this point, his integrity is intact. He responded to his wife: *"Thou speakest as one of the foolish women speaketh."* And in verse 10: *"Job did not sin with his lips."*

Job's Comforters

Job had three friends who heard of his calamity. Remembering from our study of the Imprecatory Psalms, religious men believed suffering *had* to be God's judgment on sin in the individual's life. If Job were truly righteous, all this could not have been happening. We know differently because we witnessed the two conversations in heaven, but Job did not know about them. He will go through the entire ordeal and never learn *why* it happened. Nor did his friends ever know. In their eyes, Job had to be a sinner. Their position and their theology were shaken to the core because they believed that if Job were righteous and all this had befallen him, they also might experience sudden calamity. They *had* to prove that there was sin in Job's life in order to vindicate their eastern theology.

At first because of the boils and dust, they did not recognize him. They wept and tore their robes and threw dust on their heads in typical oriental mourning. They sat on the ground for seven days and seven nights, not saying a word. Do you know anyone who would sit with you a full week because he grieved with and for you? I cannot recall this ever happening m my lifetime. Sometimes my heart longs for a return to the kind of personal relationships where people really care about people. In their own way, Job's friends cared about him. Their unselfish behavior demonstrated their genuine concern and compassion.

Job 3:1 to 41:34 is a series of dialogues among four Eastern sheiks, sitting in typical eastern fashion and discussing the verities of life. It was Job who broke the seven-day silence by cursing the day he was born. At that point, his state of mind was the lowest it will be throughout the book. It is revealed in such statements as *"Let the day perish wherein I was born."* (3:3) *"Why died I not from the womb?"* (vs. 11)

The motif begins in chapter 4 and is a continuing cycle of speeches. Eliphaz will speak and Job will give his rebuttal. Bildad will speak and Job will respond. Zophar will speak and Job will answer. Then: Eliphaz-Job; Bildad-Job; Zophar-Job. The communication deteriorates and Zophar does not respond. Throughout the cycle, each man tried to discover what was wrong in Job's life. It was thrust and parry, thrust and parry, as if they were in a fencing match.

In chapter 4, Eliphaz began by suggesting that Job could not take for himself the counsel he had offered others in trouble. Verse 3:

"Thou hast instructed many, and thou hast strengthened the weak hands. "Verse 5: "But now it is come upon thee, and thou faintest; it toucheth thee, and thou art troubled." Verse 7: "Whoever perished, being innocent? Or where were the righteous cut off?"

In verse 12 Eliphaz used an age-old method by referring to an occult experience to impress others with his religious authority.

> *Now a thing was secretly brought to me, and mine ear received*
> *a little thereof. In thoughts from the visions of the night, when*
> *deep sleep falleth on men, Fear came upon me, and trembling,*
> *which made all my bones to shake. Then a spirit passed before*
> *my face, the hair of my flesh stood up: It stood still, but I could*
> *not discern the form thereof- an image was before mine eyes,*
> *there was silence, and I heard a voice, saying, Shall mortal man*
> *be more just than God? Shall a man be more pure than his maker?*

With this story of an occult spirit experience, Eliphaz attempted to justify his argument and add validity to his claim. His accusations continued in chapter 5. Verse 17:

"Happy is the man whom God correcteth: therefore despise not the chastening of the Almighty." Verse 27: "We have searched it, so it is, hear it, and know thou it for thy good"

In chapter 6 Job was not so much answering Eliphaz as venting his anguish and remorse over the current situation. Then beginning in   7: 11, he unleashed a series of rhetorical questions, complaining with all the bitterness of his soul. In chapter eight Bildad joined the dialogue and accused Job of producing nothing but a big wind. Verses 2 and 20 sum up his argument: *How long wilt thou speak these things? And how long shall the words of thy mouth be like a strong wind? Behold, God will not cast away a perfect man, neither will he help the evildoers.* Job's reply to Bildad in chapter nine is sarcastic agreement. Finally, in 10:1 he mourned, *"My soul is weary of my life ,"* and continued to express the depths of his depression. In chapter 11, Zophar took up the challenge by accusing Job of talking too much. *"Should not the multitude of words be answered? And should a man full of talk be justified? "* (vs. 2) Verses 13-15, sum up his argument.

> *If thou prepare thine heart, and stretch out thine hands toward*
> *him; if iniquity be in thine hand, put it far away, and let not*

wickedness dwell in thy tabernacles. For then shalt thou lift up thy face without spot, yea, thou shalt be steadfast and shalt not fear.

Job's lament and response to that statement continues through chapter 14. Then in chapter 15, Eliphaz began the second cycle of speeches. He no longer showed the courtesy of his first speech but accused Job of being full of hot air saying in verse 2, " *Should a man utter vain knowledge, and fill his belly with the east wind ?*" He has now joined the others in his disdain of Job. He asked, "*What knowest thou, that we know not? What understandest thou, which is not in us? *" (vs. 9) In other words, Job, you do not have all the answers. And he continued to rebuke him even more severely.

Job's reply in chapter 16 was that he was sick of their useless talk. *Shall vain words have an end? Or what emboldeneth thee that thou answerest? I also could speak as ye do: if your soul were in my soul's stead, I could heap up words against you.* Job wished they could exchange places and that he could be the one to speak to them. They were not helping him with their words. After a few speeches that contained high thoughts and elevated ideas, Job had begun to sink back into despair. In 17:1 he complained: "*My breath is corrupt, my days are extinct the graves are ready for me.*" Job was ready to die.

Bildad's next speech is recorded in chapter 18, and in it he had no patience with Job. Beginning in verse 5, he discussed the horrible fate of the wicked. Then Job responded in chapter 19 and after the crushing burden of the heavy words of his friends, he begged,

"*How long will ye vex my soul, and break me in pieces with words? And be it indeed that I have erred, mine error remaineth with myself.*" "*Help me,*" he begged. Finding no pity, he cried out in verses 25 and 26: "*I know that my redeemer liveth, and that he shall stand at the latter day upon the earth: And though after my skin worms destroy this body, yet in my flesh shall I see God.*"

What a tremendous prophecy of the coming Redeemer! The Hebrew word is the same used in the book of Ruth, *goel.* It can be translated *redeemer, avenger,* or *defender.* Job needed all of these! Zophar's reply in chapter 20 was one of uncontrollable anger and Job responded to him by declaring them all wrong. In chapter 21, Job defends his philosophy and theology. The third cycle of speeches begins in chapter 22 with Eliphaz unleashing a scathing accusation. In verses 4-9, he gives a detailed catalogue of sins which he believed Job had committed, and summarized his argument in verse 29. Job's response is recorded in chapters 23 and 24.

PANORAMA of the OLD TESTAMENT

In chapter 25, Bildad speaks briefly. Communication among the group had broken down and deteriorated into slanderous remarks. Job responded in chapter 26 then paused as if waiting for Zophar to speak. Eliphaz has had three speeches, Bildad has had three speeches, but Zophar has had only two. When Zophar did not respond, Job began again in chapter 27. Unable to reconcile his suffering with his integrity, Job (chapter 29) turned his mind to the wisdom of God. Although he seemed to be at the end of his rope, he burst forth with a beautiful poem in chapter 29: "*Oh that I were as in months past, as in the days when God preserved me.*" Job longed for the time when his children were around him, when his servants met his needs, and he had food and good health. But those days were gone, he was out on the ashes, and his friends were reviling him. He lamented, "*I cry unto thee, and thou dost not hear me.*"

Finally, in chapter 31, Job initiated the ancient oriental final proof of honesty by calling down a curse on himself from Heaven if he is guilty. This method of self-incrimination, or self-exoneration, in Job's culture was more meaningful than swearing before a jury. The punishment for perjury against God held more terrifying consequences than perjury before a human jury. As he categorized the different activities for which he wished judgment if he were guilty, they were in specific response to the listing by Eliphaz (chapter 22) of which he believed Job to be guilty.

The seriousness of Job's oath in chapter 31 cannot be overestimated. He enumerated a series of "ifs" and following each "if", he pronounces a curse on himself *if* he was guilty of the things he mentioned in these following verses:

5: If I have walked with vanity
6: Let me be weighed in an even balance.
7: If my step hath turned out of the way
8: Then let me sow and another eat.
9: If mine heart have been deceived by a woman
10: Then let my wife grind unto another.
13: If I did despise the cause of my manservant
16: If I have withheld the poor from their desire
19: If I have seen any perish for want of clothing
20: If I have lifted up my hand against the fatherless
22: Let mine arm fall from my shoulder blade.

242

Job, fully confident of his innocence, finally said in chapter 31:40, *"The words of Job are ended."* He closed the argument. He must either suffer the sanctions he had called down upon himself or else be acquitted.

Enter Elihu

In chapter 32, we are introduced to Elihu, a fourth individual who was present, and had been listening from the sidelines. Chapter 32 begins, *then was kindled the wrath of Elihu against because he justified himself rather than God.* Elihu began to speak out self-righteously, making four speeches between Job 32:1 and 37:24. His first speech lasted through chapter 33. His second takes all of chapter 34, and the third all of chapter 35. The fourth is chapters 36 and 37. Elihu forms a transition between the speeches of Job, his friends, and the Theophany of God when He answered Job out of the whirlwind. God did not rebuke Elihu, as we read in chapter 42.

The Lord began in 38:3 by demanding, *"Gird up now thy loins like a man."* This was the challenge of an ancient belt wrestler. It was another way of saying, *"It is time to get down to business, Job!"* With that introduction, God enumerated His wonders to Job. In chapter 39, He described how His creation scorned man. In chapters 40 and 41 He asks, "How can you contend with God when you cannot even match the creatures I have made?"

Chapter 42 is the epilogue. Job confessed to the Lord, *"I know that thou canst do everything."* Having come face to face with God, Job's response is like that of Moses, Joshua, and Isaiah centuries later. In 42:5, Job said, *I have heard of thee by the hearing of the ear but now mine eye seeth thee. Wherefore I abhor myself, and repent in dust and ashes.*

After Job's repenting and confession, the Lord rebuked Eliphaz, Bildad, and Zophar, but not Elihu. God commanded them to offer sacrifices, *"and my servant Job shall pray for you: for him I will accept lest I deal with you after your folly, in that ye have not spoken of me the thing which is right, like my servant Job."* Verse 10 says, *"The Lord turned the captivity of Job, when he prayed for his friends."* Job was a gracious man considering how much he had suffered from the comments and dagger-like remarks of his three "friends." *"So the Lord blessed the latter end of job more than his beginning."* (vs. 12) Notice that he ended with twice as much as he had at the start. "So Job died, being old and full of days" (vs. 17). In the book of Job, we have the answer as to why the righteous suffer. But Job never knew why he suffered. In effect, what God had said to him was, *"You need to trust Me, Job."*

XLIII. LIVING AND LOVING

-ECCLESIASTES & SONG OF SOLOMON-

The book of Ecclesiastics contains the philosophy of a man who had everything. Chapter 1:1 identifies the author as *"the Preacher, the son of David, king in Jerusalem.* "The only person who qualifies is King Solomon. Certainly, Solomon had the wherewithal to do anything and everything he desired. His wealth was incalculable. Probably no one ever had more wives and concubines; he must have known everything possible about love and the relationships between men and women. His philosophy, as recorded in Ecclesiastics, was simply: "I have tried everything and nothing is worth anything. Vanity of vanities, everything is vain, or futile-empty.

"What profit hath a man of all his labor which he taketh under the sun? One generation passeth away, and another generation cometh: but the earth abideth forever." (vss. 3 and 4) The sun rises, the sun sets, everything happens over and over, so what is it all about anyway? In verses 13 and 14 he admitted,

> *I gave my heart to seek and search out by wisdom concerning*
> *all things that are done under heaven: this sore travail hath*
> *God given to the sons of man to be exercised therewith. I have*
> *seen all the works that are done under the sun; and, behold,*
> *all is vanity and vexation of spirit.*

In chapter 2: 1, he described another pursuit: *"I said in mine heart, go to now, I will prove thee with mirth, therefore enjoy Pleasure: and, behold, this also is vanity."* There was no pleasure in work; there was no pleasure in fun; there was no pleasure in futile enjoyment. The hedonistic life-style was simply vanity: Pleasure accomplished nothing. He tried creativity and materialism (vss. 4-8). *"I builded me houses. I made me gardens. I got me servants and cattle. I gathered me also silver and gold and treasure."* Once again, Solomon discovered it all to be vanity. Imagine! Solomon was a man who had everything: pleasure, beautiful women, creative pursuits, gold and silver, but in verse 17 he finally concluded. *"I hated life."* It was a striving after wind. Verse 18: *"I hated all my labor because I should leave it unto the man that shall be after me."* He had realized that, *"You can't take it with you."*

Chapter 3 begins Solomon's second discourse in which he came to terms with the laws which govern life. Chapters 1:1-2:26 describe the vanity of human endeavor *"Under the sun."* In chapter 3 he determined, from a human viewpoint, that there is an appointed time for everything and for every event under heaven.

His third discourse extends from 6:1 through 8:17. The central theme is that there is no satisfaction in earthly goods. Finally, in the fourth discourse (9:1-12:8), Solomon has realized that God will deal with the injustices of this life. Solomon was an old man who had tried everything. He had not lived in the *hokmah* wisdom of the Proverbs he had written. His world-view had developed around a self-centered approach to fife. He had been an egocentric person. As he looked back over his life, he realized that it had been empty, vain, futile, because it had been done outside of a proper relationship with God. The counsel given by this old man who had everything and had tried everything when he looked back over his life was, *"Remember now thy Creator in the days of thy youth."* Look at example of *merisms* in Ecclesiastesares in chapter 3:1-8

SONG OF SOLOMON

The final book in the collection of poetry is the Song of Solomon, often called *Canticles, or Songs*. Through the centuries, this little book has been looked at in many ways. Some see it as allegorical. The best approach is a combination of literal and typical interpretation. Literally, it is probably a single short incident in Solomon's life with a simple country girl. As typology, it typifies the love relationship between Christ and His bride, the Church. Despite his failures, Solomon was in some aspects, a type of Christ. Because of the intimate nature of the book, as it relates to the Personal relationship between a man and a woman, the old rabbinical requirement was that a man must attain the age of thirty before he was allowed to read it. It is a wonderful book for a husband and wife to read as they share intimate times and moments together. In addition to being used for this purpose, it demonstrates the love of Christ for His Church, and shows how the Church should respond to the love of her Master and heavenly Bridegroom. Some interesting sidelights are that the Song of Solomon mentions some twenty one varieties of *flora*. It also contains fifteen species of *fauna*. It provides extensive examples of royal luxury with its use of silver and gold and purple.

The Song of Solomon is one of eight Old Testament books not quoted from in the New Testament. The other seven are Judges, Ruth, Esther, Ecclesiastes, Lamentations, Obadiah, and Zephaniah. In John 6:31, the opponents of Jesus mentioned Nehemiah 9:15, which includes Ezra in the Hebrew Old Testament, so Ezra cannot be included in this list of eight.

XLIV. THE KINGDOM DIVIDED

Beginning with I Kings 12, we have a new era in Israel's history. The nation will be divided into a northern kingdom named Israel, and a southern kingdom named Judah. They will be two separate nations with a common border as are Canada and the United States. They will develop two distinct religious systems, two distinct political systems, and two distinct military systems. These divided kingdoms continued for 209 years, from their inception in 931 B.C., until 722 B.C. when the Assyrians invaded and dispersed the kingdom of Israel among the nations. During those 209 years, Israel and Judah had various relationships. Sometimes they fought with one another as if each were a common enemy; sometimes they formed an alliance against another enemy; at other times they were friendly. The reader will also discover that common personal names were used by the royalty of both kingdoms.

From this point in time forward, the books of I and 11 Kings become increasingly difficult to understand. This is not the fault of the inspired record. It is simply that we are unfamiliar with the method by which the kingdoms kept the records. In working out the chronology the primary requisite is that the chronological structure of that nation be clearly understood. These must be considered:

1. The year from which a king began to count the years of his reign: that is either from his actual accession to the throne, or from the year following his accession.
2. The in the calendar year when a king began to count his reign.
3. The method by which a scribe of one nation reckoned the years of the king of a neighboring nation; whether according to the system used in his own nation, or by that of the neighboring nation.
4. Whether the nation made use of co-regencies; whether or not rival rulers might have been reigning at the same time; and whether or not there was an inter-reignum.
5. Whether during the period under review, a uniform system was followed, or variations occurred.
6. A proven date during the period in question from which the years can be figured backward and forward so that the full chronological pattern can be determined.

The customs were not the same among all nations. In Assyria, Babylon, and Persia, the year a king ascended to the throne was known as his accession year. Not until the first day of the next new year did he begin to reckon his reign from his own first year. This is called the accession year system, or post-dating. In other nations, the king's first year began when he ascended the throne. This is known as the non-accession year system, or ante-dating. Any particular year of a king's reign according to the non-accession year system was one year higher than the accession year method. The first year according to the accession year system would be the second year according to the non-accession year system. In order to know exactly what is meant by a recorded date, it is necessary to understand the system used. The chronologist will discover that throughout this 209 year period, Israel and Judah alternated in the method they used for determining the first year of the king's reign.

One final consideration must be made concerning I and II Kings; that is, the method by which the author, under the inspiration of the Holy Spirit, recorded the events of these two kingdoms. He had to keep track of events in two separate nations. The author began Ws consideration with one nation and carried it on until its history overlapped the death of the monarch in the other nation. Then he went back and picked up the history of the second nation until a king there outlived the monarch of the first nation. Then, he went back and picked up that history again. In doing this, a zigzag pattern developed. His movement from one nation to the other is like rungs on a stepladder; the main vertical supports being the northern and southern kingdom. He will move back and forth from king to king until the end of the divided kingdom in 722 B.C.

Look at an example in I Kings 15. According to verses 1 and 2, Abijam reigned over Judah until 911 B.C., beginning in the eighteenth year of King Jeroboam in the north. Verse 1 says, "*Now in the eighteenth year of king Jeroboam Abijam reigned over Judah. Three years reigned he in Jerusalem.*" In 911 B.C., Jeroboam was still ruling in the north because 14:20 says, "*And the days which Jeroboam reigned were two and twenty years: and he slept with his fathers, and Nadab his son reigned in his stead.*" Jeroboam reigned from 931 to 910B.C. and Abijam's reign is from 914 to 911 B.C. Since Jeroboam was still alive at Abijam's death, the author of I Kings continued his consideration of the southern kingdom. In verse 9 ff:

And in the twentieth year of Jeroboam king of Israel reigned Asa over Judah. And forty one years reigned he in Jerusalem. And Asa did that which was right in the eyes of the Lord, as did David his father.

Asa came to the throne in the twentieth year of Jeroboam and we know Jeroboam lived only two more years. Chapter 15:24 says, *"And Asa slept with his fathers, and was buried with his fathers in the city of David his father. And Jehoshaphat his son reigned in his stead."* At that point the author turns back to a consideration of the northern kingdom starting with 15:25:

> *And Nadab the son of Jeroboam began to reign over*
> *Israel in the second year of Asa king of Judah, and*
> *reigned over Israel two years. And he did evil in the*
> *sight of the Lord, and walked in the way of his father.*
> *And Baasha the son of Ahijah, of the house of Issachar,*
> *conspired against him, and Baasha smote him at Gibbethon.*

One more point must be made. The southern kingdom had only one ruling family. From the death of Solomon in 931 B.C. to the Babylonian Captivity in 586 B.C., only one ruling family will sit on the throne of Judah except for a brief period when Athaliah usurped it. All nineteen kings: Rehoboam, Abijam, Asa, Jehoshaphat, Jehoram, Ahaziah, Joash, Amaziah, Azariah (Uzziah), Jotham, Ahaz, Hezekiah, Manasseh, Amon, Josiah, Jehoahaz, Jehoiakim, Jehoiachin (Jeconiah / Coniah), and Zedekiah, are all descendants of David. In the northern kingdom of Israel, the twenty kings who sat on the throne were from many ruling families. They were Jeroboam, Nadab, Baasha, Elah, Zimri, Tibni, Omri, Ahab, Ahaziah, Joram (Jehoram), Jehu, Jehoahaz, Jehoash, Jeroboam 11, Zechariah, Shallum, Menahem, Pekahiah, Pekah, and Hoshea. The similarity of many names in the two kingdoms also complicates the study of I and II Kings since often, without a chronological chart at hand, it is difficult to determine which kingdom the author is discussing. Since there were many ruling families in the north, it is obvious that they obtained the throne by some means other than inheritance. We will read that it was a period of intrigue, assassinations, murder, military coups, and suicide. All of which eventually brought God's judgment on the northern kingdom. See Figures 4 & 5 in the Appendix.

The Prophetic Office

It is also important to take notice of the function of the prophet during this period. In addition to being a foreteller, one who spoke of future events, his function was also to anoint God's choice as king as Samuel had done with Saul and David. Such anointing indicated to everyone that God had selected the man for his position. To be a God approved king, one must have either been a descendant of David, as were all the kings in the south, or he must have been anointed by a prophet. Not one of the twenty kings in the north was a descendent of David. This made it vital for prophets to function in the north and anoint the king which God selected. Only two, Jeroboam and Jehu, were anointed. This leads us to conclude that the other eighteen kings were there not by God's choice, but by mere circumstance. The prophet Hosea, speaking in the middle eighth century B.C., under the inspiration of the Holy Spirit, said in 8:4, *"They have set up kings, but not by me."*

This was a task for John the Baptist when the Lord Jesus Christ came. He was both a prophet and a king-maker. When he made his announcement regarding the Lamb of God, he was pointing at the One whom he knew God had selected to be His king. John the Baptist functioned in the same capacity as did the Old Testament prophets, and the Lord Jesus met the double criteria. Namely, He was a descendant of David, and He was anointed by God's prophet. The anointing took place in the baptismal ceremony when the Lord Jesus identified Himself with the movement and with the program of God. It took on an even more dramatic aspect when the Holy Spirit, in the form of a dove, descended on Him. In the Old Testament, the anointing off was symbolic of the Holy Spirit, but in our Lord's case, the Holy Spirit descended in visible form. To those of spiritual discernment who observed the scene, its impact could not be misunderstood. There was the prophet of God, the Son of God, and the Holy Spirit doing the anointing in a personal way which no Old Testament king had ever experienced.

The Kingdom Divided

Rehoboam, the son of Solomon, inherited the throne at his father's death. However, at this point in the nation's history, the people were not naturally inclined to accept Rehoboam as their king. Solomon had imposed heavy taxes and had conscripted labor for his ambitious building programs. Conscription of labor was a common practice in the ancient world. It was unpopular but a citizen could not resist. Because of these inequities, the children of Israel were discontented. Heavy taxes and conscripted labor had made them bitter toward the monarchy. Therefore, it was not easy for Rehoboam to establish himself as king over all Israel. In 12:1 we read that *"Rehoboam went to Shechem: for all Israel were come to Shechem to make him king."* This indicated a need for conciliation because Rehoboam traveled north to Shechem rather than receiving the people in Jerusalem.

Jeroboam learned that Solomon was dead and that his life was no longer threatened. With the words of Ahijah burning within him, he returned from Egypt. When Rehoboam arrived in Shechem, he encountered not only the elders of the tribes, but also Jeroboam. He had become the spokesman for the tribes, and confronted Rehoboam with the demand of verse 4: *"Thy father made our yoke grievous: now therefore make thou the grievous service of thy father, and the heavy yoke which he put upon us, lighter, and we will serve thee."* Rehoboam asked for three days in which to consider their proposal, and the people departed. He was now faced with his first major decision as king.

Rehoboam first consulted with the elders who had served Solomon. Verse 7 records their advice: *"If thou wilt be a servant unto the people this day, and wilt serve them, and answer them, and speak good words to them, then they will be thy servants forever."* God's direction and criteria for the monarchy had indicated that the king was to be a servant, a shepherd, to His people. But Rehoboam did not intend to be anyone's servant. Verse 8 says, "H*e forsook the counsel of the old men and consulted with the young men that were grown up with him, and which stood before him."* It is easy to anticipate the advice these spoiled sons of the court would give. It is recorded in verses 10and 11:

> *Thus shalt thou speak unto the people. My little finger*
> *shall be thicker than my father's loins. And now whereas*
> *my father did lade you with a heavy yoke, I will add to*
> *your yoke, my father hath chastised you with whips, but*
> *I will chastise you with scorpions.*

When Jeroboam and the elders returned on the third day, the king answered the people harshly, forsaking the old men's counsel and listening to his companions. *"Wherefore, the king hearkened not unto the people."* It is interesting to see the acts of men line up with the will of God. Proverbs 2 1: 1 says, *"The king's heart is in the hand of the Lord."* Rehoboam thought he was doing what he wanted, but all the time he was advancing the program of God who had said He would eradicate Israel from the face of the earth if Solomon did not obey. The division of the kingdom was the first step toward bringing that prophecy to pass.

When the elders of the northern tribes heard Rehoboam's response, they disavowed their allegiance with this statement (vs. 16): *"What portion have we in David? Neither have we inheritance in the son of Jesse: to your tents, 0 Israel: now see to thine own house, David."* These were the same words spoken back in 11 Samuel 20:1, when Sheba revolted. Israel had long been looking for an opportunity to split away from the house of David, and under Jeroboam, their opportunity had come. God allowed this penchant toward division to fulfill His will. It is a perfect example of how God causes even the wrath of men to glorify Him and bring about His purposes. *"It was a turn of events from the Lord."*

The ten tribes returned north and Rehoboam retreated to Jerusalem, as king over only Judah and tiny Benjamin. But he was not ready to give up. He instructed Adoram, the man who had been in charge of Solomon's conscripted labor, to go north and secure a labor force. How foolish this was. The use of conscripted labor was one of the issues leading to division. For almost forty years Adoram had been commandeering their sons to work in Solomon's building projects. He personified all that Israel was rebelling against. Not surprisingly, no sooner had he arrived in the northern kingdom than they stoned him to death. Immediately, Rehoboam gathered an army to wage war, but God sent a prophet to forbid it. Rehoboam dropped his military plans and the division became permanent.

XLV. THE SIN OF JEROBOAM, I

In I Kings 12:26-27 we learn the reasoning behind the sin of Jeroboam, (Jeroboam, I, followed later by Jeroboam, II) which Scripture so frequently mentions, when referring to him.

> *And Jeroboam said in his heart, now shall the kingdom return*
> *to the house of David: If this people go up to do sacrifice in the*
> *house of the Lord at Jerusalem, then shall the heart of this people*
> *turn again unto their lord, even unto Rehoboam king of Judah,*
> *and they shall kill me, and go again to Rehoboam king of Judah.*

Jeroboam had evidently forgotten the promise which God gave to lam, through Ahijah the prophet, saying that He would establish his house if he walked according to the ordinances of the Lord. In Rehoboam's capitol in Jerusalem was the temple of Solomon where the followers of Jehovah gathered several times a year for religious festivals, assemblies, and the Day of Atonement. Jeroboam's heart began to fear as he imagined his constituents continuing their religious and emotional ties to Jerusalem. How could he prevent it? Instead of trusting God, who had promised him a solid kingdom if he was faithful, his solution was to substitute an alternative religion *"which he had devised of his own heart."* (vs. 33) As the crux of his devised religion, Jeroboam had two golden calves fashioned. He set one up in Bethel, near the southern border of his kingdom, and the other at Dan, far up in the north. Then he announced, *"Behold thy gods, 0 Israel, which brought thee up out of the land of Egypt."*

From our twenty-first century viewpoint, we wonder how anyone could be foolish enough to believe that a golden calf could have lived, breathed, and done something miraculous in the past. But, we need to remember the land in which the people lived. Their neighbors, the Canaanites, were Baal worshipers. Much of the time they worshiped Hadad, the storm god, who was personified and riding on a bull. In Baal worship, the bull symbolized male regenerative power and virility. In this way, Jeroboam devised a syncretism religion. He took what little knowledge the people had of Jehovah, and what they believed about Baalism, the religion of the people to whom they were exposed, and knit the two together.

Knowing that the priests of the Lord in the south would not help him, he devised his own priestly system. Verse 31 says, *"And he made an house of high places, and made priests of the lowest of the people, which were not of the sons of Levi."* In addition to this, he devised his own special religious feast days. In summary, he created a satanic duplication of the worship of Jehovah. Generations to follow, his epitaph would read: *"The man who made Israel to sin."* Time and time again, throughout the history of Israel, the words would be: *"The sin of Jeroboam, whereby he made the people to sin.*

Enter the Prophet

Since Jeroboam was an anointed king, God was quick in rebuking him. Chapter 13 tells us how He sent an unnamed prophet from Judah to Bethel. Jeroboam was standing at the altar, beside the golden calf, burning incense. While he was participating in his own false system, the unnamed prophet appeared and cried out against the altar, saying,

*Altar, altar, thus saith the Lord: Behold, a child shall be born
unto the house of David, Josiah by name; and upon thee shall
he offer the priests of the high places that bum incense upon
thee, and men's bones shall be burnt upon thee.*

This is one of the remarkable prophecies in the Old Testament. Only two others use an individual's name. The other two are Cyrus, (Isaiah 45:1) and the Lord Jesus, of whom it was said, they *"shall call his name Immanuel"* (Isaiah 7:14). This prophecy, regarding the name Josiah, would be fulfilled three hundred years later. Its fulfillment is described in 11 Kings 23 and we will examine it in detail when we arrive at that time period.

To validate his prophecy, the unnamed prophet gave a sign, saying, "T*he altar shall be rent*." When Jeroboam heard this, he was furious and extended his hand as he commanded, *"Lay hold on him."* To his shock and dismay, his hand dried up and he could not pull it back. At the same time, *"The altar also was rent, and the ashes poured out from the altar, according to the sign which the man of God had given by the word of the Lord."* (vs. 5) The king then implored the man of God to pray that his hand be restored. The prophet did so and Jeroboam invited him home to dinner. However, the episode had no affect the king. He had witnessed a prophecy fulfilled, had seen his hand withered when it reached out against God's spokesman and then healed by the prophet's prayer. After all of these events, he did not repent, or change, and the false worship at Bethel continued through the years.

Following the king's invitation to dine with him, the man of God refused to eat with the king because God had instructed him not to eat or drink in that place; the northern kingdom,. Specifically Bethel. In obedience to God's command he began the journey back to his home in Judah in the southern kingdom.

At this point in the story, we are introduced to another prophet. He was old and living in Bethel where the golden calf was. This says much about how backslidden he must have been, for even the Levitical priests had left the northern kingdom. A parallel passage tells us that he was originally from Samaria. He apparently moved to Bethel to be near the new calf worship system. When his sons told him about the events of the day and of the prophet who had come up from Judah, he must have been furious at being overlooked and jealous because God had not used him when he was there at Bethel. He promptly asked, "*Which way went he?*"

His sons saddled a donkey and the old prophet caught up with the unnamed prophet as he was resting under an oak tree. He spoke warmly to him, "*Come home with me, and eat bread*" (vs. 15). At first the unnamed prophet refused, saying, *I may not return with thee, nor go in with thee: neither will I eat bread nor drink water with thee in this place: For it was said to me by the word of the Lord, Thou shalt eat no bread nor drink water there, nor turn again to go by the way that thou camest.* We learn now that he was not even to return by the same way he went up to Bethel. God never contradicts Himself. The prophet went to Bethel and prophesied by the word of the Lord while under the command of God not to eat or drink in that place. However, verse 18 records the speech of the ungodly old prophet from Bethel:

> *I am a prophet also as thou art, and an angel spake unto me*
> *by the word of the Lord, saying, Bring him back with thee*
> *into thine house, that he may eat bread and drink water.*
> *But he lied unto him.*

The old prophet tried to make the other prophet believe that he also had a vision from God. "*So he went back with him.*" (vs. 19) What a tragic example this is of obeying experience instead of the Word of God. There could not be a better example of the penalty of giving heed to experience and laying aside the Word of God. God's Word must *always* take precedence over experience. "*And it came to pass, as they sat at the table, that the word of the Lord came to the prophet that brought him back.* "God now spoke through the ungodly old prophet just as He had formerly spoken through Balaam. As the man from Judah sat back relaxing in comfort, he heard a message of doom. (vs. 21ff):

Forasmuch as thou hast disobeyed the mouth of the Lord, and hast not kept the commandment which the Lord thy God commanded thee, But camest back, and hast eaten bread and drunk water. Thy carcass shall not come unto the sepulchre of thy fathers.

After he started back home a lion met and killed him. *"His carcass was cast in the way, and the ass stood by it. The lion also stood by the carcass."*

Success against one's enemy depends upon one's relationship with God. Remember, when the Spirit of the Lord came upon Samson in his earlier years he could kill a lion with his bare hands. If I may make a spiritual application, the lion is a type of Satan who goes about seeking whom he may devour. In the Spirit of the Lord, Samson could rend him with his bare hands. In this story we see a man of God who had just proclaimed a great prophecy, had seen the power of God split the altar, had seen Jeroboam's hand wither and then healed in answer to his own prayer. But then he disobeyed and had no power against the lion. Ordinarily, a lion that had killed a man would devour him, then possibly kill and devour the donkey. This did not happen and the event was recognized as a judgment from God. As for Jeroboam, verse 33 says he *"returned not from his evil way."* He remained unaffected by all these events.

Death of Abijah

Chapter 14 describes the illness and death of Jeroboam's son Abijah. It is interesting to notice that when his son was ill, Jeroboam, I did not consult the gods he had created, but sent his wife in disguise down to Shiloh to the prophet Ahijah in this emergency. It was Ahijah who had earlier prophesied that Jeroboam would become king over the northern tribes. In this emergency, Jeroboam, I wanted information from a *real* prophet of Jehovah about the future of his ill son. God had advised Ahijah beforehand what would happen, so he was not fooled by the disguise of Jeroboam's wife. He confronted her and prophesied doom on the family and descendents of her husband, because Jeroboam,I was not as David had been, but had *"done evil above all that were before him."* As a sign that his words would come to pass, he added (vs. 12), *"when thy feet enter into the city, the child shall die."* All Israel would mourn for him. He was the only one of Jeroboam's descendants to die of natural causes, because later, God would raise up a king over Israel who would cut off all the house of Jeroboam, I.

Ahijah's words contained a complex series of prophecies. In addition to cutting off Jeroboam's house, an event validated by the immediate fulfilling of the time of Abijah's death, Ahijah saw the future down to 722 B.C. and in verse 15 he said:

> For the Lord shall smite Israel, as a reed is shaken in
> the water, and he shall root up Israel out of this good
> land, which he gave to their fathers, and shall scatter
> them beyond the river, because they have made their
> groves, provoking the Lord to anger.

The river was the Euphrates. The groves were the places where the pillars were carved in the appearance of female deities, and cult prostitution was practiced. Verse 16 continues, *"He shall give Israel up because of the sins of Jeroboam, who did sin, and who made Israel to sin."* The prophecy extended from the immediate death of the child to the cutting off of Jeroboam, I's house, and eventually on down through history to 722 B.C. Verse 17 continues: *"And Jeroboam's wife arose, and departed and came to Tirzah: and when she came to the threshold of the door, the child died."* That was the event which validated all of the other prophecies still in the future.

Following the death of Jeroboam, the author of I Kings begins a "step-ladder" history of the southern kingdom. Starting with 14:21, we read:

> And Rehoboam the son of Solomon reigned in Judah. Rehoboam
> was forty and one years old when he began to reign, and he
> reigned seventeen years in Jerusalem, and Judah did evil in the
> sight of the Lord, and they provoked him to jealousy with their sins
> which they had committed, for they also built them high places,
> and images, and groves, on every high hill, and under every tree.

This was identical to what had been happening in the North, except that in the south they had Baalism exclusively. In the north, they had a combination of Baalism and the sin of Jeroboam. Verse 24 adds:
"There were also Sodomites in the land: and they did according to all the abominations of the nations which the Lord cast out before the children of Israel." Sodomite refers to male cult prostitutes, also referred to as *dogs*.

It is obvious that rather than maintaining themselves in the religion of Yahweh, and the worship system at the temple of Solomon as God had prescribed it, the people had begun to involve themselves in the sexual aspects of Baal worship. These evil practices corrupted their minds and, as Hosea would say later: *"The spirit of harlotry has led them astray."* Because this involvement became ingrained in the people, God sent judgment on Judah and the house of Rehoboam from an outside source. This was a promised provision in the Davidic covenant.

Invasion by Pharaoh Shishak

In the fifth year of king Rehoboam, Shishak, king of Egypt, came up against Jerusalem. This was the same Shishak to whom Jeroboam fled for safety when Solomon sought his life. To understand the impact of what took place under Shishak, it is necessary to go back and read a few verses of the Davidic Covenant in II Samuel 7. God had promised what would take place when the seed of David, through Solomon, began to sin (II Sam. 7:14ff)

> *I will be his father, and he shall be my son. If he commit iniquity,*
> *I will chasten him with the rod of men, and with the stripes*
> *of the children of men; But my mercy shall not depart a way*
> *from him, as I took it from Saul, whom I put away before thee.*

Just as the chastening rod had fallen on Solomon when he began to sin, now, the chastening rod, more violent and intense this time, fell on Rehoboam. When Shishak invaded Jerusalem, he took all the treasures of the Lord's house and the king's house. He took the shields of gold which Solomon had made and carried them back to Egypt. Pharaoh Shishak recorded these and other military exploits on the temple wall in Karnak, Egypt. He recorded that he invaded Rehoboam, spoiled the king of Jerusalem, and that he took all the wealth from the temple and the king's house.

The record of Shishak's activities on the temple wall in Karnak was written in Egyptian hieroglyphics. Prior to the nineteenth century, no one was able to read them. However, this changed after one of Napoleon Bonaparte's engineers discovered the Rosetta Stone at Rosetta, Egypt, near the mouth of the western branch of the Nile. It is an oval-topped black granite slab about 3 feet 9 inches high, 2 feet 4 inches wide and 11 inches thick. The writing on its face is in three languages common to the Nile Valley. One was Greek, but the other two were unknown to the scholars of that day. Through the years many men tried to read the two languages.

Finally, a Frenchman by the name of Jean Chameleon dedicated his life to digging out the mysteries of the Rosetta Stone. He was supported by his older brother, and for twenty-three years he wrestled with the contents of the Rosetta Stone. Finally, in 1822, he published complete translations of the tri-lingual inscription. He discovered that one of the unknown languages was Egyptian demotic, the language used by the Egyptians during the time of Christ. The other was Egyptian hieroglyphics. Scholars could translate the Greek and finally could translate the Egyptian demotic. By understanding the demotic, they broke the code of the hieroglyphics, the picture language of ancient Egypt.

Thanks to the extensive efforts of those two men, and to the timely discovery of the Rosetta Stone in the providence of God, scholars were able to read the language of the Pharaohs, thus enabling future archaeologists to decipher the previously unknown historical and literary treasures of the Nile valley, among which was the record of Shishak on the temple wall in Karnak. I have had the privilege of lecturing while standing next to the Rosetta stone in the British Museum in London.

XLVI. THE DYNASTIES

The history of Israel between 931 and 722 B.C. can be divided into three distinct religious periods. The first period is *Sin of Jeroboam*, beginning in 931 B.C. and ending with the death of Omri in 874 B.C. There is a slight time overlap, but the people worshiped the golden calves in Bethel and Dan and often included Baalism.

Beginning with the ascendancy of Ahab to the throne in 874 B.C., and continuing until the death of his second son Joram in 841 B.C., is the second period of defined as the *Sin of Ahab*, when Baalism was the official religion in Israel. After the purge by Jehu in 841, until the demise of Hoshea in 722 B.C., there was the third period identified as the *Half-Reform of Jehu*. Because Jehu's appointed task was to eradicate Baalism from Israel, he obediently and zealously succeeded in that. However, he soon returned to the worship system which Jeroboam had established. He did not lead the people all the way back to the pure worship of Jehovah.

Dynasty of Baasha

You will recall that part of the prophecy given by Ahijah to the wife of Jeroboam was that his house would be cut off. Chapter 15:28ff records the fulfillment of that prophecy. Jeroboam's son Nadab was on the throne, but:

In the third year of Asa king of Judah did Baasha slay him, and reigned in his stead. And it came to pass, when he reigned, that he smote all the house of Jeroboam; he left not to Jeroboam any that breathed, until he had destroyed him, according unto the saying of the Lord, which he spake by his servant Ahijah the Shilonite: Because of the sins of Jeroboam which he sinned, and which he made Israel sin, by his provocation wherewith he provoked the Lord God of Israel to anger.

By now, two-thirds of the prophecy given to Jeroboam had come to pass. First his son had died; second, the house of Jeroboam was cut off. The third prophecy, the dispersion of Israel, would not occur until 722 B.C. The remainder of chapter 15, and all of 16, is packed with intrigue. Baasha's death is recorded along with the sin which preceded it. Elah, his son, reigned for two years in his capital at Tirzah. He was assassinated by Zimri, the Commander of one-half his chariot forces, while he was participating in a drunken orgy.

As soon as Zimri became king, he killed every male in Baasha's family and of all his relatives and friends, ending the dynasty of Baasha just as Baasha had ended the dynasty of Jeroboam. This method of securing one's position on the throne has been practiced down through the centuries. You win recall this is what made David's treatment of Saul's grandson, Mephibosheth, so unusual. Nevertheless, we recognize that although these men were acting in accordance with the expectations in their time, they were fulfilling the program of God to bring judgment on the descendants of those who failed to live by His ordinances.

The Dynasty of Omri

Zimri's coup was not popular and his reign lasted only seven days. The remaining army, under the command of Omri, heard of Baasha's assassination and besieged the city where Zimri was living. Seeing that his cause was futile, Zimri committed suicide by setting fire to the building while he remained inside. The army officers crowned Omri king over Israel.

I Kings 16:21 records that the people were not united behind Omri. Half of them preferred Tibni, the son of Ginath. So, from 885 to 880 B.C., a period of five years, there was an overlap with two kings reigning simultaneously until Tibni died and the nation united behind Omri. (vs. 22) Omri was a powerful military monarch. So powerful, that in the extant records of surrounding nations, archaeologists have discovered tablets which refer to Israel by the name "*Land of Omri.*" One of his notable accomplishments was to build the city of Samaria and make it his capital. Because Samaria was on a hill about three hundred feet above the surrounding land, the trade routes ran right by the base of the hill. In this way, the cunning and powerful Omri had a commanding position over the trade routes from his fortress in Samaria. As a result, he was secure militarily and could demand tribute and toll payments from caravans that needed to travel past his city.

Omri was a powerful and astute King by the world's standards, but "*He walked in the way of Jeroboam wherewith he made Israel to sin*" (vs. 26). One of his acts of most far-reaching significance was to arrange a marriage between his son Ahab, and Jezebel, the daughter of the Sidonian King Eth-baal. Although we previously discussed the concept of political and military alliances between reigning families, this marriage Omri arranged for his son Ahab had both immediate and potential eschatological consequences.

The Dynasty of Ahab

The marriage of Ahab to Jezebel had religious and political implications. First, the Sidonians were fervent Baal worshipers. In addition, as King, Jezebel's father, Eth-baal, was the High Priest of Baalism. This made his daughter Jezebel the High Priestess. For political expediency, the king of Israel, Ahab, would be married to a high priestess of Baal. Is it any wonder that we read in 16:31 that he *"went and served Baal, and worshiped him."* And in verse 32 that *"he reared up an altar for Baal in the house of Baal, which he had built in Samaria."* This evil union initiated the second religious period in Israel's history, known as *the Sin of Ahab*. Under Ahab and Jezebel, Baalism became the official religion of Israel. Verse 33 sums up the period by saying that *"Ahab did more to provoke the Lord God of Israel to anger than all the kings of Israel that were before him.*

Before continuing with chapter 17, it is necessary to examine the basic tenets of Baalism. Since it had become this official religion of Israel, the people were fully involved not only in the prostitution system, but also in the entire concept of Baal's control of fertility in all of its ramifications. They looked on him as the source of rain, sunshine, productive crops, and as the god of all things which multiply on the face of the earth. They believed that as long as they worshipped Baal and were faithful to him, their crops would grow, the rains would come in their seasons, and everything would be fertile and productive. This was a belief maintained from the least Israelite to the greatest, (except for the seven thousand prophets).   {I Kings 19:18}

Enter Elijah

It is against this background that we are introduced to Elijah the Prophet in I Kings 17:1: *And Elijah the Tishbite, who was of the inhabitants of Gilead, said unto Ahab, As the Lord God of Israel liveth, before whom I stand, there shall not be dew nor rain these years, but according to my word.* Only if we understand the background against which Elijah made this statement, can we understand its significance. Ahab did not believe Elijah. As a Baal worshipper, he believed that Baal controlled the rain. So, when this hairy man, girded with leather garments pointed his finger at Ahab and declared there would be no rain *"but according to my word."* the king probably chuckled. Immediately following his unusual pronouncement, Elijah turned and quickly left (vss. 2-4):

And the word of the Lord came unto him, saying, get thee hence, and turn thee eastward, and hide thyself by the brook Cherith that is before Jordan. And it shall be that thou shalt drink of the brook; and I have commanded the ravens to feed thee there.

Elijah traveled to Cherith and verse 6 says, "*The ravens brought him bread and flesh in the morning, and bread and flesh in the evening, and he drank of the brook.*" For a while, Elijah was well cared for and comfortable. Then, since there had been no rain, the brook began to dry up. Elijah learned quickly that he lived in a physical universe that was still subject to the physical laws which God had established; so when rain was withheld, the brook dried up. If He had desired to do so, God could have supplied Elijah with water from a stone as He had once done in the wilderness. But now the time had come for Elijah's faith to be tested. Have you experienced drying brooks in your life? Perhaps drying brooks of finance, or physical health, or an eroding ministry? What has been your response to them? Elijah's response was simply to be patient then obey God's command directing him to another location. He could have sat by the brook Cherith shaking his fist at God and demanding, "*Where is the food and water You promised me?*" Instead, he obeyed God's new command and went to Zarephath.

When he reached the gate of the city he met a widow. She had been faithful in giving God the first of everything, and invited Elijah to share what she thought would be her last meal. As a result of her simple faith, she and her household, and Elijah, ate for many days because "*the barrel of meal wasted not, neither did the cruse of oil fail, according to the word of the Lord, which he spake by Elijah.* Elijah's dry brook was not a dead end but a new beginning. Because he was obedient and faithful, he received a new ministry, saved a family, performed the rare miracle of raising a person from the dead and became an illustration for Christ's teaching on sovereignty in Luke 4:25, 26.

The Contest on Mount Carmel

Chapter 18 is the account of the famous Mount Carmel contest. Verse 1 says that "*It came to pass after many days, that the word of the Lord came to Elijah in the third year, saying, Go, shew thyself unto Ahab.*" The Lord was ready to send rain on the earth. After three and a half years of drought, Ahab had slowly realized that indeed it was not Baal but Jehovah who could stop the rain. Now, it was time for Elijah to make known that Jehovah was the One who also could cause the rain. Through those years, Ahab cursed God, cursed Elijah and looked everywhere for him without success. During the same time, Jezebel had destroyed the prophets of the Lord because of her anger that Elijah's prophecy had come true.

It is in James 5:17 that we learn the drought actually lasted three and one half years. In *"the third year"* in chapter 18: 1, is after three full years of drought. Quite possibly, the drought is counted as both beginning and ending at the start of a normal Palestinian dry season. It had resulted in lost crops and famine, and Ahab, as Israel's leader, was helpless. But even after this, his view of the problem was so twisted that when he met Elijah he asked (vs. 17), "Ar*t thou he that troubleth Israel?"* Elijah replied (vs. 18), *"I have not troubled Israel, but thou, and thy father's house, in that ye have forsaken the commandments of the Lord, and thou hast followed Baalim."* Then he ordered that the people of Israel and all the prophets of Baal and Ashterah be gathered together on Mount Carmel.

Ahab sent messengers throughout the land and a large number of people gathered together. In the group were four hundred fifty prophets of Baal. Just as Mount Horeb was holy to the Israelites, Mount Carmel was holy and sacred to the Baal worshipers. They believed it was his dwelling place. It was not a coincidence that Elijah called the people there to observe the contest between Jehovah and Baal. All of the odds were in Baal's favor because, as polytheists and henotheists, the Baal worshipers believed that they were in the most powerful place possible for Baal to win the battle.

Elijah said, *"Give us two bullocks; and let them choose one for themselves."* Then Elijah proposed the test (vs. 24): *"Call ye on the name of your gods, and I will call on the name of the Lord: and the God that answereth by fire, let him be God."* Why by fire? Because the Baal worshipers believed Baal was the god of fire and lightning. Now all the odds were in Baal's favor. The Ugarit tablets contain some verses of Baal poetry which say that Baal carved his castle from the rock with fire. *"The fire ate out the windows. The fire ate out the doors. The fire carved the corridors and the rooms."* Baal worshippers all believed that fire was used by Baal at his command.

Elijah spoke to the people, *"How long halt ye between two opinions? if the Lord be God, follow him: but if Baal, then follow him."* The people did not answer. But when they heard the terms of the contest, that the test would be who could call down fire, they replied, *"It is well spoken."* (vs. 24) The odds were now in favor of their god, Baal. About noon time, according to verse 27, after the false prophets had leaped about the altar and performed all of the rituals they believed necessary to call Baal's attention to their contest, Elijah began to mock them: *"Either he is talking, or he is pursuing, or he is in a journey, or peradventure he sleepeth, and must be awakened."* These caustic remarks goaded them to greater frenzy, so they continued all afternoon screaming and crying and cutting themselves until their blood gushed out. This concept of self-flagellation to attract the attention of a god, has been used by religions of every type, cult, and denomination, throughout the centuries. The Ugarit tablets, and other extant literature from ancient times, record how worshippers would cut off their fingers and throw them on the altars of Baal and Asherah in an attempt to pacify them.

But all of this self-mutilation was to no avail. About the time of the evening sacrifice (vs. 29), Elijah solemnly said, *"Come near unto me."* By this time the people began to gather in a hushed manner around the altar. Elijah repaired the altar of the Lord that had been torn down and raised an altar to the Lord with twelve stones. He dug a trench around the altar, cut the wood and the ox in pieces and laid them on it, then drenched everything with water until the trench was full. He complicated the whole situation to such an extent that no one could say it was an accident or a coincidence.

> *It came to pass at the time of the offering of the evening*
> *sacrifice that   Elijah the prophet came near, and said, Lord*
> *God of Abraham, Isaac, and of Israel, let it be known this day*
> *that thou art God in Israel, and that I am thy servant, and*
> *that I have done all these things at thy word. (vs. 36)*

Following Elijah's invocation: God of Abraham-*the God of promise;* of Isaac- *the God of miracle*, God of Israel- *the God of change* . The fire fell from Heaven, consumed the offering, the stones, the dust, and licked up the water out of the trench. When the people saw this, they fell on their faces crying, *"The Lord, he is the God,- the Lord, he is the God."* Elijah ordered the false prophets seized, dragged to the brook and executed. Ahab watched this amazing spectacle speechless until Elijah said, "Get thee up, eat and drink, for there is a sound of abundance of rain."

Ahab departed to eat and Elijah went to the top of Carmel, where he sat down and put his face between his knees. Seven separate times he sent his servant to look for a cloud. Finally, his servant reported, "Behold, there ariseth a little cloud out of the sea, like a man's hand." Only a tiny cloud but Elijah sent his servant down with a message to Ahab, *"Prepare thy chariot, and get thee down, that the rain stop thee not."* After three and one half years of drought the ground was rock hard like cement. Elijah knew that when it began to rain, flash floods would rush across the desert and sweep away everything in their path. Very soon the sky grew black with clouds, the wind began to blow, and there was a sudden downpour. Through the blinding rain, Ahab returned to Jezreel in his chariot. The hand of the Lord was on Elijah, and He girded up Elijah's loins and he outran Ahab's horses back to Jezreel. Ahab, still shocked and numbed from the day's events, looked through the blinding rain to see the prophet Elijah, racing past his speeding chariot!

XLVII. FURTHER ADVENTURES OF ELIJAH

Beginning in chapter 19:1, Ahab went back to his palace and described the day's events to Jezebel, who was still enraged over the execution of her prophets. She quickly sent a message to Elijah, saying, *"So let the gods do to me, and more also, if I make not thy life as the life of one of them by tomorrow about this time."* Elijah left Jezreel and ran for his life down to Beer-sheba, a long distance from Jezreel. After running to Beer-sheba, he went a day's journey into the wilderness. In his despondency, he was ready to have God take his life; in fact, he was considering suicide. Lying down under a juniper tree, he fell into a deep sleep from depression. He was awakened by an angel who commanded him to: *"Arise and eat."* Near to his head he discovered a jar of water and some bread. He ate, and because of his exhaustion, fell asleep again. Once again the angel awakened him, this time saying, *"Arise and eat, because the journey is too great for thee."* On the strength of that meal, Elijah traveled for forty days and nights to Horeb, the mountain where several centuries earlier, God had given the Ten Commandments to Moses. This took 40 days because Elijah was probably randomly walking, and maybe hiding, as he escaped from Jezebel to Sinai.

At this time of spiritual emptiness in his prophetic career, God led him back to the roots of Jehovah worship; to the very mountain where Moses had been given the law. To Elijah, and the people of the chosen nation, there was no more important or sacred spot on earth. It was there that the word of the Lord came to Elijah asking (vs. 9), *"What doest thou here, Elijah?"* And Elijah replied:

I have been very jealous for the Lord God of hosts; for the children of Israel have forsaken thy covenant, thrown down thine altars, and slain thy prophets with the sword, and I, even I only, am left, and they seek my life, to take it away.

God patiently and gently commanded him to go outside. Suddenly, a great wind shook the mountain, but the Lord was not in the wind. The wind was followed by an earthquake that ripped split the mountains, but the Lord was not in the earthquake. *"And after the earthquake a fire; but the Lord was not in the fire and after the fire a still small voice."* (vs. 12) When he heard the voice, Elijah realized that he was in the presence of God. As he hid his face, God repeated His earlier question, *"What doest thou here, Elijah?"* Elijah repeated his original answer word for word. Two things were out of sync with Elijah's feelings at that time. First, he was feeling sorry for himself. He believed he was all alone and that the program of God was about to perish with him. In his self pity, Elijah believed he was in dispensable. Second, he had expected a more dramatic display of intervention by God to bring about the demise of Jezebel and the monarchy of Ahab in Jezreel. God was proving that neither one of those things was true or necessary.

First, in His display of the wind, earthquake, and fire, God was, in effect, saying, *"I do not need to use spectacular displays. The people of Israel attribute those kinds of phenomena to Baal. I can bring about My will without such physical phenomena. Therefore, Elijah, hear my answer to the two dilemmas you are facing."* The first part of God's answer was: *"Jehu the son of Nimshi shalt thou anoint to be king over Israel"* (vs. 16). We will discover later that Jehu is the one who carried out the demise of the house of Ahab. Part two (same verse) was: *"And Elisha the son of Shalphat of Abelmeholah shalt thou anoint to be prophet in thy room. I have left me seven thousand in Israel, all the knees which have not bowed unto Baal, and every mouth which hath not kissed him."*

Following this Divine encounter, Elijah continued on his mission. He now realized that the house of Ahab would be exterminated, but that it would not be by a spectacular Divine intervention, storm, earthquake, or fire; but at the hand of a man whom God had already chosen to do it. Also, he now knew that he was not indispensable. God had told him that his ministry would continue through Elisha (God is salvation) who was waiting, unknowingly, to replace him.

The last three verses of chapter 19 describe the call of Elisha. Then in chapter 20, we are introduced to Ben-hadad, II, who was king of Syria from 860 to 841 B.C. He had gathered a huge army, allied with himself thirty-two king of neighboring city-states, and went to war against Samaria, Ahab's capital. While he had the city under siege, he sent a letter to Ahab announcing Its plan and purpose. Once again, we must understand the background of siege warfare. Ben-hadad's message contained the conditions under which the city could surrender to him. *"Thy silver and thy gold is mine; thy wives also and thy children, even the goodliest, are mine"* (vs. 3). When Ahab agreed to the terms (vs. 4), Ben-hadad, pushed Ahab. In verse 6 he added:

I will send my servants unto thee tomorrow about this time, and they shall search thine house, and the houses of thy servants; and it shall be, that whatsoever is pleasant in thine eyes, they shall put it in their hand, and take it away.

This final demand was too much for Ahab. After consulting with his elders, he sent back a message of refusal. Ben-hadad's response to Ahab's refusal was, *"The gods do so unto me, and more also, if the dust of Samaria shall suffice for handfuls for all the people that follow me."* In Ben-hadad's mind, he had more people than there was dust in the streets. But the battle of words was not over. Ahab's reply to that is a classic retort which is still used today. *"Tell him, let not him that girdeth on his harness boast himself as he that putteth it off.'* (vs. 11) Ahab was saying when you are putting on your armor, you do not know whether you will take it off yourself or be brought back on your shield.

Ben-hadad received Ahab's message while he was in the midst of a drunken orgy with his officers. Nevertheless, he ordered his men to take up battle positions. Meanwhile, a prophet of the Lord went to Ahab and promised that his city would be delivered. The balance of the chapter, down through verse 25, describes how the victory was won. Ahab knew the Syrians would come back and they did. But the second time, they devised a new strategy, a logical one considering their *henotheistic* theology. Instead of confronting Ahab on the hill of Samaria, they chose another arena, saying, *"Their gods are gods of the hills; therefore they were stronger than we; but let us fight against them in the plain, and we be stronger than they."* A man of God went to Ahab with a message of victory. He said,

Thus saith the Lord, because the Syrians have said, the Lord is God of the hills, but he is not God of the valleys, therefore will I deliver all this great multitude into thine hand, and ye shall know that I am the Lord.

Rather than insulting Ahab, the Syrians had insulted Yahweh with their plan and strategy. Therefore, He would show them that He *is* the God of *all creation* . Hill, valley, or plain, made no difference to Jehovah. This was to be His victory, just as the earlier battle of Jericho. But, Ahab foolishly played the role of the benevolent victor. Although it had been God's battle, Ahab, in pompous kingly generosity, spared the life of Ben- hadad for much the same reason that Saul had spared Agag almost two hundred years earlier. Because of that act of self pride by Ahab, God sent a prophet with a warning. The prophet acted out a parable; a early example of *pedegogy in biography*. When Ahab pronounced judgment on the man the prophet was pretending to be, he was told that he had pronounced judgment on himself.

Naboth's Vineyard

In chapter 21, there is a further example of Ahab's wicked personality. Numbers 26:7 makes it very clear that an Israelite was not to transfer his inheritance outside of his immediate family, but these laws of God made no difference to Ahab. As he walked around outside his palace in Jezreel, he saw the small vineyard owned by Naboth and coveted it for himself. Approaching Naboth, he tried to strike a bargain (vs. 2):

> *Give me thy vineyard, that I may have it for a garden of herbs,*
> *because it is near unto my house: and I will give thee for it*
> *a better vineyard than it; or, if it seem good to thee, I will*
> *give thee the worth of it in money.*

Naboth, a God fearing man, understood the law better than Ahab, for he replied (vs. 3), *"The Lord forbid it me, that I should give the inheritance of my fathers unto thee.* Ahab, the evil despot, was accustomed to having whatever he wanted. He was so vexed by Naboth's refusal that he returned to his palace, laid down on his bed, turned his face to the wall and refused to eat. He sulked like a spoiled cud because he could not have the godly Israelite Naboth's little vineyard for a personal vegetable garden.

We now discover that Jezebel was the real power behind the throne. When she saw Ahab in this demented state, she taunted lam, *"Dost thou now govern the kingdom of Israel?"* Jezebel had no concept of God's ideal of the king as a shepherd or servant of the people. Then she added (vs. 7), *"Arise, and eat bread, and let thine heart be merry, I will give thee the vineyard of Naboth the Jezreelite."* Naboth's doom was sealed from the very moment that the wicked Queen Jezebel promised to acquire the vineyard. She wrote official letters accusing Naboth of sin and announcing a fast because of his *"evil"* deeds. She hired worthless men to testify against lam, and had him set *"on high"*; that is, on trial. They held a kangaroo court, and innocent Naboth, framed by Jezebel, lost his life.

They were obeying the law as stated in Deuteronomy 17:2-7, for a man accused of the crime of blasphemy. But in Naboth's case he was framed. The false witnesses perjured themselves by accusing Naboth, an innocent man, of blaspheming God and the king. If Naboth had been guilty of any other crime worthy of death, his property would have gone to his heirs; but since he was declared guilty of blasphemy, it was confiscated by the king. Through this trumped up trial and execution, the vineyard of Naboth was stolen, and his inheritance taken by an ungodly king and Ws wicked Baal-worshiping wife.

Ahab went to inspect his newly stolen property and met Elijah. His greeting to the prophet was certainly not cordial, *"Hast thou found me, 0 mine enemy?"* Elijah was not his enemy, but he certainly was his nemesis. It seems that he was on the scene whenever Ahab committed a particularly flagrant sin. This time he pronounced judgment against the house of Ahab. Contrary to his normal demeanor, this time Ahab humbled himself and although God spared him, He promised that He would carry out the judgment after Ws death; and: *"In the place where the dogs licked the blood of Naboth shall dogs lick thy blood, even thine "* (vs. 19).

In I Samuel, we were introduced to Samuel who, although he was a prophet, was also a judge and a priest. In I Kings, we were introduced to Elijah. He was a man who fully personified only the prophetic office. In ancient times there were two different categories of prophets. There was the *professional prophet*, who was not only in the land of Israel and Judah, but in the surrounding nations as well. The professional prophet was in the business for personal gain. He was not called by God, but chose his vocation to be a professional "yes" man.

Contrary to the professional prophet, the *classical prophet* was one whom God had called to the prophetic office. He was a prophet regardless of financial gain, opposition, even if his message would cost him his life. Until now we have seen only the *non-writing classical prophets*. Elijah did not write a book; neither did his successor Elisha. At this period in the middle ninth century B.C., we are only exposed to confrontations between the *classical non-writing prophets*, and the *professional prophets.*

Chapter 22 is the first example of this confrontation. Although Elijah's encounter on Carmel qualifies in a larger sense. During this period, Israel and Judah were united in an alliance against their common enemy, Syria. Verse 2 records that *"It came to pass in the third year, that Jehoshaphat the king of Judah came down to the king of Israel."* If that seems strange, one always goes *"down"* from Jerusalem even to go north, and *"up"* to Jerusalem even from the north. Ahab had a military exploit in mind. He had said, *"Know ye that Ramoth in Gilead is ours, and we be still, and take it not out of the hand of the king of Syria?"* Turning to his southern counterpart, he proposed to Jehoshaphat, *"Wilt thou go with me to battle to Ramoth-gilead?"* Jehoshaphat agreed with a single reservation. Jehoshaphat was a godly king and in 22:43, we were told that *"He walked in all the ways of Asa his father"* who was also a godly man. Verse 44 records that he *"made peace with the king of Israel."*

Being a godly king, Jehoshaphat wanted assurance that the Lord was in agreement with the proposal made by Ahab. So, before making his agreement official, he requested of Ahab, *"Enquire, I pray thee, at the word of the Lord today"* (vs. 5). Ahab called his four hundred professional prophets together and asked, *"Shall I go against Ramoth-gilead to battle, or shall I forbear?"* These professional prophets knew what the king wanted to hear and they answered as one man, *"Go up, for the Lord shall deliver it into the hand of the king."* The unanimous agreement of four hundred prophets should have been convincing, but Jehoshaphat was more discerning. Recognizing them as prophets of Baal, he asked Ahab, *"Is there not here a prophet of the Lord besides that we might enquire of him?"* There was one, Micaiah, the son of Imlah, but Ahab said, *"I hate him; for he doth not prophesy good concerning me, but evil."* Even so, Jehoshaphat wanted to hear from him regarding God's will in the proposal to go against Syria. Verse 10 is a scene of what court life in that time was like. While waiting for Micaiah to appear,

> *The king of Israel and Jehoshaphat the king of Judah sat*
> *each on his throne, having put on their robes, in a void*
> *place in the entrance of the gate of Samaria, and all the*
> *prophets prophesied before them.*

They were not in the palace, but at the city gate while the prophets of Baal were performing there publicly. One of them, named Zedekiah, made a pair of large iron horns which he put on his head, then bent down and ran around as if practicing for a bull fight. Pretending to gore everyone, he shouted: *"With these shalt thou push the Syrians, until thou have consumed them."* Meanwhile, the messenger who had been sent after Micaiah, tried to influence God's prophet, saying (vs. 13), *"Behold now, the words of the prophets declare good unto the king with one mouth: let thy word, I pray thee, be like the word of one of them, and speak that which is good."* Micaiah's stern reply was, *"What the Lord saith unto me, that will I speak."* When he came before the two monarchs, Ahab asked, *"Shall we go against Ramoth-gilead to battle, or shall we forbear?"* Micaiah's first reply was said with tongue-in-cheek. *"Go and prosper, for the Lord shall deliver it into the hand of the king."* Even wicked Ahab recognized that Micaiah was being sarcastic and demanded his true answer. Then he said, *"I saw all Israel scattered upon the hills, as sheep that have not a shepherd, and the Lord said, these have no master let them return every man to his house in peace."* He went on to explain that the Lord had put a lying spirit into the mouths of the prophets of Baal because *"The Lord hath spoken evil concerning thee."* (vs.23)

Zedekiah was incensed at that remark and struck Micaiah on the cheek, asking, *"Which way went the Spirit of the Lord from me to speak unto thee?* "He meant by this that *"You are the liar, Micaiah."* Ahab was angry at his response and had Micaiah put in prison on limited rations until, he said, "he returned." He never did! Nevertheless, the king was nervous over Micaiah's words. When they went up to the battle, Ahab said to Jehoshaphat, *"I will disguise myself, and enter into the battle; but put thou on thy robes."* When the Syrians saw Jehoshaphat, they thought he Ahab. Seeing he was not, they turned aside. Ahab, being disguised, thought he was safe. However, verse 34 explains, *"A certain man drew a bow at a venture, and smote the king of Israel between the joints of the harness."* God was behind the direction of the arrow that gave him a deadly wound. Immediately, Ahab began to bleed to death, but to keep up morale, his aides propped him up in the front of his chariot while his life blood drained out. His body was taken back to Samaria, the blood was washed from his chariot and his armor washed in the pool of Samaria where the harlots bathed, "and the dogs licked up his blood according to the word of the Lord which he spake by Elijah the prophet. The year was 853 B.C.

In 2017, archaeologists discovered a biblical title: "governor of the city." A clay seal was also found showing two persons and the inscription. II Kings 23:8 names Joshua as the governor under King Hezekiah. II Chronicles 18:25 names Amon as governor under King Jehoshaphat.

XLVIII. NORTHERN KINGDOM DEVELOPMENTS

The history of the monarchy in the southern kingdom of Judah is consistent. Except for a seven year period of usurpation by Athaliah, the lineage of David continued uninterrupted through dynastic succession generation after generation, without dramatic change or rebellion. The situation was quite to the contrary in the northern kingdom of Israel. Many of the kings who ruled there usurped the throne by assassinating their predecessors. As a result, nine different dynasties ruled in Israel, of which only two: the house of Omri (fourth dynasty); and the house of Jehu (fifth dynasty) achieved long-term stability. None of the others were able to hold the throne for more than two generations, and some for only one.

An Ungodly Alliance

Israel's relationship with Judah also made an about-face after the early years of warfare. In I Kings 22, we read that Jehoshaphat made
peace with the king of Israel. Now Jehoshaphat was a godly king who did *"that which was light in the eyes of the Lord"* (vs. 43). Nevertheless, he made one tragic mistake. It is not recorded in Kings but it is recorded in II Chronicles 18:1. *"Jehoshaphat had riches and honour in abundance, and joined affinity with Ahab."* He allied himself with the family of Ahab by marriage. In addition to his two sons, Ahaziah and Jehoram, who both later succeeded him on the throne, Ahab and Jezebel had a daughter named Athaliah. Athaliah seems to have been as fervent a Baal worshiper as was her evil old mother, Jezebel.
In 2017, during an excavation between Israel and Lebanon, a tiny sculpture was uncovered. It is believed to be a sculpture of a king. Because it dates to the 9th century B.C., it could be either Ahab, Jehu, Hazael, or King Ethbaal, Jezebel's father. (I Kings 16:31)

In a moment of weakness, or political expediency, Jehoshaphat agreed to a marriage between his son Joram and Athaliah. Joram, or Jehoram as he is also called, was the heir to the throne of Judah. Athaliah's brother, Ahaziah, had succeeded his father Ahab on the throne in Israel. For the first time in their histories, the rulers of the two kingdoms would be brothers-in-law. With this background in mind, we begin with the narrative in II Kings chapter 1.

During the first year of his reign in 852 B.C. {See 1:17} King Ahaziah, while walking on his roof, accidentally fell through the lattice work. Glass windows were unknown in that time, and braided wood, looking something like the decoration on a gazebo, kept the birds out and still allowed the wind to blow through. Evidently, Ahaziah apparently tripped and fell, injuring himself severely on jagged pieces of broken latticework. To obtain the prognosis for his recovery, he called for his messengers and ordered them to go to Baalzebub, the god of Ekron, to learn if he would recover from his injuries. Baalzebub was a Philistine god and Ekron was a Philistine city. Ahaziah was not as wise as his predecessor, of seventy eight years earlier, who founded the northern kingdom of Israel. When King Jeroboam's son became ill, he sent his wife to Ahijah, the prophet of God, to learn what the prognosis would be. But, things deteriorated spiritually in the northern kingdom and King Ahaziah decided to get an answer from a pagan god.

The Angel of the Lord informed Elijah that Ahaziah was seeking information from a pagan god. Elijah immediately confronted the messengers and told them Ahaziah would die. In fear, they returned to the king who asked, *"Why are ye now turned back?"* (1:5) They explained, *"There came a man up to meet us, and said unto us, is it because there is not a God in Israel, that thou sendest to enquire of Baalzebub the god of Ekron?"* When Ahaziah asked the man's identity, they described *"a hairy man, and girt with a girdle of leather about his loins."* Ahaziah knew immediately it was Elijah.

Ahaziah sent a cohort of fifty men to arrest the prophet. Because of their insulting attitude, Elijah called down fire upon them, killing the captain and his fifty. However, Ahaziah was not deterred. He sent out a second fifty men with the same deadly result. Still, in fury, he sent a third fifty. But, in fear and respect, this captain approached Elijah with caution and instead of issuing a command, implored him to spare his men and then to accompany him to the king. Elijah may have thought, "That's more like it!" To assure him, the Angel of the Lord said: *"Go down with him."* Elijah personally delivered God's sentence of death on the king for his evil life and for attempting to consult a pagan god. Verse 17 says,

He died according to the word of the Lord which Elijah had spoken. And Jehoram reigned in his stead in the second year of Jehoram the son of Jehoshaphat king of Judah; because he had no son.

For a brief time, there were two kings with the same name on the thrones of Israel and Judah. "Jehoram" and "Joram" are variant spellings for the same Hebrew name. Both forms are used in various passages for each king. Almost certainly, one was named after the other during a time of close friendship between the two nations. The official

synchronism for Joram's accession in Israel, given in II Kings 3: 1, is the eighteenth year of Jehoshaphat. However, at the close of the account of Ahaziah (11 Kings 1:17) we read that he was succeeded by Joram in the second year of Jehoram of Judah. From this we know that the eighteenth year of Jehoshaphat's reign was the
second year of Jehoram's co-regency. These two synchronisms for Joram's succession have often been regarded as contradictory and taken as evidence of an error. We can see that this was true in the early centuries before the Christian era because of the variant data in the Greek text (Septuagint) for these reigns.

In the Septuagint, the synchronism of II Kings 1: 17 has been altered from the second year of Jehoram to the eighteenth year of Jehoshaphat to make it agree with 11 Kings 3: 1. It should be noted that if Jehoram had been the sole ruler of Judah for two years before Joram came to the throne in Israel, then Jehoram began in Judah before Joram began in Israel. In such a case, Jehoram's record should have preceded that of Joram in the book of Kings. Such, however, is not the case. As we learned earlier regarding the development in Kings of the stepladder approach, if this were not true the system would be inconsistent.

XLIX. MIRACLES OF ELISHA

From II Kings 2:1 through 8:15, we are given an extensive history of the ministry of Elisha as it related to the northern kingdom of Israel. Chapter 2 records how Elijah was taken up by a whirlwind as he was guarded by the flaming chariots. As Elisha was leaving the scene of Elijah's miraculous ascension into heaven, his earlier request for a double portion of the Spirit was granted, when Elijah's mantle fell to the earth for him. He smote the Jordan river with the mantle as he had just seen Elijah do. The river parted and Elisha crossed over to the other side. When fifty prophets who had been watching at Jericho saw this miracle, they said, *"The spirit of Elijah doth rest on Elisha."* They came to meet him, and *"bowed themselves to the ground before him"* (vs. 15). As Elisha traveled toward Bethel, he was followed by a large group of youths who taunted him, saying, "Go up, thou bald head" (vs.23), evidently mocking the ascension of Elijah and daring him to do the same. Elisha turned and cursed them in the name of the Lord. Immediately, two she bears emerged from the woods and wounded forty-two of them.

Chapter 3 begins the narrative of Jehoram as he ascended the throne of the northern kingdom following the death of his brother Ahaziah.
According to the pronouncement of the Lord through Elijah, Jehoram,

wrought evil in the sight of the Lord; but not like his father, and like his mother; for he put away the image of Baal that his father had made. Nevertheless he cleaved unto the sins of Jeroboam the son of Nebat, which made Israel to sin; he departed not therefrom.

Unfortunately for himself and for his people, he returned to the calf worship that was created by Jeroboam, the founder of the northern kingdom. The end of chapter 3 records the defeat of the Moabites, as predicted by Elisha. The text describes how the king of Moab sacrificed his oldest son, who was to reign after him, offering him up on the wall of his city as a burnt offering. From that time on, the Moabites hated the Israelites intensely. Verse 27 says, "There *was great indignation against Israel."*

Elisha and the Shunammite Woman

Chapter 4 focuses on miracles of Elisha. Evidently, he had established a regular circuit for his ministry as Samuel had. One of the towns he frequently passed through was Shunem, where there was a wealthy woman who made a practice of offering him the traditional eastern hospitality. After a time, she and her husband built *"a prophet's chamber"* on the roof of their house where Elisha could turn in and rest anytime he chose to do so. Desiring to honor her for her thoughtfulness, he learned that she was childless and promised her that at the equivalent time in the following year she would have a son. The prophecy was fulfilled and a son was born as Elisha predicted.

When the boy was old enough to follow his father to the fields, he was stricken one day with an illness that brought on unbearable pain in his head. In a short time he was dead. His mother immediately sought out Elisha who was residing on Mount Carmel. Hearing the news, he sent his servant Gehazi ahead of him with his staff with orders to lay it across the face of the child. Gehazi did so, but according to verse 31, *"there was neither voice, nor hearing."* He returned to meet Elisha and reported, *"The child is not awaked."* Because of the climate and extreme temperatures in that part of the world, it was impossible to let a corpse stay above the ground for very long. Elisha would require more time to arrive on the scene than the faster Gehazi. Gehazi ran ahead and placed Elisha's staff on the child's face as a symbol of authority so that no one would move the body to bury it. Elisha realized that when he arrived the child must be in a place where he could get to him easily, not buried. Scripture seems to indicate that the staff was placed there as a symbol of authority rather than as an instrument for resurrection.

The remainder of II Kings 4 contains two additional miracles of Elisha; the poisoned pot which was made pure, and the bread which was multiplied to feed a hundred men. This was most certainly a miracle that anticipated the two similar ones wrought by the Lord Jesus Christ when he fed the multitudes on two separate occasions. Chapter 5 is the story of the healing of Naaman, the captain of the army of the king of Syria. Naaman was a leper, a disease for which there was no known cure. He heard from an Israelite slave girl, working in his house, that there was a prophet in Samaria who could cure him of his leprosy. Naaman went to the king of Syria who sent an official letter to the king of Israel, along with ten talents of silver, six thousand shekels of gold, and ten changes of garments. He wrote: *"Now when this letter is come unto thee, behold, I have sent therewith Naaman my servant to thee, that thou mayest recover him of his leprosy"* (vs. 6).

Jehoram was beside himself with fear and frustration. He tore his clothes and cried out, *"Am I god, to kill and to make alive, that this man doth send unto me to recover a man of his leprosy? See how he seeketh a quarrel against me"* (vs. 7) He could only imagine that the king of Syria was paying him in advance to perform an impossible service because he needed an excuse to make war on Israel. Elisha, having heard about the incident, sent word to Jehoram, asking, *"Wherefore hast thou rent thy clothes? Let him come now to me and he shall know that there is a prophet in Israel."*

When Naaman, with his pompous retinue of horses, chariots, and servants, stopped before Elisha's door, the prophet did not even give
him a personal welcome. Instead, he sent his servant outside with a message. "Go and wash in the Jordan seven times, and thy flesh shall come again to thee, and thou shalt be clean" (vs. 10). Naaman was furious at this lack of Elisha's deference for his exalted position. He raved, *"Behold I thought, He will surely come out to me, and stand, and call on the name of the Lord his God, and strike his hand over the place.."* Naaman wanted a spectacular show and not a simple task. Naaman continued raving, *"Are not Abana and Pharpar, rivers of Damascus, better than all the waters of Israel?"*

Naaman wanted God's healing, but he wanted to choose the place and method. When Elisha did not comply, he left in a rage. However, his servants demonstrated more wisdom than he did. Cautiously, they approached him and suggested: *"If the prophet had bid thee do some great thing, wouldest thou not have done it? How much rather then, when he saith to thee, wash, and be clean?"* Reluctantly, Naaman obeyed and dipped himself seven times in the Jordan. When he came out of the water the seventh time, his skin was soft like a little child. With the leprosy cured, he returned and stood before the prophet's door. This time he confessed, *"Now I know that there is no God in all the earth, but in Israel."*

He wanted to give Elisha the great wealth he had brought with him, but the prophet refused despite Naaman's insistence. As soon as Naaman left, a revealing scenario of greed and covetousness occurred. Gehazi, Elisha's servant, decided to run after the chariots and ask for some of Naaman's treasure. Perhaps he rationalized that he deserved it since Elisha did not take it. Naaman stopped his chariot, and Gehazi, claiming to speak for his master, asked for two changes of clothes and a talent of silver for *"two young men of the sons of the prophets"* who had just arrived at Elisha's home. Naaman was still so overjoyed that he took two changes of clothes and two talents of silver and sent them with two servants. Gehazi hid the clothes and silver in his house and sent the servants back.

When Gehazi returned to Elisha, he was asked: *"Where have you been, Gehazi?"* Adding to his recent deception, the servant replied, *"Thy servant went no whither."* Then, with a broken heart, Elisha confronted Him with the truth. *"Went not my heart with thee?"* Gehazi was so foolish. In the next chapter, we learn that Elisha had the gift of knowing what was happening beyond his physical vision; even in the bedrooms of enemy kings. Elisha looked with spiritual eyes and saw Gehazi, consumed with lust and greed, chasing Naaman's chariot. He would never get to enjoy the things he had taken, because the leprosy of Naaman would be on him for life.

Chapter 6 begins with the miracle of the floating axe head which provided a demonstration of God's sovereignty in the physical universe. Once again the king of Syria began to wage war against Israel. As Commander in Chief of his armed forces, he detailed the battle plan against Israel to his generals and commanders; ordering them to set up camps and lay siege to the city in specific places. Elisha sent word to Jehoram regarding each strategic location. The king of Israel would then send word to his troops to stay away from the designated place. Verse 10 says that in this way he saved himself "*not once or twice,*" meaning that Elisha helped many times.

The king of Syria became enraged, believing there must be a military leak somewhere: a traitor in his inner circle of officers who was sending information about his battle plans to the king of Israel. But, one of his officers advised him, explaining: "*Elisha the prophet that is in Israel, telleth the king of Israel the words that thou speakest in thy bedchamber.*" "*Go and fetch him*" the king commanded. What followed was the invasion by large numbers of men in the Syrian army against the city of Samaria. Elisha then miraculously delivered the city from the invasion by the Syrians.

The remainder of chapter 6, beginning in verse 24, is the account of another siege by the Syrians under King Ben-hadad. We are allowed to see firsthand the experiences of the inhabitants inside the city of Samaria in their determination to wait out the invading army lurking outside the wall. Evidently, they had not prepared for a long siege because, verse 25 says, they were eating donkey's heads and dove's dung. The situation was desperate. Finally, as Jehoram, the king of Israel, was passing by walking on the wall, a woman cried out for help. "*If the Lord do not help thee,*" "Jehoram replied, "W*hence shall I help thee? O out of the barn floor, or out of the winepress?*" The king confirmed the desperate situation by saying, "*I have no grain or wine with which to help you.*" The woman answered that she and her companion had eaten her son yesterday and were to eat the other woman's child that day, but the woman had hidden her child. Hearing this story, he rent his clothes and blamed Elisha.

Perhaps from his perspective, that was logical because in the previous invasion described in this chapter, it was Elisha who allowed all the Syrians to return to their land unharmed after he had miraculously caused them to be captured by the king's soldiers. But Elisha knew the king's intentions and he turned to those in the house with him and said, "*See ye how this son of a murderer hath sent to take away mine head*" (vs. 32) In chapter 7 Elisha promises deliverance for the city, saying that the very next day there would be an abundance of flour, so much that it would sell for only a shekel per measure. Two measures of barley would sell for one shekel. Compared to 6:25, when donkeys' heads and doves' dung were selling for exorbitant amounts, we can see what abundance there would be by contrast.

When the royal officer of the court, Jehoram's right hand man, heard it, he scoffed at the prophet. Elisha's response was, "*You will see it, but you will not benefit from it.*" The remaining verses in the chapter describe how the Lord caused the Syrian army to hear the sound of chariots and horses so that they believed that the king of Israel was coming out against them with hired mercenaries from the Hittites and the Egyptians. As a result, they panicked and fled. In their haste, they left behind all of their military provisions. When the people of Samaria heard of it, they crowded through the city gates to loot the deserted Syrian camp. In the stampede at the gate, the royal officer that had rebuked Elisha for his prophecy was trampled to death under the feet of the mob rushing to get out of the city and take the supplies left by the Syrian army.

L. THE FALL OF THE HOUSE OF AHAB

We have now reached the history of the two kingdoms when they are friendly because of political and personal ties. This resulted in a situation which had tragic results in the south and came perilously close to extinguishing the lineage of David.

Jehoram Becomes King

In II Kings 8:16, *"In the fifth year of Joram the son of Ahab, king of Israel, Jehoshaphat being then king of Judah, Jehoram the son of Jehoshaphat king of Judah began to reign."* The wording here suggests an overlap (co-regency) by Jehoshaphat and Jehoram in Judah. When his father died and Jehoram was alone on the throne in the south, he did a heinous thing in the sight of God. To learn about it we must turn to II Chronicles 21:4, which says, *"Now when Jehoram was risen up to the kingdom of his father, he strengthened himself, and slew all his brethren with the sword, and divers also of the princes of Israel."* This ungodly king was in the messianic lineage of David. To secure his position he killed all of his brothers and close relatives. Not only did Jehoram commit this heinous crime, but II Kings adds: *"He walked in the way of the kings of Israel, as did the house of Ahab."* Baalism was now in Judah. Why? Verse 18 has the answer: *"For the daughter of Ahab was his wife: and he did evil in the sight of the Lord."* His wife was Athaliah, the daughter of Ahab and Jezebel. Now, she was the Queen in Judah.

Think for a moment about the continuing saga of Satan's attempt to prevent the promise of Genesis 3:15 from coming to pass. Satan is subtle and very patient. To put into the southern kingdom a woman who powerful enough to prevent the seed lineage of David from continuing, Satan began two generations earlier with Omri, king of Israel, by inducing him to arrange a marriage between Jezebel and his son Ahab. Athaliah waited patiently while her husband was co-regent with his father. Immediately after the death of Jehoshaphat, she must have begun urging him to do something quickly before his brothers took away his throne. In response, Jehoram murdered all six of his brothers and anyone else who might cause a threat to his position as king. Athaliah had now secured her husband's position in Judah and but also hers as Queen.

When we studied the life of Elisha in II Kings 2:1-8:15, following warned the miraculous ascension to heaven by Elijah, we noticed an overlap between Jehoram's reign in Judah and the ministry of these prophets. In II Chronicles 21:12ff we learn that prior to Elijah's ascension, God used him, with a written letter, to rebuke Jehoram.

And there came a writing to him from Elijah the prophet, saying, Thus saith the Lord God of David thy father, because thou hast not walked in the ways of Jehoshaphat thy father, nor in the ways of Asa king of Judah, But hast walked in the way of the kings of Israel, and hast made Judah and the inhabitants of Jerusalem to go a whoring, like to the whoredoms of the house of Ahab, and also hast slain thy brethren of thy father's house, which were better than thyself. Behold, with a great plague will the Lord smite thy People, and thy children, and thy wives, and all thy goods: And thou shalt have great sickness by disease of thy bowels, until thy bowels fall out by reason of the sickness day by day.

In 21:19

"And it came to pass, that in the Process of time, after the end of two years, his bowels fell out by reason of his sickness: so he died of sore diseases. And his people made no burning for him, like the burning of his fathers."

Second Chronicles 22:1ff records:

"The inhabitants of Jerusalem made Ahaziah his youngest son king in his stead. So Ahaziah, the son of Jehoram the king of Judah reigned. Forty and two years old was Ahaziah when he began to reign, and he reigned one year in Jerusalem."
His mother's name also was Athaliah the daughter of Omri [Granddaughter]. He also walked in the ways of the house of Ahab: for his mother was his counselor to do wickedly. Wherefore he did evil in the sight of the Lord like the house of Ahab: for they were his counselors after the death of his father to his destruction.

*He walked also after their counsel, and went with Jehoram
the son of Ahab king of Israel to war against Hazael king
of Syria at Ramoth-gilead. And the Syrians smote Joram.
And he returned to be healed in Jezreel because of the wounds
which were given him at Ramah.*

The two kingdoms, Israel and Judah, now had relatives on their respective thrones. Joram, the son of Ahab, was king in Israel. His sister, Athaliah, was Queen mother in Judah, and his nephew, Ahaziah, the son of Athaliah, was king in Judah. Uncle and nephew then joined together to go to battle against their common enemy, Syria. Joram was wounded and went to Jezreel to recover. Shortly after that, Ahaziah decided to visit him and traveled north to see him. At that point in time the narrative changes focus.

Jehu's Coup

t was now time for God to act. Remember how He had instructed Elijah to anoint Jehu king of Israel? That instruction had been passed to Elisha. In fulfillment, Elisha sent one of the sons of the prophets to Ramath-gilead to find Jehu and speak to him alone, saying, *"I have anointed thee king over Israel."* After pouring the anointing oil on his head, the young man was to leave and run like the wind. Second Kings 9:4ff describes how he carried out Elisha's command. He spoke and then he opened the door and ran.

*Thus saith the Lord God of Israel, I have anointed thee king
over the people of the Lord, even over Israel. And thou shalt
smite the house of Ahab thy master, that I may avenge the
blood of my servants the prophets, and the blood of all the
servants of the Lord, at the hand of Jezebel. For the whole
house of Ahab shall perish: and I will cut off from Ahab
every male heir and I will make the house of Ahab like
the house of Jeroboam the son of Nebat, and like the house
of Baasha the son of Ahijah: and the dogs shall eat Jezebel
in the portion of Jezreel, and there shall be none to bury her.*

When questioned by his companions, Jehu repeated the young prophet's words. Immediately, the men removed their clothes to make a "red carpet" for Jehu. They blew a trumpet and shouted, *"Jehu is king."* He was anointed and appointed to be God's man for the spiritual revolution in the north. It was no wonder his men were pleased. They had served him well and with him as king, their positions in the kingdom were automatically elevated.

But there was one problem. Joram was currently the king of the northern kingdom. Jehu's actions would be tantamount to treason. It was to be a military *coup*. But, it was a God-ordained military *coup* because the man on the throne was not a God-ordained king. The time had come to fulfill the prophecy made by Elijah to Ahab years ago in Naboth's vineyard. Jehu mobilized his forces and began to drive his chariots toward Jezreel where the king of Israel was recuperating and enjoying a visit by his nephew, the king of Judah. The man in the watchtower of Jezreel saw the approaching chariots and reported them to the king who ordered him to send a horseman to inquire whether it was a friend or enemy. If it was an enemy, the gates of the city would be closed.

Jehu replied to the messenger's question by suggesting if he wanted to save his life he had better join them. The messenger joined Jehu. A second messenger received the same advice and also joined Jehu. By this time, the watchman recognized that by the way the charioteer drove his chariot it must be Jehu, whose reputation preceded him. Not knowing about the anointing of Jehu, there was no reason for Joram to distrust him. He and Ahaziah, each in his own chariot, went out to meet Jehu where he was waiting by the vineyard of Naboth. As they approached, Joram called out, *"Is it peace, Jehu?" "And he answered, what Peace, so long as the whoredoms of thy mother Jezebel and her witchcrafts are so many?"* Hearing these words, Joram shouted to his nephew, *"There is treachery, 0 Ahaziah."* At that time, Jehu shot an arrow into the Joram's back and he crumpled in his chariot. Turning to an officer, Jehu commanded, *"Take up and cast him in the portion of the field of Naboth the Jezreelite."* When he turned and saw Ahaziah, the king of Judah escaping in his chariot, he decided to kill him also. Jehu pursued Ahaziah and shot him. Ahaziah died and his servants carried him in his chariot back to Jerusalem for burial.

The Death of Jezebel

Leaving Naboth's vineyard, Jehu drove toward the city of Jezreel. Jezebel already knew what had happened. When Jehu arrived in his chariot, she screamed through the window at him: *"Had Zimri peace, who slew his master?"* That was a reference to the slaying of Elah by Zimri years earlier. Zimri, you recall, lasted only seven days as king. Looking up toward the window, Jehu called out, "Who is on my side?" Several officials looked down. They knew their lives depended on which side they chose. *"Throw her down,"* Jehu commanded them. They picked up the aged Jezebel, who had painted her eyes and adorned her head before going to the window, and threw her down to the street below. When she landed in a broken heap, Jehu and his men ran over her with their chariots. As they did, her blood was splattered on the wall and on the horses as they trampled her underfoot.

Jehu entered the city as the conquering monarch. He ate and drank, then said, *"Go, see now this cursed woman, and bury her: for she is a king's daughter."* (9:34) But those who went could find nothing except her skull, her feet, and the palms of her hands. The dogs had eaten the rest of her body. When they returned and told Jehu, he said, *"This is the word of the Lord which he spake by His servant Elijah the Tishbite, saying, in the portion of Jezreel shall dogs eat the flesh of Jezebel."* Elijah's prophecy to Ahab which was made years before in Naboth's vineyard was now fulfilled.

LI. REFORMATION IN ISRAEL AND JUDAH

After assassinating the kings of Israel and Judah, and taking the throne of Israel according to the word of the servant of Elisha, Jehu still had two divinely appointed tasks ahead of him; to destroy the house of Ahab, and to rid the land of Baalism. After learning that Ahab had seventy sons in Samaria (probably by women of his harem), Jehu sent word to the elders and to those responsible for raising the young princes, challenging them to declare the best qualified son as king and to engage in battle against him and defend Ahab's dynasty. After all, they had the advantage of horses, chariots, armor, and a walled city. After holding counsel together, the officials decided they could not prevail against this "usurper" who had already killed two kings. In fear, they sent a message of surrender. Jehu commanded them to decapitate Ahab's seventy sons and send their heads to him. After they obeyed, Jehu put the severed heads in two baskets and sent them to Jezreel with instructions to place them in "two heaps" at the entrance to the city. Second Kings 10:11-17 completes the narration of how Jehu eliminated everyone who was related to or associated with Ahab.

With the first task completed, Jehu turned quickly to eliminating Baalism. The description of that effort begins in 10:18. He was much too crafty to let his intentions be known. If he had announced that he was going to kill every Baal worshiper, it probably would have been difficult to find one. Instead, according to verse 18, "*Jehu gathered all the people together, and said unto them, Ahab served Baal a little; but Jehu shall serve him much.*" He ordered all the priests of Baal to be summoned and those all who worshiped Baal. "*Let none be wanting [missing]: for I have a great sacrifice to do to Baal. whosoever shall be wanting, he shall not live.*" But, the Scripture adds, "*Jehu did it in subtlety, to the intent that he might destroy the worshipers of Baal.*"

Jehu proclaimed a solemn assembly for Baal throughout the land. Verse 21 says "*The house of Baal was full from one end to another.*" Then, to be sure the Baal worshipers could be easily recognized, he supplied garments for them. He stationed his men around the house of Baal and threatened that if they allowed any Baal worshiper to escape, "*he that letteth him go, his life shall be for the life of him.*" (vs. 24) When the sacrifices to Baal were completed, he ordered his men to begin the slaughter. After slaying all the Baal priests and worshipers, his men burned the images of Baal and razed his house. Verse 28 concludes, *"Thus Jehu destroyed Baal out of Israel."*

The period in Israel's history, dominated by the sin of Ahab, ended in 841 B.C. However, Jehu did not continue to complete his religious reforms. Verse 29 says, *"Howbeit from the sins of Jeroboam the son of Nebat, who made Israel to sin, Jehu departed not from after them, to wit, the golden calves that were in Bethel, and that were in Dan."* But, as a reward for the work he had done, the Lord promised Jehu the longest dynasty Israel was to experience: four generations. Because of his incomplete obedience, his reign of twenty-eight years
was troubled by harassment from neighboring nations. Verse 31 is his epitaph:

> *"But Jehu took no heed to walk in the law of the Lord God of Israel with all his heart, for*
> *he departed not from the sins of Jeroboam, which made Israel to sin."*

The period in Israel that began in 841 and lasted until 722 B.C., was the *half-reform of Jehu*; because that is exactly what it was, a half return, and not a full return, to the worship of Jehovah.

South in Judah, reform was delayed because of the influence of Ahab's daughter Athaliah. Second Kings 11contains the story of her usurpation and downfall. As soon as she learned of the assassination of her son Ahaziah by Jehu, she began to murder her grandchildren and secured her position as Queen. This had been Satan's plan: to destroy the lineage of David. It almost succeeded! But God was faithful to His promises in Genesis 3:15 and II Samuel 7. In 11: 2:

> *But Jehosheba, the daughter of King Joram, sister of Ahaziah,*
> *took Joash the son of Ahaziah, and stole him from among the*
> *king's sons which were slain; and they hid him, him and*
> *his nurse, in the bedchamber from Athaliah, so he was not slain.*

Satan's glee over the work of the evil queen must have turned to dismay when Joash was rescued. God's promise was safe, embodied in the life of a helpless infant. Athaliah had reigned in Judah for six years, from 841 to 835 B.C. In her seventh year Jehoiada the priest gathered together the royal bodyguards, and instructed them to surround the young Joash with weapons in their hands and to put to death anyone who went within their ranks. These personal bodyguards were to be with Joash wherever he went. Finally, they brought Joash, the only remaining descendant of David into the temple and placed the crown on his head.

They anointed him king and clapped their hands shouting, *"God save the king."* (vs. 12) When Athaliah saw that she had a living grandson, and that the crown had been placed on him, she rent her clothes and screamed, *"Treason, treason."* What nerve it took for this wicked woman who had murdered her own grandchildren and usurped the throne, to call this treason when the rightful heir was crowned. The soldiers dragged her to the horse gate of the king's house and slew her there. Jehoiada made a covenant between the Lord, the king, and the people. He reestablished the worship of Jehovah. Joash was seven years old when he became king of Judah.

Joash reigned for forty years. Second Kings 12:2 tells us he *"did that which was right in the sight of the Lord all his days wherein Jehoiada the priest instructed him."* The high places were not removed, but Joash was concerned about the Lord's house. He made arrangements with the priests whereby anyone whose heart the Lord touched might bring money in to repair and refurbish the temple. It had been broken up by the sons of Athaliah who had also taken objects dedicated to Jehovah and used them in the worship of Baal.

When in the twenty-third year of his reign, the work still had not been started Jehoiada took a little chest and bored a hole in the lid. He placed it on the right side of the altar and instructed the priests who guarded the threshold to put into it all the money brought in to the temple. When sufficient money had been collected, they hired workmen, bought timber and other materials, and repaired the house of the Lord. At about that time, Jerusalem was threatened by Hazael, the king of Syria who had just captured Gath. Joash bought him off with a great amount of dedicated things which had been saved from the time of Jehoshaphat, including gold from the treasury of the temple and of the palace.

Second Chronicles 24 adds further information about the reign of Joash (Jehoash). In II Kings 12:2, we read that Joash did right as long as Jehoiada the priest instructed him. In 11 Chronicles 24:15ff, we learn that after Jehoiada died at the advanced age of 130, the princes of Judah began to flatter Joash and influence him. Their hearts were still with Baalism and under their influence the house of God was once again neglected and the people began worshiping Asherim and other idols. As a result, *"wrath came upon Judah and Jerusalem for this their trespass"* (vs. 18). Still the Lord tried to reach them, because,

He sent prophets to them, to bring them again unto the Lord,
and they testified against them; but they would not give ear.
And the spirit of God came upon Zechariah the son of Jehoiada
the priest, which stood above the people.

The prophet Zechariah rebuked them in the name of the Lord for their transgressions, pointing out that they were not prospering *"because ye have forsaken the Lord"* and *"he hath also forsaken you"* (vs. 20). In verse 21 we read a tragic statement: *"They conspired and stoned him with stones at the commandment of the king in the court of the house of the Lord."* The year was aound 797. King Joash had forgotten the kindness of Jehoiada and approved the murder of his son. Zechariah's dying words were, *"The Lord look upon it, and require it."* {See Luke 11:51}

After that, God's chastening rods were turned on Joash. From then on it was all downhill for his monarchy. The Syrians attacked with a very small band (II Chron. 24:24), and the Lord delivered a very great army of Judah into their hands, *"because they had forsaken the Lord God of their fathers."* Joash's people then turned against him, leaving him alone and sick. Two of his servants conspired and murdered him in his bed because of the blood of Zechariah.

The reign of Joash's son Amaziah is covered in greater detail in II Chronicles than in II Kings. One of his first acts after being placed on the throne was to kill his father's murderers. However, II Chronicles 25:4 says, he spared their children because he knew the law of Moses said fathers should not be put to death for the sins of their sons, nor sons for their fathers (Deut. 24:16). Each man must die for his own sin.

Second Chronicles 25:5 informs us that Amaziah numbered the men of war in Judah; 300,000. Then, to strengthen himself he went to the northern kingdom and hired 100,000 Ephraimites for one hundred talents of silver. A man of God came to the king and said, *"Let not the army of Israel go with thee; for the Lord is not with Israel."* Amaziah complained because he had already paid them. But the man of God said, *"The Lord is able to give thee much more than this."* Reluctantly, Amaziah sent the mercenaries home; but they were so angry that they raided Judah as they departed. The king paid dearly for his lack of faith and his confidence in numbers by hiring the mercenaries to add to his army. With his own men, he went into the Valley of Salt and struck down 10,000 Edomites and captured another 10,000 alive Then, led them to the top of a cliff and commanded his men to throw them off.

Although he was descendant of the royal house of David, and included in the Davidic Covenant, he practiced henotheism. When he returned home from the war with the Edomites, he brought the gods of Seir and set them up as his gods. He bowed down, and burned incense to them. Look at I Chronicles 14:12 for a comparison between King

Amaziah and his ancestor King David, the man who was the spiritual role model for all the kings who would follow. After defeating an enemy, David burned their gods. He wanted nothing to do with the gods of other nations. Contrariwise, Amaziah, one of his progeny, worshiped the gods of the army he had defeated. God angered at his foolish and wicked idolatry, sent a prophet to ask (II Chron. 25:15), *"Why hast thou sought after the gods of the people, which could not deliver their own people out of thine hand?"*

As he was speaking, the king asked him angrily, *"Art thou made of the king's counsel? Forbear, why shouldest thou be smitten? "* The prophet replied, *"I know that God hath determined to destroy thee.*

Soon afterward, Amaziah sent a declaration of war to Joash, the king of Israel. Even though the king of Israel tried to appeal to him not to start something he could not finish, accusing him of pride because of his defeat of the Edomites, and warning, *"Why shouldest thou meddle to thine hurt, that thou shouldest fall, even thou, and Judah with thee? "* (vs. 19) Amaziah would not listen because of pride. It was God's will to chastise him for worshipping the Edomite gods. The armies of Israel and Judah met in battle. Judah was quickly defeated and every man fled to his tent. Joash captured Amaziah and took him to Jerusalem. He tore down 600 feet of the wall around Jerusalem, from the gate of Ephraim to the corner gate. He took the gold, silver, and the utensils, even hostages, and returned to Samaria. Amaziah was now a crushed and defeated man. God's judgment had fallen heavily on him. Rebellion was in the air and the people of Jerusalem began to conspire against him. He fled for his life to Lachish, but he was pursued and assassinated. His constituents (and assassins) took Uzziah, his sixteen-year-old son, and crowned him king: Jeremiah 34:7. Google the *Lachish Letters*.

At this point in time, we must begin with the narrative in 11 Kings 14:23: *"In the fifteenth year of Amaziah the son of Joash king of Judah, Jeroboam the son of Joash king of Israel began to reign in Samaria, and reigned forty and one years."* This king of Israel is usually referred to as Jeroboam, II, because he was named after the founder of the nation of Israel, Jeroboam, I. It was a suitable name for him because verse 24 says, "He *did that which was evil in the sight of the Lord, he departed not from all the sins of Jeroboam the son of Nebat, who made Israel to sin."* He took the throne and practiced the old religion of Jeroboam, I by instituting the worship of the golden calves at Bethel and Dan. As evil as he was, there was a strange irony about Iam. Archaeologists have discovered coins from the middle ninth century B.C., with the name of Jeroboam, II on them. The inscription reads, *"Jeroboam, the servant of God."* It is one thing for a man to call himself a servant of God, for it may or may not be true. It is quite another thing when God calls a man His servant. Militarily, Jeroboam, II was a great king. He expanded the northern kingdom to almost the same geographical size as had been promised to Abraham and was accomplished by David when he was king over both Israel and Judah.

His contemporary in the south was Uzziah. With the combined exploits of King Jeroboam, II and King Uzziah, the two nations reached an economic level which had not been attained since the time of Solomon, and a geographical expansion not reached since the time of David and Solomon. Outwardly, it was an era of tremendous prosperity, but inwardly it was a time of spiritual decadence and decay. What reforms the nations had experienced in the past had been half-hearted and superficial.

LII. THE RISE OF ASSYRIA

Beginning with the accession of Jehu to the throne of Israel, the Assyrians, who had become increasingly influential among the surrounding nations, began to exert extensive military and political pressure on the northern kingdom. Archaeologists have unearthed a six foot high stela known as Shalmanezer's obelisk. It was carved by order of Shalmaneser, 111, the king of Assyria between 858 and 824 B.C. Its pictorial section shows Jehu bowing down and paying tribute, so he would not invade Israel. From the reign of Shalmaneser, 111, onward in history, the Old Testament shows consistent and increasing pressure on Israel by the Assyrians until they completely destroyed and dispersed the nation in 722 B.C. Some of the other Assyrian kings who had impact during this period were Shalmaneser, IV, who reigned from 782 to 773 B.C.; Tiglath-pileser, 111, also called Pul (745-727); Shalmaneser, V (727-722); Sargon, II (721-705); Sennacherib (704-681); Esarhaddon (681-660); and Ashurbanipal (669-633). It was Judah who dealt with those kings who reigned after Shalmaneser, V. There were three others, but their influence was not as extensive as that of their predecessors.

In 2014, ISIS destroyed the Shrine of Jonah in Mosel. On the mound there, archaeologists discovered the remains of the palace of the Assyrian King, Esarhaddon. (I I Kings 19:36-37; Isaiah 37:37, 38.)

When we study the Old Testament, we often think of Israel and Judah as if they operated in a historical vacuum. Although they were of utmost importance because God was working through them, they were tiny nations in the civilized world. To put Israel and Judah in a historical context, we should know what was happening in the rest of the world between 900 B.C. and 700 B.C.

Between 900 B.C. and 800 B.C., the Phoenicians settled in Cyprus and the Dorians conquered the city of Corinth. The Iliad and the Odyssey, the Greek epics ascribed to Homer, were written. Ashurbanipal, II, of Assyria, rebuilt the capital city of Calah, and designed a new palace with highly descriptive ornate wall paintings. The favorite sport in Calah was hunting Eons from chariots. Between 800 and 700 B.C., the Greeks settled on the coast of Spain. In Crete a rivalry developed among the ancient city-states. In 753, the foundations of the city of Rome were laid. A woman began to reign as high priestess of

Thebes in Egypt, and Apollo began to be worshiped in Delphi. Up in Assyria, construction began on the royal palace in Nineveh. The Babylonians produced a five tone and a seven tone scale as well as the earliest known written music. This was a hymn written in cuneiform on a tablet discovered in Samaria. In Greece, music became part of daily life. Homer referred to highly developed battlefield surgery. Spoke wheels and horseshoes began to be used in Europe. In Assyria, the military began to use animal bladders as aids to swimming in warfare.

The first recorded Olympic Games were in 776, although they had possibly existed since 1350. They were celebrated every fourth year and featured horse-racing, wrestling, boxing, the pentathlon, and running. The *hoplitodromos*, a race carrying a shield and spear, is an illustration in Hebrews 12:1. Grecian vases show the runner throwing off these items to run faster. Romulus, the first king of Rome, divided the year into ten months and his successor, Numa Pompilius, who according to fable, reigned from 715 to 672 B.C., added January and February.

Second Kings 15:1 introduces Azariah, {Uzziah}. His reign is also in 11 Chronicles 26. Everything considered, he was a good king. He waged war with great power. He had skillful men who could create engines of war to be used for shooting arrows and throwing large stones. It appears that he had catapults and machinery that could shoot a number of arrows at a time. Although through most of his life he was a great king and one who sought God, unfortunately, verse 16 begins a sad account. Because of his accomplishments, Uzziah became proud. As a result, he acted corruptly and was unfaithful to the Lord. He had come to think that nothing could stand in his way; that he could do anything; even perform the office of the priest. So, he entered the temple, planning to burn incense on the altar. In the provisions made for a king in Deuteronomy 17, we read that he was to have his personal devotional copy of the law of God. If he had been consistent with his devotional copy of the law, he would have remembered that Numbers 16:40 commanded,

> *To be a memorial unto the children of Israel, that no stranger*
> *[i.e. layman], which is not of the seed of Aaron, come near to*
> *offer incense before the Lord, that he be not as Korah, and his*
> *company: as the Lord said to him by the hand of Moses.*

When Uzziah, who was of the lineage of David and not Aaron, entered the temple to offer incense, the priests, led by Azariah, tried to stop him. When he would not stop, God struck him with leprosy. He remained a leper, isolated in his house for a number of years while Jotham Ms son served as co-regent and actually reigned over Judah. Jotham must have learned a lesson from his father's experience because chapter 27:2 tells us that *"He did that which was right in the sight of the Lord, according to all that his father Uzziah did. Howbeit he entered not into the temple of the Lord."* He became a mighty warrior king, walking obediently before the Lord his God. Jotham was co-regent with his father from 750 to 739 B.C., and reigned by himself from 739 to 735 B.C.

While Uzziah was reigning in Judah, prior to being isolated with leprosy, other intense activities, recorded in II Kings 15, were taking place in the North. Zechariah, the son of Jeroboam, 11, the fourth generation monarch who had been promised to Jehu, became king over Israel but reigned for only six months. According to verse 9-10,

> *He did that which was evil in the sight of the Lord, as his fathers*
> *had done: he departed not from the sins of Jeroboam, the son of*
> *Nebat, who made Israel to sin. And Shallum the son of Jabesh*
> *conspired against him, and smote him before the people, and*
> *slew him, and reigned in his stead.*

Shallum reigned for one month. In a *coup*, Menahem assassinated him and became king in his place. Menahem reigned ten years and he also did evil in the sight of the Lord. In verse 19 we are introduced to Pul, {Tiglath-pileser}, the king of Assyria. When he threatened Israel, Menahem bought him off with a thousand talents of silver so *"that his hand might be with him;"* To obtain this much silver, everyone in the kingdom was assessed fifty shekels of silver. *"So the king of Assyria turned back and stayed not there in the land"* (vs. 20). After ten years, Menahem died and his son Pekahiah became king. He reigned for two years and also did evil. Then Pekah, one of his military officers, assassinated him in the palace at Samaria. Pekah sat on the throne for twenty years and he also did evil, departing not from the sins of Jeroboam. Pekah ironically was in turn assassinated by Hoshea, who became Israel's final king.

The growing threat of Assyria was also affecting political decisions in Judah. II Kings 16 describes the reign of Ahaz, the son of Jotham. Ahaz reigned for sixteen years beginning at age twenty, but he *"did not that which was fight in the sight of the Lord his God, like David his father"* (vs. 2). Ahaz was so evil that he began to walk in the ways of the kings Israel. He participated in human sacrifices and we learn from II Chronicles 28, that he made molten images to Baal, offered sacrifices, and burned incense under every green tree in the land. II Chronicles 28:3 reports that he was even *more* abominable than the nations whom the Lord had driven out before the children of Israel. Which is another way of saying that Ahaz was worse than the Canaanites that Joshua had been commanded to destroy.

II Chronicles records some activities of Ahaz which are not included in II Kings. Verse 5 says that God delivered him into the hand of the king of Assyria. We also read in verse 10 that following a battle with Pekah, the king of Israel, a prophet of God named Obed rebuked Pekah and his elders when they attempted to keep captives from Judah and Jerusalem as slaves. The elders of Israel obeyed the prophet, verse 14 says and *"left the captives and the spoil before the Princes, and all the congregation. "*

In verse 16 we read, *"At that time did king Ahaz send unto the king of Assyria to help him."* We need to return to II Kings 16 for additional details about this very important event. Second Kings 16:5 says that *"Rezin, king of Syria and Pekah son of Remaliah king of Israel came up to Jerusalem to war and they besieged Ahaz, but could not overcome him."* Israel and Syria attacking Jerusalem, was Ahaz's motivation for seeking an unwise alliance with the Assyrians. He took the silver and gold from the house of the Lord, and the king's house, and sent these treasures to Assyria as a bribe for the king. So, Tiglath-pileser went to war against Damascus, killing Rezin the king. He also captured several cities of Israel and took many of them as captives. It was about this time that Hoshea conspired against Pekah, probably motivated by his loss to the Assyrians. He was, however, too weak to oppose the Assyrians. Hoshea became a vassal king, and was forced to pay tribute to Assyria as his predecessors had.

The agreement Ahaz made with Tiglath-pileser would have later consequences for Judah. II Chronicles 28 describes how the Edomites, and later the Philistines, devastated Judah because Ahaz had *"transgressed sore against the Lord"* (vs. 19). Tiglath-pileser came, but afflicted him rather than strengthening him. Verse 21 says *"He helped him not."*

LIII. SIEGE OF TWO CITIES

The king of Assyria continued to be very aggressive toward the two kingdoms. At the request of Ahaz, and in consideration of his generous tribute payments, he moved from his victory in Damascus down into Israel. While Tiglath-pileser was still at Damascus, Ahaz had gone up to greet him. While there, he admired an elaborate pagan altar and sent some of his priests to make a replica and place it in the temple at Jerusalem. Not only did he offer sacrifices on it, but he also dismantled some of the worship objects in the temple that had been constructed by Solomon, making God's temple a place of heathen worship. Verse 18 says he did these things *"for the king of Assyria."*

The End of the Divided Kingdom

By the time of the events recorded in 11 Kings 17, Tiglath-pileser had passed from the scene and Shalmaneser, V was king of Assyria. The king of Israel, Hoshea, whom you recall had become a vassal to Assyria, decided it was time to rebel. He did by refusing to send the customary tribute to Assyria and sought an alliance with Egypt. It was a bad move by Hoshea. The king of Assyria captured Hoshea and put him in prison. Then he besieged the city of Samaria for three years, from 725 to 722 B.C. In 722, the city was taken. Verse 6 says he *"carried Israel away into Assyria, and placed them in Halah and in Harbor by the liver of Gozan, and in the cities of the Medes."* This verse brings to a close the history of the nation of Israel and ends the 209 year period of the divided kingdom. Although the Assyrians were accustomed to conquest, as they expanded their campaigns throughout the known world, they did not have enough troops to occupy every city or nation they defeated. This has been a major difficulty experienced by conquering armies: how to keep the conquered nations under control. The Assyrians had an answer. They mixed up the populations in the cities they conquered.

Origin of the Samaritans

Second Kings 17:24ff is a summary of this military tactic as it was used by the Assyrians in Samaria:

"And the king of Assyria brought men from Babylon, and from Cuthah, and from Ava, and from Hamath, and from Sepharvaim, and placed them in the cities of Samaria instead of the children of Israel: and they possessed Samaria, and dwelt in the cities thereof."

The king of Assyria sent the wealthy and influential people of Israel to other conquered areas and took captives from other nations and sent them to Samaria. The result was a new mixed race of people who became known as the Samaritans. From 722 B.C. to the time of our Lord Jesus Christ as recorded in John 4, the inhabitants of the land of Samaria were a hated people. They were mixed racially and religiously (see II Kings 17:26-34). The Jews who lived in the south had nothing to do with them. There was as little contact as possible between the two nations.

In II Kings 17:7-18, God lists the reasons why He allowed the Assyrians to disperse the nation of Israel. They feared other gods;
 they walked in the customs of the nations whom the Lord had driven out; they did things secretly which were not right; they built high places; they set for themselves sacred pillars; they served idols. The Lord gave them many warnings through the prophets, saying, *"Turn ye from your evil ways, and keep my commandments,"* but they did not listen. They stiffened their necks. They followed vanity and went after all the heathen gods that surrounded them. They forsook the commandments of the Lord and made molten images, especially the two calves. They worshiped all the host of heaven (astrology) and served Baal. They made their sons and their daughters to pass through the fire; that is, they offered their own children as human sacrifices. They practiced divination and enchantments. In the end, the Lord was so angry with Israel (vs. 18) He removed them from His sight. None was left except the tribe of Judah. In 722 B.C., the divided kingdom ended. The period known as *Judah Alone,* began.

Ahaz, the king of Judah, died in 715 B.C. and his son Hezekiah inherited the throne, although they were in a co-regency since 728. Unlike his father, Hezekiah was a godly king and brought about many important reforms in Judah. He removed the high places, cut down the images, and cut down the brazen serpent which Moses had made in the wilderness because it had now become an idol (II Kings 18:4). Hezekiah rebelled against the king of Assyria and did not serve him. This was not received well by the Assyrian king who had profited by his invasion and conquest of Israel. His appetite for riches had been whetted by the wealth that flowed into his coffers because of Ahaz's submission to his predecessor and consistent payment of tribute.

In retaliation, after his conquest of Israel, he continued to move south, invading various cities in Judah. Finally realizing that the very center of his kingdom, Jerusalem, was in jeopardy, Hezekiah began a construction program which would preserve the integrity of the city if it came under siege. II Chronicles 32 records that he sent men throughout the land to stop up the springs of water so that there would be no fresh water for an invading army. Then, for their personal use, he ordered a tunnel dug out to the Pool of Siloam. The passageway went underground for 1200 cubits so that when the gates of Jerusalem were shut, they could go through the tunnel without being observed by the Assyrians and obtain fresh water from the pool, and bring it back underground into the city. The pool of Siloam was camouflaged from above so that the Assyrians did not even know it was there.

On the wall of the tunnel was one of the oldest extant samples of Hebrew writing, dating from 701 B.C., describing how the tunnel was a masterful feat of engineering. A group of men began on each end and met in the middle of the hewed out tunnel. The inscription, called the Siloam inscription, was discovered and cut from the rock in the tunnel so it is now preserved in a museum in Israel. It records the feat and the fact that the tunnel was 1200 cubits long. Since we know it measures 1800 feet, we have contemporary evidence that a cubit equaled 18 inches.

By that time Shalmaneser had died and Sennacherib became king of Assyria. We read in II Kings 18:13: "*Now in the fourteenth year of king Hezekiah did Sennacherib king of Assyria come up against all the fenced cities of Judah and took them.*" The year was 701. In panic, Hezekiah sent money, silver, and treasure, to the king of Assyria; everything that he could find in the house of the Lord. He even took the gold from the doors of the temple and from the doorposts which had been overlaid with gold leaf. It only served to whet Sennacherib's appetite and he laid siege to Jerusalem.

The record of the siege is recorded in 11 Kings 18. The messenger sent from Sennacherib to Hezekiah was named Rab-shakeh (probably a title) and his taunt is quoted in verse 19ff. Isaiah 36 and 37 also records these events, since Isaiah's period of greatest activity and influence occurred during Hezekiah's reign. Jerusalem was shut up tight against the hordes of Assyrians camped outside the wall. Many of the city's inhabitants were sitting on top of the wall watching the events outside. No military activity was taking place because Sennacherib had sent his messenger to try to negotiate a peaceful surrender with Hezekiah. That would have been to his advantage because he was in a hurry to conquer the remaining cities of Judah and return to Assyria as soon as possible. Because he did not want to be involved in a long siege, Rab-shakeh gave a compelling speech, filled with propaganda, to entice the people of Jerusalem to surrender. The following s a summary of his taunts:

"What good has it done you to look to Egypt for support? Their military system is so weak it is like a reed that if a man leans on it, it will break and its sharp end will pierce his hand. Or, if you are trusting in the Lord your God, is it not He whose high places and altars Hezekiah has taken away?"

Rab-shakeh did not understand that what Hezekiah had removed was the Baal objects. His reforms actually opened the way for the power of God to work miraculously in behalf of Jerusalem. Rab-shakeh continued: *"Make a bargain with my master. I will give you 2000 horses if you are able to set riders on them."* What he meant was, even if I gave you 2000 horses you would not have enough men to ride them and fight against us. You are so weak militarily you do not have enough people to repulse even one official of my master's servants. Am I now come up without the Lord against this place to destroy it? The Lord said to me, Go up against this land, and destroy it.

Rab-shakeh used every psychological ploy to discourage the people of Jerusalem. In fact, his taunts had so much effect on the people sitting on the wall that Eliakim, Hezekiah's representative, asked Rab-shakeh to: *"Please speak in Aramaic because the elders understood it and not in Judean (or Hebrew) because of all the people on the wall."*

Rab-shakeh replied to that (vs. 27): *"Hath my master sent me to thy master, and to thee, to speak these words? Hath he not sent me to the men which sit on the wall?"* I am to speak to all, he said, because you and your people are doomed to eat your own dung and drink your own urine. This was a terrible thing for the people to hear. Then: *Hear the word of the great king, the king of Assyria: Thus saith the king, Let not Hezekiah deceive you; for he shall not be able to deliver you out of his hand, Neither let Hezekiah make you trust in the Lord.* Trust in us and surrender to us, he said, and you will each have your own vine and fig tree and drink water from your own cistern. But he added:

> *Until I come and take you away to a land like your own land,*
> *a land of corn and wine, a land of bread and vineyards, a*
> *land of oil olive and of honey, that ye may live, and not die,*
> *and hearken not unto Hezekiah, when he persuadeth you,*
> *saying, The Lord will deliver us .*

Rab-shakeh concluded by reminding them that there was no god that had ever delivered his people from attack by the Assyrians, so why should they think their God would do any better. That taunt had so much impact on the people and the elders that they went to

Hezekiah with their clothes tom. They were convinced that Rab-shakeh spoke the truth and that they did not stand a chance of holding out against an Assyrian siege.

II Kings 19:1 records that when Hezekiah heard their report, *"He rent his clothes, and covered himself with sackcloth, and went into the house of the Lord."* After pleading his case before the Lord, he sent messengers to Isaiah who returned a very comforting message from Jehovah to Hezekiah. Because the servants of Sennacherib have blasphemed Me, the Lord said, I am going to send a rumor that will cause him to return home. There he will fall by the sword in his own land. The fulfillment of that prophecy is recorded in 19:37. In the meantime Sennacherib, who was fighting against Libna, sent messengers once again to meet with Hezekiah. They carried a letter which reiterated some of the salient points of the previous taunts. After reading the letter, Hezekiah went into the temple and spread it out before the Lord. In effect he prayed, *"These men of Assyria have blasphemed You and I pray, Lord, deliver us from their hand."* Again Isaiah sent to him, saying (vs. 20), *"That which thou hast prayed to me against Sennacherib king of Assyria I have heard."*

Reading through to verse 32, we can see that Isaiah told Hezekiah that the king of Assyria would not come to the city, or even shoot an arrow inside it. Hezekiah's heart must have been relieved and comforted at the hearing of those words. Their fulfillment is recorded in verse 35 where we read that "the Angel of the Lord went out, and smote in the camp of the Assyrians an hundred and fourscore and five thousand [185,000]." Sennacherib, unsuccessful in his attempt to capture Jerusalem, returned home and lived at Nineveh until 681 B.C. In that year the earlier prophecy was fulfilled, as recorded in verse 37. As he was worshiping in the house
of his god, two men killed him and Esar-haddon his son became king in his place.

Sennacherib recorded many of his activities on an artifact known as the *Taylor prism*, also called the *Prism of Sennacherib*. It can be seen in the British Museum. It is a small clay cylinder containing an account of Sennacherib's eight campaigns. It includes the capture and destruction of the city of Babylon in 689 B.C., and his expedition down the east coast of the Mediterranean Sea toward Egypt in 701. He gives the number of Palestinian cities captured, and carefully lists all of the spoil that he took. Regard his Jerusalem campaign, this what he wrote: *I shut up Hezekiah like a caged bird.* He gives no reason for not having captured Jerusalem, nor does he mention a disaster having befallen any of his army, which caused his retreat without winning a victory. This was the hand of God. Sennacherib was the most powerful monarch in the world at that time, and there is absolutely no reason why he could not have captured Jerusalem. Typical of the monarchs of his day, he did not record the negative aspects of his campaigns. He mentions the siege, shutting Hezekiah up *"like a bird in a cage."* But he did not capture him. This is a tremendous piece of extant evidence proving the biblical account of Sennacherib's invasion in 701 B.C.

The remaining years of Hezekiah's life are recorded in 11 Kings 20. He became extremely ill and the Lord said to him through Isaiah, *"Set thine house in order, for thou shalt die, and not live."* (vs. 1) Hezekiah tearfully pleaded for an extension of his life and the Lord replied, *"I have heard thy prayer, I have seen thy tears: behold, I will heal thee."* He promised to add fifteen years to his life and to save Jerusalem from the Assyrians *"for mine own sake, and for my servant David's sake."* Isaiah instructed him to place a lump of figs on the boil that was killing him and he would be healed. Hezekiah, doubting, asked for a sign that he would be healed within three days. In response, Isaiah gave him a choice: *"Shalt the shadow go forward ten degrees, or go back ten degrees?"* He was referring to the sundial where the shadow goes forward, so Hezekiah asked to let it turn backward. God complied with this request, and for the second time, He intervened in the movement of the physical universe He had done to honor the prayer of Joshua. Hezekiah later acted foolishly by displaying all his treasure to emissaries from Babylon. Isaiah prophesied to him (vs. 17) that the day would come when all that his fathers had laid up in store would be carried away to Babylon.

In 2015 and 2018, two seals were discovered near the temple mount. One is inscribed, "Isaiah the prophe...(missing one letter)" and the other, "of King Hezekiah of Judah" which because of their proximity, provides extant evidence supporting the many verses containing their names.

LIV. JUDAH'S FINAL YEARS

After Hezekiah's death, a new evil and idolatrous period began in the nation of Judah. Manasseh, who succeeded his father, Hezekiah,
began a reign of terror. This depraved monarch ruled for fifty-five years until 642 B.C. and then was succeeded by his son Amon, who reigned just two years until 640 B.C. Manasseh was the most evil of all the kings to sit on the throne of his ancestor David, and his reign marked the beginning of Judah's final downfall. Right down until the end (and even beyond), the Lord continued to send His prophets to warn His people in an attempt to call them back to repentance before it was too late.

The Reign of Manasseh

For a complete perspective on the monarchy of Manasseh, we must look both at II Kings 21 and II Chronicles 33. We will begin in II Kings 21. Manasseh reigned for fifty-five years and committed evil in the sight of the Lord like *"the abominations of the heathen, whom the Lord cast out before the children of Israel."* (vs. 2) Scripture says he was worse than the Canaanites whom Joshua drove out. He erected altars to Baal. He made the Asherah; these were the wooden idols representing female deities, many with six and eight breasts symbolizing fertility, just as Ahab the king of Israel had done. What tragedy to read that a king of David's lineage is being compared to the evil king Ahab of the northern kingdom. Manasseh worshiped *all* the hosts of heaven. He practiced astrology. He erected heathen altars in the house of the Lord. He made his sons to pass through the fire; he was offering his own sons as human sacrifices. He practiced witchcraft, used divination, and dealt with mediums and spiritists. He was involved in occult practices, many of which survive to our own day but which God condemned centuries before in Deuteronomy 18:9-12. Verse 16 sums up his life by saying *"Manasseh shed much innocent blood."* Tradition records that he martyred Isaiah by placing him in a hollow log and sawed it in half.

As a result of Manasseh's evil practices, many people suffered. He ingrained the worship of Baal in the hearts of the people, that never again could they, or would they return wholly, with mind and heart, to the worship of Jehovah. The religious history of Judah goes from one extreme to the other. Hezekiah had been able to bring his good influence to bear after the evil reign of his father Ahaz. But each wave of reform took longer to accomplish and each one was more a mental acquiescence than a heart change. The people seemed to respond like robots with little conviction, by accepting the religious practices of the one on the throne at that time. But, because of his *long* reign, Manasseh was able to thoroughly ingrain Baalism as the official religion of the land.

Manasseh's Repentance

Second Chronicles 33 gives us an interesting postscript to the life of Manasseh. Because Manasseh had made Judah and its inhabitants to sin *"worse than the heathen, whom the Lord had destroyed before the children of Israel"* and because neither he nor the people would listen when God spoke to them through the prophets, verse 11 says He allowed the Assyrians to attack, capture Manasseh, and carry him in chains to Babylon. The Hebrew says, "hooks through his lips and bronze chains." Prior to recent discoveries, critics pointed to this statement as an error in the Bible because it associated Assyria with Babylon. However, we now know from secular history the Assyrians had captured Babylon just prior to this time and made it an Assyrian province. Later, Manasseh humbled himself before the Lord, repented, and the Lord brought him back to Jerusalem. *"Then Manasseh knew that the Lord was God."* (vs. 13)

After this conversion experience in his old age, he removed the heathen artifacts from the temple, returned the altar of the Lord, and began to worship Jehovah. He also commanded all the people of Judah *"to serve the Lord God of Israel."* But by that time, they were so wedded to Baal that they only gave lip service to the king's new edict. There is no doubt that Manasseh saved his own soul by his belated repentance, but it was too late to save his nation. Not even his son Amon followed his later example.

When Amon ascended the throne at the age of twenty-two, he restored his father's carved idols and worshiped them. Verse 23: *"Amon trespassed more and more"* until after only two years, his servants conspired and assassinated him in the palace. The people then slew Amon's murderers and made his young son Josiah, who was only eight years old, king of Judah.

Josiah's Good Reign

Josiah reigned from 640 until 609 B.C. and was the last godly king of Judah. Second Kings 22:2 says *"he did that which was right in the sight of the Lord and walked in all the way of David his father."* In his eighteenth year, he became concerned about the physical condition of the Lord's house and made preparations for its restoration. He was influenced by the preaching of Jeremiah who recorded that he began his prophetic ministry in Josiah's thirteenth year (Jer. 1:2). While the work on the temple was in progress, Hilkiah found a copy of the book of the law. It had disappeared during the long evil era of Manasseh and Amon, but evidently some pious priest, at the risk of his life, had hidden a copy in the temple. Shaphan the scribe carried it to the palace and read it in the hearing of the king. When Josiah heard the words of the law, he tore his clothes and realized how far the nation had departed from God's laws and how deserving was, *"the wrath of the Lord that is kindled against us"* (vs. 13).

Josiah could have responded in another way, making excuses that he was doing his best, but the Book of the Law was not available to him before that time. Josiah did not respond in that manner. When he heard God's laws he mourned and began to direct his life and the religious system of the nation by it. Because his heart was right, God told him (vss. 19-20):

> *Because thine heart was tender, and thou hast humbled thyself before the Lord, when thou heardest what I spake against this place, and against the inhabitants thereof, that they should be come a desolation and a curse, and hast rent thy clothes, and wept before me, I also have heard thee, saith the Lord. Behold therefore, I will gather thee unto thy fathers, and thou shalt be gathered into thy grave in peace; and thine eyes shall not see all the evil which I will bring upon this place.*

Chapter 23 contains the record of Josiah's reforms. He emptied the temple of all the items used for worshiping Baal, Asherah, and everything used by the astrologists, and burned them outside the city. He did away with the evil priests and broke down all of the houses of the male cult prostitutes along with the places where the women wove garments for the Asherah. He defiled all the high places, and finally, went up to Bethel and destroyed the infamous calf altar that had such a long history dating back to Jeroboam, I.

Following this fulfillment of the three hundred year old prophecy which had been made the day the altar at Bethel was dedicated, Josiah celebrated a Passover. Verse 22 says there had not been such a God honoring Passover since the days of the Judges-at least six hundred years before! But even with all of Josiah's efforts, the people's hearts were not entirely returned to the Lord. The resulting tragedy of the reign of Manasseh is revealed in verse 26:

"Notwithstanding the Lord turned not from the fierceness of his great wrath, wherewith his anger was kindled against Judah, because of all the provocations that Manasseh had provoked him withal."

The damage that Manasseh had done was not undone by his later conversion. His evil life had damned the entire nation. Judah would soon reap what Manasseh had sown. Verse 27 goes on to say, and the Lord said, *"I will remove Judah out of my sight, as I have removed Israel, and will cast off this city Jerusalem which I have chosen, and the house of which I said, My name shall be there."*
The year was 623 B.C. and the time was becoming shorter for the nation of Judah to exist. Doom was already visible on the horizon.

The Surrounding Nations

it helps us to know what was happening in the civilized world during this period. If we place Judah at the center of a clock face, we can look down to about seven o'clock and see the land of Egypt, a tremendous power in the late seventh century B.C. Up at the top and fanning out from about ten o'clock over to two o'clock is Assyria, the number one power in the world at that time. Going over to three o'clock we see the rumblings of neo-Babylon under the leadership of the Chaldean General, Nabopolassar. When he seized the throne, the Babylonians were able to throw off the yoke of Assyrian occupation. The man who followed Ashur-banipal on the throne of Assyria in 633 B.C., was more of a scholar than a military leader. In God's plan for the southern kingdom, the demise of Assyria began because of his weakness.

We know from Isaiah 10:5ff, God had earlier used the Assyrians as His chastening rod on the northern kingdom. When they did not acknowledge they were being used by Him, but assumed they were victorious in their own strength, God would soon punish and destroy them. For this historical event He used the Babylonians. In 614 B.C., with assistance from the Medes, the Babylonians defeated Asshur and Calah. In 612 they conquered Nineveh With that victory, the resistance of the Assyrian army was broken. In 609 B.C., Pharaoh Necho sent his armies up along the Mediterranean seacoast to join in the engagement, giving military aid to the Assyrians.

The Death of King Josiah

When King Josiah learned that Necho was leading his troops north to help the Assyrians, he attempted to stop him at Megiddo. For the details of what happened, we must turn to II Chronicles 35, where we read in verse 21 that Necho sent messengers to Josiah, saying:

What have I to do with thee, thou king of Judah? I come not against
thee this day, but against the house wherewith I have war. For
God commanded me to make haste: forbear thee from meddling with God, who is with me,
that he destroy thee not.

Although verse 22 suggests that God was speaking through Necho, Josiah did not listen. Perhaps his heart also was becoming lifted up in pride. Whatever the reason, he disguised himself and went out to
battle against Necho on the plain of Megiddo. In the conflict, he was wounded by the arrows from the archers and taken back to Jerusalem to die. Based on 11 Chronicles 34:28, and the similar verse in II Kings which promised peace to Josiah, it would appear that peace was God's perfect will for him, but defeat and death were His permissive will when he attempted to involve himself in world affairs which God was controlling. Necho continued his advance toward the north with a series of battles until he was defeated at the Battle of Carchemish in 605 B.C., four years after the death of Josiah. That battle was a major historical event. It was the turning point in the power struggle for the world. It was a bloody battle and its outcome had been predicted by Jeremiah in chapter 46. The Egyptians returned to Egypt after their defeat. After conquering Assyria and Egypt, Babylon was the number one power in the known world. Prior to his defeat at Carchemish, Necho discovered that the people of Judah had placed Jehoahaz on the throne. He imprisoned him in Hamath; replaced him with Eliakim, the son of Josiah; changed his name to Jehoiakim; imposed a levy of one hundred talents of gold on Judah; and brought Jehoahaz to Egypt where he died.

The ruins of Carchemish are on the West bank if the Euphrates river in Turkey. After Nineveh was overrun by the Babylonians in 612 B.C., the capitol was moved to Haran. When the Babylonians captured Haran in 608, the Assyrian capitol was moved to Carchemish.

Babylonian Invasions

Nabopolassar ruled over Babylon from 625 to 605 B.C. His General was Nebuchadnezzar. After his decisive victory at Carchemish in 605, he turned south into Judah and entered the city of Jerusalem as a conqueror. He carried hostages back to Babylon, including many of the young men from the leading families, including Daniel and his friends about whom we read in Daniel chapter 1. Returning to Babylon, Nebuchadnezzar succeeded Nabopolassar as king, while Jehoiakim was king in Jerusalem. Jehoiakim agreed to pay Nebuchadnezzar tribute money, but after three years he rebelled and refused to send another payoff. In 598-597, when no tribute was received, Nebuchadnezzar returned to Jerusalem in anger. He learned that Jehoiakim had died and his son Jehoiachin was king. Nebuchadnezzar laid siege to the city, carried Jehoiachin and his family captive to Babylon; and placed his uncle, Zedekiah, another son of Josiah, on the throne. (II Chronicles 36:8-10)

II Kings 24:20 tells us Zedekiah also rebelled against the king of Babylon. Nebuchadnezzar returned in 588 B.C. and besieged Jerusalem for two years. In 586 the Babylonian army broke down the walls, burned the temple, the palace, and the city. They carried many of the inhabitants into temple in Babylon, along with all the valuable treasures from the destroyed temple. This climactic event was the fulfillment of all the earlier prophecies which the Lord had made concerning the destruction of the city and temple if His people continued their idolatry and rejection of His Law. The prophecies were fulfilled accurately and precisely. (II Kings 25:1-12; 22)

During recent archaeological excavations near Robinson's Arch on the Temple Mount, a small weight was discovered. It was inscribed
beka, in Hebrew. This weight is believed to be the beka referred to in Exodus 38:26 as equivalent to half a shekel during the time of Moses and the tabernacle. The weight that was discovered is believed to date to the time of the first temple and used to weigh the temple tax during that time.

LV. AFTERMATH OF JUDAH'S DEFEAT

We have arrived at the historical point in time when the inhabitants of Judah were taken to Babylon in captivity. There is a certain irony in the fact that God called Abram from the geographical area which came to be known as Babylon. He promised Abram a progeny which would become a great nation, as numerous as the stars of heaven and the sand of the sea, and would inherit the land of Canaan to which Abram went. Now, as captives, they were back in the land from which God had called their forefather, Abram.

The World Outside of Babylon

While the Jews were captives in Babylon during most of the sixth century B.C. (605-539) many changes were occurring throughout the civilized world. Aesop was writing his timeless fables; the theater at Delphi was under construction; the Delphic oracle and its priestesses were at the height of their influence; Pythagoras, the philosopher and mathematician, was developing his phythagorean theorum; Confucius was teaching in China; Buddha left his home to devote himself to philosophy and asceticism and preached his first sermon in 521 B.C.; the temples of Apollo at Corinth and of Olympian Zeus in Athens, were under construction.

From this era come the first reports of papyrus being used in Greece. Just a little later, the Persians would be wearing tight fitting leather clothes. In Babylon, the banking business was being practiced. Nebuchadnezzar was building his palace with its terraced gardens, presumed to be the legendary hanging gardens, one of the seven wonders of the ancient world. He also built a tunnel more than half a mile long connecting the palace and the temple of the sun. The other six "wonders" are: The Great pyramid at Giza; the Colossus at Rhodes; the Temple of Artemis; the statue of Zeus; the mausoleum of Halicarnassus; and the lighthouse at Alexandria. Later, Darius, I would use pontoon bridge warfare to cross the Bosphorus. He would also establish the city of Persepolis and explore the Indian seacoast. The Greek philosophers were adopting the theory that the earth is a disc covered by a dome of sky.

Conditions of Captivity

While all these things were occurring in the civilized world, the Jews were captives in the land of Babylon. Ezekiel and Daniel were prophesying and encouraging the people. They were not slaves, as they had been in Egypt. They were subject to forced labor, but they also had a certain amount of freedom and many of them prospered in the land of their captivity. Their primary hardship was the fact of their exile, their homesickness for Jerusalem and the temple, and their inability to participate in the festivals and other facets of worship that God had originated for them. (See Psalm 137)

Lamentations Over Jerusalem

As the captives were being led away to Babylon in 586 B.C., leaving the smoldering city behind, there was an eye-witness of the situation in Jerusalem immediately following Nebuchadnezzar's conquest. We can find his account in the book of Lamentations. Because of the religious and political nature of Jeremiah's prophesies, which had been misconstrued as pro-Babylonian by the leaders in Judah, the Babylonian conquerors allowed him to choose between going to Babylon, or staying in Jerusalem. Jeremiah chose to remain. He witnessed what was prophesied fifty-five years earlier by the prophet Zephaniah (1:18):

> *Neither their silver nor their gold shall be able to deliver them in*
> *the day of the Lord's wrath; but the whole land shall be devoured*
> *by the fire of his jealousy: for he shall make even a speedy riddance*
> *of all them that dwell in the land.*

This prophecy had at last been fulfilled. Nebuchadnezzar and his generals went back through the broken wall and carried the people away to Babylon. Jeremiah, the weeping prophet, walked around the city, sat down and scanned the desolation which lay before his eyes, as he recorded what he witnessed and felt. Beginning in Lamentations 1:1:

> *How doth the city sit solitary that was full of people! how is she*
> *become as a widow! she that was great among the nations, and*
> *princess among the provinces, how is she become tributary! She*
> *weepeth sore in the night, and her tears are on her cheeks: among*
> *all her lovers she hath none to comfort her. all her friends have dealt treacherously with*
> *her, they are become her enemies.*

In this melancholy lament, Jeremiah personified the city of Jerusalem as if it was a woman. She had been a princess; now she was a widow. Even the city seemed to be weeping. Her lovers which she followed became her enemies and had dealt treacherously with her. In Hosea 2:5, Hosea had personified Judah as a harlot. The harlot's wages she had received were those things that cities and nations are interested in, viz., bread, water, wool, flax, and oil. Jerusalem had sold herself for those things to the surrounding nations and became involved in the worship that praised Baal for providing them. Jeremiah followed up on Hosea's personification and said that all the nations Jerusalem had involved herself with, and whose gods she had worshiped, moved in against her just like a man who dealt treacherously with his adulterous lover.

Jeremiah continued in verse 4: *"The ways of Zion do mourn, because none come to the solemn feasts: all her gates are desolate."* By writing, *"the ways,"* he means the roads. It is as if the roads into Jerusalem previously rejoiced when pilgrims came up to worship Jehovah, but now they were abandoned, vacant and desolate. So, even the roads were mourning. What a difference! Think back to II Samuel 15:2. When Absalom was meeting people at the gate to turn their hearts away, there was activity. The Judges were there, the people were entering to present their cases before the king. But now Jeremiah said, *"Her gates are desolate."* This was because there had not been justice in the gates for scores of years.

Look at Amos 5:10. Although Amos gave his message to the northern kingdom prior to the invasion of the Assyrians, the principle still applies because the same thing was happening in the south in Jerusalem. Amos said, *"They hate him that rebuketh in the gate, and they abhor him that speaketh uprightly."* There must have been individuals of integrity in the gate who attempted to stand for principles of justice and for the worship of Jehovah. But the major portion of the population hated them. They were so corrupt that they abhorred the man who spoke with integrity. In verse 12, Amos accused them of accepting bribes. They also *"afflict the just, and, most of all, they turn aside the poor in the gate."* The judges in the gate were turning aside the poor because they could not afford to pay the bribes. The whole system of justice that God had prescribed was being perverted. What a difference from what we saw earlier when Boaz could sit in the gate in Bethlehem and enjoy the fellowship of the other elders; when he could discuss the matter of redeeming the land with a nearer kinsman, and everything was done the way God had outlined it. Times had changed dramatically since then because, rather than justice being in the gates, evil and perversion were there. God *had* to judge it.

Jeremiah continued by saying, *"her priests sigh, her virgins are afflicted, and she is in bitterness."* Is it a surprise that her virgins were afflicted? When the Babylonian soldiers ravaged the city they ravaged the women. Verse 5ff summarizes the reasons behind it all.

> *"Her adversaries are the chief, they are in charge. Her enemies prosper. And why has it happened? For the Lord hath afflicted her for the multitude of her transgressions: her children are gone away into captivity before the enemy."*

Verse 9 adds this. "She *remembereth not her last end.*" The Israelites did not consider their future. Moses had been the pleasures just the opposite." He did not want to "*enjoy the pleasures of sin for a season*" (Heb. 11:25). The inhabitants of Judah wanted the pleasures of sin for a season, so they were now paying the price.

Verse 10 says that other nations have entered her sanctuary. Those whom God had said could not even join the congregation had defiled the sanctuary. As Jeremiah looks around, he mourns and cries (vs. 12): Doesn't anybody want to comfort us? We are destroyed, in agony, miserable and suffering, but no one seems to care. In verse 17 he says that the Lord had commanded those around about Jacob to become adversaries. This is a fulfillment of the Davidic covenant in which God had promised chastisement for disobedience. Jeremiah 2:7 states very explicitly that God abandoned all the sacred items in the temple He had told Solomon to make for His worship. We learned earlier that His house had been polluted by objects of Baal worship, and the people had mistreated the things He had designed, caring nothing for them. So now He abandoned them and delivered them into the hand of the enemy. It is reminiscent of the battle in 1075 B.C. when God *allowed* His Ark to be taken by the Philistines. It isn't that God could not have stopped the Babylonians from destroying the temple, His glory had departed. It was an empty building that had been used to worship the false gods they had imported from the surrounding nations. Without God's presence, it was a hollow shell.

In verse 14, Jeremiah summarized his interaction with the false prophets during Ms earlier ministry. He reminded the inhabitants of Judah that these professional prophets had seen false and foolish visions. Their preaching was not that which would bring repentance.

When we study his book, we will see that Jeremiah preached God's message and was opposed by the "yes men," the professional prophets, and those who did not agree with his God given message. If the people had accepted Jeremiah's message, they would have prevented what he was describing in Lamentations. Because they heeded the false prophets instead, they were reaping the present disaster. Jeremiah's heart must have been broken when he mentioned in verse 20 the cannibalism that took place inside the city. The carnage and cannibalism which had been prophesied earlier had happened. In chapter 3, beginning with verse 12, Jeremiah began to personify himself as the city of Jerusalem. God had aimed His bow and set him as a target. It reminds me of the time God determined to destroy Ahab. He could not escape; a random arrow pierced the joint of his armor. In a similar way, Jeremiah felt that an assassin's arrow had entered his inward parts. He continues in verse 16 to say, *"He hath also broken my teeth,"* making himself the recipient of an imprecatory Psalm. Psalm 3:7 contains this imprecation against the enemies of God.

Verse 40 says, *"Let us search and try our ways, and turn again to the Lord."* This summarizes the basic message he had given over and over. Verse 44 adds, *"Thou hast covered thyself with a cloud that our prayer should not pass through."* God had hidden Himself from His apostate people. Earlier, He had said through Hosea to the northern kingdom (5:15): *"I will go away to my place, and will not return again."* Now it has happened to Judah. God had gone away; He had departed from the temple; He had withdrawn His hand of protection from Jerusalem, the beautiful city, and allowed the Babylonians to invade bringing destruction and devastation.

Chapter 4 contains specific details regarding the Babylonian invasion. In verse 5, Jeremiah says that those who had eaten delicacies and dressed in purple were reduced to sitting in the ash pit. Earlier, Amos had given such a message to *"the cows of Bashan,"* those heavy women who ordered their husbands to go out and work hard and cheat some more to bring in more money and more expensive food for them. There were also people like that in Jerusalem, but the days of fancy food and other delicacies were over. They were now eating each other, because of the judgment of God against them. Compassion was gone and women boiled their own children (vs. 10).

In verse 12, Jeremiah wonders who could believe that adversaries could enter the gates of Jerusalem, or that the city would fall. It was wrong to say that no army could take Jerusalem, because that was what happened when God withdrew His hand. The professional prophets and the evil priests who had shed the blood of the righteous in her midst (vs. 13) were now wandering blind in the streets. Those who were so pious, holy, and pure that they would not even speak to those beneath them were crying, *"Depart, unclean, depart, do not touch us,"* because they were defiled by death and corpses and cannibalism on every hand. There was no escape, Jeremiah says in verse 18: *"They hunt our steps, our end is near, our days are fulfilled; for our end is come."* Chapter 5 continues (vs. 2): *"Our inheritance is turned to strangers, our houses to aliens."* This is a fulfillment of Zephaniah 1:13. Verse 4 complains that they must even pay for their water and their own wood is sold to them. Verse 12: *"Princes are hanged up by their hands."* The Babylonians hung them up by their thumbs in the middle of the streets. They put the young men to work in the grinding mills and the young people had to carry loads of wood to serve their new masters.

In Lamentations, the prophet Jeremiah summarizes the horror and cruelty which the inhabitants of the beautiful city of Jerusalem suffered at the hands of the Babylonians. His heart was broken because he knew that if the people had heeded his earlier warnings and messages from God, this would not have happened. But in the program of God, because of His earlier prophecies based on their failures to obey His ordinances, this final calamity was inevitable! God's request in Jeremiah 6:16 should have been obeyed.

LVI. BABYLON THE GREAT

As the captives from Judah made their weary, dreary journey to Babylon, they must have felt even more helpless and hopeless when they caught their first glimpse of the most magnificent city which had been built until that time. Approaching from the north, with the River Euphrates on their left and the setting sun to their right, they observed walls of such magnitude that no military engine of war was capable of breaching them. The walls were sixty to eighty feet high and every sixty feet was a tower which sustained the wall and stored implements for warfare. The walls were 45 feet thick and served as an expressway for chariots to drive around the wall while fending off any approaching enemy or carrying military supplies from the towers to the points of defense. Chariots would be driven six abreast-a phenomenon never before achieved. The city had no parallel in the ancient world.

The Euphrates flowed beneath the walls and at the same time filled a oat that surrounded the city. The huge gate bars which went down to the bottom of the river bed prevented enemies from using them as an entrance point. Penetration of the city was all but impossible except by permission from within. The circumference of the wall measured eleven miles and formed the perimeter of the city. Daniel, Ezekiel, and later all the captives, probably entered through the Ishtar Gate in the northern wall. This gate is on public display in the British Museum.

Assuming that the captives did pass through the Ishtar Gate, they immediately entered upon a road called the *Processional Way*. This main artery through the city was constructed of limestone squares measuring 31/2 feet on each side. Each square had an engraving which read, *"To the honor of Marduk, the god of Babylon."* The Processional Way was bounded by orange brick sidewalks. Anyone who thought of escaping would soon notice that the orange sidewalks were bordered by walls 40 to 60 feet high.

The Palace

Continuing along this route, the captives would eventually see the blue and orange enameled brick palace of Nebuchadnezzar. This was another one of the wonders of the ancient world. Whether in Egypt, Assyria, or Babylon, a new monarch would very often erase the name of his predecessor from every edifice he had erected and place his own name on it instead. There were at least two reasons for this. First, it was done to personally take credit for the construction. Second, it was done to erase the memory of the previous monarch from the inhabitants. Nebuchadnezzar's palace had walls 135 feet thick, and he had prepared in advance against his successor erasing his name by inscribing every brick used in the first thirty-five feet into the wall with his name. The only way one could erase the name of Nebuchadnezzar was to knock down 35 feet of his palace wall.

The Temple

Continuing down the Processional Way, one would come to the intersection with Marduk Way, where the famous temple, known as the *Temple Between Heaven and Earth*, was located. It was built as a ziggurat. Its size was overwhelming. The lowest pedestal was white, above it was a black one, and above that a yellow one. The lower one was 300 feet square. Each section became narrower and narrower until, after ascending all the stairs, one arrived at a small place of worship at the apex where, as their idolatrous worship system said, "The gods of heaven would commune with the priestesses in the temple." This function was carried out by the priests and the priestesses. The sexual activities involved were similar to Baal worship. After contemplating all these wonders, then seeing the Hanging Gardens of the palace, it is not surprising that Nebuchadnezzar would say *"Is not this great Babylon that I have built for the house of the kingdom by the might of my power, and for the honour of my majesty?"* (Dan. 4:30).

LVII. DANIEL AND NEBUCHADNEZZAR

No other book in the Old Testament has been maligned by critics as much as the book of Daniel. But be encouraged, because it will stand on its own. It can be analyzed from linguistics; it can be analyzed from knowledge of the historical period in which Daniel lived; and it can be analyzed from the prophecies contained therein. These validate that Daniel was a historical character and that he did write his book in the sixth century B.C. The reason skeptics want to give the book a late date, is that they cannot believe that Daniel would be able to prophesy as accurately as he did about the nations which would succeed the Babylonian empire.

Daniel tells us *"in the third year of the reign of Jehoiakim king of Judah Nebuchadnezzar king of Babylon came unto Jerusalem, and besieged it."* He was using the Babylonian dating system and this is in 605 B.C. He emphasized the fact that it was the Lord who gave Jehoiakim into Nebuchadnezzar's hands. We read earlier how Jehoiakim finally refused to continue being a vassal after paying tribute for three years.

The balance of Daniel 1 contains the testing given to Daniel and his three friends, Hananiah, Mishael, and Azariah, regarding their participation in eating the Babylonian food which Nebuchadnezzar insisted upon. These young men appeared to be bright, motivated and alert, and naturally, Nebuchadnezzar had great plans for them. By eating only vegetables and drinking water, and refusing the king's wine and other delicacies which may have included pork and foods forbidden by the law of Moses, these four young men were able to look better at the time of testing than those who had participated in the king's menu. As a result, these four men were put into the king's personal service. In that capacity no one in the entire realm was better than Daniel, who was renamed Beltashazzar; Hananiah, renamed Shadrach; Mishael, named Meshach; and Azariah, whose new name was Abednego.

Nebuchadnezzar's Dilemma

Nebuchadnezzar, like all other monarchs of the period, was surrounded with professional prophets. However, he was more astute than many of the other kings who would possibly say: "This is the dream I had." Then they would ask their prophets to interpret it. If the same dream had been given to ten different men in secret, there would have been ten different interpretations. How difficult would it be to interpret a dream if no one knew the dream?

In chapter 2, Nebuchadnezzar threw a red herring into the interpretation by calling his wise men around him and stating in (vs. 3): *"I have dreamed a dream and I am anxious to understand it."* The Chaldean wizards gave their usual answer (vs. 4): *"Tell thy servants the dream, and we will shew the interpretation."* This time, Nebuchadnezzar was firm. He insisted that he wanted to know both what the dream *was* and the *interpretation*. This was too much for them. They complained that no monarch had ever asked such a thing from any wizard before. However, to Nebuchadnezzar, it was being quite logical. If a wizard was capable of interpreting a dream, why could he not also tell what the dream was? So, Nebuchadnezzar would not budge, but insisted, *"If you do not tell me what the dream was and its interpretation I am going to cut off all your heads and make your houses dunghills."*

Unfortunately, none of the wizards were able to accommodate the king. In his anger, he sent orders throughout the land to kill all the wise men, so Daniel and his three friends were included. When Daniel learned the reason for the command, he asked for a reprieve in order to have time to supply the king with the information he had requested. Verse 17 tells us that he went back to his house and told his three friends about it so they could all pray together about the matter and seek compassion from God in order that they might not be destroyed in the execution of all the wise men of the land.

The Dream

Verse 17 says that the mystery of the dream was revealed to   Daniel in a night vision. Because God gave him the interpretation, Daniel prayed and blessed God (vss. 20-23). He then went in and spoke to the king, who asked,

"Art thou able to make known unto me the dream which I have seen, and the interpretation thereof" No one can do that, Daniel disclaimed modestly, *"But there is a God in heaven that revealeth secrets, and maketh known to the king Nebuchadnezzar what shall be in the latter days"* (vs. 28).

Daniel began to describe the awesome statue with the head of gold, the breast and arms of silver, the stomach of bronze, the legs of iron, and the feet made of iron and clay. He told Nebuchadnezzar that while he watched in his dream, a stone cut without hands struck the statue on its feet of iron and clay crushing them, then the iron, the bronze, the silver, and the gold, all crumbled down at the same time and were crushed together where they became like chaff on the summer threshing floor, and the winds carried them away so that not a trace of them was found. The stone that struck the statue suddenly became a great mountain that filled the whole earth. Daniel told him exactly what his dream was, even though he had not revealed it. God designed this scenario to give credibility to Daniel and bring glory to Himself. Daniel gave the king the interpretation beginning with verse 36. *"Thou, 0 King art a king of kings: for the God of heaven hath given thee a kingdom, power, and strength, and glory. Thou art this head of gold."*

The head of gold was Babylon and it ruled the civilized world from 605 to 539 B.C. *"After thee shall arise another kingdom, inferior to thee."* That would be Medo-Persia. It was in power from 539-333 B.C. Then a third kingdom of bronze would rule over the earth. This would be Greece, ruling the world from 333 to 167 B.C. The fourth kingdom, strong as iron, would be Rome. The interpretation continued throughout chapter 2, and Nebuchadnezzar responded (vs. 46) by falling on his face and giving homage to Daniel. He gave orders to present Daniel with gifts, offerings, and incense. And as he gave homage he said, *"Your God is a God of gods, and a Lord of kings, and a revealer of secrets, seeing thou couldest reveal this secret."*

Then the king promoted Daniel. Following his promotion, Daniel asked that the king would promote his three friends also.

LVIII. GOD AND NEBUCHADNEZZAR

Chapter 3 begins with a description of how Nebuchadnezzar created an image of gold 60 cubits high. Its breadth was 6 cubits. The 90 ft by 9 ft statue was erected in the plain of Dura in the province of Babylon. His dream was the inspiration and motivation. His ego was inflated as he remembered Daniel saying, *"You are the king of kings and the head of gold."* His immediate impulse was apparently to make a golden statue of himself. After erecting the huge statue of himself, the king gave in instructions that when the musical instruments were played, everyone must bow down. And according to verse 6, *"whoso falleth not down and worshippeth, shall the same hour be cast into the midst of a burning fiery furnace."* Everyone bowed down except Shadrach, Meshach, and Abednego.

We do not know where Daniel was. Perhaps he was back in the king's court, or on a diplomatic mission. Shadrach, Meshach, and Abednego did not bow down. Influential men approached Nebuchadnezzar (vs. 12) and reported, *"These men have not regarded thee: they serve not thy gods, nor worship the golden image which thou hast set up."* The king went into a rage and gave orders for Shadrach, Meshach, and Abednego to be brought to him. Then (vs. 15), he personally instructed them to fall down on their faces and worship the statue, threatening that if they did not, they would be thrown into a furnace of blazing fire. He foolishly asked, *"Who is that God that shall deliver you out of my hands?"*
Remember what he said in 2:47? That the God of Daniel was the Lord of kings? Evidently, he had forgotten there was a God in heaven who had him in His hands, and that he had his throne only because God allowed him to be there. Shadrach, Meshach, and Abednego answered the king and said: *"We are not careful [or, we do not need to answer thee in this matter. If it be so, our God whom we serve is able to deliver us from the burning fiery furnace, and he will deliver us out of thine hand, 0 King. But if not, be it known unto thee, 0 king, that we will not serve thy gods, nor worship the golden image which thou hast set up."* Regardless of whether or not they were delivered, those three godly Israelites declared, "We are not going to serve your gods because God has told us not to bow down before gods. Whether or not He chooses to deliver us, we are not going to do so."

Nebuchadnezzar went into an insane frenzy! He had the furnace heated seven times hotter than it had ever been. The soldiers tied up the three men and threw them in. The blazing heat was so intense that those who took them to the entrance were killed just from the heat roaring out of the door. Nevertheless, the three bound men walked freely inside the furnace fully clothed. From where he was seated, Nebuchadnezzar looked through the flames and saw four men walking around. Turning to his officials in panic, the King asked *"Did not we cast three men bound into the midst of the fire?"* They replied, *"Yes we did."* The King said, *"I see four men loose and the form of the fourth is like the Son of God."* Then, when he called the men to come out, they were totally unsinged. When Nebuchadnezzar saw they were unharmed, he worshiped the God of heaven and made a decree (Nebuchadnezzar loved decrees.) saying that anyone who says "*anything amiss against the God of Shadrach, Meshach, and Abednego, shall be cut in pieces, and their houses shall be made a dunghill.*"

Nebuchadnezzar's Humiliation

Chapter 4 begins by describing another of Nebuchadnezzar's dreams and it was a warning from God. In his dream, he saw a tree great and large, strong, and reaching to the sky. It was visible to the ends of the earth with beautiful foliage and abundant fruit. The beasts of the field were enjoying the shade under it, the birds dwelt in its branches, and all living creatures were feeding themselves from it. As Nebuchadnezzar watched, a holy one descended from heaven and shouted (vss. 14-17):

> *Hew down the tree, and cut off his branches, shake off his leaves, and scatter his fruit: let the beasts get away from under it, and the fowls from his branches: Nevertheless leave the stump of his roots in the earth, even with a band of iron and brass, in the tender grass of the field, and let it be wet with the dew of heaven, and let his portion be with the beasts in the grass of the earth: Let his heart be changed from man's and let a beast's heart be given unto him; and let seven times pass over him. This matter is by the decree of the watchers, and the demand by the word of the holy ones: to the intent that the living may know that the most High ruleth in the kingdom of men, and giveth it to whomsoever he will, and setteth up over it the basest of men.*

Nebuchadnezzar was troubled by the dream and asked Beltashazzar (Daniel) to interpret it. Daniel was afraid to tell him, saying, *"My lord, the dream be to them that hate thee, and the interpretation thereof to thine enemies."* It is a terrible dream! Nebuchadnezzar insisted and demanded to know the interpretation. The tree, Daniel said, is you. You have grown powerful and great, and your splendor is like the giant tree. When the angelic messenger said "chop it down," this means you are going to be driven from your kingdom. You will live in the fields like a beast for seven years. But, because the stump was left, this means when the time is over, you will regain your throne. Daniel continued by adding (vs. 27), *"Break off thy sins by righteousness, and thine iniquities by shewing mercy to the poor; if it may be a lengthening of thy tranquility."* With this statement, Daniel gave Nebuchadnezzar the hope of forgiveness, saying that if he would repent, God would possibly relent and extend his days.

Everything happened to Nebuchadnezzar as Daniel prophesied. Verse 28 says, twelve months went by and Nebuchadnezzar did not change. Remember the principle in Scripture that when judgment does not fall immediately, the individual seems to think it never will? It took 700 years for the Canaanites, 400 years for the Amalekites, fifteen years for Hophni and Phineas, two years for Amnon, and a single day for Agag. Nevertheless, judgment did come. In the case of Nebuchadnezzar, it came in one year. I am sure that by the end of four or five months, he had completely dismissed the prophecy by Daniel from his mind. Then one day, walking on the roof, he looked over his magnificent city and exclaimed in vs. 30: *"Is this not great Babylon that I have built for the house of the kingdom by the might of my power, and for the honour of my majesty?"* While the words were in his mouth, a voice came from heaven and said, *"The kingdom is departed from thee."* Judgment was immediate. He was driven from mankind and roamed the fields like a wild beast. His hair grew like eagle's feathers, and his nails grew like bird's claws. Verses 34 through 37 contain the personal testimony of Nebuchadnezzar after the seven year period was over and he began to worship the *"King of heaven, all whose works are truth, and his ways judgment; and those that walk in pride he is able to abase."*

LIX. DANIEL'S LATER LIFE

A long period of time elapsed between chapters 4 and 5. In chapter 5 we read that Belshazzar gave a great feast in 539 B.C. We must take some time here to examine the names and dates of the kings of the Babylonian period. We know Nabopolassar reigned from 625 to 605 B.C. and was replaced by Nebuchadnezzar, who reigned from 605 to 562 as recorded in II Kings 24 and 25, and also in the book of Daniel. He was followed by Amel-Marduk, from 562 to 560 as recorded in II Kings 25:27-30, and Jeremiah 52:31-34. After him, came Neriglissar from 560 to 556 B.C. Neriglissar was followed by Labashi-Marduk. He reigned for only one year, 556 B.C., and was succeeded by Nabonidus who reigned from 556 until 539 B.C.

Nabonidus was an explorer and lover of archaeology. He enjoyed digging and excavation. He was slightly interested in military activity, but he spent most of his time away from the city of Babylon in the Arabian oasis of Tayma. Because of his various personal interests, he left his son Belshazzar in charge in the capitol. This has been called an error in the book of Daniel. Until recent archaeological discoveries at Tayma, no "scholars" believed there was a king named Belshazzar. Archaeology revealed that Nabonidus placed his son Belshazzar on the throne of Babylon because he was away from the city for extended periods of time. The fact that Belshazzar understood that he was second in command is borne out by the narrative in chapter 5, which records that he promised to make Daniel number three in the kingdom if he interpreted the handwriting. Chapter 5 is a tremendous chapter for the defense of inspired Scripture. With the information we have at our disposal, thanks to the archaeological records, the historical accuracy of the book of Daniel has been established.

The Demise of Babylon

While Belshazzar was holding a feast for a thousand of his nobles, and was drinking wine in their presence, he was unaware that Cyrus,
King of Persia, the powerful military genius, was gathering his troops north of the city and was in the process of digging a canal from the Euphrates and into the adjoining swamp.

This canal subsequently diverted the Euphrates into the swamp; Cyrus and his soldiers marched into the city of Babylon on the dry river bed. Herodotus, the Turkish historian born in 484 B.C., gives the full account of the invasion of Cyrus in *Histories 1.189-191.*

Seventy years earlier, the Babylonians and the Medes had used the Tigris River to conquer Nineveh. Now, Cyrus was diverting the Euphrates so that he could conquer Babylon on the dry river bed. While the soldiers were digging north of the city, and while the Euphrates was drying up, lowering the water level which ran through the center of the city, Belshazzar and his nobles were reveling inside the palace. With a drunken command, Belshazzar called for the golden vessels to be brought which had been taken as loot by Nebuchadnezzar back in 586 B.C. before he destroyed Solomon's temple. As the revelers drank wine from them, they praised the gods of gold, silver, bronze, iron, wood, and stone (vs. 4). As they shouted their drunken praises, a man's hand appeared on the wall and began to write on the plaster. When the king saw it, he was so frightened that his face grew pale and his knees began to knock. The hand continued to write and verse 8 indicates that no one in the room could understand it. Belshazzar was desperate and his nobles were dumbfounded. No one knew what to make of the mysterious and eerie event.

Finally, the queen entered and called Belshazzar's attention to the fact that there was a wise old man who had served Nebuchadnezzar, and that the power of God was still on him to interpret such things. Belshazzar sent in haste for Daniel. Daniel entered the room and began to tell Belshazzar the history of his ancestor Nebuchadnezzar. Everyone trembled and feared before him, and Daniel said, but *"When his heart was lifted up, and his mind hardened in pride, he was deposed from his kingly throne and they took his glory from him because of his pride."* Daniel continued, Nebuchadnezzar was driven from men to five like the beasts *"till he knew that the most high God ruled in the kingdom of men, and that he appointeth over it whomsoever he will."* (vs. 21) Nebuchadnezzar had to be shown that truth, Daniel said, by having his vision divinely interpreted for him and then living for seven years as an animal. Then when he returned, he knew that God was ruler over all mankind. But, Daniel continued, *"thou his son* [descendant], *0 Belshazzar, hast not humbled thine heart, though thou knewest all this"* (vs. 21)

Belshazzar knew! He had been told of Nebuchadnezzar's experience by word of mouth and had read what had been written about the event. Daniel said, *"Even though you knew, you exalted yourself against God."* Nebuchadnezzar had to be shown and his judgment was *remedial.* Belshazzar, although he knew, rebelled. In view of this, his judgment was to be punitive. In the stunned silence of the frightened guests, Daniel read the mysterious writing on the wall.

"God hath numbered thy kingdom, and finished it. Thou art weighed in the balances, and art found wanting. Thy kingdom is divided, and given to the Medes and Persians" Daniel 5:30 concludes, *"In that night was Belshazzar the king of the Chaldeans slain."*

Darius the Mede captured the city in 539 B.C. The Babylonians were defeated and replaced by the Medes and the Persians exactly as the statue in Nebuchadnezzar's vision had visually prophesied. Herodotus and Xenophon describe this event on October 12, 539.

The Lions' Den

Chapter 6 is the narrative of Daniel in the lions' den later during the Medo Persian period. When this occurred, he was a old man, probably abound eighty. After more than fifty years, the other wise men in Babylon were still conspiring against him. They maneuvered King Darius into signing a decree which they could use to trap Daniel because they knew his singular commitment to Jehovah. Darius quickly realized his error, but had to carry out his decree because according to the law of the Medes and Persians, once enacted, it could not be cancelled. Daniel was captured while he was in prayer and imprisoned in the lions' den. A large stone was rolled over the opening and sealed by the king's signet ring. Early next morning, the king went running to the den. He ordered the den unsealed and was overjoyed to find that Daniel was alive. Daniel explained in verse 22, *"My God hath sent his angel, and hath shut the lions' mouths."* Darius, in anger, turned on the conspirators and threw all of them in the lions' den along with their families. Before they hit the floor of the lion's den, the lions crushed them with their teeth and jaws.

Chapters 7 and 8 are flashbacks to the years of Belshazzar. Chapter 9 contains a tremendous prophecy. Because of the intricate accuracy of its fulfillment, we have confidence in the historic and predicted accuracy of the book of Daniel. Reading in 9:25:

> *"Know therefore and understand, that from the going forth of the*
> *commandment to restore and to build Jerusalem unto the Messiah*
> *the Prince shall be seven weeks, and threescore and two weeks: the*
> *street shall be built again, and the wall, even in troublous times."*

Sixty-two weeks and seven weeks total sixty-nine weeks. The Hebrew word here is *shabua,* which is "a period of seven." Most scholars will agree that this is a period of seven years, a *heptad,* so it is sixty-nine periods of seven years each. Multiplying 69 x 7 is 483 years. We know that the commandment to rebuild the city and wall, recorded in Nehemiah

2:1, was on the first of March, 444 B.C. The day on which Messiah was cut off was March 25, 33 A.D.

The prophetic calendar consists of 360 days per year, so we must multiply 360 x 483 prophetic years for a total of 173,880 predicted days. As we check this out on the Julian calendar, we must take the 444 years from the command to rebuild the wall of the city down to the year zero. Then add the 33 years A.D. from the year zero to the crucifixion of Christ for a total of 477 years. However, since the year zero is 1 B.C. and 1 A.D., we must subtract one year, leaving a total of 476 years according to the Julian calendar. When we multiply 476 years x 365 days, we have a total of 173,740 days. There were 116 leap year days, so we add those and also add the 24 days covering the interlude between the March 1, date for the command to build the city and the wall, and the March 25, date of our Lord's crucifixion.

By counting every day, we have a total of 173,880 days, exactly the same as the 173,880 predictive days prophesied by Daniel in 9:25. This is one of the most tremendous prophecies in the entire Old Testament. Daniel predicted *to the day* the date of the crucifixion of the Lord Jesus Christ, 173,880 days in the future!

Chapter 10 records that Daniel was still alive in the third year of Cyrus king of Persia. Historians confirm this was 536 B.C. Daniel continues with some additional prophecies through the rest of the book and prophecies which have eschatological significance. The third year of Cyrus, in 536 B.C., gives us the parameters for the date of the book of Daniel, viz., 605 to 536 B.C., during which time he served in Babylon under the Babylonians and the Persians.

LX. THE VISIONS OF EZEKIEL

Daniel had been taken to Babylon at the time of Nebuchadnezzar's first invasion of Jerusalem in 605 B.C. Ezekiel was taken during the second invasion in 597 B.C. Daniel lived in the palace and was trained for government service. Ezekiel lived with the captives. He was 22 when Daniel was taken captive eight years earlier.

Ezekiel introduces himself in Ezekiel 1:1 by saying, *"In the {his} thirtieth year, in the fourth month, in the fifth day of the month, as I was among the captives by the river of Chebar."* This was the fifth year of King Jehoiachin, who was also a captive in Babylon. Although Nebuchadnezzar had replaced him on the throne in Jerusalem with his uncle, Zedekiah, Ezekiel's dating system corresponded to Jehoiachin's reign.

In chapter 1, we are introduced to Ezekiel's unusual vision of the wheels within the wheels. Following this vision and introduction to God, he heard God's voice say (2: 1): *"Son of man, stand upon thy feet, and I will speak upon thee."* Ezekiel carried this title-Son of man-throughout the book. God addressed Ezekiel in this way, and Ezekiel explains, *"The spirit entered into me when he spake unto me, and set me upon my feet, and I heard him."* God began to describe to Ezekiel how the house of Judah had rebelled against him. He said that regardless of whether they heeded His message, they would *"know that there hath been a prophet among them."*
He was to say what God told him to say. Continuing in chapter 3, God commanded:

"Son of man, eat what thou findest; eat this roll, and go speak unto the house of Israel. Then I did eat it. And he said thou art not sent to a People of a strange speech and of an hard language, but the house of Israel."

The exiles would understand his speech but they would be unwilling
to listen. And in the event that Ezekiel might become dismayed or discouraged, *"I have made thy face strong against their faces, and thy forehead as an adamant harder than flint."* (vss. 8-9). Ezekiel was to take all of God's words into his heart and then, whether or not the people would listen, say to them, *"Thus saith the Lord God."* After that, Ezekiel said, *"the spirit took me up, and I heard behind me voice of a great rushing, saying,*

Blessed be the glory of the Lord from his place." Then he sat among the captives at Telabib on the river Chebar *"astonished among them"* for seven days. At the end of that time the Lord spoke to him (vss. 17-18):

> *"Son of man, I have made thee a watchman unto the house of*
> *Israel: therefore hear the word at my mouth, and give them*
> *warning from me. When I say unto the wicked, Thou shalt*
> *surely die; and thou givest him not warning, nor speakest to*
> *warn the wicked from his wicked way, to save his life; the*
> *same wicked man shall die in his iniquity, but his blood will*
> *I require at thine hand."*

God goes on to say in verse 19, that if Ezekiel does warn them and they do not respond, *"Thou hast delivered thy soul."*

The Cherubim and Wheels

The whirlwind, great cloud, and fire that was unfolding itself and coming out of the north, which Ezekiel saw in his opening vision, were symbols of coming judgment. The four living creatures were the heavenly cherubim as we discover in 10:1-22. Each one of them had four faces-a lion, an ox, a man, an eagle. The lion, symbolizing strength at its greatest, the ox, service at its meekest, man, signifying intelligence at its fullest, and the eagle, showing spirituality at its highest. The four faces looked north, south, east, and west, seeing everything. Their appearance was like burning coals of fire-this showed total holiness. They moved as a flash of lightning, symbolizing sheer swiftness.

Then Ezekiel witnessed a strange new marvel: four awesome wheels, one beside each cherub, having a vast circumference reaching from heaven to earth and connecting those heavenly beings with this world below. As an additional curious feature, each wheel was criss crossed, a wheel within a wheel, one revolving north and south, the other revolving east and west, so that neither cherub nor wheels needed to turn as they ran with lightning speed between heaven and earth. The huge rims of the wheels were full of eyes that looked simultaneously in every direction. Most amazing of all, the life of the cherubim was in the wheels so that the wheels expressed with preciseness the will of those heavenly beings. Moreover, as the wheels joined earth with heaven, so in like manner the cherubim joined the wheels with the very throne of God. Then, Ezekiel heard a voice from the firmament above the cherubim. Looking up, he saw the likeness of a throne *"as the appearance of a sapphire stone."* On the throne sat the fire enveloped Supreme Being.

The meaning of all this symbolism apparently was pending judgment. But behind and above the coming judgment, were the vast all seeing wheels of divine government and the flaming cherubim, the mighty super intelligent executives of the divine will. The purpose was to show that behind the events that take place on earth are the operations of the Supreme power in Heaven; the overruling will and purpose of the infinite Jehovah God.

The entire book ties in with the opening vision. The message confronts us on every page. Seventy times we find the refrain, *"That they shall know that I am Jehovah."* In connection with the judgment on Jerusalem, it was repeated twenty-nine times. In connection with the judgments on Gentile nations, it was said seventeen times. All those events were permitted by Jehovah and through them He made Himself known. It is He who overrules all events. All this is supplementary to the theme of Daniel that God is the Most High who controls the future. As repeated three times (Dan. 4:17, 25, 32), *"that the living may know that the Most High ruleth in the kingdom of men and giveth it to whomsoever He will."* Keep these two concepts in mind: God overrules all events; and gives kingdoms to whom He will.

Pedagogy in Biography

Some of the prophets were a pedagogy in biography. (Remember the prophet that Ahab encountered on the road.) What they did became a teaching, didactic, experience for the people. Because of this, the prophets had to endure unusual hardship so that their lives and experiences could be pedagogy in biography to those around them. Very often, the only way the prophet could get his message across was to be a living, walking example of the message which God used him to deliver. Since Ezekiel was going to be a pedagogy in biography for the exiles in Babylon, he would have some hard days to live through and hard experiences, as he provided himself a visual aid for the prophecies he would deliver to the exiles.

His first experience as a pedagogy in biography is found in chapter 4. He was instructed to take a brick, lay it on the ground and inscribe the word *Jerusalem* on it. Making believe that the brick was the city of Jerusalem, he was to build a siege wall, lay up a ramp on the side, pitch toy camps around it, and place battering rams against it all around. He would design a miniature city with soldiers and engines of war. The reason for this is given in verse 3. It was to be a sign to the house of Judah. Keep in mind that this was prior to the final invasion of Jerusalem by Nebuchadnezzar in 588-587 which lasted until 586 when the city wall as breached. Ezekiel's prophecy in these verses was between 592 and 589.

Nebuchadnezzar had not devastated the city and temple. This was a prophecy to the inhabitants in exile that he would do this a few years later.

Ezekiel was commanded to lie on his left side for 390 days to bear the iniquity of the house of Israel, and when those days were over he was to lie on his right side and bear the iniquity of the house of Judah for forty days. What a personal sacrifice! Four hundred and thirty days immobilized, first on his left side and then on his right side. So Ezekiel did not move or roll over, God tied him in position.

For nourishment, he was to eat peasant's food, cooked over his own excrement. Ezekiel protested. "That is too much. That is unclean!" This was to symbolize the pollution in that Israel and Judah had defiled themselves with. God relented and allowed him to substitute cow's dung for human dung (vs. 15).

Verse 16 summarizes the meaning: "I will break the staff of bread in Jerusalem, and they shall eat bread by weight, and with care: and they shall drink water by measure, and with astonishment." There would also be cannibalism. Ezekiel 5:10 says, "*The fathers shall eat the sons and the sons shall eat the fathers.*" This fulfills Leviticus 26:29 when God gave them the "if-but" principle. Since they did not
obey, they would suffer the consequences of His judgment.

Chapter 8 is one of the most frightening in the entire book. We travel with Ezekiel, guided by God, to peer inside the temple in Jerusalem and become eye witnesses of the occult evil practices taking place within. According to verses 3-6,

> *He put forth the form of an hand, and took me by a lock of mine head, and the spirit lifted me up between the earth and the heaven, and brought me in the visions of God to Jerusalem, to the door of the inner gate that looketh toward the north; where was the seat of the image of jealousy, which provoked to jealousy. And, behold, the glory of the God of Israel was there, according to the vision that I saw in the plain. Then said he unto me, Son of man, lift up thine eyes now the way toward the north. So I lifted up mine eyes the way toward the north, and behold northward at the gate of the altar this image of jealousy in the entry. He said further more unto me, Son of man, seest thou hat they do, even the great abominations that the house of Israel committeth here, that I should go far off from my sanctuary? But turn thee yet again, and thou shalt see greater abominations.*

Verses 7-10, continues:

*And he brought me to the door of the court. And when I looked,
behold a hole in the wall. Then said he unto me, Son of man,
dig now in the wall: and when I had digged in the wall, behold
a door. And he said unto me, Go in, and behold the wicked
abominations that they do here. So I went in and saw, and
behold every form of creeping things, and abominable beasts,
and all the idols of the house of Israel, portrayed upon the wall
round about.*

This evil graffiti detailed explicitly their occult, licentious practices. As Ezekiel continued to watch, he saw seventy men involved in the evil things. Then in verse 12:

*Then said he unto me, Son of man, host thou seen what the
ancients of the house of Israel do in the dark, every man in the
chambers of his imagery? For they say, The Lord seeth us not,
the Lord hath forsaken the earth.*

This vision continues in chapter 9 where we read of a unique occurrence; the progressive departure of the glory of Jehovah. First from the holy of holies to the temple threshold (9:3); then from the threshold to the up-bearing cherubim (10:18); then out of Jerusalem to the Mount of Olives (11:23). The tragic illustration is obvious. The harlot city of Jerusalem became God forsaken. But even in the midst of, and following His judgment, God's grace and patience were still present because in chapter 43:2-5 we see in the future temple the glory of the God of Israel. He will return and fill the house again. I am reminded of Hosea 5:15 where God said, *"I will go away and return to my Place until they acknowledge their guilt and seek my face. In their affliction they will earnestly seek Me."* **Until** is the key word. In the time of the Millenial temple, Christ will return and fill the temple with His glory. (Matthew 25:31)

Another outstanding feature in Ezekiel is that Jehovah eventually becomes sanctified in Israel before all nations. He says, *"I will sanctify my great name, which was profaned among the heathen, which ye have profaned and the heathen shall know that I am the Lord when I shall be sanctified in you before their eyes"* (36:23). When we studied the call of Abram, confirmed in Isaac and Jacob, we saw that God chose Israel to be a Theocratic nation which would reveal Him to the surrounding nations. Throughout the centuries, Israel continued to disregard the covenant relationship until God turned them over to the Assyrians and Babylonians. In 722 B.C. and 586 B.C., the divine election became divine rejection as God, who had chosen them as sons, scattered them into all the surrounding nations as slaves. Now, Ezekiel will show us that Jehovah will turn this failure into ultimate triumph bigger than the earth itself. The very last verse of the book tells us of a new Jerusalem bearing the name of Jehovah Shammah, "Jehovah is there" (48:35). God will bring final glory for Himself.

LXI. PROPHECIES AND ALLEGORIES

More on Ezekiel

Another example of pedagogy in biography is in chapter 12. The word of the Lord came to Ezekiel again reminding him that he was living in the midst of a rebellious house. He described them as having *"eyes to see, and see not; they have ears to hear, and hear not: for they are a rebellious house."* God commanded Ezekiel to prepare baggage for exile. He was to pretend to go into exile by day so that all the exiles could see him. "Perhaps, when you do this, they will consider their ways."

Beginning in verse 5, God commanded him to dig a hole in the wall, to put his baggage on his shoulder and go out through the wall at evening like an exile so the people would see him. However, he was to cover his eyes so he could not see the land because *"I have set thee for a sign unto the house of Israel."* Ezekiel recorded, *"I did so as I was commanded."* This was symbolic of two things. First, of the final invasion when Nebuchadnezzar demolished and burned sections of the wall of Jerusalem in 586, and led the captives back out through it. Second, it was symbolic of those inside the wall trying to escape without being observed by the Babylonians. Even the prince would put his baggage on his shoulder; he would try to dig through the wall, sneak out, and get away without being seen. Ezekiel carried out the instructions; then God told him what to reply when the people asked why (vs. 11). *"Say, I am your sign: like as I have done, so shall it be done unto them: they shall remove and go into captivity."* "Them" referred to the people still back in Jerusalem. If the captives in Babylon thought it would soon be over and they would soon be going back to their homeland, they were wrong. The worst had not happened yet. Even the prince was going to try to dig through the wall to get away. But he would not succeed, because God prophesied in verse 13: "

"My net also will I spread upon him, and he shall be taken in my snare: and I will bring him to Babylon to the land of the Chaldeans; yet shall he not see it, though he shall die there."

Think back to verse 6. Ezekiel was told to cover his face so he could not see the land. Looking at the historical event as it happened shortly after Ezekiel's pedagogic illustration, we read in II Kings 25:6-7:

> *So they took the king, and brought him up to the king of Babylon to Riblah, and they gave judgment upon him. And they slew the sons of Zedekiah before his eyes, and put out the eyes of Zedekiah, and bound him with fetters of brass, and carried him to Babylon.*

The Allegory of the Cast-Off Infant

In chapter 16, God reminded Israel that when He found her she was like a cast-off newborn baby whose umbilical cord had not yet been cut. She had not been washed, but was a bloody newborn that was not wanted. God said, "I came along and saw you there squirming in your blood and *"I said unto thee live."* God caused her to prosper like the plants of the field and grow into beautiful womanhood. Then the Lord began to draw the analogy between Himself and Israel, His bride. *"I spread my skirt over thee, and covered thy nakedness."* This symbolism was demonstrated in the book of Ruth when Boaz spread his skirt over Ruth as symbolic of accepting her as his wife. *"I sware unto thee, and entered into a covenant with thee, saith the Lord God, and thou becamest mine."* Verses 9 through 13 describe how He cleansed her and beautified her with silk, embroidery, gold, jewels, a beautiful crown, and fed her with the finest of foods. Verse 14 says that her fame went forth among all nations because of her beauty which *"was perfect through my comeliness, which I had put upon thee, saith the Lord God."* The downfall of His people begins in verse 15. God said, *"Thou didst trust in thine own beauty, and played the harlot because of thy renown, and pouredst out thy fornications on every one that passed by."* God had made her beautiful, but she became a harlot. We will learn more about this in the book of Hosea.

The Lord gives more details regarding the reasons for His complaint. She had taken all of the beautiful things He had given her, made images of them, and gave them to her paramours. She took the sons and daughters she had borne to Him (God) and sacrificed them to idols. She had not remembered that He rescued her when He found her *"naked and bare, and wast polluted in thy blood."* She did not even behave as harlots usually do in accepting wages for her harlotry. Instead, *she paid* her lovers with the beautiful things God had given her. So the Lord said He will bring judgment upon her because of her lewdness.

He will gather the lovers with whom she had evil relationships (the heathen nations) and they will destroy her.

Ezekiel's style of prophetic utterance has many characteristics. Ezekiel portrayed nations under the personification of animals, plants, and specific types of people. Jerusalem and Samaria were prostitutes (23:2-3); the house of David was a lion's den (chapter 19) or a vine (19) or a cedar (17). Egypt was a cedar (31) or a crocodile (32). In chapter 17, the Chaldeans were pictured as eagles. Ezekiel is also unique in his *writing* style. He uses interrogative sentences: for example, *"Son of man, seest thou what they do?"* He also used the proverb, the parable, and the allegory. A typical proverb is *"The fathers have eaten sour grapes, and the children's teeth are set on edge"* (18:2). Another is *"As is the mother, so is her daughter."* (16:44) The use of allegory is seen in chapter 16, which we have just examined concerning Judah as the foundling child. For an example of a parable, study the Messianic parable of the cedar tree: 17:22-24.

We will finalize our study of Ezekiel in chapter 28 where he gives a complete description of Satan anywhere else in Scripture. Many object to the application of this chapter to Satan. They criticize but in their efforts to relate the unusual language to the historic kings of Babylon and Tyre, their attempts fail. The important question is, why are these two prophecies addressed to the historic kings of Babylon and Tyre if they are descriptive of Satan? Three reasons:

1. There is to be seen in the characters and careers of these monarchs the wicked character and career of Satan.
2. Satan fulfilled his evil administration in and through these earthly kings who ruled over his earthly dominions.
3. The rulers of Tyre and Babylon appropriated to themselves divine honors. We find this aspect in Isaiah 14 as well as Ezekiel 28. Look at the extraordinary description in Ezekiel 28:11-19:

"Thou sealest up the sum, full of wisdom, and perfect in beauty."

"Thou wast in Eden the garden of God."

"Every precious stone was thy covering." Verse 14 says that his place was: *"the holy mountain of God"*

"In the day that thou wast created" Two times (vss. 13 and 15) his

unusual origin is referred to. This is certainly inappropriate if applied to the king of Tyre. The Bible states Adam was created. The posterity of Adam were not created, they were born.

"Thou art the anointed cherub that covereth" (vs. 14). Regardless how this verse is spiritualized, there is no way to deal satisfactorily with the designation of *cherub* outside its application to a spirit being. In every instance where cherubim appear in the Bible, they are always in very close proximity to God. Usually, they are bearing the throne of God when He manifests Himself in His glory. They are guardians of the inaccessibility of the Holy Presence of God. More references are: Ezekiel 1; Psalm 18; Exodus 25:20; I Chronicles 28:18. There is no reasonable way these descriptions can be spiritualized to apply to the king of Tyre.

"I have set thee so; thou wast upon the holy mountain of God" (vs. 14). This most likely signifies the divine presence of God and His glory around whose feet Ezekiel beheld the appearance of fire (1:27). And as Moses saw earlier (Exod. 24:10, 17): *"Under his feet as it were a paved work of a sapphire stone.. And the sight of the glory of the Lord was like devouring fire."*

"Thou wast perfect in thy ways from the day thou wast created, till iniquity was found in thee." (vs.15). This is certainly unsuitable and inappropriate to apply to the King of Tyre. He was not originally perfect, or created, or later fall from some previous condition of perfection. However, it is an accurate description of the career of Satan. Colossians 1:16 and Ephesians 6:12, compared with Job 1:6 and 8:44, presuppose the fall of Satan from an original state of righteous. Isaiah 14:13-16 also describes Satan's fall and his attempt to usurp the prerogatives of God.

"Thine heart was lifted up because of thy beauty thou hast corrupted thy wisdom by reason of thy brightness." (vs.17). First Timothy 3:6 and Isaiah 14 contain information about his pride. Satan's fall and condemnation began with pride. *"Therefore I will cast thee as profane out of the mountain of God: and I will destroy thee, 0 coveting cherub, from the midst of the stones of fire. I will cast thee to the ground. I will bring thee to ashes and never shalt thou be any more"* (vss. 16-10). The fate predicted for Satan in Revelation 12:7-9 and 20:10 is the same as the words of God written by the prophet Ezekiel.

LXII. THE DECREE OF CYRUS

The year 539 B.C. was a turning point in the lives of the exiles. We read in Daniel 5 how in that year Cyrus led the Medo-Persians into Babylon, killed Belshazzar, and became the dominant world power (the chest and arms of silver). The Persians had an unusual government policy. Whenever they conquered a country where they found captives who had been taken from their homelands, they released those captives. This was unique in the military world at that time and possibly was developed by Cyrus because he records this policy on an artifact known as the *Cyrus Cylinder*, a cuneiform tablet in the British Museum. In 2010 the tablet was taken on tour to Tehran and viewed by more than one million Muslims and considered to be an ancient testimony to human rights. This discovery validates the policy as recorded in the last chapter of II Chronicles and the first chapter of the book of Ezra.

This Persian policy takes on more dramatic implications when we remember that Isaiah 45, written about 150 years earlier, predicted this very event. Verse 1 states,

> *"Thus saith the Lord to his anointed, to Cyrus, whose light hand*
> *I have holden, to subdue nations before him; and I will loose the*
> *loins of kings, to open before him the two leaved gates; and the*
> *gates shall not be shut."*

Throughout chapter 45, there are indications that God was the cause
the victories which Cyrus enjoyed, and especially the victory at Babylon when Belshazzar's loins were loosened so that his knees knocked together. Verse 13 says, *"He shall build my city"* (that is, Jerusalem, referred to in Isaiah 44:28) *"and will let go my captives not for price nor reward, saith the Lord of hosts."* This is a wonderful prophecy. We know from the Cyrus cylinder that this proclamation was made in 539 B.C., the same year Babylon was defeated and Belshazzar was slain. We can also tie this date to the historical account contained in II Chronicles 36:22, 23 where the historian relates, under the inspiration of the Holy Spirit:

> *Now in the first year of Cyrus king of Persia, that the word of*

the Lord spoken by the mouth of Jeremiah might be accomplished, the Lord stirred up the spirit of Cyrus king of Persia, that he made a proclamation throughout all his kingdom, and put it in writing, saying, Thus saith Cyrus king of Persia, All the kingdoms of the earth hath the Lord God of heaven given me, and he hath charged me to build him an house in Jerusalem, which is in Judah. Who is there among you of all his people? The Lord his God be with him, and let him go up.

Except by the sovereign hand of God, why would this man, the pagan ruler of the Medo-Persian Empire make such a proclamation? In anticipation of it, Isaiah prophesied almost 150 years earlier (48:20): *Go ye forth of Babylon, flee ye from the Chaldeans, with a voice of singing declare ye, tell this, utter it even to the end of the earth, say ye, the Lord hath redeemed his servant Jacob.* Not only did Isaiah prophesy the event, but God commanded the exiles to get out of Babylon when the proclamation is made.

We can read in II Chronicles 36:22ff, and in Ezra, references to the promises in Jeremiah 25:11ff:

And this whole land shall be a desolation, and an astonishment; and these nations shall serve the king of Babylon seventy years. And it shall come to pass, when seventy years are accomplished, that I will punish the king of Babylon, and that nation, saith the Lord, for their iniquity, and the land of the Chaldeans, and will make it perpetual desolations.

For additional insight, read Ezekiel 24:1-2:

Again in the ninth year, in the tenth month, in the tenth day of the month, the word of the Lord came unto me, saying, Son of man, write thee the name of the day, even of this same day: the king of Babylon set himself against Jerusalem this same day.

I am amazed at the preciseness of this verse, because God is very emphatic to Ezekiel regarding the month, the day, and the year. But God also emphasized this back in II Kings 25:1:

And it came to pass in the ninth year of his reign, in the tenth month, in the tenth day of the month, that Nebuchadnezzar king of Babylon came, he, and all his host, against Jerusalem, and pitched against it, and they built forts against it..

This was the year 589-588 B.C., which began the two-year siege of Jerusalem until the eleventh year of the king. Not only did Jeremiah prophesy the Babylonian captivity in Jeremiah 25:11-12, but as an eyewitness, he recorded the fulfillment of it in 52:4:

> *And it came to pass in the ninth year of his reign, in the tenth*
> *month, in the tenth day of the month, that Nebuchadnezzar*
> *king of Babylon came, he and all his army, against Jerusalem,*
> *and pitched against it, and built forts against it round about.*

It is apparent that this date is a valuable piece of information which God wants us to have. Otherwise, He would not have mentioned it in so many places. Why is there such a particular and repeated emphasis on the year, the month, and the day, as we have seen in these various passages? To find out we will turn to Haggai 2:15 ff:

> *And now, I pray you, consider from this day and upward, from*
> *before a stone was laid upon a stone in the temple of the Lord:*
> *Since those days were, when one came to an heap of twenty*
> *measures, there were but ten: when one came to the pressfat for*
> *to draw out fifty vessels out of the press, there were but twenty.*
> *I smote you with blasting and with mildew and with hail in all*
> *the labours of your hands; yet ye turned not to me, saith the*
> *Lord. Consider now from this day and upward, from the four*
> *and twentieth day of the ninth month, even from the day that*
> *the foundation of the Lord's temple was laid, consider it.*

And now the most important words, the last line of verse 19: *from* **this day** *will I bless you.*

We know that the prophet Haggai was writing in 520 B.C. (Haggai 1:1) Looking back to the edict of Cyrus in 539-538 B.C., we also know that the captives returned from Babylon, under Zerubbabel, to Judah in what is classified as the first return. From the time they arrived back home in Jerusalem, until 520 B.C. when the book of Haggai was written, the temple was still not rebuilt although the edict of Cyrus had commanded that the temple should be rebuilt. The Jews who returned under Zerubbabel, apparently misunderstood or inferred from their Scriptures, that the temple could not be rebuilt until the desolations period of seventy years, which had been predicted by the prophet Jeremiah, had expired.

They were saying, *"The time has not come."* To them, the time that Jehovah's house should be built had not come. Haggai 1:2 says: *"Thus speaketh the Lord of hosts, saying, the people say the time is not come, the time that the Lord's house should be built."*

We read God's reply to their excuse in Haggai 2:18-19: *"Consider now from this day will I bless you."* The astounding fact is that from the date emphasized by Jeremiah, Ezekiel, and the author of II Kings 15:1, the tenth day of Tebeth in 589 B.C. until Haggai's date, the 24th day of Chisleh, 520 B.C., was a span of exactly 25,200 days which, when divided by 360 days (which is the prophetic year in Scripture) equals exactly seventy years. Through the prophet Haggai, the Spirit of God indicated the end of the seventy years of desolation, to the very day, as predicted by Jeremiah in chapter 25.

LXIII. THE FIRST RETURN

Ezra

Turning to the book of Ezra, we can see that following the decree of Cyrus in 539 B.C., Zerubbabel recruited a large number of people for the return from Babylon to Jerusalem and Judah. The actual number of recruits is given in Ezra 2:64 as 42,360. In addition to these, were male and female servants numbering 7,337, plus 200 singing men and women, for a total of 49,897. Royal encouragement was given to Zerubbabel and his large company of pilgrims when Cyrus took all of the articles of the house of the Lord, which Nebuchadnezzar had carried away from Jerusalem, and gave them back to Zerubbabel, to be placed in the rebuilt temple.

Worship Restored

In Ezra 3, we learn that upon arriving back in Jerusalem, the people immediately set up an altar and began their new life by celebrating the Feast of Tabernacles. After many years, the restoration of the prescribed worship of Jehovah had begun. They prepared burnt offerings on the altar, but verse 6 says, *"The foundation of the temple of the Lord was not yet laid.* In the remainder of chapter 3, we read of a half hearted attempt to lay the foundation for the new (2nd) temple, but when the old men, who had known the magnificence of Solomon's temple prior to 586, 45 to 50 years earlier saw it, they saw this meager attempt so dismal in comparison to the original that they wept. However, other people began to praise. There was such a confusion of sounds, with some weeping aloud and other shouting for joy, that the difference could not be distinguished.

The Chronology in Ezra

Beginning in chapter 4, there is a section which was written in fifth century Aramaic. From 4:8 through 6:18, and in 7:12-26, we can read these Aramaic portions. They tend to validate the book of Ezra
and give it the fifth century B.C. date which scholars believe to be correct. Beginning in chapter 4, the first five verses detail for us chronologically what occurred after the return to

the land. The enemies of Judah and Benjamin heard that the people of the exile were building a temple. They went to Zerubbabel and asked to help with the project. Zerubbabel refused (vs. 3). He told them, "We are going to do this ourselves because the king of Persia has commanded us to complete this project." However, the inhabitants of the land discouraged the people of Judah and frightened them through hired counselors who frustrated them all the days of Cyrus and until the reign of Darius, king of Persia.

Two kings are mentioned here: Cyrus, king of Persia, who reigned from 539 to 529 B.C., and Cambyses (529-522). Darius, mentioned here in verse 5 was Darius, I who reigned from 522 to 485 B.C. Ahasuerus, whose Persian name was Xerxes reigned from 485 to 465 B.C. Verse 7 mentions Artaxerxes, who ruled from 465 to 424. To complete the Persian chronology beyond the listing of Ezra, there was Darius, II (424-404), Artaxerxes, II (404-359), Artaxerxes, III (359-338), Arses (338-335), Darius, III (335-331). In the time of Darius, III, the Persian Empire was overthrown by Alexander the Great, ending the kingdom of silver and initiating the kingdom of Greece; the belly and thighs of brass, as prophesied in the dream of Nebuchadnezzar.

Returning to the narrative in Ezra 4, we learn that the enemies of the Jews frustrated their attempts to build the temple until the reign of Darius, I who ascended the throne in 522 B.C. Earlier, we read that Haggai dated his book to the second year of Darius, in 520 B.C., at which time God began to bless the people and the seventy years of desolation predicted by Jeremiah came to an end.

Beginning in verse 6, Ezra picks up a different narrative, mentioning Xerxes, who reigned from 485 to 465, during whose reign the events of Esther took place. Then in verse 7, he mentions the reign of Artaxerxes (465-424). In relating the opposition which took place during the reign of Artaxerxes, Ezra was recording events that occurred during his own lifetime. The events about the return and original attempt to rebuild the temple, and the opposition under Cyrus and Xerxes, were historical to Ezra. As the author of the book, he recorded them under the inspiration of the Holy Spirit as historical events. To place Ezra historically, look at chapter 7:1, 6, and 8 in 458-457 B.C.:

How after these things, in the reign of Artaxerxes king of Persia, Ezra went up from Babylon; and he was a ready scribe in the law of Moses, and he came to Jerusalem in the fifth month, which was in the seventh year of the king.

Opposition to the Wall

In Ezra 4:7, he relates some events that occurred during his lifetime. The chapter records an attempt to rebuild the wall which predated, by a short time, the successful rebuilding of the wall by Nehemiah. The inhabitants of the land, the evil opponents of the Jews, were angry when they saw the Jews attempt to rebuild the city walls. The earlier decree of Cyrus to allow the rebuilding of the temple was a decree of religious freedom. They were not at that time given permission to rebuild the walls. That would have been a decree of military freedom, because once a city had its walls intact, it was able to resist a military invasion or a siege for one to two years. The Persians at that time had not allowed the Jews to rebuild the walls.

What went on in Israel was of no concern to those in control in Persia. So, following the completion of the temple in Jerusalem, the Jews attempted to rebuild the wall. Needless to say, their enemies did not want this. They sent a letter to King Artaxerxes: vss. 12-13:

The Jews which came up from thee to us are come unto Jerusalem, building the rebellious and the bad city, and have set up the walls thereof, and joined the foundations. Be it known now unto the king, that, if this city be builded, and the walls set up again, then will they not Pay toll, tribute, and custom, and so thou shalt endamage the revenue of the kings.

In verse 14 we see the false piety and false loyalty those inhabitants were pretending to have toward Artaxerxes, saying that they were in the service of the king,: *"And it was not meet for us to see the king's dishonour, therefore we have sent and certified the king."* In verses 17-22, we read the order from Artaxerxes that the work on the walls should cease. When the opposition received the document, they sent an armed militia to force the inhabitants of Jerusalem to stop the work on the walls.

Review of Earlier Opposition

In chapter 5, Ezra looked back historically and says it was the preaching of the post-exilic prophets, Haggai and Zechariah, who in 520 B.C. motivated the people to resume work on the temple. Then he gives additional information about the nature of the opposition. In verse 3, the leaders of the opposition, with Tatnai, their governor, questioned Zerubbabel, *"Who hath commanded you to build this house, and to make up this wall?"* Zerubbabel

informed them that the decree authorizing them to return and rebuild the temple had been issued by Cyrus in the first year of his reign. Tatnai then sent a
letter to Darius requesting the royal archives be searched to see if the Jews were telling the truth and to send them his decision.

The Decree of Darius

In chapter 6, we read that Darius had the archives searched and in one of the fortresses they found an abstract of Cyrus's earlier decree. Isn't it interesting that in 520 B.C. they could look into their ancient filing system and find a document written nineteen years earlier. Verses 3-5 give details of Cyrus's commands concerning the temple as quoted by Darius in his reply to Tatnai. He continued in verse 7, *"Let the work of this house of God alone; let the governor of the Jews and the elders of the Jews build this house of God in his place."*
Darius went on to say that he was making an additional decree to Tatnai and his allies. The full cost of the rebuilding was to be paid from the royal treasury out of the taxes of the provinces. And it was to be done without delay! Those opponents of the Jews, the citizens of a Persian province, had to pay taxes to Persia and now they were told their tax money would be used to further the work they were trying to stop. King Darius went further and ordered that whatever the Jews needed for offerings for their God, whether rams, bulls, lambs, goats, or fine oil, was to be given to them without fail on a daily basis. Finally, the king said that any man who violated his edict would have a timber taken from his house and he himself would be impaled and his house would be made a heap of refuse.

We know from secular history that the Persians had unique methods for torture; so this statement in Ezra is historically accurate. The torture of impalation, they inherited from the Assyrians who had invented it. This method had been known for a couple of centuries. What appeared to be opposition in the beginning, God used for His glory in the end so that the opposition became a source of blessing when the enemy had to provide the resources which resulted in   completion of the new temple. Chapter 6 describes the celebration that marked the completion.

LXIV. THE SECOND RETURN

More About Ezra

Chapter 7 begins with the second return of more exiles to Jerusalem under the personal leadership of Ezra. The first return was led by Zerubbabel and culminated in the completion of the new temple. Chapter 7 begins in 457 B.C., almost sixty years after the rebuilt temple was completed in 516 B.C.

The World in Ezra's Time

When Ezra returned to the land of Judah in the middle fifth century B.C., other major events were happening throughout the civilized world. Soldiers and judges in Athens began to receive regular salaries. The temple of Zeus was completed in 460 B.C. Herodatus, the father of history, was born in 485 B.C. and died in 424 B.C. Buddha died in 480 B.C. Confucius died in 479. Socrates was born in 470 and Euripedes, the Greek dramatist, was born in 484 B.C.

All of the Persian Wars occurred during that era. When the Persian army was defeated by the Greeks at Marathon in 490 B.C., this event was the origin of the marathon race. The Persians defeated the Spartans at Thermopylae in 480. Xerxes, I, burned Athens. In the same year, the Acropolis was destroyed. The Athenians destroyed the Persian fleet in the battle of Salamis in 480 B.C. In Esther, these Persian Wars also impacted on events. The Ionian war occurred in 499-494 B.C., and the building of the first temple of Saturn in Rome was completed in 498 B.C. In addition to these things, many significant medical accomplishments were taking place. The Indian surgeon, Sisrata, performed cataract operations in 500 B.C. Hippocrates, the Greek physician, was born in 460 B.C. This was only three years before Ezra led the exiles back to Jerusalem in the second return.

Ezra returned to Jerusalem with a letter that taxes could not be imposed on the Jews, nor could tolls be collected from them by the nations through which they passed as they returned. The letter also provided that if anyone disobeyed its instructions, they would be either executed, banished, or have their goods confiscated. With that letter safely in hand,

Ezra returned to Jerusalem with 1500 men, 38 Levites, and 220 helpers, for a total of 1,758 people. Ezra would not ask the king for troops to protect their small party from robbers lest he (Ezra) appeared to have no faith in his God. His explanation is in chapter 8:22-23:

> *I was ashamed to require of the king a band of soldiers and*
> *horsemen to help us against the enemy in the way. Because we*
> *had spoken unto the king, saying, The hand of our God is upon*
> *all them for good that seek him; but his power and his wrath is*
> *against all them that forsake him. So we fasted and besought*
> *our God for this: and he was entreated of us.*

Verse 31 sums up how God listened to their entreaty: *"The hand of our God was upon us, and he delivered us from the hand of the enemy, and of such as lay in wait by the way."*

Almost immediately after his arrival, Ezra learned that the sons of the Jews had taken the daughters of the local people as wives and had merged with the peoples in the land, in opposition to what God had commanded. Ezra 9:1 reports that the priests and the Levites, as well as the rank and file of the people, had married into the families of the Canaanites, the Hittites, the Perizzites, the Jebusites, the Ammonites, the Moabites, the Egyptians, and the Amorites. Most of these were descendents of those whom under Joshua's leadership were to have driven out a thousand years earlier, but they were still around. The warning given in Joshua's time, that if they were not driven out they would infiltrate the people and cause them to sin, was still coming to pass a thousand years later. Through their own sin and lust, these exiles were reaping the disobedience their ancestors sowed a millennium before.

When Ezra heard about it, he went into deep mourning, tearing his garments and plucking out his hair and beard. Then he sat down appalled at what was happening. He could not believe what he was seeing. These people had been in bondage in Babylon because of their sins and now, by God's grace and provision, they had been allowed to return to their homeland. They had been empowered to rebuild their temple with tax money; they had experienced God's blessing and promises; now, despite all of this, they still disobeyed by marrying the daughters of the local pagan people.

Verse 4 says that there gathered unto him *"every one that trembled at the words of the God of Israel, because of the transgression of those that had been carried away; and I sat astonished until the evening sacrifice."* In vs. 5, Ezra said, *"I arose up from my heaviness; and having rent my garment and my mantle, I fell upon my knees, and spread out my hands unto the Lord my God."* Ezra was embarrassed and ashamed and in this way, he united himself with the exiles in their sins. Although personally innocent, he prayed in confession, *"Our iniquities are increased over our head, and our trespass is grown up unto the heavens."* Notice how Ezra assumed the role of intercessor and participant. As he pleaded on behalf of the people, he included himself so that somehow God might see his personal plea and as a substitutionary and a national plea. In his prayer, he reviewed some of the history of the nations of Judah and Israel, summing it all up in verse 10 by asking, *"O our God, what shall we say after this? For we have forsaken thy commandments."*

The people were back in their land with every reason to praise God.
But again they sinned and acted in disobedience. Ezra continued his prayer in verse 13ff:

> *And after all that is come upon us for our evil deeds, and for*
> *our great trespass, seeing that thou our God hast punished us*
> *less than our iniquities deserve, and hast given us such deliverance as this; Should we*
> *again break thy commandments, and*
> *join in affinity with the people of these abominations?*

"Can there be any remnant to escape?" he asks. *"Will you not now be angry to the point of destruction? We are guilty and cannot stand before You."* While Ezra was praying, chapter 10 records that the people began to come forward and weep and confess their sins. As they came forward in repentance, Ezra instructed them to put away their foreign wives. Then, Ezra recorded the names of those who sinned. Forever and eternally, their names are recorded in the last chapter of Ezra as those who sinned and disobeyed God.

LXV. NEHEMIAH THE BUILDER

The book of Nehemiah continues the historical narrative which began in Ezra. The opening events occurred in the twentieth year of King Artaxerxes, who came to the throne in 465 B.C. The year was 445 B.C. and Nehemiah, whose job was cup-bearer to the king, was in Susa, the summer capital of the Persian kings. While he was there, he had visitors who had been to Jerusalem. Nehemiah asked them about conditions there and received this tragic report (vs. 3):

> *"The remnant in the provinces are in great affliction and*
> *reproach: the wall of Jerusalem also is broken down, and*
> *the gates thereof are burned with fire."*

It had been 141 years since the gates were burned and the walls torn down by Nebuchadnezzar in 586 B.C. We have read how the opposition hindered those who first returned under Zerubbabel and later returned with Ezra.

Nehemiah apparently had a fine reputation with Artaxerxes and was usually cheery. However, after receiving news from his homeland, Nehemiah's countenance had fallen. When he went in before the king, Artaxerxes looked at him and noticed a difference. "Are you sick?" he asked. *This is nothing else but sorrow of heart,"* He responded (2:3). Nehemiah said, *"I was very sore afraid."* It is no wonder he was afraid, because there was no room for a sad heart, or a sad face, in the inner sanctuary of a Persian monarch. They hired men who were happy and could keep them happy. If one exhibited a sad face, the result was often instant execution. However, Nehemiah explained to the king the reason for his sorrow, and the monarch's reply was, *"For what dost thou make request?"* Those words indicated the royal intention was to provide the necessary help for Nehemiah's concern. Before replying, Nehemiah said, *"I prayed to the God of heaven,"* Notice that he did not try to respond in his own wisdom. After praying, he asked for, and received, time off, a passport, building materials, and an armed escort.

The Wall Rebuilt

Nehemiah returned to Jerusalem with *some few men* and almost immediately work began on the wall. But again, as with all of the previous endeavors, they were also opposed, mocked, and despised by the inhabitants of the land. Nehemiah 2:19 summarizes this. Chapter 4:6 gives the secret of success for the rebuilding of the wall. It was because, *"the people had a mind to work."* They worked even while preparing for opposition. As we read in 4:18: *"For the builders, everyone had his sword girded by his side, and so builded."* Nehemiah kept a trumpeter ready to sound the alarm in case the enemy approached. Chapter 5:14, records that Nehemiah was the governor in Judah for twelve years; from 444 to 432 B.C.

Chapter 6 describes the tactics used by the opposition. Nehemiah was also told of a threat to his life and was advised to seek safety in the temple. His reply was, *"Should such a man as I flee? And who is there, that, being as I am, would go into the temple to save his life? I will not go in"* (vs. 11). Verse 13 explains that the man who warned him had been hired to do so in order that Nehemiah might become frightened and flee for his life, so they might be able to make an evil report against him. But Nehemiah acted wisely. He responded spiritually and scripturally, because he *knew* that God was protecting him. He did not fear when he heard about the "trumped-up" assassination attempt. Finally, in verse 15 we read that the wall was completed in just fifty two days. Verse 16 reports:

> *And it came to pass, that when all our enemies heard thereof,*
> *and all the heathen that were about us saw these things, they*
> *were much cast down in their own eyes: for they perceived that*
> *this work was wrought of our God.*

So, even through opposition, God was glorified when the Walls of Jerusalem were rebuilt in 444 B.C. after fifty-two days of consistent effort because the people had a heart to work.

Continuing in chapter 8, we discover that Ezra was still in Jerusalem. You recall that he had made his return, which we know as the second return, in 458-457 B.C. We do not know how many returned with Nehemiah in 445-444 B.C., because the words are, *some few men,* but we can call this the third return. At that time, Ezra had been there for about thirteen years. In chapter 8, Ezra and Nehemiah formed a team to continue to reform the people. Verse 9 states that Nehemiah was the governor and Ezra was the priest and scribe. Then an extensive description of the teaching, reforms, and organizations, introduced in the post-exilic community.

Chapter 13 records the sinful alliance between the priesthood and the opposition leader. This occurred after 432 B.C. when Nehemiah

was not in Jerusalem. He reports in verse 6 that he had returned to Persia to take up Its responsibilities to the king, but after a suitable length of time, he once again obtained leave of absence from the king to return to Jerusalem. When Nehemiah returned, he discovered that some of the priests had left Jerusalem, and the temple service, and began to work in their own fields. He brought them back and made certain that the tithes were collected regularly to take care of them. He observed that the Sabbath was not being kept, and he set that matter in order. He also discovered that some of the Jews, including members of the high priest's family, had married women from Ashdod, Ammon, and Moab. He contended with them, cursed them, and actually hit some of them, then pulled their hair out as he made them aware that they must not give their daughters, or their sons, to the inhabitants of the land. With that fury of reformation activity, Nehemiah's ministry drew to a close.

With the completion of the events in the book of Nehemiah, we have come to the end of the historical period of the nations of Israel and Judah. Only Malachi lived after the time of Nehemiah, or at the earliest during Nehemiah's latter years. So, generally speaking, the inspired record of the history of Israel and Judah came to an end in the times of Nehemiah and Malachi, in around 400 B.C.

LXVI. THE STORY OF ESTHER

We have one more historical book to consider. Even though Esther follows Nehemiah in the English structure of the Old Testament, the events in the book occurred prior to Nehemiah's time, beginning in the third year of King Xerxes, which was approximately 483/482 B.C. Historically the book of Esther occurs about twenty-five years prior to Ezra's return to Jerusalem. The events which transpired must be considered in light of Isaiah's earlier prophetic command which said: *"Flee Babylon"* (48:20)

Isaiah had instructed the people to *flee Babylon*, when Cyrus defeated the Babylonians. But, as he tried to recruit all the exiles, Zerubbabel was able to recruit fewer than 50,000 to return with him. Ezra, a little later, following the time of Esther, was able to put together about 1700 people to return with him. Finally, those who returned with Nehemiah were "some few men." It can only be assumed that the people who had gone into exile to Babylon had become very comfortable in their situation by the time Cyrus captured the city in 539 B.C. Because of this, they remained there for years under the Persian monarchs. But, it was a comfort in disobedience because they had not obeyed the command of God through Isaiah to return to Judah when the seventy years in exile ended in 539 B.C.

The events in Esther must be seen as taking place in Persia, and involving a large number of Jews who had not followed the command of God. They were living in disobedience away from Jerusalem and apart from the worship system God had ordered through Moses; under a foreign monarchy, rather than being in Judah under the priesthood and under God.

The book of Esther begins by introducing King Xerxes, also called Ahasuerus. We know from history that he had been involved in intense military activity and suffered defeat at the hands of the Greeks, at the battle of Marathon in 490, and very shortly would experience another defeat at Thermopylae, in 480, and again at Salamis in 479. Meanwhile, he had sought refuge by banqueting, partying, and in his harem. The story begins in his third year, at about 482 B.C. The party described by the author lasted for 180 days. When the six month party ended, he gave a special seven-day banquet and sent a command to Queen Vashti, who was evidently very beautiful, to come out and expose herself to his drunken friends. She refused with dignity, and the king became very angry.

Verse 12 sums up his reaction by saying: *"his anger burned in him."* He ordered his wise men to check the law books and see what could be done to this queen who did not obey his command. The wise men informed Xerxes that Queen Vashti had not only wronged the king, but also all the princes and all the people in the provinces, because her conduct would become known. When the other women saw that Queen Vashti was not punished for saying "no" to the king, they would *all* have contempt for their husbands and refuse to do their bidding because their queen had refused. This event, they claimed, would have a domino effect which would end up with a Persian women's liberation movement. They said (vs. 19):

> *If it please the king, let there go a royal commandment from*
> *him, and let it be written among the laws of the Persians and*
> *the Medes, that it be not altered, That Vashti come no more*
> *before king Ahasuerus; and let the king give her royal estate*
> *unto another that is better than she.*

When the king's edict became known all the women would say; *"Great is the king."* They would give honor to their husbands and there would be no rebellion from the wives. The advice pleased the king and the princes. Implementing this advice, Xerxes sent letters to all his provinces so that every man should be master in his own house. Vashti was dethroned, and her crown was taken away.

Esther is Chosen

In chapter two the search for a replacement began. The king's overseers went to all of the provinces in Persia seeking beautiful young virgins and taking them to the harem in Susa. There must have been many broken hearted young men throughout the kingdom, because the king had first choice of the beautiful women in the land, and took whomever he pleased for himself. But they were powerless to stop him and the young lady who most pleased the king, would become queen in the place of Vashti.

In verse 5 we are introduced to Mordecai, a Jew of the tribe of Benjamin. He was responsible to care for Esther, his uncle's daughter, because she had neither father, or mother. Although she was his cousin, he took her as his own daughter. When the command seeking beautiful young women was carried out, Esther, who must have been very beautiful, was taken into the palace. She so pleased the Chief Eunuch in the harem, that he provided her with the best cosmetics, the finest food, and gave her the choicest handmaidens. She did not tell anyone she was a Jewess, because Mordecai had instructed her earlier not to make that known. Mordecai paced back and forth in front of the harem every day to see if he could hear some news, or rumors, about how things were proceeding in the palace. Verse 12 says that each girl chosen was commanded to go in to the king after twelve months of preparation.

The eunuchs and handmaidens used the twelve months preparing the women so they could spend a night with the king. For six months they rubbed them down with oil and myrrh, and then for six months with spices and cosmetics. The girl would go to the king in the evening and in the morning she would return to the second harem. After that first night, she would live in the harem unless the king had been so pleased, that he summoned her by name at a later time. Finally, Esther's turn came and she was taken to the king. Verse 16 says *"He loved her more than all the women."* He placed the royal crown on her head and made her his queen in the place of the deposed Vashti. Then he gave a great banquet in Esther's honor and summoned all the princes.

Mordecai Saves the King's Life

As time passed, Mordecai became almost a permanent fixture at the king's gate. He had probably been there for so long that the officials disregarded his presence. So it was that he overheard two of the king's officials, who guarded the door, plotting to assassinate Xerxes as he passed by. He revealed the plan to Esther, who informed the king in Mordecai's name. The king investigated and found that the plot was true and hanged both of the assassins. Then, as with all other official acts which took place in the Persian court, it was documented and filed away in the official archives.

Haman Plots Revenge

Chapter 3 introduces Haman, the Agagite {see Exodus 35:12.}. He was a proud man with political aspirations. He advanced in the Persian bureaucracy until eventually he had authority over all of the princes who served with him. All of the servants at the king's gate would bow down to him when he went in to the palace because the king had commanded everyone to do so. But Mordecai would never bow down. Finally, others asked him (vs. 3) why he transgressed the king's command and he told them he could not because he was a Jew. When Haman became aware of Mordecai's defiance, he was filled with rage. When he learned that he was a Jew, he was not content to take vengeance on Mordecai alone, but determined to destroy all of the Jews in the Persian Empire.

Verse 7 gives us another piece of chronological information. The king met Esther in the *seventh* year of his reign, which would have been after his defeat at Salamis in 479. Now, *five years* after his marriage to Esther, as recorded in 3:7, in the twelfth year of the king, lots were cast to decide when, using Haman's plan, they would destroy all of the Jews. The lot fell on the month Adar. Haman cast lots until he could arrive at the most strategic month for the attack to take place. Then he said to the king (vss. 8-9):

> *There is a certain people scattered abroad and dispersed among*
> *the people in all the provinces of thy kingdom; and their laws*
> *are diverse from all people; neither keep they the king's laws:*
> *therefore it is not for the king's profit to suffer them. If it please*
> *the king, let it be written that they may be destroyed: and I will pay*
> *ten thousand talents of silver to the hands of those that have the*
> *charge of the business, to bring it into the king's treasures.*

Evidently, Haman was a very wealthy man and the king was intimidated because he was devastated psychologically. This was due in part to the military disasters which had befallen him and his drunken revelry which had debilitated him physically and mentally. He did not question Haman's statement, but gave him his signet ring, saying, *"Do with them as it seemeth good to thee."* These plans to commit genocide against the Jews were written in the laws of the Medes and the Persians, and sealed with the king's signet ring. Letters were sent to all the provinces ordering them to annihilate the Jews, both young and old, women and children, in one day-the thirteenth day of the twelfth month, the month of Adar. In addition to destroying the Jews, they were to confiscate their possessions. Verse 14 says that a copy of the edict was issued as law in every province, and couriers ran throughout the entire land. Meanwhile, the king and Haman sat down together to drink and to discuss matters of state. At last, Haman thought, he was to be recognized as a political genius.

When Mordecai heard about the edict (chapter 4), he rent his garment, put on sackcloth and ashes, and began to cry loudly throughout the streets of the city. He walked all the way to the king's gate, but did not go inside because the kings of Persia did not allow any unhappiness inside the gate. No one was to enter clothed in sackcloth. The mourning spread throughout the land when the Jews in the provinces heard that they were to be annihilated.

Finally, queen Esther's maidens and the eunuchs told her about Mordecai's behavior. Then she also was in great anguish. She sent him new garments, but he did not take off his sackcloth. She called her personal attendant, and sent him out to learn exactly what was wrong. Mordecai related to him all that had taken place and the exact amount of money Haman had promised to pay the king for the destruction of the Jews. (The king's treasury must have been emptied by his military expenditures and losses on the battlefield.) He gave him a copy of the edict to show to Esther in hope that she would go in to the king and ask him to reverse it. When Esther heard the story, she sent a message back to Mordecai explaining that according to the law, anyone who went to the king without being summoned was put to death unless he held out his golden scepter. Then she added that the king had not summoned her for thirty days. King Xerxes was a man of ultimate and absolute power. Drawings on the Persian walls show him sitting on the throne with his sceptre at his side. His son Artaxerxes often stood behind him and in front of the throne was a censor of burning incense. No one was allowed to come near to King Xerxes.

When Mordecai heard, he said, *"Think not that thou shalt escape in the king's house, more than all the Jews. For if thou altogether holdest thy peace then shall deliverance arise to the Jews from...?* At that point we would expect to read "God." But God's name never appears in the book of Esther. Instead, the writer says *"another place."* Then he added, *"Who knoweth whether thou art come to the kingdom for such a time as this?"* Perhaps Esther, he was saying, God, knowing in advance what Haman would do, placed you in the kingdom to stand in the breach and save the lives of all the Jews. Esther commanded Mordecai to assemble all of the Jews and hold a three-day fast. She and her maidens would fast likewise and then she would go in to the king even though she had not been summoned, which was not allowed according to the Persian law. She closed by saying, *"And if I perish, I perish."*

Esther's Strategy

On the third day, Esther, dressed in her most beautiful royal robes, stood in the doorway of the inner sanctuary where Xerxes was sitting on his throne opposite the entrance. She must have been frightened, knowing that in the next few seconds she would either be condemned to death, or invited into the royal presence of Xerxes, the mightiest monarch on earth. Although the word *"God"* is never mentioned in the book of Esther, the Holy Spirit has a marvelous way of presenting the story so that we can see the sovereign hand of God in all these events. Just as Ruth *"happened"* on the field of Boaz, and just as the king in the next chapter will *happen* to find a particular record describing the heroism of Mordecai, so now in 5:2 it *happened* that when the king saw Esther *"she obtained favour in his sight."* Once again we see how the king's heart is in the hand of God. Xerxes extended the golden sceptre to Esther and she *"drew near, and touched the top of the sceptre."*

Following this welcome by Xerxes, the Holy Spirit allows us to hear the conversations that occurred between Haman, Xerxes, and Esther, in the king's inner chamber. Through this divinely inspired Book, we are allowed to witness events in the court of Xerxes, almost as silent participants in the scenarios which were played out. When Esther touched the top of the sceptre, the king asked, *"What is thy request? it shall be even given thee to the half of the kingdom."* Esther replied, *"If it seem good unto the king, let the king and Haman come this day unto the banquet that I have prepared for him."* Notice that Esther did not speak out immediately against Haman. We read earlier how the king and Haman sat down together to drink. They were both friends and political allies. Esther, knowing the ways of the court, did not make an overt accusation against Haman. She appealed to Haman's ego and to the king's love of parties, by inviting them to a banquet.

When the banquet which Esther organized ended, and as they finished their wine, the king again asked Esther what her request was and she replied (vs. 8):

"If I have found favour in the sight of the king, and if it please the king to grant my petition, and to Perform my request, let the king and Haman come to the banquet that I shall prepare for them, and I will do tomorrow as the king hath said".

Following this strategic move she invited them to another party. Haman went home that evening glad and pleased in his heart. He had banqueted with the king and queen, and he had been invited to another banquet scheduled for the next day. But as he walked out the gate he saw Mordecai, who as always, was not standing up, trembling, or bowing before him. His anger burned again, but he controlled himself and continued his journey home. After arriving home, he began calling his friends together to brag about himself, his possessions, his promotions, and his second invitation to Esther's banquet. Then he confessed that because of Mordecai the Jew, he could not really enjoy anything. His wife and friends suggested that he build a gallows fifty cubits high (75 feet) and ask the king to hang Mordecai on it. The suggestion pleased Haman and he ordered the gallows constructed.

Mordecai is Honored

The first few verses of chapter 6 take us into the king's bedroom on the evening between the two banquets to which he and Haman had been invited. God once again intervened and afflicted Xerxes with insomnia. He ordered that the book of records - the chronicles - be read to him. Among all the records kept by the Persians, the man who selected the scroll (or tablets) just *happened* to take the one that contained the account of the assassination plot and Mordecai's intervention which had occurred five years earlier. After hearing of Mordecai's heroism, the king asked, *"What honour and dignity hath been done to Mordecai for this?"* He was told, *"There is nothing done for him."* By that time it was early morning and Haman had just arrived in the court to petition the king for permission to hang Mordecai on the gallows. Calling him in, Xerxes asked, *"What shall be done unto the man whom the king delighteth to honour? "* In his egotism, Haman was certain that Xerxes could only be referring to him. I can imagine him wrinkling his forehead and scratching his head in thought before saying (vss. 8-9):

*Let the royal apparel be brought which the king useth to wear,
and the horse that the king rideth upon, and the crown royal
which is set upon his head: And let this apparel and horse be
delivered to the hand of one of the king's most noble princes,
that they may array the man withal whom the king delighteth to
honour, and bring him on horseback through the street of the
city and proclaim before him, Thus shall it be done to the man
whom the king delighteth to honour.*

The king approved the idea and said to Haman, *"Make haste and do even so to Mordecai the Jew."* Haman had no choice. No one could defy Xerxes and live. He did as the king demanded and proclaimed Mordecai's honor throughout the city. But he was so humiliated after it was over, that he returned home with his head covered, unrecognized, and mourning. When he described his disappointment to his wife and friends, they said (vs. 13): *"If Mordecai be of the seed of the Jews, before whom thou hast begun to fall, thou shalt not prevail against him, but shalt surely fall before him."* As this omen was uttered, the king's servants arrived to escort him to Esther's second banquet. It was to be Haman's last meal.

Haman is Exposed

As they were enjoying the banquet and drinking their wine, the king again asked Esther (7:2): *"What is thy petition, queen Esther, and it*
shall be granted thee: even to the half of the kingdom." This time Esther answered (vss. 3-4):

> *If it please the king, let my life be given me at my petition, and*
> *my people at my request: For we are sold, I and my people, to be*
> *destroyed, to be slain, and to perish. But if we had been sold for*
> *bondmen and bondwomen, I had held my tongue, although the*
> *enemy could not countervail the king's damage.*

Then the king demanded, *"Who is he, and where is he, that durst presume in his heart to do so?"* Esther pointed her finger to *"this wicked Haman."* Haman, whom the king had trusted, was visibly shaken and terrified. Xerxes stood up in anger and walked into the cool palace garden to clear his head from the effects of the wine and contemplate the situation. Esther remained on her couch when suddenly, Haman, sensing his doom by the king's demeanor, prostrated himself on the couch before Esther to beg for his life. At that moment, Xerxes returned, and seeing Haman by Esther on the couch, exclaimed, *"Will he force the queen also before me in the house?"* As he spoke the words, the servants *"covered Haman's face."* Haman was history. When someone was sentenced to die in the presence of a Persian monarch, his face was immediately covered. It would never be seen again. One of the eunuchs quickly spoke up and informed the king of the gallows which Haman had made for Mordecai, *"who had spoken good for the king."* Then the king said, *"Hang him thereon."* So they hanged Haman on the gallows that he had prepared for Mordecai.

The Jews are Spared

Chapter 8 informs us that even though because of the law of the Medes and Persians the date of annihilation could not be rescinded, a new decree was made which allowed the Jews to defend themselves. When the Persians attacked the Jews on the 13th of Adar, the Jews fought back fiercely. Esther 9:16 says that the Jews killed 75,000 of those who hated them. But, it adds, they did not take any spoil. Because the Jews were disobedient and had stayed behind in the land, all these things came about and 75,000 people were slain because of the Jews' disobedience. God intervened and allowed Esther to perform in a heroic manner. As we have seen before, innocent people often suffer when God's people are disobedient.

Purim is Established

The remainder of chapter 9 tells how, as a result of the annihilation of the enemies of the Jews, the feast of Purim was established. Even now, it is celebrated (usually on February 28th) as a remembrance and a memorial. It is a memorial, celebrated year by year, which validates the historical accuracy in the book of Esther.

LXVII. TWO EARLY PROPHETS

Obadiah

Conservative scholars date the writing of Obadiah to approximately 840 B.C. Assuming this is correct, he is the first of the writing prophets. His was a message of Judgment on the land of Edom. Obadiah is probably mentioned in II Chronicles 17:7, because the dating of the book and the dating of Jehoshaphat's reign would be in the same historical time-frame. Verses 11 to 14 of the book form the pivotal dating key, and probably refer to the invasion by the Philistines, which is recorded in II Chronicles 21:16ff. The name Obadiah means, worshiper of Yahweh. The book was addressed to the Edomites, who were the descendents of Esau.

In verse 3, God said, *"The pride of thine heart hath deceived thee, thou that dwellest in the clefts of the rock, whose habitation is high; that saith in his heart, Who shall being me down to the ground."* The root sin of pride is evident here. The Edomites lived in Petra, the cave city built high in the mountains. If can still be visited today by horseback. In those days, there was no way an invading army could bring them down from those highly elevated dwelling places. As a result, they felt very secure. Yet in verse 4, God said, *"Though thou exalt thyself as the eagle, and thou set thy nest among the stars, thence will I being thee down, saith the Lord."* By contrast, he said, if thieves and robbers came they would ruin you. But they would only steal until they had enough. They could carry off only so much.

From I Samuel 14:47, we know that King Saul fought against the Edomites. Later (11 Sam. 8:13-14) King David subdued them. In II Kings 8:20, we read that Edom revolted, and in fact at a later time, they encouraged Babylon, as reported in Psalm 137:7. The Edomites continued in existence through the time of Christ. They were tolerated and ruled by the Roman Caesars, who called them Idumeans. Herod the Great, who became king of Judah in 37 B.C., was an Idumean. It was he who had the children of Bethlehem slaughtered shortly after the birth of the Lord Jesus. Finally, in 70 A.D., when the Romans invaded Jerusalem under Titus, Edom helped the inhabitants of the land and was annihilated.

Among the reasons for the prophesied destruction of Edom, and among the reasons they were hated, is narrated in verse 10ff: *"For thy violence against thy brother Jacob thou shalt be cut off forever."* They stood aloof when strangers carried away Jacob's wealth and foreigners entered his gates and cast lots upon Jerusalem. Edom stood with the invaders. In God's evaluation, they should not have gloated over their brother's calamity. Obadiah was probably describing the invasion by the Philistines in 845 B.C. However, in the prophetic-perfect sense, Obadiah could also have been looking down to 586 B.C. We know from Psalm 137:7, that the Edomites were pleased when the Babylonians sacked Jerusalem. They actually *helped* catch those who tried to escape and turned them over to the Babylonians. For these reasons, for the violence done to their brother Jacob, the Edomites were promised total destruction.

Verse 15 begins the eschatological section. Assuming that Obadiah was the first of the writing prophets, this is the first mention in the Old Testament of the *Day of the Lord*. Your dealings, he said, *"shall return upon thine own head."* The final comparison is made in verse 18 where Obadiah says, *"The house of Jacob shall be afire, and the house of Joseph aflame."* It would be a destructive fire and flame, because the house of Esau was going to be stubble. The allusion is that of a farmer going out to burn the stubble from his field. Verse 18 continues by prophesying total destruction: *"There shall not be any remaining of the house of Esau."* The final result, as indicated in the concluding verses, was regarding the descendents of Judah, *"They of the south shall possess the mount of Esau."* Eventually, when all who oppose God are destroyed, the Jews will inhabit the lands of their enemies and dwell in them forever.

Joel

There are many suggested dates for the authorship of the book of Joel. The conservative date of 835 B.C., would place Joel in the time of the reign of Athaliah. The occasion for the prophecy was a devastating locust plague and drought, as recorded in chapter one. Because of this natural calamity, and in view of the imminent coming of the *Day of the Lord*, of which the locusts, plague, and drought, were only forerunners, Joel called the people to national repentance. Conditional to their repentance, was immediate security and blessing; then a future outpouring of the spirit of prophecy. It would be poured out upon all the faithful, after which time a new era of righteousness and peace would begin.

Joel's prophecy can be divided into two sections. In the first (chapters 1 and 2) there is the national call to repentance on the basis of God's judgment; and, the promise of deliverance and blessing in the *Day of the Lord*. The second (chapter 3) indicates judgment on the enemies of Israel. In the first division, the unprecedented plagues of locust and drought are described while everyone is called to lament their effects. The priests were especially addressed because it was necessary to suspend the daily sacrifice. This calamity was only a forerunner of the great *Day of the Lord* which was to come. The army of locusts was a graphic demonstration of the future hosts of the Lord who would be sent in judgment. But, it could be averted by humble repentance after which would follow the promises of God. The central theme is the phrase "The Day of the Lord." It is a unique eschatological phrase first used in Obadiah and now reiterated again and again by Joel (1:15; 2:1, 11 & 31; 3:14,18). The spiritual significance can be found in the nature and purpose of the Day of the Lord. It will be a day of wrath, and a day of judgment upon the wicked, and a day of salvation for the righteous.

Assuming the early date for Joel, it would be just a little over one hundred years later that the Assyrians would invade and destroy Israel. The locusts were forerunners of this event. It is interesting that over and over again, Joel personified the locusts as if they were an army of invading Assyrians. Sometimes it is difficult to delineate between what is a real locust and what is a real Assyrian. For example, in 2:3: *"the land is as the Garden of Eden before them, and behind them a desolate wilderness; yea, and nothing shall escape them."* Certainly locusts can do that, but the Assyrians did it as well. *Like the noise of chariots on the tops of mountains shall they leap, they shall climb the wall like men of war.. They shall run to and fro in the city; they shall run upon the wall, they shall climb up upon the houses; they shall enter in at the windows like a thief. Who can abide it? (2:5ff)*

The eschatological significance of the impending Assyrian invasion is closely intertwined with the reality of the locust invasion because, as terrible as the locusts were the invasion by the Assyrians would be even worse. However, there was still hope for deliverance from Assyria. In verse 12ff, God said, *"Also now turn ye even to me with all your heart, and with fasting, and with weeping, and with mourning: And rend your heart, and not your garments."*

In later centuries an individual could buy a garment for rending. Jews loved to rend their garments so others could look and say, that man must be in deep mourning. Since many liked to do that so frequently, tailors designed garments that could easily be rent. They may not have had such garments in Joel's time. Nevertheless it had become a more or less automatic act which did not mean anything. It was not from the heart, but only for outward show. In effect, God said, "I don't care about your garment, the outward show; rend your heart because you have disobeyed Me." The irony in the book of Joel is that the inhabitants of the land were looking for the *Day of the Lord* as a day of deliverance. But Joel was of the saying, "You are all wicked and you should not be anticipating the *Day of the Lord,* because for you it will be a day of darkness, gloom, sadness, and judgment." Chapter 3 continues when God says, *"I will also gather all nations."* He is going to bring them into the valley of Jehoshaphat and enter into judgment with them there on behalf of Israel, whom they scattered among the nations and divided *His* land.

With this prophecy, the book of Joel begins to conclude as he reiterates again in 3:18: *"It shall come to pass in that day, that the mountains shall drop down new wine and the hills shall flow with milk."* The parallel passage here is Isaiah 66:19-24, as the prophet looks down through the corridors of time, beyond our present age, toward the time when Israel will be restored. This is a common theme throughout the Minor Prophets, because, even though it was necessary for them to prophesy God's judgment on His chosen people, they did not lose hope. There was always a light at the end of the tunnel. They knew that one day God would restore the remnant to the land, and would bless them there. The Apostle Peter quoted Joel 2:29-32 in Acts 2:17-21.

LXVIII. JONAH

As we switch from the ninth century prophets to the eighth century prophets, we will begin with Jonah. We know from II Kings 14:25, that Jonah prophesied during the time of Jeroboam, II, who reigned from 793 to 753 B.C. Based on some of the historical events which occurred in the early years of Jeroboam, II's reign, we can date Jonah's experience at Nineveh to the early eighth century B. C.

Historicity of Jonah

Without spending a great deal of time regarding the authenticity of the book and historicity of the person of Jonah, it is sad to say that some Christians, although very few, view the book as mythological. These believe that Jonah is no more historical than the books of Greek mythology. The two prevailing views are: *allegorical* and *literal*. The literal view is synonymous with the historical one. The allegorical says that Jonah symbolizes Israel. Israel was called to make God known to the world, both in message and by conduct. They failed in their responsibility and were destroyed. Judah was swallowed up into the Babylonian exile. This was symbolized by Jonah who was swallowed by the fish, and vomited back up three days later. In this same way, the exiles from Judah, who were swallowed up by Babylon, were later vomited back up and returned home. There are no valid reasons to believe that the book is anything but historical. It presents its materials as historical, not as parables or allegories. Also, the ancient Jews believed it as historical. The book of *Tobit 14:4* records this fact and so does Josephus in *Antiquities 912.2*. Furthermore, Jonah is mentioned in II Kings 14:25 as a historical person. Finally, the Lord Jesus Christ acknowledged Jonah as historical. He pointed to Jonah's experience in the fish as a type of His death, burial, and resurrection. He also used the repentance of Nineveh as a sign of judgment on His generation (Matt. 12:39-41):

"An evil and adulterous generation seeketh after a sign, and there shall no sign be given to it, but the sign of the prophet Jonas: For as Jonas was three days and three nights in the whale's belly, so shall the Son of man be three days and three nights in the heart of the earth. The men of Nineveh shall rise in judgment with this generation, and shall condemn

it: because they repented at the preaching of Jonas; and, behold, a greater than Jonas is here."

Those who doubt the words of Christ, say that He knew Jonah was not a real character. But because the people did not know, He accommodated His words to their ignorance by giving them illustrations which they believed to be true. If this is true, then we cannot believe anything the Lord Jesus Christ said, even regarding His divine origin, or the necessity of redemption.

There is also a fallacy creeping into doctrinal statements today which says that the Bible is inerrant in "all matters of revelation." This is the subtle leaven of heresy. This seemingly innocent statement asserts that the Bible is not necessarily accurate in matters that are not revelatory. For example, matters concerning creation, history, and science. This belief is a companion to skepticism and atheism. The Bible *is* the inspired Word of God and it *is* inerrant. Although it is not designed to be a scientific text, or history book, where it does touch on these subjects it is without error. I must believe that Jonah was a historical person and that the events contained in the book actually occurred in the early part of the eighth century B.C. during the time of Jeroboam, II in the northern kingdom, if I am to be true to the words of my Savior, the crucified, buried, and risen Son of God.

Why the Book of Jonah?

The first questions one might ask are, "Why do we have the book of Jonah? What is its purpose?" In answer to these questions, I can say that until now, we have dealt primarily with the nations of Israel and Judah mentioning the surrounding nations only when these two came in contact with them. We know that Jeroboam II was a strong king and that because of his power the Assyrians were not in control of Israel in any official capacity other than receiving tribute. However, they were an ever present threat on the northern horizon. The book of Jonah has as its main purpose to show us that God is interested not only in the Israelites, but in the Gentile world as well. We know that Israel had a three-fold purpose in the program and plan of God. First, they were the recipients and custodians of the true revelation of God (Exod. 3; Psalm 47:19-20; Romans 3:1-2). Second, Israel was to exhibit to the world the true religion and morality of Yahweh, through separation from other nations and by her obedience, righteousness, and holiness (Lev. 20:24-26; Deut. 7:6). Third, the major aspect of Israel's ministry was to prepare the way for the Messiah.

A few of the Old Testament prophecies we have not considered (Isa. 2; 45; 66; Micah 4; Zechariah 8 and 14) concerning the salvation of the Gentile nations, are not for the Old

Testament dispensation, but to a period in the future Messianic era. True missionary activity was possible only after the cross of Jesus Christ (John 12:20-24; Acts 1:4-8). Israel frequently did welcome proselytes, but there was no command in the Old Testament for Israel to act as a missionary nation actively recruiting. We know there were always strangers and aliens, non Israelites among them, but the burden was always on them. Foreigners had to demonstrate the initiative to become proselytes, and they would do so for a variety of reasons. It was only at a later time, when the Pharisees came into existence, that an outreach was begun to bring people into Judaism. Jesus rebuked the Pharisees because their motives were not pure (Matt. 23:15).

The book of Jonah demonstrates that God is interested in the Gentile world and not only in His chosen people Israel. Jonah's place in the Old Testament canon allows us to see very graphically that God is willing to send His emissary, chosen by Him at His will, to the most wicked and violent nation on earth. Chapter 1:1-2 says: *"Now the word of the Lord came unto Jonah saying, arise, go to Nineveh, that great city, and cry against it; for their wickedness has come up before me."* When Jonah responded improperly to the call of God, he became a type of those who do not respond in obedience when God calls them to special service. For this reason, Jonah has become one of the most maligned prophets in the Old Testament. Although I believe that Jonah did not respond properly, I also believe that only as we understand the historical, religious, and military background of the book, can we totally comprehend the reasons why he did not want to go. By looking at his failure as another human being, with the same

First, I believe that Jonah did not want to go because the Assyrians were the most wicked, violent people in the entire world. History books are filled with graphic descriptions regarding their battle tactics. After a military encounter, they forced the subdued people to kneel down, then they came from behind and either clubbed them in the head or decapitated them. Usually they decapitated them so the soldiers would have evidence of the number they killed. The Assyrians paid their soldiers based on the number of dead. They took pride in their cruelty and not only cut off heads, but also the hands of those they conquered. They would tear out their tongues, and often flayed the leaders of a city while they were alive.

They usually made giant mounds of corpses, heads, and hands, and left them behind as macabre evidence of Assyrian superiority. It was the Assyrians who invented the torture of impalation. They might spare a captive long enough to take him back to one of their cities where outside the city wall, he would be impaled lengthwise on a long stick put through his mouth and down through the stomach. Because of their ingenuity, the victim might live for a day or two as he slowly slid down the stake. It is known that they surrounded the city with stakes holding both captives and criminals. As a visitor approached the city, he was sickened and terrified by the sight of dead bodies impaled on hundreds of stakes. The Assyrians were more violent and cruel than any nation on earth and Jonah knew this. When God told him to go to Nineveh, his immediate response was one of fear. He reacted just as we probably would have if we knew what could happen if we went to such a city.

Second, I believe that Jonah did not want to go because he knew the Assyrians were henotheistic. In the past, the Assyrians had subjugated Israel, especially in the time of Jehu, an ancestor of Jeroboam, II, some fifty years earlier. Because of their victories over Israel, and because they were henotheistic they believed their gods were stronger than the Israelite God. Jonah must have thought to himself, "How can I go up to this powerful nation and tell people who believe their gods are stronger than Yahweh that our God is going to destroy their city in forty days?" Jonah must have thought, "They will never, ever, believe me!" Many books on Old Testament archaeology contain pictures taken from inside the ancient palace walls showing the Assyrians carrying back the gods of other lands on their shoulders to their own cities, where they placed them in their temples as part of their worship system. Jonah knew that this was their policy and he knew that because of the past history and involvement of the Assyrians and Israelites, they would be reluctant to believe that the Israelite God could overpower their gods.

Third, Jonah knew that since his people had special spiritual knowledge, they had added responsibility. They had been given responsibility for the oracles of God; they had in their hands the truth of God in written form. God had said many times over, "You only have Me." We will see that this is to be a theme later in the Minor Prophets. In numerous ways, God pointed out that He had chosen them and that they were unique. Jonah knew that with such knowledge and insight about the worship and truth of Jehovah, that if he went to the Assyrians, who had no light or knowledge of the true God, and they repented, there would be judgment on his own people who had not repented at his preaching.

Centuries later, our Lord Jesus Christ said in Matthew 12, that because Nineveh had repented at the preaching of Jonah and *"a greater than Jonah is here"* their judgment would be the greater. We must keep in mind that Jonah's message did *not* contain a provision for repentance, but from his later statements in regard to his knowledge about God, we know that Jonah believed that the possibility for repentance existed, and that the possibility for God to relent existed because of His great love. (Isaiah 45:22-24)

Jonah knew that if for some unknown reason, illogical as it may have seemed, Assyria did repent, and if, because of God's love and grace and long-suffering, He did not destroy them, then their most powerful enemy would be spared and would continue to be a threat to the security of Israel. Throughout the previous century, Assyria had been a constant threat. Even now, during the reign of Jeroboam II, they were a growing threat. This was the ideal opportunity, in terms of the mentality and thought processes of a national zealot such as Jonah probably were to see the possibility of the elimination of the natural enemy of Israel. Why then should he go preach to them and risk the possibility that they would repent? Although we may rebuke Jonah for his unwillingness to go, as we examine these four possibilities, we can understand.

LXIX. THE RUNAWAY PROPHET

More on Jonah

Jonah 1:3 tells us that *"Jonah rose up to flee from the Presence of the Lord."* This is the same description that is used of Cain in Genesis 4:16. We must remember that in the eighth century B.C. he did not have the complete revelation of God as we have. He should, however, have known Psalm 139, which David had written over two hundred years earlier, could have read:

"Whither shall I go from thy spirit? Or whither shall I flee from thy presence? If I take the wings of the morning, and dwell in the uttermost parts of the sea; even there shall thy hand lead me, and thy right hand shall hold me."

Jonah should have known this, yet it was to the uttermost part of the sea that he was headed. When I read of him as a prophet of God, trying to flee from the presence of God, there is a hint of henotheism in the theology of Jonah; believing that somehow by leaving Israel, he could escape the influence and call of God. Jonah left Israel and went south to Joppa, a city on the Mediterranean seacoast and located a ship which was going to Tarshish. {Southern Spain?} He paid the fare and boarded the ship bound for Tarshish, fleeing from the presence of the Lord. The seriousness of this sin is in the fact that it was so well planned. We can ask God's forgiveness for our sins of ignorance, but those of a high hand, those committed after lengthy and strategic planning, are the ones judged most severely. We can see this type of sin in Jonah. He did not run blindly away. He had to stop and think: "Where can I go to get far away from God? I know, I will go to Tarshish! How do I get there? There is a commercial port at Joppa." And so his thought processes would go. When he got there, he had to find a ship that would take him as a passenger. Then after finding the right ship, in the crowded harbor, he paid the required fare and boarded the vessel. No sooner was the ship out into the Mediterranean Sea than the Lord, not nature, hurled a great wind onto the sea and there was such a storm that the ship was in danger of breaking up. This threat was a real source of fear to the mariners. We know from underwater photographs that the sea bottom there is covered with thousands of *amphora* and wooden ships wrecked many centuries ago. They were victims of storms such as the one which threatened Jonah and the crew. Along with the hundreds, possibly thousands of others, the ship on which he had taken passage was about to sink to the bottom of the Mediterranean.

The frightened sailors, who were polytheists and henotheists, began to call on their gods. At the same time, they began to throw cargo overboard to lighten the ship. Because of Jonah's disobedience, innocent merchants were suffering great financial loss. While these men were praying to their gods, Jonah was asleep in the hold of the ship. I believe it was a sleep of depression. He was guilt ridden and sleeping the sleep of escape. The captain went below and awakened him, saying, *"Get up! How can you sleep? Call on your god! We are calling on ours. Perhaps yours can save us from perishing!"* He used the name god in its pagan sense. He was not at this point talking about Jehovah.

As superstitious pagans, the crew began to realize that something, possibly an omen, had happened to bring the storm upon them. They also believed that someone on board had brought this evil upon them. So, they began to cast lots to discover who it could be, From Proverbs 16:33 we know that *"The lot is cast into the lap, but the whole disposing thereof is of the Lord."* Because the Lord was active in this affair, the lot fell upon Jonah. When the lot fell, they turned and demanded from Jonah a reason for the storm. Notice in verse 8 how they directed the questions at him. *"For whose cause is this evil upon us? What is thine occupation? Whence comest thou? What is thy country? Of what people art thou?"* Their questions struck Jonah like rapid hammer blows. Jonah's answer is in verse 9. *"I am an Hebrew; and I fear the Lord, the God of heaven, which hath made the sea and the dry land."* Notice that he confessed his creationist theology.

He had already told them that he was fleeing from the presence of the Lord, so now the frightened seamen asked, *"How could you do this?"* As henotheists, they could understand his thinking that he could flee from God's presence. But now that he admitted to believing in a Creator-God, who must therefore be mightier than all gods, those pagan sailors asked, *"How could you do this?"* Following Jonah's testimony that he worshiped Yahweh, who created the earth and the sea, they asked what they should do with him in order that the sea might become calm. Verse 11 says it was becoming increasingly stormy with waves crashing over the bow of the ship. Jonah's reply was to offer him as a sacrifice. He said, *"Take me up, and cast me forth into the sea; so shall the sea be calm unto you: for I know that for my sake this great tempest is upon you."*

What a thought for Jonah to realize that his disobedience might cause the death of every man aboard and the cargo of the merchant who was shipping it to Tarshish. The men were not yet willing to throw Jonah overboard. They dug in their oars and rowed desperately to get back to land, but could not. The storm only became worse but still they did not want to harm God's prophet. Verse 14 says, *"They cried unto Yahweh."* The pagan sailors now used the sacred four consonant name Yahweh {YHWH}. They had evidently become believers in the Lord God of heaven. *"O Yahweh, we beseech thee, let us not perish for this man's life, and lay not upon us innocent blood: for thou, 0 Yahweh, hast done as it pleased thee."* They acknowledged the sovereignty of Yahweh and unwillingness to harm His prophet. After asking God's forgiveness, they picked up Jonah and hurled him into the sea which immediately *"ceased from her raging."* Verse 16 says, *"The men feared Yahweh exceedingly, and offered a sacrifice unto Yahweh, and made vows."*

Verse 17, which should be verse 1 of chapter 2, *"Now the Lord had prepared a great fish to swallow up Jonah. And Jonah was in the belly of the fish three days and three nights."* Some see the fish as a punishment on Jonah. We should realize, however, that had it not been for the great fish, Jonah would have drowned when he was cast into the raging sea. God sent the fish to save him. It is often true that the immediate discomfort, the immediate trials and tribulations that appear so overwhelming, are ultimately the means of blessing. I am sure that when the jaws of the huge fish closed around Jonah, and he slid into the darkness of the whale's belly, he thought, "This is it! There can be no more terrible experience than this." Yet, this terrible experience was the means of his salvation.

When you read the book of Hosea, you will notice that he called the valley of troubling (Achor) a door of hope. In addition to being the means of preservation, Jonah's experience in the whale allowed him to become a type of Christ. Had Jonah known, as the fish swallowed him, that because of his experience, the Lord Jesus, almost eight hundred years later, would refer to this event as typifying His death, burial, and resurrection, Jonah would have considered himself greatly blessed to be pedagogy in biography.

While in the belly of the fish, Jonah began to pray. In his prayer, he quoted from Psalms 42 and 69. Evidently, he had studied these and now claimed them as his own. Verse 4 reveals that Jonah gained confidence that God was going to rescue him because he said, *"I will look again toward thy holy temple."* This is interesting because Jonah lived in the north. As God's prophet, he must have made occasional trips to Jerusalem. Now, from the belly of the whale, he expressed confidence that he would once again look on God's holy temple. Verse 10 says, *"The Lord spake unto the fish, and it vomited out Jonah upon the dry land."* God appointed the fish to swallow Jonah then He commanded the fish to vomit him up. Everything in creation except man always obeys God.

LXX. JONAH'S SECOND CHANCE

In chapter 3, we read that *"the word of the Lord came unto Jonah the second time."* The fish had vomited Jonah on the Mediterranean seashore some distance from Nineveh. It is possible that he was bleached white like the sailor we just read about. If so, he must have been a striking sight to the superstitious Assyrians in Nineveh. He certainly was "a sign." Jonah traveled to Nineveh, which, the Scripture says, was *"an exceeding great city, a three days walk."* I am always amazed at the remarks of the critics who look for excuses not to believe the Word of God. Many have said that Jonah could not be the author of the book because he used the past tense *"was"* in verse 3. This was a literary style as Jonah was looking back on the event after it had occurred. We have a similar occasion of this style in Luke 24:13: *"And behold, two of them went that same day to a village called Emmaus, which was from Jerusalem about threescore furlongs."* This does not mean that Emmaus was not there at that time. It is a way of referring to something that had previously happened.

The three days probably referred to the length of time necessary to go through the city and see everything. Jonah entered the distance of
about one day's walk" and began to preach. His message was *"Yet forty days, and Nineveh shall be overthrown."* In the original language he used only six words. If you are a student of numerology, you see this is an appropriate number for the message because it is the number of man. I wonder if Jonah preached in Assyrian, or Hebrew? In either case, the inhabitants of the city understood it. So it just may be that God gave him that brief six word message in Assyrian and he memorized it, because it appears that he had nothing else to say except these six words. There was no provision for repentance in his message. But, surprisingly enough, verse 5 tells us, the people believed Yahweh. They ordered a fast and put on sackcloth from the greatest to the least of them. When word reached the king, he arose from his throne, laid aside his royal robe and covered himself with sackcloth.

Skeptics have pounced on this verse because, they say, "Ashurbanipal, II, was king of Assyria in the time of Jonah. How could he use the *"king of Nineveh?"* There was no king of Nineveh." Once again, this is literary style. If we read I Kings 21:1, we see that Ahab was referred to as *king of Samaria.* He was king of Israel. In II Chronicles 24:23 we read that when the Syrians came up against the princes of Judah and Jerusalem, they sent the spoil to *the King of Damascus.* There was no king of Damascus; there was a king of Syria, of which Damascus was the capitol, as Samaria was the capitol of Israel and Nineveh was the capitol of Assyria.

The king issued a proclamation calling for a fast and commanded that both man and beast be covered with sackcloth, and that all men should call on Yahweh, turning from their wicked ways and their violence. This was certainly a good prescription for reform, and we know that through this admission of violence, they were well on their way to the repentance God expected. We know that no deliverance was promised, because the statement in verse 9 says *"Who can tell if God will turn and repent, and turn away from his fierce anger, that we perish not?"* The Assyrians were not stiff necked. They did not rebel, but humbled themselves before God, not even knowing what the outcome would be. Verse 10 says, *"God saw their works, that they turned from their evil way; and God repented of the evil, that he had said that he would do unto them; and he did it not."* This is the verse that Jesus referred to in Matthew 12:41, when He said that the inhabitants of Nineveh repented at the preaching of Jonah, a real historical person!

Chapter 4 provides some insights into the personality of Jonah. Based on possibilities three and four, which were mentioned earlier, Jonah was unhappy because Nineveh was not destroyed. It is interesting that because of the preaching of Jonah, the people of Nineveh repented and God did not destroy them. Then sixty years later, in 722 B.C., He used the Assyrians to destroy Israel. A missionary from Israel was the means of salvation and preservation for the heathen nation which three-score years later, destroyed the nation from which the missionary came. It just might be, that the Assyrians were on the borderline of destruction because of their wickedness, as the Canaanites had been earlier. But in God's plan, He needed to preserve them and delay their destruction, in order to use them as His instrument of judgment against Israel sixty years later (Isaiah 10:5). Complex as it is we know that everything must work together in God's sovereign program in order for His purposes to come to pass. No doubt, Jonah knew that he would be an unwelcome individual when he returned to Israel and they discovered that because of him, God did not destroy their enemies, the Assyrians.

After delivering his message, Jonah sat down outside the city and in great anger prayed, *"Take, I beseech thee, my life from me; for it is better for me to die than to live."* He remembered he had said in verse 2, that God would be kind and compassionate. In verse 4, God asked whether he had good reason to be angry. In other words, God said, "Jonah, are your personal feelings more important than my over-all program?" As he waited, Jonah made a shelter where he could sit down east of the city and watch to see whether or not God would destroy it.

While Jonah sat outside in his little shelter, under the blazing sun, God appointed a plant to grow up over him. It grew as large as a shade tree over his head and added greatly to his comfort. Jonah was very happy about the plant as it protected him from the sun, but immediately, God appointed a worm to attack the plant at dawn on the next day. The plant died and the sun came up, along with a scorching east wind from the desert, to burn down on Jonah's head. He became faint and wanted to die, saying, *"It is better for me to die than to live."*

Once again God asked, *"Doest thou well to be angry?"* And he replied, *"I do well to be angry, even unto death."* God's response was, *"Thou hast had pity on the gourd, for the which thou hast not laboured, neither madest it grow; which came up in a night and perished in a night."* Jonah saw the injustice. He saw himself as happy and secure in the shelter of the plant. Suddenly the worm had attacked and destroyed it. And now he thought, "I just cannot tolerate this kind of injustice. I am ready to die. Then in effect God said, "Look at Nineveh. It is a large city that has taken scores of years to build for both human and animal comfort. Now you want it destroyed. You want to see judgment fall on this city that took so long to build. Yet, when I destroyed the plant, that took only a day to create, you were angry, and it was made *only* for your own physical comfort. How logical is it that you would be so angry and want Me to destroy a large city when you are so angry because I destroyed a single plant? And how unjust are you? Should I not have compassion on Nineveh *'wherein are more than six score thousand persons that cannot discern between their right hand and their left hand, and also much cattle?'"*

There is a four-part lesson in the book of Jonah. First, God will save anyone. He apparently saved the heathen sailors on board the ship; and He saved the wicked Assyrians in the city of Nineveh. Second, we saw how very patient God was with His prophet. He did not strike him down when he first refused to obey but used a series of circumstances to bring him back into the center of His will. Third, it is not by power or by might that men are saved, but by God's grace. As Jonah said in 4:2: *"I knew that thou art a gracious God and merciful, slow to anger, and of great kindness, and repentest thee of the evil."* Fourth, God is telling us to care about *all* men. Because of Jonah's disobedience, many people suffered; and because of his selfish attitude, many more would have suffered. God wants us to love *all* men, especially those of the household of faith (Gal. 6:10).

K. A. Kitchen, the renowned Egyptologist, wrote in Chapter One of *The Bible and the World*, that archaeologists are fortunate if they can excavate 2-5% of any site. The excavation of Nineveh uncovered 2.9 square miles. If this is 3% of the original city 2,800 years ago, the original city was 96 square miles, the size of Savannah, GA, with a population of 150,000 living in typical city wide distances from each other, with wide streets and public parks. This is similar to Nineveh, with small family dwellings and a population of 120,000 children, plus their parents. 2% would be 145 square miles. Either percentage is a reasonable estimate for the major city of the world's most powerful military nation.

LXXI. HOSEA LIVES HIS MESSAGE

Hosea follows Jonah chronologically and his book dates to about 760 B.C. As with the other eighth century prophets, he was thoughtful enough to provide the names of the kings who were in power during the time of his prophetic and symbolic ministry. The book is easily divided into two sections. Chapters 1through 3 consists of a symbolic narrative, with chapters 4 through 14 containing various addresses given by the prophet. Internal evidence indicates that he wrote the book after the occurrences described. In his older years, he looked back on the events of his lifetime, beginning with his marriage to Gomer, and wrote about his life and recorded his prophetic messages.

Why Hosea's Experience?

God considered Himself as the husband in His relationship to Israel. You recall Ezekiel's allegory of His having found her lying abandoned in a field and made her His own. Other relevant verses are Exodus 34:15, Isaiah 62:5, Jeremiah 3:14, and an assortment in Hosea. The idolatry which Israel was so prone to follow is called whoredom and adultery. In the infidelity of Israel, there seems to have been no way that God could adequately express His heartbreak to this stiff-necked people. In the same way, it was impossible for God to transmit His message to the prophet, unless the prophet had a similar experience, in a finite sense, to what God had experienced in an infinite way. Hosea's role had to be one of total involvement in the kind of rejection God had experienced. This was possible only by his experiencing the heartbreak of having an unfaithful wife.

Gomer was a pure woman at the time of her marriage. Hosea had no reason to believe she would not be a faithful wife. This position allows us to accept the book as literal and historical. It eliminates the moral difficulty of a prophet of God marrying a harlot. It gives proper recognition to Hosea's love for his wife as a genuine affection, not something artificial or symbolic as would be the case if the marriage were contracted only for the purpose of the pedagogy in biography, symbolizing a spiritual lesson to Israel. It also better explains the close relationship between Hosea's experience and the lesson it is intended to teach about Israel's unfaithfulness; because we will discover that God saw Israel as pure in the beginning and then becoming unfaithful to Him later. So, for this to be a true symbolism, Hosea's relationship to Gomer, in the beginning, had to be pure.

Chapter 3 gives additional support to this view. The narrative reveals that Hosea took back the wife he had rejected in chapter 2 because of her adultery. The rejection does not seem justifiable if Hosea had married Gomer knowing her to be a harlot. It would not be logical to reject her later if he knew from the beginning that she was prone to harlotry and adultery.

All human relationships can be described by one of three levels of intimacy. The first is that of mere acquaintance. One is not concerned about the number of acquaintances one has, and it is very difficult to be hurt deeply by a casual acquaintance. The second level is friendship. Some have only a very few close friends throughout their lives with whom to share their hearts and feelings, while other more gregarious persons may have many friends. At the third level of intimacy, there is room for only two people; this is the husband-wife relationship. At this level, if one additional person comes into the arrangement, the relationship is damaged or destroyed. When that relationship is broken, Scripture describes it by the ugliest word possible - *adultery*. Hosea selected this word in describing his wife Gomer, and the nation of Israel.

Hosea's prophecies were given to him during the reigns of Uzziah, Jotham, Ahaz, and Hezekiah. These kings ruled in Judah between 790 B.C. and 686 B.C. The king in Israel was Jeroboam, II, who reigned from 793 to 753 B.C. We read earlier that Jeroboam II's era was one of spiritual depravity. There was no justice in the gate; the religious worship combined that of Baalism and the sin of Jeroboam I. It was against this background of religious harlotry that Hosea began to preach. (See II Kings 14:23-26.)

After Hosea took Gomer as his wife, she conceived (vs.3) and bore him a son. This may have been the only child he fathered. The Lord said to him (vs. 4): *"Call his name Jezreel, for yet a little while, and I will avenge the blood of Jezreel upon the house of Jehu, and will cause to cease the kingdom of the house of Israel."* In verse 5, He said that he would *"break the bow of Israel;"* that is, He would destroy them. Any military power they thought they could exert would be destined to fail. Then (vs. 6) Gomer conceived again and gave birth to a daughter. Since Hosea is not mentioned as the father, this may already have been a child of harlotry. God said, *"Call her Loruhamah: for I will no more have mercy upon the house of Israel."* We know from what happened thirty eight years later, that He did not forgive them. Then He added (vs. 7): *I will have mercy upon the house of Judah, and will save them by the Lord their God.* Because of the Davidic Covenant, Judah was allowed to return from captivity in Babylon, not by bow, sword, battle, or horsemen, but by the grace of God through the edict of Cyrus, king of Persia. Verse 8 says that when she had weaned Loruhamah, she conceived and gave birth to a son; evidently this was another child of harlotry. God said, *"Call his name Loammi, for ye are not my people, and I will not be your God."* This time, her adultery was discovered.

Verse 10 is a reminder of God's promise to Abram, which was given so many centuries earlier, when God said,

> *"The number of the children of Israel shall be as the sand of the sea, which cannot be measured nor numbered; and it shall come to pass, that in the place where it was said unto them, Ye are not my People, there it shall be said unto them, Ye are the sons of the living God."*

This is eschatological in its implications and is followed by the prophecy of verse 11:

> *Then shall the children of Judah and the children of Israel be gathered together, and appoint themselves one head, and they shall come up out of the land, for great shall be the day of Jezreel.*

After realizing that his wife had given birth to two children, who were probably not his, Hosea's heart began to break. Now, God began to work through Hosea, so that when he preached to the people, about the heartbreak of God over the adultery of the nation, it would not only be God's message, it would be *his* message. His heart was broken, as God's heart was, and now God's feelings would be transmitted and presented through the shattered life of Hosea to the people. The message of God would be real and framed by Hosea's own experience. In Hosea 2:5 God says, *"Their mother hath played the harlot."* This is similar to Ezekiel's allegory where the faithless wife said it was her lovers who gave her bread and wool and oil. It was a picture of Israel who believed that Baal, the god of fertility, was providing the produce of the land. Not so, God stated, *(vs. 8): "I gave her corn, and wine, and oil, and multiplied her silver and gold, which they prepared for Baal."* God had provided abundantly for Israel as He had promised throughout the Old Testament, but instead of recognizing His bounty, they attributed it to Baal. Because of this sin and ingratitude, God says in verse 9 that He will take it all back. The produce of the land is His, He was responsible for fertility and growth, and to prove it, He was going to take it back. Then let them see if Baal will help them!

We are almost on holy ground in the book of Hosea, because when he writes, we get to almost see into the heart of God as He is stirred by His love for Israel and at the same time His justice and holiness require judgment. So often, He seemed about to drop the hammer of judgment, then, in love and grace, gave them one more chance. It is as if a man, whose wife has been guilty of adultery, is about to divorce her in his anger; but as she is leaving, he remembers how much he loves her and says, *"Come back. I forgive you."* Then she sins again, and again his heart is broken. He is angry and threatens divorce and again calls her back. In Hosea, we see that God's love and grace are extended during the promise of judgment. He begs them to repent so that He may allow them to return.

In verse 14, we read what I believe is God's love song of forgiveness and return. His use of the word *"will"* here speaks of His covenant love, *"hesed."* God's lovingkindness: *"I will allure her, and bring her into the wilderness, and speak comfortably to her."* The scenario is that of a man speaking to his sweetheart, determined to woo her to love him; or, the appeal of a man to a wife whose love has grown cold. He wants to take her back to the place of memories, the honeymoon place, which in Israel's case was the wilderness. There He would give her vineyards, *"and the valley of Achor for a door of hope."* This statement refers to the punishment, or *"troubling"* on Achan because of his sin (josh. 7:24-26) and how it opened a door of hope for Israel to go up and be victorious at Ai. So now, though God will trouble Israel by taking away the crops, this troubling will be a door of hope if it results in bringing them back to Himself. It is an eschatological promise, for later on *"She shall sing there, as in the days of her youth, and as in the day when she came up out of the land of Egypt. It shall be in that day."* (vs. 16), declared the Lord, looking to the future, *"That thou shalt call me Ishi, and shalt call me no more Baali."* In other words *"husband"* rather than *"master"* because, (vs. 17) *"I will take away the names of Baalim out of her mouth."*

Beginning in verse 18, when God restores Israel, He will undo all of the judgments of the earlier part of chapter 2 by giving abundant blessings. Verse 23 ends with a statement of His sovereignty: *"I will sow her unto me in the earth."* The concept of sowing, as we will see further in Isaiah is another way in which God viewed His nation;
but this time, they will not bring forth wild or bitter grapes, but good
ones. He will say to them, *"Thou art my people,"* and they will respond , *"Thou art my God."* See Ezekiel 37:21-24.

Chapters 1 and 2 have described Hosea's heartbreak of an adulterous marriage. He has separated himself from Gomer, and she has gone her way into the world to earn her living as a harlot. If one were to ask Hosea, at that time, what was the worst thing that ever happened to him, he would probably say, "my marriage to Gomer." But much later, after completing his prophetic ministry, he might then say, "What a blessing it was, because it allowed me to preach God's message with a depth of feeling and emotion I could never have known."

Until this time Hosea experienced only the first half of his personal pedagogy in biography. At the beginning of chapter 3, God said to him, *"Go love a woman beloved of her friend, yet an adulteress."* How surprised Hosea must have been, having lived through his tragedy and having put the heartbreak behind him. But God was saying, "Hosea, you are only half finished. " You have learned so far how to preach against the nation that has played the harlot, but you have not yet experienced the depth of forgiveness and love required to *"bring the harlot back."*

With His covenant love, God is going to draw the nation back to Himself and in order to deliver that message Hosea must physically and emotionally experience the bringing back of the harlot to his life and home. Hosea was told to seek out his former wife and bring her back. I can hardly fathom the depth of love this required of Hosea. Gomer had been gone for years living as a harlot. The depth of love required to restore her is almost beyond comprehension. Hosea is about to experience, in a finite way, the infinite love of God for His harlot nation that allows Him to seek out and bring her back. In obedience to God's command, Hosea went out and searched through the marketplace for the woman who had left so long ago. Perhaps he began in the better part of town and walked through to the slums. Finally, he saw a dirty, abused woman whom he recognized as the one he had loved and married many years before. His heart went out to her and he sought out the cruel man she served, and evidently, by the con text, owned her. Hosea appears here as a type of Christ. The woman who was once his wife was under the power of another. It does seem unfair that he should have to pay for his own wife, but it is a picture of the Lord Jesus Christ, our Creator of the world, who shed His blood to pay the ransom.

Verse 2 says, *"I bought her for fifteen pieces of silver."* That was *one half* the price of a slave. She was old, tired, her beauty was gone, and she was not worth much to her master. She had passed the prime of life and was not in demand by the men who would come to seek such women. In addition to the silver, Hosea gave an omer and a half of barley. That was food for animals and impoverished peasants. No doubt it was what the master fed the harlots who worked for him. Hosea wrapped his cloak about her, and led her through the streets back to his home.

In order to purify and purge Gomer from the lustful appetites which had driven her to a life of harlotry, Hosea placed a set of restrictions upon her. Verse 3 says that he told her: *"Thou shalt abide for me many days; thou shalt not play the harlot, and thou shalt not be for another man: so will I also be for thee."* To completely restore Gomer, Hosea denies himself his conjugal rights for as long as it takes to purge her from the desire for adultery.

Hosea's actions demonstrate how Gomer is a type of Israel. God is going to send the same nations she had sought out to be her lovers to be her enemies. After they have abused and defeated her, then He will seek her out and bring her back home to Himself. Hosea is a type of the heavenly Father in His h*esed*, His long-suffering covenant love. God sums it up in verse 4: *"For the children of Israel shall abide many days without a king, and without a prince."* Notice the fourfold discipline of verse 4. First, t*hey shall remain many days without king or prince.* When Zedekiah, the last king of Judah died in Babylon, there was no longer a king on the throne of Judah from that time until now. The only rightful Heir to the throne was crucified, so the first phase of the discipline is still continuing. Israel has no king or prince. Second, w*ithout sacrifice.* When Titus invaded Jerusalem in 70 A.D., and destroyed the temple, all of the animal sacrifices ended.

Quoting the late Messianic Jew evangelist, Dr. Hyman Appelman, you can ask any orthodox Jew today, *"Where is the blood?"* Since 70 A.D. their worship system has been spiritualized. Third, W*ithout sacred pillar.* I believe this refers to the teraphim, and sexual activities in pagan worship. Fourth, *Without ephod or household idols.* The ephod was probably destroyed when Nebuchadnezzar invaded Jerusalem. The criteria for discipline began then and it exists until this time. It will continue until the Lord returns, gathers Israel and reestablishes them in the land. Verse 5 begins *"Afterward."* Then the sons of Israel will return and seek the Lord their God and David their king. In the last days they will come trembling to the Lord and recognize His goodness.

LXXII. GOD'S INDICTMENT OF ISRAEL

More in Hosea

Among the many benefits which the writing prophets provided in their books is the great insight they supply into the religious, political, and military customs of the times in which they lived. Hosea 4:11-14 is a graphic display of what those days when Baal was worshipped were like. Verse 11 says, *"Whoredom and wine and new wine take away the heart" (or, the understanding)*. The total Baal experience had become completely ingrained in their lives. Did you ever try to reason with an addict? The drug user is not a rational person; understanding has been taken away. That is how it was with Israel. They were so involved in their licentious system that they could not be reasoned with. They loved it and would not listen to a message which asked them to have it any other way.

"My people ask counsel at their stocks, and their staff declareth unto them." In other words, they are involved in what today would be the same as ouija boards, palm reading, crystal balls, and spiritism. God said that it was this spirit of harlotry which led them to go astray from His truth. They offered sacrifices on the tops of mountains and burned incense under oak, poplar and terebinth trees because their shade was pleasant. Hosea was speaking of the groves constructed for the worship of Baal. These were areas where there were trees, as well as artificial tree trunks, planted by the Baalists and carved to look like female deities. When a man wanted to worship with a prostitute, he took her out into the groves because the shade sheltered them. *"Therefore (vs. 13) your daughters shall commit whoredom, and your spouses shall commit adultery."* These people had adopted the Canaanite religious system which decreed, by law, that at some time in her life, *every* woman must sit in the Baal temple until she was selected by a "worshiper" and money was paid by him for her sexual services. If the women waited until they were old, they might sit for a long time before they were chosen. Many went while they were young. These were the *daughters and spouses.*

Verse 14 continues, *"I will not punish your daughters when they commit whoredom, nor your spouses when they commit adultery."* And we ask why? God said it is because the men also go apart with harlots and offer sacrifices with temple prostitutes so that all of people without understanding are ruined. Since Israel sinned to the point where she appears to be beyond hope, Hosea then turns Its words of warning to the south: *"Though thou, Israel, play the harlot, yet let not Judah offend"* (vs. 15). Do not go up to Gilgal, he warns, or to Bethavin. These were popular centers of Baal worship. Do not take an oath in the Lord's name in those idolatrous places. Then he spoke the tragic words of verse 17: *"Ephraim is joined to idols; let him alone."* Although the Assyrians did not destroy them until thirty-eight years later, there is no saving the nation of Israel, because the people will continue their idolatrous activities until their dying breaths. {Ephraim is another name of the northern kingdom.}

Chapter 5 continues with the refrain of judgment. Verse 9 says *"Ephraim shall be desolate."* Therefore, God continues in verse 12: *"Will I be unto Ephraim as a moth, and to the house of Judah as rottenness."* Like a moth in a closet of woolen clothes, He will weaken them militarily. But when they realize what has happened, instead of turning to Him for strength, which was the purpose of His remedial judgment, Israel turned to Assyria and its king. He could not heal you, the Lord says, and because you did not respond correctly to my judgment, I am going to come in as a lion and when I tear you to pieces, there will be none to deliver you."

Following His plea for return in 6:1-3, we have God's lament of wounded love, beginning in verse 4. God calls out, *"O Ephraim, what shall I do unto thee? 0 Judah, what shall I do unto thee?"* I can understand men crying out, *"What shall I do to be saved?"* But here God is saying, *"What shall I do to save men?"* *"Your goodness is like the morning cloud and the early dew."* They are beautiful, but too feeble to produce any harvest. They come briefly, then disappear. The word *"goodness"* (loyalty) comes from a root word which means a bending of the neck in submissiveness. He is saying, "You seem to submit yourselves to Me, but it does not last. You come back then sin again. You have done it so often, it does not mean anything. What shall I do with you?"

In chapter 7 we learn that it was not only the common people who committed these sins. Verse 3 says, *"They make the king glad with their wickedness, and the princes with their lies."* We know that Jeroboam, II was an evil king, and this seems to indicate that he was involved in all of the wicked practices in the city. *"They are all adulterers."* They are *"sick with bottles of wine. There is none among them that calleth unto me. All their kings are fallen."* These statements are a reference to the fact that the history of the northern kingdom is one of assassinations and military *coups*. None of the kings of the north, from Jeroboam I to Hoshea, worshipped Jehovah or did right in His sight. Verse 8 continues, *"Ephraim, he hath mixed himself among the people; Ephraim is a cake not turned."*

Looking at Israel from the outside, in the time of Jeroboam, II, we would see prosperity, an expanding monarchy and territory.

We will learn in Amos that materially the people were living very well. But decay was eating away at the heart of the system and it had only thirty-eight more years until captivity and dispersion. Ephraim did not know this, because no one was listening. Wine and harlotry had taken away their understanding. They were oblivious that they were dying. So, God said, *"Ephraim is a cake not turned."* If I forget a pancake on the griddle, then return and lift up a corner to see it black and hardened, what do I do? Even though it looks good on top, it is ruined underneath. Throw it down the garbage disposal! Symbolically, this is what Hosea says will happen to Israel. Verse 9 continues, *"Strangers have devoured his strength, and he knoweth it not. Yea gray hairs are here and there upon him, yet he knoweth not."* The nation is unaware of how it has been weakened by its moral degeneracy and inner rottenness. It is like a man who walks around with a head of gray hair and thinks he still looks like a teen-ager because he has not looked in the mirror. The gray hairs spoken of here are indicative of moral decay. It has spread throughout the system, but, Israel does not even know it.

"When I began to bring chastening rods upon Ephraim," God said, she became like a silly dove without sense. She ran to Egypt and to Assyria. She went everywhere except back to Me where there was genuine deliverance. Like Elijah, when King Ahaziah sent to inquire of Beelzebub, the Lord is saying to Ephraim, *"Is there not a God in Israel?"* Verse 14: *"They have not cried unto me with their heart. They wail on their beds, but only for the sake of grain and new wine."* They are concerned only with poor harvest, heartbroken because there is no grain or new wine with which to worship Baal. They are not crying because God rejected them. *"Even though it was I who strengthened their arms, they devise mischief against Me."* Through this entire indictment we can trace the theme of Psalm 1, which teaches that *godless thinking* leads to *careless speaking* which in turn leads to *godless living*. That principle applied to Israel, and it applies today.

Finally, God says (verse 16), *"they are like a deceitful bow."* If you pull back the string on a bow, expecting the arrow to fly toward the target, and it veers off to the side, you have used a deceitful bow. In the Old Testament, there are sixteen different words for sin and one of them means *"to miss the mark,"* or, to fall short and go astray. Throughout all the years, this is what Israel did. She was a deceitful bow who missed God's mark.

In 9:15, God once again looks at Ephraim, but this time as a man would look at his bride, and says, *"All their wickedness is in Gilgal."* Gilgal was a major center of Baal worship;

and like a jealous lover, God says, *"there I hated them."* This statement is an illustration of a man, walking outside his house, and seeing, against an upstairs window shade, the shadow of his wife in another man's arms. As the truth of her unfaithfulness strikes his heart, he will remember the location, and never forget that place. From that time on he could say, "I began to hate her there." God looked at the harlotry Israel practiced at Gilgal and said, *"there I hated them: for the wickedness of their doings I will drive them out of mine house, I will love them no more."* Finally, in 11:1 we read, *"When Israel was a child, then I loved him, and called my son out of Egypt."* Although God was speaking of Israel, Matthew, under the inspiration of the Holy Spirit, said that Israel was personified as the Lord Jesus Christ and that He fulfilled this prophetic statement when He was called out of Egypt with his parents. (Matthew 2:15).

In verse 5, Hosea prophesies that Assyria is going to be their king. But as God contemplates the judgment, He cries out (vs. 8) *"How shall I give thee up Ephraim? How shall I deliver thee, Israel?"* His compassions are kindled within Him and He says, *"I will not execute the fierceness of mine anger."* He will not destroy Ephraim but will bring them like birds from Egypt, and they will dwell in their own houses. With that eschatological statement, God looks beyond the impending Assyrian invasion to occur in 722 B.C. and said, *"I will regather them."* In chapter 13:14, His mercy again breaks forth and He promises, *"I will ransom them from the power of the grave; I will redeem them from death: 0 death, I will be thy plagues; 0 grave, I will be thy destruction."* It is from this Old Testament verse that Paul writes his *paean* of victory over death recorded in First Corinthians 15:55. God finally says, as Hosea must have said about Gomer (14:4): *I will heal their backsliding. I will love them freely, for mine anger is turned away from him.*

LXXIII. AMOS GOES TO ISRAEL

Amos was a contemporary of Hosea, but where Hosea majored on the religious adultery of Israel, Amos stressed their social sins. Both prophets, whose ministries were thirty to forty years prior to the Assyrian conquest, placed themselves in the breach. It was as if the nation of Israel was rolling downhill like a giant snowball, gathering momentum as it's people involved themselves in more wickedness, injustice, and idolatry, until it was about to plunge over the edge of a chasm and disappear forever into the gorge below. Hosea and Amos were the prophets who attempted to stop the downward course of this giant juggernaut by calling the nation to repentance.

The messages of Hosea and Amos contained all the prerequisites for repentance. They pointed out both national and individual sins; they warned that judgment was soon to come; they stated that God was willing and ready to accept them if they would repent and return. The Lord, in His longsuffering *hesed* love, was waiting to take them back if they returned to Him. But, because of the sins of the people, and of their kings who consistently led them astray and participated   they would not return. As God had said in Hosea 11:2, the more often He sent the prophets to them the more often they turned away.

The Date of Amos

Amos dated his prophetic ministry to a well known catastrophic and historical event. We know from verse 1, that he prophesied two years before the earthquake, but wrote the book some time afterward. Zechariah 13:5, 240 years later, recalled this earthquake, saying, *"Ye shall flee, like as ye fled from before the earthquake in the days of Uzziah king of Judah."* The prophecies of Amos concerned Israel during the days of Uzziah, king of Judah and Jeroboam, II, king of Israel. Second Kings 14:23-26 and II Chronicles 26, give us information about these kings. We know from previous study, Uzziah was co-regent with his father from 790 until 767 and reigned alone from 767 to 739 B.C. Jeroboam, II reigned from 793 until 753, being co-regent with Jehoash from 793 until 782. Because these reigns overlap between 767 and 753, we know Amos's activities occurred during the fourteen or fifteen years.

Amos had a unique presentation. He was a sheepherder from Tekoa, in the southern kingdom, where there had been spiritual reform under Uzziah. The word used for sheepherder is not the usual word. It is used only one other time in II Kings 3:4 to describe Mesha the king of Moab as a sheep breeder who was able to pay the king of Israel {Ahab} 100,000 lambs and the wool of 100,000 rams. You can use Google to learn about the archaeological discovery regarding this event. So, God sent Amos, the owner/manager of super size herds, to preach in the north against its corrupt and evil worship of Baal. Amos would not be welcome, and neither would his message, because he was sent from the south to preach God's judgment against the nation of Israel. However, to ease the shock and reduce rejection, he used a psychological approach which would get the ear of his listeners. He launched his words of judgment against Israel by beginning to call down God's judgments on the enemies of Israel, which were the surrounding nations. Amos began in verse 3 with *"For three transgressions, and for four."* This is ascending numerology. He did not mean that there were only three or four transgressions. He meant there were ascending numbers of transgressions which were continuing at that very time. Throughout the book, and especially in the early pronouncements of judgment upon the surrounding nations, we will see God as the Master Chess Player moving and judging the nations.

Hosea was alive and living out his pedagogy in biography. Even Jonah may have been still alive. Tiglath-pileser was growing up in northern Assyria with dreams of conquest. Isaiah and Micah were growing up in the southern kingdom. Against this background, Amos, obeying the call of God, left his herds and sycamore figs in Tekoa and journeyed north to pronounce God's judgment against the nation of Israel, the northern kingdom. His preaching began with judgments against three natural and historical enemies of Israel. It then ascended to God's judgment on three distant relatives of Israel. It then advanced to Judah, the close relative in the south. Finally, the Israelites were declared ripe for judgment.

First, he called down God's judgment on Damascus, the capitol of Syria. He mentioned the historical individuals, saying, *"I will send a fire into the house of Hazael."* Hazael was the king of Syria from 841 until 806 B.C. It *"shall devour the palaces of Ben-hadad."* Ben-hadad was the name of the predecessor of Hazael and the name of his son who reigned from 806 to 770. Then verse 5: *"I will break also the bar of Damascus, and cut off the inhabitant from the plain of Aven, and him that holdeth the sceptre from the house of Eden: and the people of Syria shall go into captivity unto Kir, saith the Lord."* Amos prophesied the destruction of all Syria's symbols of power and military might, including the huge gate-bar that kept invading armies from storming into the city. Isaiah, in chapter 17 will later duplicate this prophecy which was initiated by Amos. I am sure that when the inhabitants of Israel heard God's judgment on Damascus, they screamed out a giant shout of approval. Then Amos moved on, saying in verse 6, *"Thus saith the Lord, "For three transgressions of Gaza and for four."* Gaza was the major city of the Philistines and I am sure the people raised more cheers after hearing judgment pronounced against their historic enemy who, back in 1010 B.C., killed King Saul and Jonathon.

As Amos continued through verse 8, he mentioned three more major cities of the Philistines. The only one not mentioned, among the five city pentapolis, was Gath. God also promised to cut off the inhabitants from Ashdod, Ashkelon and Ekron. Amos then called God's judgment down upon Tyre, the capitol of Phoenicia. Keep in mind that Jeroboam, II was the great-grandson of Jehu, who had Jezebel, the daughter of a Phoenician king, thrown out of the window. There would be more cheers at hearing of Phoenicia's downfall. God said, *"I will send a fire on the wall of Tyrus, which shall devour the palaces thereof"* (vs. 10). We discussed the *Ugarit* tablets which contained Canaanite poetry demonstrating that Baal used fire constructively. The tables would be turned on the Phoenicians, who were ardent Baal worshipers, because they would discover that Baal did not control fire but Jehovah did and He would turn it against them. In verse 11, Amos began to pronounce judgment on the closer relatives of Israel by saying, *"For three transgressions of Edom, and for four."* He mentioned that Edom had played the traitor by pursuing her brother, Israel, with the sword. He said, *"I will send a fire upon Teman."* Teman was the capital of Edom. We read earlier that Obadiah took up used this same theme in his short but powerful book.

In verse 13: *"For three transgressions of the children of Ammon, and for four."* The Ammonites were descendents of the incest between Lot and his daughter. We learn here that the Ammonites were to expand their territories at any cost. Amos says that the Ammonites ripped open the pregnant women of Gilead. They killed everyone and tried to practice genocide so they could expand their borders. Amos 2:1 begins the promise of judgment against a third near relative of Israel. The Lord says, *"For three transgressions of Moab, and for four."* The Moabites were also descendants of the incest between Lot and his other daughter. God is concerned with what enemies do to each other. He said, *"Because he burned the bones of the king of Edom into lime."*

By now, the cheers must have been long and loud because the Israelite audience had heard judgment pronounced against six surrounding nations. Perhaps they were even saying, "Jehovah is the kind of God we want. We need a God who will punish our enemies." Amos then brings the message a little closer to home. Verse 4 says, *"For three transgressions of Judah, and for four."* That must have produced cheers, because there was no love lost between the northern and southern kingdoms, even though during the time of Jeroboam, II and Uzziah, the kingdoms were prosperous and there was a relative peace. God said (vs. 5): *"I will send a fire upon Judah, and it shall devour the palaces of Jerusalem."* We know this prophecy would be fulfilled in 586 B.C.

Because the theme of Amos, following these pronouncements, will deal specifically with what an ideal citizen should be; what God expects of men; and the social injustices He condemns, we should look at Psalm 15 where King David described the ideal citizen.

> *Lord, who shall abide in thy tabernacle? Who shall dwell in thy holy hill? He that walketh uprightly, and worketh righteousness, and speaketh the truth in his heart. He that backbiteth not with his tongue, nor doeth evil to his neighbour, nor taketh up a reproach against his neighbor. In whose eyes a vile person is condemned; but he honoureth them that fear the Lord. He that sweareth to his own hurt, and changeth not. He that putteth not out his money to usury, nor taketh reward against the innocent. He that doeth these things shall never be moved.*

As Amos continues his narrative, we will see that the Israelites have fallen far short of God's description of an ideal citizen. A New Testament complement is I John 3:17: *"But whoso hath this world's good, and seeth his brother have need, and shutteth up his bowels of compassion from him, how dwelleth the love of God in him?"* With the cheers going up around him, Amos brought the message home to their hearts beginning with 2:6: *"Thus saith the Lord, for three transgressions of **Israel**, and for four."* Suddenly, there was dead silence. You could have heard a pin drop as the audience thought *"What? Not us!"* Amos had gone around in a large circle, drawing the noose tighter around the necks of the Israelites. God said,

> *"I will not turn away the Punishment thereof; because they sold the righteous for silver, and the poor for a pair of shoes. They trampled on the heads of the helpless and turned aside the humble. A man and his father resorted to the same prostitute."*

This probably referred to the prostitution in the Baal temples. Verse 8 refers to the custom of taking a man's garment as pledge for a debt. Deuteronomy 24:10-13 is very explicit regarding this practice. In those times, people would often sleep outdoors, and the cloak was all that protected them from the elements. Deuteronomy 24:10 says, *"When thou dost lend thy brother anything, thou shalt not go into his house to fetch his pledge."* The debtor was obliged to bring it out to him. Verse 13 is very explicit, *"In any case thou shalt deliver him the pledge again when the sun goeth down that he may sleep in his own raiment, and bless thee."* The creditors in Israel were taking garments taken as pledges. They often took the garments into the Baal temples and spread them before the altars, and lying on them when they purchased the services of the temple prostitutes. The wickedness was widespread because even the ungodly priests charged innocent people exorbitant fees which they could not pay, then went in to their homes and confiscated the wine, on the pretext of putting it in the house of Baal. Instead, they sat around inside the temple, carousing and drinking wine which was to have been given to their gods.

Beginning in verse 9, Amos reminded them of the things God had done in the past. It is a historical summary beginning back in 1446, explaining how they corrupted everything God planned for their well being. He had raised up Nazarites, dedicated men who, among other requirements, were not to drink wine. *"But, ye gave the Nazarites wine to drink. You did not want them to serve Me."* They also *"commanded the prophets, saying, Prophesy not."* The Lord was obviously wearied by their sin. Verse 13 says, *"Behold, I am pressed under you, as a cart is pressed that is full of sheaves."* The picture is that of an overloaded cart whose axles are about to buckle. Verses 14 through 16 describe the future battle with the Assyrians in 722 B.C. and demonstrate that regardless of how powerful the Israelites may believe themselves to be, in that day when the enemy attacks, the places of refuge will be destroyed. It will not matter how fast a person runs, he win not reach safety. The stalwart man, the one most powerful in battle will weaken and fall. Even the mighty man will not be able to save his life. The archer will not be able to stand his ground.

As their army retreats, those in the rear will be overrun. No one will be able to escape, not even the one who rides a horse. Even the bravest man will flee naked. So vicious and terrible will be the onslaught of the Assyrians that not even the most courageous will stand. After hearing this description, the people's hearts should have
failed them from fear. After listening to the prophecy of their impending doom, they appeared to have the attitude that "It cannot happen to us; it will not be in our lifetime."

Amos 3:2 reminds Israel of God's sovereign election and the special position that required the moral responsibility indicated in Exodus 19:6: *"And ye shall be unto me a kingdom of priests, and an holy nation."* This is a statement of the Old Testament concept that spiritual rights and privileges bring with them added responsibility for the recipients. Notice the words of Psalm 147:19-20:

"He sheweth his word unto Jacob, his statutes and his judgments unto Israel. He hath not dealt so with any nation: and as for his judgments, they have not known them."

The Lord Jesus describes this same concept in Luke 12:48:

But he that knew not, and did commit things worthy of stripes, shall be beaten with few stripes. For unto whomsoever much is given, of him shall be much required and to whom men have committed much, of him they will ask the more.

LXXIV. A TRUE PROPHET AND HIS MESSAGE

More in Amos

Amos 3:8 says, *"The lion hath roared, who will not fear? The Lord God hath spoken, who can but prophesy?"* As one walking in a jungle fears to hear the lion's roar, so much more should one fear the words of Almighty God that were spoken in judgment. Likewise, when God speaks and puts His hand on an individual for service, that one must speak out and proclaim His Word. How was it possible for hearers to determine whether or not the one speaking was a true prophet? The land was filled with false prophets and not all of them used the various heathen methods of divination. Some would prophesy in the name of the Lord and claim to have received His message through a dream or vision. However, the Lord provided several biblical tests for validating the claims of a prophet.

First, the true prophet spoke only in the name of *Yahweh*. This was the validation Amos used in 3:8. Second, the true prophet spoke only by *revelation.* If a prophet claimed to speak on behalf of *Yahweh*, but practiced sorcery or divination, he was to be rejected as a false prophet. Third, the true prophet of God could be identified by his *personal testimony* and moral character. His lifestyle marked him as a true prophet of God. The false prophet was a mercenary who prophesied for money (Micah 3:5, 11). He was often a drunkard (Isa. 28:7). He was often profane and wicked (Jer. 23:11). He often conspired with others to deceive and defraud (Ezek. 22:25). He often committed adultery, walked in lies, and supported evildoers (Jer. 23:14). His overall lifestyle was one of immorality and misconduct (Jer. 23:15). More than all else, he was a religious opportunist. Fourth, the true prophet was conscious of a *definite call* experience. We will see that Amos recognized this by giving his personal testimony in 7:14-15. Fifth, his message was *always in harmony* with all previous revelation. Sixth, whatever the true prophet prophesied eventually *came to pass*. There would be an event in the future that would confirm that he spoke for God.

Amos continued to prophesy God's impending judgment on Israel by looking to the future through the Assyrian conquest. On that day, God said (vs. 14), *"I will also visit* (punish) *the altars of Bethel."* Bethel, you recall, was the site of one of Jeroboam, I's golden calves.

Is it not ironic that Bethel, which means "house of God" and which had such a sacred history in connection with the patriarchs, especially Jacob and his vision of the ladder, should have been a place defiled by the sin of Jeroboam? God said, *"The horns of the altar shall be cut off and fall to the ground."* Verse 15: *"I will smite the winter house with the summer house; and the houses of ivory shall perish, and the great houses shall have an end, saith the Lord."* Several years ago, the British Museum displayed the ivory panels that had been excavated from this time period. I was fortunate to be there to view them. With these words by Amos, there is proof of the prosperity in that time. There is more evidence from archaeology of the opulent lifestyle during that time. Many of the residents owned *second homes* in the hills from which to escape the heat of summer.

In chapter 4, Amos addresses the obese women of high society, saying, *"Hear this word, ye kine of Bashan that are in the mountain of Samaria."* These women would recline on their ivory beds, drinking wine and nagging their husbands for even more riches. As a result, their husbands oppressed the poor and crushed the needy. What a picture we have here of the blatant social injustice being perpetrated by the Israelites. There was no middle-class society in Israel. There was the elitist group, the wealthy and powerful people; and there were the very poor, who were oppressed and exploited by the rich. But the Lord swore in His holiness that, *"The days shall come upon you, that he will take you away with hooks, and your posterity with fishhooks."* This was a reference to the Assyrian practice of putting hooks through the lips of their captives before leading them away. The next verse describes them being led out single file through a hole in the city wall. Historically, we know that this is exactly what happened when the Assyrians invaded.

Knowing that Israel was not going to repent, the Lord spoke sarcastically through Amos: "Go ahead and do what you love to do. Go to Bethel where I learned to hate you. Go to Gilgal. Take your tithes and your thank offerings of leavened bread." Evil had completely permeated the nation of Israel. Everything was leavened, and in Scripture leaven is always a symbol of evil (Matt. 16:6; I Cor. 5:6-9). These things were what Israel loved to do, because they ritualized the outward show of worship, sacrifice, and the licentious activities that went with the system.

Read carefully Amos 4:6-11 where the Lord lists all that He has done to bring them back. There is a momentum and tempo to this section which keeps increasing. Over and over the refrain is repeated, *"Yet have ye not returned unto Me."* See the methods God used: Verse 6 ff: *"I gave you cleanness of teeth and lack of bread. I have withholden the rain from you when there were yet three months to the harvest. I have smitten you with blasting and mildew."* The gardens, vineyards, and orchards were ruined. Insects also attacked them.

Notice the ascending severity of the chastisements. Famine, then drought then blight. Verse 10: There was a plague *"after the manner of Egypt. Your young men have I slain with the sword."* This was comparable to the Passover night in Egypt. Finally, verse 11: *"I have overthrown some of you, as God overthrew Sodom and Gomorrah."* Think of the evil in those cities which motivated God to destroy them. Now because the same evil is present, He has to destroy Israel. Five awesome opportunities were presented, but, *"yet have ye not returned unto me, saith the Lord. Therefore, thus will I do unto thee, 0 Israel: and because I will do this unto thee, prepare to meet thy God 0 Israel."*

The Israelites were to be special people, but God had demonstrated that being divinely elected did not mean they could sin with impunity. Amos 3:2 showed that God *must* punish Israel because of its unique position in the world. Because Israel was chosen then failed in her responsibility, the punishment was all the more severe. Chapter 5 has the tone of a funeral dirge. Amos says, *"Hear ye this word which I take up against you, even a lamentation of the house of Israel."* Verses 2 & 3 are prophetic because while Amos is speaking, Israel is prosperous; but he envisions the nation as fallen and forsaken. In this statement he foresees the Assyrian invasion and their brutal conquest.

Verses 4-7 are God's plea for Israel to return to Him. Once again, as in Hosea, we see God's emotions churning between His love for Israel and His holiness which demands judgment upon them. In the last verse of chapter 4, God demonstrated that He has powers men cannot duplicate, by forming mountains, creating wind, and identifying Himself as the Lord God of hosts. This is a military term and is appropriate for God to use when predicting judgment. But in 5:4, He pleads once again, *"Seek ye me, and ye shall live"* God is speaking as a wounded father, or rejected lover. In verse 5, He begs them not to go back to Bethel. He has already warned that He is going to destroy Bethel, so He pleads, *"Seek the Lord, and ye shall live; lest he break out like fire in the house of Joseph."* {Ephraim and Manasseh.; see Genesis 48:1 and Hosea 4:17.}

God has been identifying Himself to Israel in various ways, and in 5:8-9, He shows Himself to be the omnipotent Creator. Then, beginning in verse 10, He goes on to describe Israel. *"They hate him that rebuketh in the gate, and they abhor him that speaketh uprightly."* These evil Israelites hated the righteous man who pointed out their injustices or any official who sought to uphold justice in the gate. Verse 11 continues by saying, that because of their ruthless collection of the heavy fines and taxes they impose on the poor, they are going to soon witness their own luxurious houses and pleasant vineyards taken by others. Little did they realize how soon the Assyrians would be living in their houses and drinking their wine! God was well aware of their transgressions. "They afflict the just, they take a bribe, and they turn aside the poor in the gate from their sight" (verse 12). Yet the Lord had prescribed through Moses how business and judgment should be transacted in the gates. Look at Deuteronomy 16:18-19:

> *Judges and officers shalt thou make thee in all thy gates, which the*
> *Lord thy God giveth thee, throughout thy tribes; and they shall*
> *judge the people with just judgment. Thou shalt not wrest judgment, thou shalt not respect*
> *persons neither take a gift. For a gift doth blind the eyes of the wise, and pervert the words*
> *of the righteous.*

God said that judges must not accept bribes, but in 5:12 Amos said, *"they take a bribe, and they turn aside the poor in the gate from their right."* Why? Because the poor did not have money to pay a bribe and therefore, their cases were ignored, ruled against, and they were pushed aside by those whose money had met the needs of the judges. But in verses 14 and 15, they are once again offered the opportunity to repent:

> *Seek good, and not evil, that ye may live: and so the Lord, the God*
> *of hosts, shall be with you, as ye have spoken. Hate the evil, and*
> *love the good, and establish judgment in the gate: it may be that*
> *the Lord God of hosts will be gracious unto the remnant of Joseph.*

In verse 18, Amos echoes the earlier theme of Joel when he rebukes his listeners for desiring the Day of the Lord. The Day of the Lord is a day to be feared by the ungodly, not hoped for. For the unrepentant sinners. *"The day of the Lord is darkness, and not light."* There will be no escape from it. The one who tries will be like a man fleeing from a lion then meeting a bear. If he reaches his house safely, he will suddenly be bitten by a serpent. There will be no escape in the Day of the Lord; judgment will come!

In verses 21 and 22, the Lord tells His hatred for hypocritical worship. *"I hate, I despise your feast days."* God refused to accept their offerings; He did not want to hear their hymns; their rituals were part of Jeroboam's system, not the one He had given to Moses. {I Kings 12:31-33}Verse 24 is the key thought of Amos: *"Let judgment (justice) run down as waters, and righteousness as a mighty stream."* Remember, God delights in these. See Jeremiah 9:24. For parallel passages, see James 2:26; also Psalm 97:2, which say that righteousness and justice are the foundation of God's throne. These must be present in a person's life before his worship is acceptable to God. Righteousness and justice were not present in the gates of Israel, so the Lord said of their worship, *Take it away. I hate and reject it!*

LXXV. VISIONS AND OPPOSITION

More in Amos

Beginning in chapter 7, Amos describes five visions. The first is a *locust swarm* forming to devour the spring crop after the king had received his share. When Amos saw the pending destruction he prayed, *"O Lord God, forgive by whom shall Jacob arise for he is small?"* God relented at Amos's intercession and said He will not send the locusts. The second a *great fire* that dried up the sea and devoured the land. Again, Amos interceded because Israel was small, and again the Lord relented and restrained His hand of judgment. Vision 3 was a *plumbline.* A plumbline is a string with a heavy weight attached to determine whether a vertical object is perfectly upright. The Lord was about to inspect Israel with a plumbline. Israel was not straight when measured by His plumbline and He determined not spare them any longer.

To understand this concept, look at Isaiah 28:17: *"Judgment also will I lay to the line, and righteousness to the plummet"* (plumbline). God hangs the plumbline in the midst of Israel and it reveals how far the nation is leaning away from the standard God had established. Israel was a leaning wall that will eventually collapse. When this vision is seen, Amos does not intercede. He has nothing to say, because he knows that size has no relationship with integrity. Justice can be practiced by one person or by an entire nation. In verse 9, Amos prophesies about the devastation which will be wrought by the Assyrians, but says the invasion will be preceded by judgment on the house of Jeroboam II. That occurred in 752 B.C., when Shallum assassinated Jeroboam's son Zachariah and usurped the throne by claiming it for himself.

Confrontation

When Amos said these things, the priest of Bethel, Amaziah, had heard enough of Amos and reported his last words to the king, saying, *"Amos hath conspired against thee in the midst of the house of Israel, the land is not able to bear all his words."* He accused Amos of having prophesied both the assassination of the king and the invasion and captivity of Israel. After his report to the king, he returned and confronted Amos. *"Go home, Seer."* He commanded. *"Prophesy in Judah and not in Bethel. It is the king's chapel, and it is the king's court."* The humble herdsman, knowing God's hand was on him, stood before Amaziah with his eyes blazing. He looked at the godless priest who served at Bethel where Jeroboam, I had put one of his golden calves, and was now even more polluted by Baalism, and gave his testimony: *"The Lord took me as I followed the flock, and the Lord said unto me, Go, prophesy unto my people Israel."* In effect Amos said," Are you saying to me, 'Do not prophesy against Israel'? (vss.16-17): Amos continued:

> *Therefore thus saith the Lord, Thy wife shall be an harlot in the*
> *city, and thy sons and thy daughters shall fall by the sword, and*
> *thy land shall be divided by line, and thou shalt die in a polluted*
> *land: and Israel shall surely go into captivity forth of his land.*

Because of his disrespect for the prophet of God, four curses were pronounced against the godless priest by Amos.

Rotten Fruit

Chapter 8 describes the fourth vision of the *summer fruit*. We can best understand this illustration by understanding the summer climate in Israel. Summer fruit does not last. When the temperature soars, it turns black and rotten. God said this was the condition of Israel; like a basket of summer fruit, rotten and worthless, ready to be thrown into the garbage. In 8:2-3, Amos reported the conclusion of the vision:

In verse 4, Amos again turned his attention to the greedy merchants who exploited the poor people. They were impatient with the Sabbaths because they had to close down their businesses. *When will it be over so we can start trading again?* The indictment goes even farther. Not only were they impatient about closing down in order to "worship," they were seeking ways of *"making the ephah small, and the shekel great."* In this way, they were altering the system of weights and measures. Amos tells what was happening in both sides of a transaction. Viz., merchants were using baskets smaller than a normal bushel and when a customer came, they would fill the smaller bushel and charge the customer for a normal bushel. For weighing products in a transaction, the shekel was used on one side of the scale.

When dishonest customers wanted to *buy* produce, they would use an oversize shekel, telling the merchant their shekel was standard weight. E.G., if the merchant to believe the shekel weighed an ounce, he gave the dishonest customer what he believed was an ounce, but the amount of grain on the other side of the scale was more than the ounce for which the customer was charged. A picture by Norman Rockwell shows a butcher with his thumb on the scale while the little old lady on the other side has her finger underneath it, each is trying to cheat the other. But it was not a joke in Amos's day, because no one could be trusted in the marketplace. In Amos's day there were no official controls on weights and measures. A wealthy man could even buy the helpless for money. And if he needed a pair of shoes, he could sell a slave for just the necessary amount. He could rob the poor by selling grain to them from which only part of the chaff had been removed. In Amos's day, dishonest merchants increased the weight of the wheat by mixing some of the chaff back into it. God abhors such practices and Amos says (vs. 7): *"The Lord hath sworn by the excellency of Jacob, Surely I will never forget any of their works."*

In verse 11, Amos predicted a different kind of famine, *"not a famine of bread, nor a thirst for water, but of heating the words of the Lord."* God was going to return to His place and when He did, the voice of the prophets would no longer be heard in the land. All who had sworn by the false gods would fall *"and never rise up again"* (vs. 14). Chapter 9 describes Amos's fifth vision. The altar involved is the one established by Jeroboam, I, where all the kings of the north had worshiped. Symbolically, an altar was a place of mercy because a substitutionary sacrifice was offered there. In I John 2:2 Christ is our *"propitiation,"* and in Hebrews 9:5 the same Greek word is translated *"mercy seat."* Christ is our mercy seat, our altar, where God the Father placed our sins on His sinless Son. When the altar of God is despised, there is judgment on the one who
despises it. Israel worshiped at Jeroboam's altar because they had despised God's altar. So, it became a place of judgment. In his vision, Amos saw God standing beside it and giving instructions for its destruction.

In the vision, God said there was no way possible that the people could escape from His judgment, regardless of where they hid themselves. Even after their captivity, they would be slain because *"I will set mine eyes upon them for evil, and not for good"* (vs. 4). Beginning in verse 5, He reaffirmed His omnipotence and His control over the physical universe. In verse 7 He took them to task for their belief that they were a unique people. They took much pride in that. The Lord affirmed throughout the Old Testament that they were His special Exodus people. Now He asks, *"Have not I brought up Israel out of the land of Egypt and the Philistines from Caphtor, and the Syrians from Kir?"* In other words, God said: "You are no longer special. I have brought other nations from other places just as I did you. Because of your wickedness you are, so far as I am concerned, just like the Philistines or the Syrians or the Ethiopians." No longer did it have special meaning to be an Exodus people. But even after this, in verse 8, He again confirmed the Davidic covenant.

> *Behold the eyes of the Lord God are upon the sinful kingdom, and I
> will destroy it from off the face of the earth; saving that I will not
> utterly destroy the house of Jacob, saith the Lord.*

Although Israel would be completely destroyed in 722, the nation of Judah would still be protected because of the Davidic covenant.

Amos 9:11 begins an eschatological section describing how the fallen booth of David would again be raised up and be rebuilt as in the days of old. So, at the time of national restoration, Israel can look forward to the return of a converted remnant. Again, as with all of the true prophets, there is left to the listener a ray of hope, a fight at the end of the tunnel. After God's judgment has fallen, He will continue to be faithful with His *hesed* love and honor the Davidic covenant as He promised in 11 Samuel 7. {Acts 15:13-18}

LXXVI. ISAIAH, THE UNIVERSAL PROPHET

Isaiah's prophetic ministry begins in the year 739 B.C., which he identified as *the year that king Uzziah died.* He probably began his ministry in the last years of Uzziah's reign, but then received his official call into prophetic service at the time of Uzziah's death. Chapter 1:1 reveals that his activity extended through the reigns of Jotham, Ahaz, and Hezekiah Isaiah was prophesying and preaching for at least forty years. Rabbinic tradition says that he was murdered by Manasseh. We are familiar with the historical political and religious sins against which Isaiah preached. The situation in Judah was similar to what it had been in Israel during the reign of Jeroboam, 11. Because Isaiah began his prophetic ministry in 739, we know that he was an eyewitness to the Assyrian invasion and conquest of the northern kingdom in 722. The inhabitants in Judah were given a visual demonstration of what God's judgment could do. This should have provided impact to the prophetic messages by Isaiah which commanded them to repent.

Isaiah Spans History

It is difficult to analyze and summarize all of the truths in this wonderful book. Isaiah's broad scope of revelation, deals with everything from Satan, in eternity past (Isa. 14), to beyond the church age, to the New Heaven and the new earth (Isa. 66). No other prophet in the Old Testament has Isaiah's span of knowledge, history, and prophecy. Without his prophecies, there would be a significant void in our knowledge of future events including those events that preceded the Advent of the Messiah. He was given unusual insights into the life of Messiah. He wrote of the virgin birth, His deity, and His eternal kingdom. He spoke of His humanity as the Root of Jesse, and wrote of His righteous reign and that He is the Mighty God. He wrote about His vicarious suffering, death, and His reign as king during the millennium. It is because of the book of Isaiah, that we are able to put together the sufferings of Christ and the glory that should follow. If the other prophets had been able to completely understand the book of Isaiah, they would have seen that Messiah was both to suffer and to reign. Even Isaiah, however, was not allowed to see the Church Age. As the Apostle Paul said, it was a mystery. {Ephesians 3:3-6}

Many attempts have been made to discredit the book of Isaiah. The most popular is the deutero-Isaiah position which theorizes that the first thirty-nine chapters were written by the historical Isaiah, but chapters 40-66 were written by a pious forger at a later date. This is an attempt to discredit the prophecies contained in the latter section of the book. The following verses should prove that Isaiah wrote the 66 chapters. John 12:37-40 quotes Isaiah 53:1 and Isaiah 6: 9,10:

{53:1}But though he had done so many miracles before them, yet they believed not on him: That the saying of Esaias the prophet might be fulfilled, which he spake, Lord, who hath believed our report? And to whom hath the arm of the Lord been revealed?
{6:9, 10}; Therefore they could not believe, because that Esaias said again. He hath blinded their eyes, and hardened their heart, that they should not see with their eyes, nor understand with their heart,
and be converted, and I should heal them.

In the gospel of John we have the assurance that Isaiah wrote both the first half and the second half of the book which bears his name.

Beginning in 1:2: *"Hear, 0 heavens, and give ear, 0 earth."* The Lord personifies the heavens and earth, calling on them to witness His complaint against the nation. He compares His people to rebellious children who have turned their backs on His goodness. Even dumb oxen and asses, He said, know where their meals come from, *"but Israel doth not know, my people doth not consider."* Verse 4 contains a seven-fold indictment describing Israel's sins. This is a negative use of the number seven, suggesting that Judah is complete in sin.

*"**Ah sinful nation.**"* The first. {See Exodus 19:6.}
*"**A people laden with iniquity**."* The second.
*"**A seed of evildoers**."* The third. *{Compare it with Genesis 21:12.}* *"**Children that are corrupters**."* The fourth. {See Deut. 14.}
*"**They have forsaken the Lord**."* The fifth. {See Deut. 32:11ff.}
*"**They have provoked the Holy One of Israel**"* The sixth.
*"**They are gone away backward**."* The seventh.

This is the seven-fold indictment of sin. There is no hope left for them. They had reached the point of no return. Verse 5 discusses their chastisement. Have you not had enough? "The *whole head is sick, and the whole heart faint.*" In verse 6 He compares them to lepers, completely covered with sores and oozing wounds and they have done nothing to clean up or bandage them. As an illustration, God compares their spiritual infirmity to this most revolting physical infirmity. I am reminded of the classic novel, *The Picture of Dorian Gray*, who from all outward appearances, went through life as beautiful and unmarred as he was while in his youth. But, he was living such a sinful life, that the portrait in his attic, took on the characteristics of his inner self, until it was too hideous to look at. Such was the situation in Judah. In verses 7-9, Isaiah, with his prophetic eye, saw the destruction of Judah and described it as if it were a present reality. His audience must have looked around and wondered what he was talking about. They could see only their outward prosperity; but Isaiah saw their inner rottenness and the destruction to which it would lead. God then compared His own people to Sodom and Gomorrah who, because of their wickedness, were wiped off the face of the earth.

Because they had fallen so low, He rejected their sacrifices and their feasts. He wanted nothing to do with their outward hypocritical worship. He could no longer endure them, and *"It is iniquity, your appointed feasts my soul hateth: they are a trouble unto me. I am weary to bear them."* Notice God's use of the word *"your"* These were not God's festivals. He rejected them because they were not from the heart but a man-made religious observance. Neither would He hear their prayers because their hands were stained with the blood of injustice. Like Lady Macbeth, who cried, *"Out, damned spot,"* after she encouraged Macbeth to kill Duncan, so the hands of Judah could not be cleansed of their iniquities.

Beginning in verse 18 we have a courtroom scene. God said, *"Come now, and let us reason together."* This is a way of saying, "come let's reach a reasonable legal settlement." These descendants of Jacob were His covenant people. The covenant, as presented in the book of Deuteronomy, was an agreement that He would be their God and they were to be His people. It was a legal document. Now, speaking in legal language, God said, "Can we arrive at a solution to this?" *"Though your sins be as scarlet, they shall be as white as snow, though they be red like crimson, they shall be as wool. If ye be willing and obedient, ye shall eat the good of the land."* This is another version of the earlier *"if-but"* principle which was presented in Leviticus 26. *"But if ye refuse and rebel, ye shall be devoured with the sword: for the mouth of the Lord hath spoken it. How is the faithful city become an harlot! It was full of judgment; righteousness lodged in it; but now murderers. Thy princes are rebellious."* When God looked, He saw there was corruption in government; everyone loved a bribe; everyone chased after rewards; no one defended the orphan or listened to the widow's plea.

In verse 29, there is a shift to the personal approach. *"They shall be ashamed of the oaks (terebinth) that ye have desired."* The site of the terebinth was the location where temple prostitutes worked. "Ye shall be confounded for the gardens that ye have chosen." The temple gardens where the harlots provided their services for the "worshipers." Chapter 3:24 contains a heart-rending prophecy about the Babylonian Captivity.

> *It shall come to pass, that instead of sweet smell there shall be*
> *stink; and instead o a girdle a rent, and instead of well set hair*
> *baldness; If and instead of a stomacher a girding of sackcloth; and*
> *burning instead of beauty.*

God's Vineyard

Beginning in chapter 5, we have one of the most beautiful allegories in Isaiah. In verse 1, God is speaking to the Son. There are two divine Persons mentioned in this allegory.

> *Now will I sing to my well beloved a song of my beloved touching*
> *his vineyard. My well beloved hath a vineyard in a very fruitful*
> *hill. And he fenced it, and gathered out the stones thereof, and*
> *planted it with the choicest vine, and built a tower in the midst of*
> *it, and also made a winepress therein: and he looked that it should*
> *bring forth grapes, and it brought forth wild grapes.*

This allegory presents Israel and Judah and, as we can see in the parallel passage in Matthew 21:33ff, the program of God for them in His plan for the ages. He had planted Israel and Judah like a vineyard in the earth so that they might bring glory to Him. Then, when He sought their worship, including the love which He expected to come back to Him, shown symbolically by going to get grapes from His vineyard that He might enjoy the fruit, He found instead bitter wild grapes. Throughout the Old Testament, God consistently asked, *"What more could I have done?"* In this allegory, He provided a protected territory; removed the stones (the Canaanites); planted it with the choicest vine (His chosen people); and in the midst He built a tower, symbolic of the law. It was a tower of protection providing shelter from invaders. Historically the law, when obeyed, protected the inhabitants from the very sins He was forced by His Holiness to condemn them for. He *"also made a winepress therein,"* symbolic perhaps of the temple where He could enjoy the worship of His people. After all this special care, they perverted everything and brought forth only wild grapes. Look at the New Testament parallel in Matthew 21:33ff to see what happened.

> *Hear another parable: There was a certain householder, which*

planted a vineyard, and hedged it round about, and digged a
winepress in it, and built a tower, and let it out to husbandmen,
and went into a far country: And when the time of the fruit drew
near, he sent his servants to the husbandmen, that they might
receive the fruits of it. And the husbandmen took his servants, and
beat one, and killed another, and stoned another.

This should remind us of Hosea 11, where God said that the more He sent prophets, the more they went from them. 21:36 continues:

Again, he sent other servants more than the first. And they did
unto them likewise. But last of all he sent unto them his son, saying, They will reverence my
son. But when the husbandmen saw
the son, they said among themselves, This is the heir; come, let us
kill him, and let us seize on his inheritance. And they caught him,
and cast him out of the vineyard, and slew him. When the lord
therefore of the vineyard cometh, what will he do unto those husbandmen? They say unto
him, He will miserably destroy those
wicked men, and will let out his vineyard unto other husbandmen,
which shall render him the fruits in their seasons.
Jesus saith unto them, Did ye never read in the scriptures, the
stone which the builders rejected, the same is become the head of
the corner. This is the Lord's doing, and it is marvelous in our eyes?
Therefore say I unto you, the kingdom of God shall be taken from
you and given to a nation bringing forth the fruits thereof.

Finally, in verse 45, "And when the chief priests and Pharisees had heard his parables, they perceived that he spake of them." Of course they did, because they were familiar with Isaiah 5:5-7:

I will tell you what I will do to my vineyard: I will take away the
hedge thereof, and it shall be eaten up, and break down the wall
thereof, and it shall be trodden down: And I will lay it waste; it
shall not be pruned, nor digged, but there shall come up briers and
thorns: I will also command the clouds that they rain no rain upon
it. For the vineyard of the Lord of hosts is the house of Israel, and
the men of Judah his pleasant plant. And he looked for judgment,
but behold oppression: for righteousness, but behold a cry.

God had once said to Moses, "I have heard the cry of My people at the hands of the Egyptians," but now He says, "I am hearing the cry of the oppressed at the hands of their own people." In Isaiah 5 and Matthew 21, we can see, in an allegorical format, God's total Old Testament program as it related to Israel and Judah.

Isaiah's Official Call

In chapter 6, Isaiah records his official call to prophetic service. It was in the year that king Uzziah died. *"I saw also the Lord sitting upon a throne, high and lifted up, and his train filled the temple."* We have seen pictures of monarchs ascending the steps to their thrones and pulling behind them a majestic red velvet train. The Pre-incarnate Son of God (John 12:41} had a magnificent train in Isaiah's vision. It is so magnificent that it fills all of the temple. The seraphim stood above the throne crying one to another, *"Holy, holy, holy, is the Lord of hosts: the whole earth is full of his glory."* So awesome was the presence of the Lord that the foundations of the temple shook and trembled. This was a climactic event in Isaiah's life. Until this, Isaiah thought of himself as a righteous man. He also had a close relationship with the monarchy and was a welcome figure in the palace. Suddenly, he was allowed to see the holiness of God. Like everyone else in the Old Testament, who had a personal encounter with the Angel of the Lord, he fell on his face and for the first time, saw himself as he really was. He cried out, *"Woe is me for I am undone; because I am a man of unclean lips."* That was the leper's cry, "Unclean, unclean!" *"For mine eyes have seen the King, the Lord of hosts."* Our Lord will appear this way during His 1,000 year reign. When Isaiah saw himself as he actually was, and also knew Judah was decadent, permeated with sin, hypocrisy, and injustice, he realized that everything must be destroyed. God sent one of the seraphim from the heavenly altar to purge his lips with a flaming red hot coal. It was a symbolic cleansing of Isaiah's life.

Now, being cleansed and prepared for service, as a vessel fit for the Master's use, God's call for service came to Isaiah. He asks, *"Whom shall I send, and who will go for us?"* Immediately Isaiah volunteers, *"Here am I, send me."* After being touched by the coal, there could be no other response to the call of the Holy Trinity. The job will not be easy. The people will hear without understanding, and see without perceiving. Their hearts will remain fat, while their ears are deaf and their eyes will be closed to the truth. God was going to bring judgment on them, but, He told Isaiah, to compound their judgment, "We are to sending *you* to preach to them. They will not see or hear, and their hearts will be hardened so they cannot repent and be healed." In the New Testament, the Lord Jesus confirms this prophecy to the disciples when He explained why it was He spoke in parables. He presented the truth, but His enemies would not understand it because their hearts were evil and unbelieving. They were ready for the judgment which would soon come upon them from the Roman legions under Titus in 70 A.D.

Prophecies of the Christ

In Isaiah 9:2, we read prophecies about the first half of the ministry of the Lord Jesus Christ, which came 750 years later. *"The people that walked in darkness have seen a great light. They that dwell in the land of the shadow of death, upon them hath the light shined"* When this prophecy is read by our Lord in Matthew 4:16, He stopped reading at Isaiah verse 2. The Jews in Capernaum waited for verses 3 through 7. Unknown to them, verse 2 is the first advent. Verses 3-7 will be in the Second Advent with the Church Age between verses two and three. In 9:6-7:

For unto us a child is born, unto us a son is given: and the government shall be upon his shoulder. And his name shall be called Wonderful, Counsellor, The mighty God, The everlasting Father, The prince of Peace. Of the increase of his government and peace there shall be no end, upon the throne of David, and upon his kingdom, to order it, and to establish it with judgment and with justice from henceforth even forever. The zeal of the Lord of hosts will perform this.

As an Old Testament prophet, Isaiah was not aware of the future Church Age, so his message includes the first and second advents of the Lord Jesus Christ. (Col. 1:26; I Peter 1:11)

An Outline

Because space prevents coverage of the entire message of Isaiah, this is an outline to help in your study of Isaiah's wonderful book.

Section One
I. Prophecies concerning Judah and Jerusalem. 1-12
II. Prophecies of judgment against the nations. 13-23
               Against Babylon, Assyria, Philistia, Moab, Damascus, Ethiopia,
  Egypt, Edom and Arabia, Jerusalem, and Tyre
III. God's judgment upon the earth and establishment of the
   future kingdom. 24-27

In the latter chapters of Isaiah, we are introduced to Jehovah's three servants: viz., Cyrus, Israel, and Messiah. Beginning in 52:13, where Isaiah says, *"Behold, my servant shall deal prudently, he shall be exalted and extolled, and be very high,"* is a prophecy of the future of Messiah. I am sure that as Isaiah wrote these verses from 52:13 through chapter 53, he must have wondered how to reconcile the sufferings of Christ, as he wrote about them in chapter 53, and the glory which he described in chapter 9. As we look back in retrospect begin to grasp the span of prophecy given to Isaiah, we must stand in awe at this great man of God and the vision which was given him to record for us. The span and scope of his prophecies cannot be overestimated. The original sin of Lucifer, the invasion of the Assyrians, the invasion of the Babylonians and the exile, the return of the remnant under Cyrus, the virgin birth of the Messiah, Messiah's suffering, His return in glory, the re-establishment of the Davidic kingdom, the return of Israel to the land, and finally the new heavens and new earth and the establishment of Israel forever as a nation under God in the new earth (Isa. 66:22). How can we comprehend such things? A lifetime of study in these sixty-six chapters would not be enough!

LXXVII. THE PROPHETIC MINISTRY OF MICAH

Micah, a contemporary of Isaiah, was the last eighth century B.C. writing prophet. His book contains three prophetic sermons, each distinguished from the other by the introductory word, *"Hear."* These are in: 1:2; 3:1; & 6:1. These three prophetic messages can be differentiated by the content and point of view. Each contains a description of the spiritual corruption, an announcement of imminent judgment, and the glorious future of Israel.

The first, announces a general judgment on Israel because of their sin. The second, after Micah pronounced divine judgment on the nation's leaders, the wicked princes and false prophets, predicts the future hope of the messianic kingdom. The third is an admonition to repentance and the promise of future deliverance and salvation. Micah listed the essential requirements of true religion and acceptable worship; viz., to do justly, to love kindness (mercy) and to walk humbly with God (6:8). In both the Old and New Testament economies, this was a summing up of the cardinal principles of genuine religion. From the days of slavery in Egypt, until the exile in Babylon more than eight centuries later, God attempted to teach His people the nature of acceptable religion and worship.

Over and over, the prophets pointed out that the people had misunderstood the entire concept, because they only involved themselves in the *outward* religious practices but did not do justly, did not love kindness, and did not walk humbly with their God. They were consistently unjust to their fellow Israelites until their cries went up to God in heaven. They did not demonstrate mercy. They turned aside the widows and orphans, and finally their pious and stiff-necked attitude caused such self-pride that they never walked humbly with God. When they did, it was only temporary. As God said through Hosea, *"What shall I do with you because your goodness is like the morning cloud and the morning dew?"*

Micah's Times and Prophecies

Because Micah prophesied during the time of Jotham, Ahaz, and Hezekiah (1:1), we know he lived during the time of the destruction of Israel in 722 B.C. Realizing that the sins being committed were going to bring destruction on the north and the south, he compelled them to begin practicing the religion which God expected of them. Micah ranks with Isaiah in regard to the quantity of predictions he made concerning Israel's future and the advent of the Messiah and Messiah's kingdom. Among the predictions made by Micah were: the destruction of Samaria in 722; the invasion of Judah by Sennacherib; the destruction of Jerusalem and the temple in 586; the years of exile in Babylon; the return of the exiles from captivity; the future peace and supremacy of Israel; and, most amazing of all, the birth of Jesus Christ in Bethlehem.

Isaiah and Micah present the two most unmistakable prophecies about Jesus Christ. Isaiah foretold His birth to a virgin (7:14). Micah described the geographic location of His birthplace (5:2). When the Magi came from the east inquiring where the king of the Jews was to be born, they received an immediate answer from the Jewish scribes and priests (Matt. 2:5). Micah uses the same words as Isaiah to predict that during the time of Messiah's reign there would be worldwide peace for man and beast.

Beginning in 1:2, God, through Micah, calls on all the people and on the earth itself, to witness against the sin of His people as He speaks from His holy temple. Verses 3 and 4 give us some insight into the omnipotence of God. He: treads on the high places of the land; mountains melt under him; valleys split and run down like wax when it is close to a fire and like water when it is poured down a steep hill. We know this will literally happen when the Lord Jesus Christ returns and places His feet on the Mount of Olives. The mountain will split and all of the mountains will collapse. They will melt, and the low places will be raised up. But here, Micah uses these physical phenomena as symbolism of the future destruction on the nations of Israel and Judah. He says, *"This is for the transgression of Jacob."* Isn't it interesting that the prophet uses the old name of Jacob, not Israel, because the old name described his old character? Even Esau said, *"He is rightly named Jacob because he has supplanted me these two times.*

God said His people are supplanters and He cannot use the new name He gave Jacob at Penuel, because these evil descendants of Jacob do not deserve the new name which means, *prince of God.* Then He uses the names in parallel fashion, *"And for the sins of the house of Israel. What is the transgression of Jacob? is it not Samaria?"* Remember in Amos 8:14: *"They that swear by the sin of Samaria and say, Thy God, O Dan, liveth."* This is a reference to the worship of the golden calves which was established by Jeroboam, I, back in 931/930 B.C. Micah continued, *"What are the high places of Judah? Are they not Jerusalem?"* Decades later, during the reign of Josiah in the southern kingdom, we read (II Chron. 34:3-4):

*For in the eighth year of his reign while he was yet young, he
began to seek after the God of David his father. And in the twelfth
year he began to purge Judah and Jerusalem from the high places,
and the groves, and the carved images, and the molten images.
And they brake down the arms of Baalim in his presence: and the
images, that were on high above them.*

So it is obvious that all of the people, north and south, were polluted with their idolatrous worship. Because of their sins, God says, *"I will make Samaria a heap."* We know that Micah began to prophesy after 739, but before 730, because he links his ministry with Jotham, who reigned from about 750 as co-regent with his father Uzziah (who died in 739), until 730, but he does not mention Uzziah. He made an accurate prediction regarding the destruction of Samaria in 722 B.C., which occurred about a decade after the time he preached this message in 1:7:

*All the graven images thereof shall be beaten to pieces, and all the
hires thereof shall be burned with the fire, and all the idols thereof
will I lay desolate: for she gathered it of the hire of an harlot, and
they shall return to the hire of an harlot.*

This is the same message Hosea preached approximately thirty years
earlier in 2:5. The same sinful Baal-inspired activities were still continuing. Realizing this, Micah began a personal lament, saying, *"Therefore I will wail and howl, I will go stripped and naked."* This is interesting because his contemporary, the prophet Isaiah, had been instructed by God to go barefoot and naked. That was Isaiah's example of pedagogy in biography. In Isaiah 20:2-4:

*At the same time spake the Lord by Isaiah the son of Amoz, saying,
Go and loose the sackcloth from off thy loins, and put off thy shoe
from thy foot. And he did so, walking naked and barefoot. And the
Lord said, like as my servant Isaiah hath walked naked and bare-
foot three years for a sign and wonder upon Egypt and upon Ethiopia; So shall the king of
Assyria lead away the Egyptians prisoners, and the Ethiopians captives, young and old,
naked and barefoot, even with their buttocks uncovered, to the shame of Egypt.*

Isaiah's pedagogy in biography was a visual object lesson regarding the future captivity of Egypt and the defeat of Egypt by the Assyrians. Now, Micah laments, saying the whole scenario is so terrible, that he also must go mourning, lamenting like the jackets and mourning like the ostriches. Why, Micah? Verse 9 says *"Because her wound is incurable."* It was bad enough when it was in Israel, but now it had come down to Judah, it had even reached Jerusalem, the location of the temple of Jehovah. Then Micah said in verse 10: *"Declare ye it not at Gath, weep ye not at all."* The exact translation is, *"weeping, weep not."* Then, *"In the house of Aphra roll thyself in the dust."* He used a term we know as *paronomasia.* This is a satirical play on words. What he says is, *"In the house of dust, roll in the dust."* The balance of chapter one has several examples of paronomasia.

In chapter 2, Micah reiterated the theme of Amos, his predecessor from several decades earlier. His message is, there is oppression by the upper classes. He says, *"Woe to them that devise iniquity, and work evil upon their beds!"* There is an interesting contrast here between evil men and godly men. The evil man schemes iniquity on his bed, whereas the godly man says, *"My tears have been my meat day and night, while they continually say unto me, where is thy God?"* (Psalm 42:3). The ungodly man may spend his night planning schemes of iniquity for the dawn, but the godly man lies in sorrow and heartbreak if he has offended God. His tears stream down his face and he says they are his meat night and day. What a dramatic contrast! Continuing his description of the evil man *"When the morning is light, they practice it, because it is in the power of their hands. And they covet fields, and take them by violence."* This is reminiscent of I Kings 21, where Jezebel conspired to take Naboth's vineyard and seized it for her sullen husband, Ahab.

In verse 6, *"Prophesy ye not, say they to them that prophesy."* The inhabitants of the land were commanding the prophets of God not to speak. That also happened, you recall, in the time of Amos when he was confronted by Amaziah, the priest of Bethel. But, he said, *"They speak out because if they do not, their reproaches shall not be turned back. Is the spirit of the Lord straightened? Are these his doings? Do not my words do good to him that walketh uprightly?"* (vs. 7) The Word of God is not going to do any good for the evil man who will not listen. But the one who walks uprightly, who loves God's Word and looks into it as a mirror, then makes needed changes, the Word does good because he is an upright man. Continuing with verse 8, *"Even of late my people have risen up as an enemy."* It was bad enough when the Israelites had to worry about invading armies from the surrounding nations, but now the people in the land have become so wicked that they would strip the robes from their fellow Israelites. There were muggers in the streets stealing personal belongings from unsuspecting people. Even the wounded soldiers, returning from war, were not safe from vandals. The wealthy found reasons to evict

424

women, probably widows, from their homes. The people, seeking religious support for their wickedness, wanted prophets who would talk to them of wine and strong drink (vs. 11). *"He shall even be the prophet of this people."*

Chapter 3 opens with an address to the heads of Jacob leaders, rulers, priests and princes. Micah asked, *"Is it not for you to know judgment?"* That was a rhetorical question because of course it was. That was their business. But, Micah continued, *"You hate the good, and love the evil."* They were like cannibals, tearing the skin from God's people and eating the flesh from their bones, chopping them up like meat for the pot. Even so, when the mistreated cry to God, He will not answer because even they have practiced evil. Do you remember what God said earlier, *"I will go and return to my place"* That threat by God is the theme of Micah 3. *"Thus saith the Lord concerning the prophets that make my people err."*

Micah addressed the professional prophets, the yes men of his day. When they have something to bite with their teeth, they cry peace. Their politics and their messages were determined by the satisfaction of their appetites. Do you remember how Ahab asked his professional prophets, *"Shall we go up against this city?"* And they replied as one man, *"Go up."* They knew who signed their paychecks. The only man who spoke for God was the one who never prophesied good things concerning Ahab. The verse continues and Micah denounces the fury of the evil prophets against those who, *putteth not into their mouths.* In fact, they even declare "Holy War" against them. But, verse 6 continues, God would make sure their prophecies would fail.

Following his exposure of the false religious system and its leaders, Micah began to speak for himself. His words in verse 8 were dangerous and inflammatory. He had rebuked the false prophets, and he spoke the Word of God saying their prophecies would not come true and that their contrived methods of divination would fail. When they failed, they would be embarrassed and ashamed. Then he said, *"I am full of power by the spirit of the Lord, and of judgment and of might, to declare unto Jacob his transgression, and to Israel his sin."* Filled with courage and the power of the Spirit, Micah addressed the heads of Jacob and rulers of Israel. You *"abhor judgment, and pervert all equity."* The corrupt politicians twisted everything out of shape for their own advantage. *"They build up Zion with blood and Jerusalem with iniquity."* (vs. 10) Notice the synonymous parallelism in his words.

The heads there of judge for reward, and the priests thereof teach for hire, and the prophets thereof divine for money. Yet will they lean upon the Lord, and say, is not the Lord among us? None evil can come upon us.

(Parallel passages are in Judges 18:4 and I Chronicles 28:3.) What a false security those professional prophets had, *"None evil can come upon us,"* they said. But Micah retorted, *"Zion will be plowed as a field.* "With the spiritual eye, he looked into the future to 586 B.C. when *"Jerusalem shall become heaps and the mountain of the house as the high places of the forest."* Read Lamentations to see how this came to pass exactly as Micah had prophesied.

Chapter 4 is eschatological and demonstrates the ultimate triumph of God's grace. Verses 1-3 are identical with Isaiah 2:2-4 except for a very few words. This similarity has resulted in some controversy. Some scholars believe that Micah originated this section and then Isaiah borrowed it. Another group believes Micah copied from Isaiah. A third group believes that both men borrowed from some original document. Still another group says that Micah wrote it and a redactor inserted it at a later time in both Isaiah and Micah. The position I believe is the conservative one which says that, since they are not *quite* the same, both men received independent revelations of this tremendous truth. I believe the Holy Spirit inspired Isaiah to write Isaiah 2:2-4, and also inspired Micah to write Micah 4:1-3.

Micah says in verse 4, that a time is coming when every man will sit under his own vine and fig tree, and there will be no one to make him afraid. This is a tremendous promise, when considered alongside the prophecy of future destruction. Once again, it is the light at the end of the tunnel. Micah had prophesied that Samaria, Jerusalem, and the temple, would be destroyed. But, immediately following these statements, he exclaimed this promise of comfort and future restoration when every man would sit under his own vine and no one would have anything to fear.

> *In that day, saith the Lord, will I assemble her that halteth, and I will gather her that is driven out, and her that I have afflicted, And I will make her that halted a remnant and her that was cast far off a strong nation: and the Lord shall reign over them in mount Zion from henceforth, even for ever. (Micah 4:6-7)*

This is very similar to the cry of the people back in Hosea 6:1-2.

> *Come, and let us return unto the Lord: for He hath torn, and He will heal us; He hath smitten, and He will bind us up. After two days He will revive us. In the third day He will raise us up, and we shall live in His sight.*

God gave the inhabitants of the land, through Micah, the assurance that even though He must afflict them, the judgment would actually be remedial since there will be a time when He would regather them. Continuing in verse 10, Micah made a prophecy which would be fulfilled more than 140 years later. *"For now shalt thou go forth out of the city, and thou shalt dwell in the field, and thou shalt go even to Babylon."* This is tremendous; who would have thought it could happen? At that time, Assyria was the dominant power. A little later, Egypt would become strong. Who, except God's prophet, was allowed to look far enough into the future to know that Babylon would become a power strong enough to defeat Assyria and then take them captive? And if someone could have comprehended this prophecy, who would have thought that after becoming captives in Babylon, they would be allowed to return? But, verse 10 continues, *"There shalt thou be delivered, there the Lord shall redeem thee from the hand of thine enemies."* Not only did Micah prophesy the captivity in 586, but the later release under Cyrus in 539 B.C.

Chapter 5, verse 2 contains the outstanding prophecy regarding the birthplace of the Lord Jesus Christ. This is especially meaningful because of the insignificance of the city of Bethlehem. The prophecies, from Micah's vantage point in about 730 B.C., look down through the corridors of time to 722, 586, 539, the birth of Christ, and to the Millennial Kingdom. The balance of chapter 5 is eschatological and details the vengeance which will be carried out on the nations which have not obeyed God.

All 16 verses in chapter 6 contain God's controversy with unfaithful Israel. We saw this theme earlier in Isaiah 5, when God asked *"What more could I have done?"* This seems to be a recurring theme in the messages of the prophets. Micah was similar to many of his predecessors in using the technique of historical review. God often used this method to remind His people of everything He had done for them. As creator, He called upon the mountains and the foundations of the earth to hear His controversy against them. Micah continued his explanation about true worship (vss. 6-7):

> *Wherewith shall I come before the Lord, and bow myself before the high God? Shall I come before him with burnt offerings, with calves of a year old? Will the Lord be Pleased with thousands of rams, or with ten thousands of rivers of oil? Shall I give my firstborn for my transgression, the fruit of my body for the sin of my soul?*

The priests of Moloch would build a fire in the hollow brazen replica of Moloch until it was red hot. Then, without showing any outward emotion, the worshipers would place their firstborn on the idol's outstretched red hot hands and watch emotionless until the child fell into the fire below. "Must I do that?" Micah asked, "To atone for my sin?" Look at the beauty of verse 8: *"He hath showed thee, 0 man what is good; and what doth the Lord require of thee, but to do justly, and to love mercy, and to walk humbly with thy God?"* In the balance of the chapter, Micah echoes Amos in condemning unjust business practices. Can God justify short measures, wicked scales, and deceptive weights? What these evil businessmen sow, they will also reap. They will eat without being satisfied and lose what they save. They will be given over to destruction. God said to the entire nation that He would *"make thee a desolation, and the inhabitants thereof an hissing"* (vs. 16).

Micah 7:2 laments that the godly person had perished from the land. None was righteous among them. Each man waited for bloodshed and they hunted one another with a net. The illustration is of the hunter who used a net to ensnare his prey. The men of Judah were so evil, that they would hide while waiting for their prey, a fellow Israelite. David similarly described the wicked in Psalm 10:8, 9:

> *He sitteth in the lurking places of the villages; in the secret places doth he murder the innocent, his eyes are privily set against the poor. He lieth in wait secretly as a lion in his den; he lieth in wait to catch the poor, he doth catch the poor, and draweth him into his net.*

The treachery which was prevalent was both eschatological and historical. Listen to the words of Micah as he describes the decline in family relationships.

> *Trust ye not in attend, put ye not confidence in a guide: keep the doors of thy mouth from her that lieth in thy bosom. For the son dishonoureth the father, the daughter riseth up against her mother, the daughter in law against her mother in law, a man's enemies are the men of his own house. (7:5, 6)*

This was a foreshadow of what life will be in the Tribulation period which Christ spoke of when He said that a man's enemies will be those of his own household (Luke 21:16).

Micah knew the only source of hope: *"Therefore I will look unto the Lord, I will wait for the God of my salvation, my God will hear me"* (vs. 7). The balance of the chapter is eschatological. Micah looked forward to that future day and spoke for both Israel and Judah as a united nation when he said,

Then she that is mine enemy shall see it, and shame shall cover her
which said unto me, Where is the Lord thy God? mine eye shall
behold her: now shall she be trodden down as the mire of the streets. In the day that thy
walls are to be built, in that day shall the decree be far removed.

What tremendous eschatological promises about the time when God's ways, and His mistreated people, will be vindicated. Parallel passages are in Zechariah 2:2; 14:4-10; Ezekiel 47:13; 48:30-35. Finally, Micah said the other nations will be ashamed when they see what our God is like (vss. 18-20):

Who is a God like unto thee, that pardoneth iniquity, and passeth
by the transgression of the remnant of his heritage? he retaineth
not his anger forever, because he delighteth in mercy. He will turn
again, he will have compassion upon us; he will subdue our iniquities; and thou wilt cast
all their sins into the depths of the sea.
Thou wilt perform the truth to Jacob, and the mercy to Abraham,
which thou hast sworn unto our fathers from the days of old.

LXXVIII. NAHUM THE ELKOSHITE

Our study now continues on into the middle of the seventh century B.C., where we meet the prophet Nahum. In the Septuagint, Nahum follows Jonah as a complementary book. Both books concerned the Assyrians (Ninevites), but while Jonah described how they repented in his day, Nahum is completely prophetic. Nahum's book was written while Assyria was still strong. The best estimate for the date of Nahum is somewhere between 663 and 612 B.C. We arrive at this from internal evidence and the history of Assyria, considering the historical date of the destruction of Nineveh by the Babylonians.

Unlike his predecessors, Nahum did not name the king who was on the throne during his ministry; perhaps this was because the focus of his message was not on Judah but on Nineveh. However, Nahum was probably prophesying prior to the time of Josiah and Jeremiah. If so, the evil king Manasseh and later his son Amon would have been reigning in Jerusalem. Manasseh, you recall, had been taken away with hooks to Babylon, which was an Assyrian stronghold.

It may be that the preaching of Nahum, regarding the destruction of Nineveh, provided inspiration and encouragement for good king Josiah, who began his reign very soon after Nahum's time. It would have been natural for Josiah to come to the throne and continue to pay tribute to the Assyrians because his father and grandfather had done so. It is possibly that Nahum's preaching, with encouragement from Jeremiah, that Nineveh was going to be destroyed, encouraged Josiah to begin his national reforms.

Verse 1 begins, *"The burden of Nineveh. The book of the vision of Nahum the Elkoshite."* This was an area near Capernaum. God, through Nahum, introduced Himself as an avenging God. *"He reserveth wrath for his enemies."* Verse 4 introduces God as all-powerful. *"He rebuketh the sea, and maketh it day."* Reading this, one thinks of the Red Sea experience during the Exodus. *"And drieth up all the rivers. "* We are reminded of the drying up of the Jordan river. *"Bashan languisheth and Carmel."* Those were the revered sites of Baal according to the authors of Canaanite poetry. *"The flower of Lebanon languisheth."* The flowers wither for lack of water. It is Yahweh, not Baal, who controls the rain. *"The mountains quake at him."* Remember how Mount Horeb was quaking and smoking when the people feared (Exod. 19:18) *"The hills melt and the earth is burned at his presence, yea, the world, and all that dwell therein. His fury is poured out like fire, and the rocks are thrown down by him."* I am reminded of Elijah on Horeb as God went before him and the mountains split. (I Kings 19:11)

In verse 7 there is an obvious change of tone: *"The Lord is good, a stronghold in the day of trouble; and he knoweth them that trust in him."* Praise God that we are the children of the Creator and not His enemies. I would not want to be on the opposite side, as described by Nahum in verses 2-6. Have you ever stopped to think how wonderful it is that the One who's whirlwind and storm are His way, with clouds underneath His feet, who can dry riverbeds and cause mountains to melt, is our heavenly Father, and we are His children because of the Lord Jesus Christ? What a tremendous thing it is going to be to live in eternity, to see Jesus Christ our Savior face to face, and throughout all the ages to come, to have the Creator, the omnipotent, omniscient, omnipresent God, shower us with all of His abundant goodness and rewards through Jesus Christ. This is the God we love, know, and serve. The same God of whom Nahum speaks, who was going to destroy Nineveh, is our heavenly Father. Verse 8 provides details of Nineveh's destined destruction. *"But with an overrunning flood he will make an utter end of the place thereof, and darkness shall pursue his enemies."*

We know that according to the *Babylonian Chronicle* the city wall of Nineveh was breached by the Babylonian army in 612 B.C., at a time of unusually high tides in the Tigris and Khoser rivers. Verse 13 might have been especially encouraging to King Josiah. *"For now will I break his yoke from off thee, and will burst thy bonds in sunder."* Although they had been under Assyrian oppression for many years, God was going to break it loose and tear off their shackles of occupation and tribute payments. Hearing such a prophecy may have encouraged Josiah to begin his reform. After Josiah began his spiritual reforms, Ashurbanipal died, and the Assyrian monarch who followed him, was more of a literary man, a student of history, and a lover of the finer things, rather than being a military opportunist. God used this lack of interest in military affairs as a way for Assyria to go into decline as a world power so that Nineveh could be destroyed by the Babylonians in 612 B.C.

Verse 15: *Behold upon the mountains the feet of him that bringeth good tidings that publisheth peace! 0 Judah, keep thy solemn feasts, perform thy vows: for the wicked shall no more pass through thee; he is utterly cut off.* Good news! There will be peace. Judah can celebrate her feasts and pay her vows. The wicked one is cut off completely. What a note of encouragement this must have been. Yet it was still a *prophetic event*. Nineveh would not be cut off until 612 B.C., but Nahum said that Assyria *is* cut off completely. In God's eyes and therefore in the prophet's eyes, it was already done.

Chapter 2 is the prophetic description of the siege and destruction of Nineveh by the Babylonians. Various archaeological discoveries support Nahum's description. Among these are: The Babylonian Chronicle and the writings of Diodorus Siculus (ca. 20 B.C.) As Nahum writes, we can see what is happening in the city and around the walls. The shields of the mighty men are smeared red with blood. The warriors are dressed in scarlet. The chariots, covered in polished, flashing steel, race madly in the streets. The defenders of the city run to the wall to prepare its defenses. The gates of the river are opened by the invaders and the city is destroyed. Nineveh was once like a pool of water; an oasis in the desert. But now, all people flee from it and no one will look back on its destruction. *"Plunder the silver and gold,"* Nahum says (vs. 9). There is no limit to the treasure. There is wealth of every kind, and every desirable object.

The treasures of Nineveh, Khorsabad, Calah, and Assur were beyond compare; not only because of the riches which they brought back from their many conquests, but also because of the literary masterpieces which were collected by the Assyrians. The library of Ashurbanipal, which was destroyed, held 100,000 tablets. Among these tablets was the Chaldean flood epic. It was a storehouse of literary treasure which was obliterated. Only recently have men uncovered Assyrian cities and found some of these ancient tablets which were not destroyed. Verse 10 describes the sickening fear that gripped the Ninevites when they contemplated their destruction. Then verse 11 asks, *"Where is the dwelling of the lions, and the feeding place of the young lions?"* This is another example of the exactness of Nahum's prophecy. Only a person on the scene at the time would have known the facts in this verse. Recent archaeological discoveries have revealed that in the cities of Nineveh and Asshur, were lions' dens, built there because the Assyrians loved the sport of lion hunting. They went on expeditions, to capture lions alive and bring them back. They fed them in their dens until the king wanted some sport. Then they would turn a lion loose so the king could hunt it from his chariot. Many of the bas-reliefs contain carvings showing the king in his chariot, with his spear in hand, chasing a lion. Nahum had an exact knowledge of the lifestyle of the Assyrian monarchs in the late 7th century B. C. These are in the British Museum.

Chapter 3 describes the causes for the downfall of Nineveh. It is ironic how very similar this chapter is to the book of Lamentations, where Jeremiah later laments (586 B.C.) over the destruction of Jerusalem. The two ravaged cities sound very much alike.

Woe to the bloody city! It is all full of lies and robbery, the prey departeth not; the noise of a whip, and the noise of the rattling of the wheels, and of the prancing horses, and of the jumping chariots. (3:1,2)

The description continues: horses charging; swords flashing; spears gleaming; many slain; a mass of corpses; countless dead bodies. All this *"Because of the multitude of the whoredoms of the well favoured harlot, the mistress of witchcrafts, that selleth nations through her whoredoms, and families through her witchcrafts"* (vs. 4) When it happens everyone will say, *"Nineveh is laid waste; but no one will grieve for her."* The prophet asks, *"Whence shall I seek comforters for thee?"* God asks in vs. 8, *"Art thou better than populous No?"* No refers to No-ammon, which was another name for Thebes. That ancient city was captured by Ashurbanipal in 663 B.C. Nahum 3:8 is one of the key verses for dating the book. Nahum lived *after* 663 and looked back in time to the defeat of Thebes by Ashurbanipal. And, he lived *before* 612 because he looked forward to the future defeat of Nineveh.

No-ammon (Thebes) was situated by the Nile River. Ethiopia and Egypt were her allies. The inhabitants became exiles, going into captivity by the Assyrians. The young children were dashed to pieces on the stones of every street. They cast lots for the honorable men to see who would take them as prisoners for bounty. All the great men were bound with fetters. Some were hanged and dragged away. Verse 19 summarizes: *"There is no healing of thy bruise; thy wound is grievous: all that hear of thee shall clap the hands over thee; for upon whom hath not thy wickedness passed continually?"* There have been nations and men down through history whose deaths have resulted in handclapping. The Assyrian capitol was not an exception. It is interesting that God used the same phrase for Nineveh that He had used for His own people? In Micah 1:9, God said, *"Her wound is incurable."* He was speaking of Israel because her sins had come to Jerusalem. Like an arm with gangrene there was no saving it. The only solution was radical surgery, amputation. When Israel's wound was incurable the nation was amputated.

LXXIX. ZEPHANIAH

Nahum had prophesied prior to the time of Josiah. Zephaniah tells us in verse 1 that he was a prophet in the days of Josiah. And, that he is the great, great, great, grandson of King Hezekiah; the only prophet who was a descendant of royalty. Josiah's reign lasted from 640 to 609. Zephaniah's prophecies were made prior to 623 B.C.

His prophecy is judgment, and its central theme is the coming Day of the Lord. He began by announcing a universal judgment on Judah in particular and on the world in general. He described the Day of the Lord as an overwhelming terror in which God's wrath was going to consume the whole earth. Because his interest was primarily in His own people in the land of Judah, the first part of his message was directed to them. Then he turned to all the surrounding nations: the Philistines, the Moabites, the Ammonites, the Ethiopians (Egyptians), and the Assyrians. His presentations were almost the exact reverse of the presentations given by Amos.

When the evil king Manasseh died, he was succeeded by his son Amon, who reigned for only two years. Amon was so wicked, that he was assassinated by his servants. His son Josiah, who was only eight years old, was placed on the throne of Judah. At that time, the nation was in a sad state; a totally ruinous spiritual condition resulting from the evil influence of Manasseh and Amon. In II Chronicles 34:3 we learned that as early as his sixteenth year, Josiah's heart was turned to the Lord and he began a program of moral and spiritual reforms. No doubt much of his encouragement and motivation, which included tearing down the various altars and high places, came from Zephaniah and perhaps a knowledge of the prophesies of Nahum. Josiah was the one of whom the man of God spoke in scolding Jeroboam, I at the altar in Bethel where he said, referring to the one who would destroy the altar about three hundred years later, *"Behold, a child shall be born unto the house of David, Josiah by name"* (I Kings 13:2). So the king on the throne in the time of Zephaniah, was the fulfillment of the earlier prophecy by the unnamed man of God. Josiah was a good king and he would continue to reform the nation until he was killed in 609 trying to intervene and stop Pharaoh Necho from leading his armies up the Mediterranean coast. At that time, Necho took the whole land of Judah as a protectorate until 605 B.C.

After describing in detail all of the evil practices in Jerusalem upon which His judgment would fall, God said (vs. 12) that He would search Jerusalem with lamps to flush out and punish *"the men that are settled on their lees."* They were like stagnant bitter wine. And, being stagnant in spirit, they were saying in their hearts, *"The Lord will not do good, neither will he do evil."* God detests a neutral attitude! Remember what the ascended Christ said to the church at Laodicea in Revelation 3:16? *"Because thou art lukewarm, and neither cold nor hot I will spew thee out of my mouth."* He is an active God, concerned about His creation. The men described in verse 12 were deists. Deism believes that there may be a God somewhere, but He is so far out there in space, He has no concern for His creation. God will not do good or evil. God replied, *"I will show you whether I am concerned. I will see to it that your wealth becomes plunder for someone else."* Their houses would become desolate; they would build but not inhabit them. They would plant vineyards but not drink the wine. Everything they had would become plunder for the Babylonians. Zephaniah repeated the theme that the other Minor Prophets had proclaimed throughout their ministries; viz., everything owned by the inhabitants of Judah would very soon belong to an invading army.

In Zephaniah 1: 14, the prophet repeated what other minor prophets, especially Joel, had talked about regarding the Day of the Lord. He pointed out that it was near and coming very quickly. He said that it will be a day of wrath, trouble, distress, destruction, desolation, darkness, gloom, clouds. He went on to describe what will happen in the future during the battle of Armageddon. It will be similar to the soon coming invasion of the Babylonians against Judah, but it will be a day that will bring distress on all men.

Verse 18 confirms that nothing a man does will help him in that day. It is impossible to purchase God's mercy with riches of silver and gold. Throughout history kings had been able to pay off the Assyrian and Babylonian monarchs with their silver and gold to prevent them, temporarily, from invading their land. But when the Day of the Lord comes, silver and gold will not suffice. Returning to the immediate future, Zephaniah said in 2:3: *"Seek ye the Lord, all ye meek of the earth."* The ones who supported Josiah in his efforts at reform responded to this. They were the ones who backed him as he sought to bring the nation back from the idol worship established by his father and grandfather. They were the ones who carried out God's ordinances and His justice. They sought righteousness and humility. They quickly reacted to the message of Zephaniah in 2:3.

Verse 4 begins the prediction of judgment on all the nations of the world. Gaza will be abandoned, including Old Ashkelon, Ashdod, and Ekron. Throughout chapter 2, Zephaniah called for God's judgment on the nations that had oppressed His people during the previous centuries. At the beginning of chapter 3, Zephaniah directed his prophecy and judgment against Jerusalem, calling it a tyrannical city. His scathing rebuke in verses 3 and 4, identified four categories of leaders: the princes, the judges, the prophets, and the priests. The princes were like roaring lions. The judges were like wolves at evening. They starved during the day and at night, under protection of darkness, like wolves they stealthily walked around and crouched to attack the poultry in the barns. The prophets were reckless and treacherous men. He was referring to the professional prophets, the "yes men." The priests had profaned the sanctuary. In the southern kingdom they had brought in images so the people could worship Baal in the temple of Jehovah. It was this evil that Josiah would soon be successful in purging from the land.

Verse 8 picks up again with the eschatological theme. God said, *"My determination is to gather the nations."* Compare this with Ezekiel 38:9. Then, in Zephaniah 3:9, *"For then will I turn to the people a pure language, that they may all call upon the name of the Lord,"* In verse 13, *"The remnant of Israel shall not do iniquity."* Think of Micah 4:4, where God talks about the time when Israel will be restored, and where He described the time of Israel's restoration. Zephaniah says in 3:14, 15: *"Sing, O daughter of Zion; shout, O Israel; be glad and rejoice with all the heart, O daughter of Jerusalem. The Lord is in the midst of thee."*

The final verse of the book of Zephaniah summarizes the eschatological predictions when God says,

"At that time will I bring you again, even in the time that I gather you: for I will make you a name, and a praise among all people of the earth, when I turn back your captivity before your eyes, saith the Lord."

This is similar to the earlier promise in Micah 7:10: *"Mine enemy shall see it, and shame shall cover her which said unto me, Where is the Lord thy God?"* With these eschatological promises of a future return and restoration, Zephaniah ended his prophetic message to the inhabitants of Judah.

LXXX. HABAKKUK AND THE WAYS OF GOD

Habakkuk prophesied prior to 605 B.C., which was the date of the first invasion of Jerusalem by General Nebuchadnezzar. We know that he prophesied after the fall of Nineveh in 612, because Assyria is not included. The Chaldeans were at that time rising to power as indicated in 1:5-6. This evidence gives us the date of 612 to 605 B.C. However, we can narrow it down even more because we know that from 612 to 609, Josiah was on the throne and his reforms in the land were still in effect. However, following his death at Megiddo in 609, at the hands of Pharaoh Necho, Jehoahaz took the throne. Pharaoh Necho replaced him with Jehoiakim, who ruled from 609 to 597. {I Kings 24:31-34} Jehoiakim was a wicked king. The spiritual conditions described in verses 2-4 could not have applied to the time of Josiah, but do fit very well with what would have taken place during the reign of Jehoiakim. Based on these facts, we can assume that Habakkuk prophesied between 609 and 605 B.C.

Habakkuk was confronted with what he believed to be an ethical dilemma. In the first chapter, he was concerned over the rampant sin and iniquity going on unchecked in the land of Judah. He wondered why God did not do something about this corruption which was not being punished or judged. God informed Habakkuk that He planned to punish the iniquity of Judah very soon and that the instrument He would use would be the Chaldeans, a ruthless, aggressive, violent nation. This information only increased Habakkuk's dilemma. He was completely perplexed, because he could not reconcile the problem of how God, in His righteousness and holiness, could use such a wicked nation, the Chaldeans, to chasten His chosen people Judah. He knew Judah deserved punishment, but how could God use
the Chaldeans who were *more* wicked than Judah?

The prophet presented his problem to the Lord and then said, "*I am going to sit in a high tower and wait for You to answer me.*" When the answer came, Habakkuk learned that God dealt with men through His law, "*The just shall live by his faith.*" The proud and wicked would perish. Evil, by its very nature is self destructive, but the righteous individual shall live in his faithfulness. Just As the Assyrians described in Isaiah 10:5ff, the Chaldeans, in their blind arrogance and pride, were completely ignorant that they were the chastening rod of God to be used against His sinful nation, and because of their ruthlessness, and failure to acknowledge God, they too were doomed to destruction. God's reply to Habakkuk implied that the righteous, godly, man exercises a continuous and abiding confident trust in God even in the face of all adversity and trial, and in every circumstance of life. To Habakkuk, this meant that the just lived in faithfulness both in a time of spiritual declension, such as he was currently experiencing in Judah, and in a time of national calamity which he was commissioned to prophesy.

Beginning in chapter 1, Habakkuk looked around and said, *"How long shall I cry, and thou wilt not hear!"* There was violence in Jerusalem. The law was being ignored. Justice was not upheld and the wicked surrounded the righteous. When justice was attempted, it was twisted and perverted. In verses 5 & 6, God said,

"I will work a work in your days, which ye will not believe, though it be told you. I raise up the Chaldeans, that bitter and hasty nation, which shall march through the breadth of the land, to possess the dwelling places that are not theirs."

Their horses were swifter than leopards. They were dreaded and feared. They were a violent people, moving like a giant horde across the ground and collecting captives like sand. They mocked at kings and laughed at fortresses. They had no problem overcoming walls but swept in like the wind and then passed on leaving the city like a field after a swarm of locusts. In the balance of chapter 1, Habakkuk presented his ethical and moral dilemma to the Lord and then said he would build a little tower or guard post and keep watch until God spoke to him in 2:1. The Lord answered with a command in 2:2:

Write the vision, and make it plain upon tables, that he may run that readeth it. For the vision is yet for an appointed time, but at the end it shall speak, and not lie: though it tarry, wait for it because it will surely come. It will not tarry.

He was speaking of the invasion of the Babylonians. Then in verse 4, God instructed, *"The just shall live by his faith."* It was from this obscure passage in Habakkuk that the Apostle Paul developed the theme in the New Testament. In Romans 1:17, Galatians 3:11; and also is included in Hebrews 10:38.

Beginning in 2:6, God assured Habakkuk that He would also later judge the Chaldeans. He described their destruction with five *woes*. Verses 6-8 contain the first *woe* because of their plunder, their blood, and their violence. Verses 9-11 contain the second *woe* because of their greed, pride, and cruelty. Verses 12-14 contain the third *woe* because of their bloodshed and iniquity. Verses 15-17 contain the fourth *woe* because of their debauchery and the devastation which they inflicted on every nation. Verses 18-20 contain the fifth *woe* because of their idolatry. Verse 18 asks: *"What profiteth the graven image that the maker thereof hath graven it?"* How foolish it is for a man to think he can carve something out of wood and then worship it. (cf. Isa. 44:12-19) The Chaldeans collected gods from everywhere and worshiped the gods from nations they defeated. Verse 19 says,

"Woe unto him that saith to the wood, Awake, to the dumb stone, Arise, it shall teach! Behold, it is laid over with gold and silver, and there is no breath at all in the midst of it. What a contrast is contained in verse 20: *"The Lord is in his holy temple: let all the earth keep silence before Him."*

Chapter 3 is a Psalm of praise to God for His greatness and His judgments. Verses 17-19 form a beautiful climax to his prophecy and a fitting testimony to Habakkuk's faith:

Although the fig tree shall not blossom, neither shall fruit be in the vines; the labour of the olive shall fail, and the fields shall yield no meat; the flock shall be cut off from the fold, and there shall be no herd in the stalls: Yet I will rejoice in the Lord, I will joy in the God of my salvation. The Lord God is my strength, and he will make my feet like hinds' feet, and he will make me to walk upon mine high places.

LXXXI. JEREMIAH: THE WEEPING PROPHET

Habakkuk was the last of the *pre-exilic* prophets who prophesied prior to the *exilic* prophets, Ezekiel and Daniel. The three Minor Prophets remaining to be examined are *post-exilic*: Haggai, Zechariah, and Malachi. However, one major prophet spanned the last years of the kingdom of Judah and lived on into the exilic period. Jeremiah's ministry began in the thirtieth year of Josiah, in 627 B.C. Following this early beginning, he prophesied of the Chaldean invasion and victory over Judah, and witnessed it in 586 B.C. The Appendix to his prophetic ministry in chapter 52, ended in 560 B.C.

In 1;1, 2, we read: *The words of Jeremiah the son of Hilkiah, of the priests that were in Anathoth in the land of Benjamin: To whom the word of the Lord came in the days of Josiah the son of Amon king of Judah, in the thirteenth year of his reign.* The historical account of Josiah's reign was studied when we examined II Chronicles. In that book, there is an interesting comment in chapter 34:8 which says, *"In the eighteenth year of his reign, when he had purged the land, and the house, he sent Shapan to repair the house of the Lord his God."* The repair of the temple and the discovery of the law which resulted from it, occurred five years after Jeremiah's prophetic ministry began. the encouragement of Jeremiah's gave Josiah the encouragement to carry out his reforms and repairs.

We read earlier how the preaching of Nahum, that Assyria was to be destroyed (although Nahum preceded Josiah), gave him written encouragement. Then, the preaching of Zephaniah in Josiah's early years, gave him further encouragement that God was with him. Finally, the prophetic ministry of Jeremiah, crystallized everything for Josiah; and I am sure, gave him the confidence that God would be a constant source of strength, as he fulfilled the earlier prophecy of the unnamed man of God, in the time of Jeroboam I, and purged the land of idol worship. To validate that Jeremiah had a very long ministry, verse 3 says:

It came also in the days of Jehoiakim the son of Josiah king of Judah, unto the end of the eleventh year of Zedekiah the son of Josiah king of Judah, unto the carrying away of Jerusalem captive in the fifth month.

Jehoiakim reigned from 609 to 597 and Zedekiah from reigned 597 to 586. Jeremiah was an eyewitness to all the invasions of Nebuchadnezzar in 605, 598-597, and 588-586. He was allowed to stay in Jerusalem after the captivity. As the author of the book of Lamentations, he looked upon the desolation in Jerusalem after the Babylonians had ravished it.

Beginning in verse 4, Jeremiah records the circumstances of his call to the prophetic ministry. *"Then the word of the Lord came unto me,*
saying, Before I formed thee in the belly I knew thee." He was a man who was sovereignly selected by God before he was born; even before he was conceived. His reply was, *"Ah, Lord God! Behold, I cannot speak, for I am a child."* Pleading his lack of ability as an eloquent orator is reminiscent of Moses' response to his call by Yahweh at the burning bush. But the Lord said to Jeremiah, *"Say not that I am a child: for thou shalt go to all that I shall send thee, and whatsoever I command thee thou shalt speak."* Age and oratory would not determine his success because God would put His words into the prophet's mouth. Neither was fear to silence him because he had the Lord's promise of deliverance. His ministry would be far reaching, extending beyond Judah *"To root out, and to pull down, and to destroy, and to throw down, to build, and to plant."* God used rural farming terms to the young prophet from Anathoth. His first prophecy evidently followed soon after. *"Out of the north an evil will break forth upon all the inhabitants of the land."*

It was from the north following the battle at Carchemish in 605, Nebuchadnezzar first invaded the land of Judah. In verses 18, 19:

> *Behold, I have made thee this day a defenced city, and an iron*
> *pillar, and brasen walls against the whole land, against the kings*
> *of Judah, against the princes thereof, against the priests thereof,*
> *and against the people of the land. And they shall fight against*
> *thee; but they shall not prevail against thee; for I am with thee,*
> *saith the Lord, to deliver thee.*

Jeremiah was going to need this spiritual encouragement and Divine physical strength later on, because his entire ministry would be beset by open and vicious opposition.

Jeremiah's central theme would be that the coming judgment at the hand of the Chaldeans was from God. They were His chastening rod, because the inhabitants of the land had become so evil. This agrees with the theme of Habakkuk. Their messages were the same: the Chaldeans are coming and God is allowing it because they are His chastening rod to judge the violence and wickedness in the city. However, Jeremiah's message had a somewhat different tone. He followed up his predictions of the invasion by saying, "*Do not resist the Babylonians; You must not resist but bow your heads in submission. God is sending them to chasten you, so take the punishment you deserve. The Lord will deliver you when He is ready.*" The people of Judah did not want to hear this message. They wanted to resist the invading army. They would not recognize Jeremiah's message was coming from God, so they accused him of being a traitor. Throughout his entire ministry, he was rejected by everyone as a man who preached treason. Jeremiah was a weeping prophet because he was rejected because he saw the calamity that was coming on the land; and because he preached a message which no one wanted to hear.

To outline the book, we must understand that his prophecies are not arranged in chronological order. His prophecies under Josiah in chapters 1-20, are followed in chapter 21 by a prophecy given during the reign of Zedekiah, Judah's final king. Between these two, there were three others on the throne: Jehoahaz in 609, Jehoiakim (609-597), and Jehoiachin in 597. The reigns of these three kings were omitted. Chapters 35 and 36 precede 27-34 chronologically. Many reasons have been advanced to explain why the book is arranged in such an order. Some expositors, Kyle for example, have suggested that Jeremiah arranged his book topically according to subject matter. Other expositors have said that certain portions circulated independently, in small separate collections, and were later gathered together. Still others explain the character of the book by the nature of its composition, saying that the earlier prophecies were destroyed and were re-dictated with additions (36:32, for example), while later prophecies were collected and edited by Baruch. Finally, Unger believes that because the book was written in stages, it was not arranged in strict chronological order.

Jeremiah's reasons for the arrangement are not easy to ascertain. The general arrangement of the prophecies is discernable because they are divided based on the subject matter. Those concerning Judah and the future Messianic kingdom, come first in chapters 1-45. These are followed in 46-51, by prophecies concerning foreign nations. The final chapter is an historical Appendix. The following listing is arranged according to the reigns of the rulers under which Jeremiah prophesied.

1. Prophecies under Josiah and Jehoiakim, 2-20
2. Prophecies only under Jehoiakim, 25-27; 35-36; 49:1-33
3. Prophecies under Zedekiah, 21-24; 28-34; 37-39; 49:34-51:64

4. Prophecies under Gedaliah, 40-42
5. During his life in Egypt, 43-44
6. In the Historical Appendix, 52

Space does not permit analyzing all fifty-two chapters in the book of Jeremiah. I will some of the highlights of the book, primarily as they concern the theme of his message, including a few of his personal encounters with the leaders in Judah.

One central thought in Jeremiah's message is found in 6:16: "*Thus saith the Lord, Stand ye in the ways, and see, and ask for the old paths, where is the good way, and walk therein, and ye shall find rest for your souls.*" This is an echo of David's earlier cry in Psalm 25:4, 5, "*Shew me thy ways, 0 Lord, teach me thy paths. Lead me in thy truth, and teach me: for thou art the God of my salvation; on thee do I wait all the day.*" The people's response to the Lord's plea through Jeremiah was, "*We will not walk therein.*" We see the stiff-necked rebellion by the inhabitants of Judah because they were so steeped in Baalism that they did not want to be involved in the true worship of Jehovah. Jeremiah called them back to the Lord again and again, but they continued to rebel and stiffen their necks.

Because of their responses, God continued in chapter 7 to call them murderers and adulterers who swore falsely and offered sacrifices to Baal. Then He asks, "*Is this house, which is called by my name become a den of robbers in our eyes? Behold, even I have seen it, saith the Lord.*" (vs. 11) God then draws their attention back about 460 years to the historic battle of Aphek in 1075 B.C., saying, "*Go ye now unto my place which was in Shiloh, where I set my name at the first, and see what I did to it for the wickedness of my people Israel.*" That was the time period of Eli and his two wicked sons, Hophni and Phineas, when because of the evil in the land, God allowed the Philistines to capture the Ark and destroy the place of worship at Shiloh. Evidently, the tabernacle and altar were salvaged because they remained at Nob where the priests served God until they were slain by Doeg the Edomite during the reign of Saul. These cultic objects were then moved to Gibeon where they remained until Solomon completed the temple and placed them in storage.

Because of their stubbornness, the Lord instructed Jeremiah not to pray for the people (7:16). God was not going to hear them because of their wickedness. He determined to bring judgment on them and therefore it was too late for intercession. In verse 15 God said He was going to do to them just as He had done to Ephraim. They knew what had happened to Ephraim (Israel/Samaria), back in 722, when God allowed the Assyrians to invade them. Now, He was saying, He was going to do to them as He had done to Shiloh and to Ephraim, destroy them! "Jeremiah, God exclaimed, "Do you see what they are doing down there in the streets? They are baking cakes to the queen of heaven." As late as Jeremiah's time, the Babylonian religion (established back during the time of Nimrod) was still around, and promoting the worship of the queen of heaven. Even the children were participating. As we studied earlier, central to that system was the worship of Tammuz who, according to their myth, was virgin born. This was Satan's ancient counterfeit to confuse the prophecy about the true virgin-born Son of God.

Seeing all that was happening, Jeremiah exclaimed in 9:1: " *Oh that my head were waters, and mine eyes a fountain of tears, that I might weep day and night for the slain of the daughter of my people!"* This is one of the verses used to identify Jeremiah as the weeping prophet. Verse 14 says, they *"have walked after the imagination of their own heart, and after Baalim, which their fathers taught them."* Jeremiah wept because he must deliver the message of judgment and because he knew it would go unheeded.

In the midst of Jeremiah's weeping, because of his knowledge about what would happen to the nation he loved, God added in chapter 15 that there would be four kinds of doom: *The sword to slay; the dogs to drag off, the birds of the sky; and the beasts of the earth to devour and destroy.* Knowing that all of these things would surely come to pass, because the people would not repent, Jeremiah prayed for himself (15:15-16):

0 Lord, thou knowest: remember me, and visit me, and revenge me of my persecutors; take me not away in thy longsuffering: know that for thy sake I have suffered rebuke. Thy words were found, and I did eat them; and thy word was unto me the joy and rejoicing of mine heart: for I am called by thy name, 0 Lord God of hosts.

Because of Jeremiah's intimacy with God, and his knowledge of His ways, he did not fit into the evil clique of mockers and merry makers. He could not involve himself in their activities. Because God's hand was on him, he was alone.

Jeremiah continued to proclaim the words that God gave him. Just as he had been forewarned, his hearers remained stubborn and stiff necked. Following one message, we read the response by people in 18:8. They said: *Come, and let us devise devices against Jeremiah: for the law shall not perish from the priest, nor counsel from the wise, nor from the word from the prophet. Come and let us smite him with the tongue, and let us not give heed to any of his words.* They planned to use slander as a weapon against Jeremiah and he turned to the Lord with his lament (vss. 19-20):

Give heed to me, O Lord, and hearken to the voice of them that contend with me. Shall evil be recompensed for good? For they have digged a pit for my soul. Remember that I stood before thee to speak good for them, and to turn away thy wrath from them.

In the remainder of chapter 18, he called down imprecations on the land. Beginning in chapter 19, God gave Jeremiah a command to go and buy a potter's earthenware jar, then to take it out into the valley of Ben-hinnom. He was to stand by the potsherd gate and preach, saying: *Hear ye the word of the Lord, O kings of Judah, and inhabitants of Jerusalem; Thus saith the Lord of hosts, the God of Israel; Behold I will bring evil upon this place, because they have forsaken me.* His sermon continues with several accusations, such as: verse 5: *"They have built also the high Places of Baal."* It reaches a climax in verses 8 and 9, *"I will make this city desolate. I will cause them to eat the flesh of their sons and the flesh of their daughters."* This would happen because of the siege by Nebuchadnezzar against the city in 588, that would last for two years until 586, when the wall was breached (II Kings 25:1-4).

God instructed Jeremiah that when he had finished preaching, *"Then shalt thou break the bottle in the sight of the men that go with thee. Thus saith the Lord of hosts; Even so will I break this people and this city, as one breaketh a potter's vessel, that cannot be made whole again."* In chapter 20, Jeremiah recalls how when the priest, who was the chief officer in the temple, heard about this sermon, commanded that Jeremiah be beaten and put in stocks. When he was released the next day, Jeremiah said to him, *"The Lord hath not called thy name Pashur, but Magormissabib."* This name meant "terror on every side." This was prophetic because Jeremiah continued in verses 4-6:

For thus saith the Lord, Behold, I will make thee a terror to thyself, and to all thy friends: and they shall fall by the sword of their enemies, and thine eyes shall behold it: and I will give all Judah into the hand of the king of Babylon, and he shall carry them captive into Babylon, and shall slay them with the sword. Moreover I will deliver all the strength of this city, and all the labours thereof, and all the precious things thereof, and all the treasures of the kings of Judah will I give into the hand of their enemies, which shall spoil them, and take them, and carry them to Babylon. And thou, Pashur, and all that dwell in thine house shall go into captivity: and thou shalt come to Babylon, and there shalt thou die, and shalt be buried there, thou, and all thy friends, to whom thou hast prophesied lies.

In chapter 21, we learn that King Zedekiah sent messengers to Jeremiah to learn what was going to happen. The request which the king made to Jeremiah was (vs. 2): *Inquire, I pray thee, of the Lord for us; for Nebuchadnezzar king of Babylon maketh war against us; if so be that the Lord will deal with us according to all his wondrous works, that he may go up from us.* I am sure that Zedekiah knew the history of his nation and, for example, how Hezekiah had been saved from the invading Assyrians by turning to God through Isaiah. But, Jeremiah presented God's message that this time there would be no deliverance, because the Lord Himself was against them to punish them. Then he gave this counsel:

Behold, I set before you the way of life, and the way of death. He that abideth in this city shall die by the sword, and by the famine, and by the pestilence: but he that goeth out, and falleth to the Chaldeans that besiege you, he shall live, and his life shall be unto him for a prey.

The king and nation rejected Jeremiah's words for the way of life which God had presented; viz., surrender.

LXXXII. REJECTED AND PERSECUTED

The events of chapter 26 occur *"In the beginning of the reign of Jehoiakim."* This was in 609 B.C., although in the prophet's earlier years, the response of the leaders to his message even then, was as intense in its opposition as it would be later on. The Lord said to him in verse 2, *"Stand in the court of the Lord's house, and speak unto all the cities of Judah."* God encouraged and commanded him not to omit a word. Perhaps they would listen and everyone will turn from his evil way. But God said, *"You shall say to them that if they will not listen and turn from their evil ways, then will I make this house like Shiloh."* (vs. 6)

Kill the Prophet!

The priests and the professional prophets also, along with all the people, heard Jeremiah speak those words. When he brought this pronouncement of doom on them, they agreed together against him, saying (vss. 8-9): *Thou shalt surely die. Why hast thou prophesied in the name of the Lord, saying, this house shall be like Shiloh, and this city shall be desolate without an inhabitant? And all the people were gathered against Jeremiah in the house of the Lord.* When the leaders of the city heard what was going on, the princes assembled together from the palace and sat down in the gates as judges. The priests and prophets quickly accused Jeremiah saying, *"This man is worthy to die; for he hath prophesied against this city, and ye have heard with your ears."* (vs. 11)

Jeremiah's defense is in verses 12-15.

The Lord sent me to prophesy against this house and against this city all the words that ye have heard. Therefore now amend your ways and your doings, and obey the voice of the Lord your God, and the Lord will repent him of the evil that he hath pronounced against you. As for me, behold, I am in your hand: do with me as seemeth good and meet unto you. But know ye for certain, that if ye put me to death, ye shall surely bring innocent blood upon yourselves, and upon this city, and upon the inhabitants thereof- for of a truth the Lord hath sent me unto you to speak all these words in your ears.

The verdict of the princes, who were backed by the people, was, *"This man is not worthy to die: for he hath spoken to us in the name of the Lord our God."* They did not want to take any chances. Then certain ones of the elders added their viewpoint, saying,

Micah the Morashtite prophesied in the days of Hezekiah king of Judah, and spake to all the people of Judah, saying, Zion shall be plowed like a field, and Jerusalem shall become heaps, and the mountain of the house as the high places of a forest. Did Hezekiah king of Judah and all Judah put him at all to death? Did he not fear the Lord, and besought the Lord, and the Lord repented of the evil which he had pronounced against them.

The elders did not understand that Micah was *not* making that prophecy to Hezekiah for *his* time, but was prophesying the future destruction under Nebuchadnezzar which was soon to come. Those at Jeremiah's trial would soon be witnesses and captives. It was for them that Micah had made the prophecy. They misunderstood this, but at least their application was correct, because they assumed that Hezekiah responded properly to the preaching of Micah.

In chapter 27, Jeremiah became a participant in *pedagogy in biography*. God commanded him to make a yoke for his neck and to walk around wearing it. When the people asked him what the yoke was for, he was to say this:

I have given all these lands into the hand of Nebuchadnezzar the king of Babylon .And all nations shall serve him. And it shall come to pass, that the nations and kingdom which will not serve that same Nebuchadnezzar the king of Babylon, and that will not put their neck under the yoke of the king of Babylon, that nation will I punish, with the sword, and with the famine, and with the pestilence, until I have consumed them by his hand. Therefore hearken not ye to your prophets nor to your diviners, nor to your dreamers, nor to your enchanter, nor to your sorcerers, which speak unto you, saying, Ye shall not serve the king of Babylon: For they prophesy a lie unto you, to remove you far from your land, and that ye should perish. But the nations that bring their neck under the yoke of the king of Babylon, and serve him, those will I let remain still in their own land.

Jeremiah spoke these words to King Zedekiah, while imploring him to obey and *"Bring your necks under the yoke of the king of Babylon, and serve him and his people, and live. Why will ye die?"* (12-13a) His plea to the king and then to the priest, continues throughout the chapter; but still they did not heed. Jeremiah continued to walk around preaching while wearing the yoke on his neck. Chapter 28:1 introduces us, in the same year, to the "yes man" false prophet.

"Hananiah, the son of Azur the prophet, which was of Gibeon, spake unto me in the house of the Lord in the presence of the priests and of all the people. Thus speaketh the Lord of hosts, the God of Israel, saying, I have broken the yoke of the king of Babylon. Within two full years will I bring again into this place all the vessels of the Lord's house, that Nebuchadnezzar king of Babylon took away from this place and I will bring again to this place Jeconiah the son of Jehoiakim king of Judah, with all the captives of Judah that went into Babylon for I will break the yoke of the king of Babylon.

This was the message the people wanted to hear and which Jeremiah had denounced before. In verses 6-9 Jeremiah gave his reply:

Amen: the Lord do so: the Lord perform thy words which thou hast prophesied. Nevertheless hear thou now this word that I speak in thine ears. The prophets that have been before me and before thee of old prophesied both against many countries, and against great kingdoms. The prophet which prophesieth of peace, when the word of the prophet shall come to pass, then shall the prophet be known, that the Lord hath truly sent him.

When Hananiah heard this, he reached over and broke the yoke from Jeremiah's neck. Then, he used Jeremiah's broken yoke to demonstrate *his own* message, saying, *"Thus saith the Lord, even so will I break the yoke of Nebuchadnezzar from the neck of all nations within the space of two full years."* (vs. 11)

Jeremiah departed without his yoke; but God gave him some additional words for Hananiah. He first described the yokes of iron which would be on the necks of the nations brought under the power of Babylon. Then, He added a personal message for the false prophet (vss. 15, 16):

Hear now, Hananiah; the Lord hath not sent thee, but thou makest this people to trust in a lie. Therefore thus saith the Lord; Behold, I will cast thee from off the face of the earth: this year thou shalt die, because thou hast taught rebellion against the Lord.

The chapter concludes, *"So Hananiah the prophet died the same year in the seventh month."* The "yes man" false prophet died with along with his false message of hope.

Chapter 32 begins *"in the tenth year of Zedekiah king of Judah."* This was in 587 B.C.; during the siege, but just prior to when Nebuchadnezzar breached the wall of Jerusalem, in 586, ending the siege, destroying the city, and the temple. Zedekiah had put Jeremiah in prison because he prophesied that when the Babylonians invaded the city, the king would be taken captive. While he was imprisoned, God instructed him to buy a field at Anathoth. This was another object lesson, demonstrating the prophet's faith in God's assurance that there would be a time after the invasion and return from exile, when *"Houses and fields and vineyards shall be possessed again in this land."* (vs. 15) In chapter 33, while Jeremiah was still confined in prison, the word of the Lord came to him again.

God gave His prophet a wonderful promise, *"Call unto me, and I will answer thee, and shew thee great and mighty things, which thou knowest not."* Then, He gave Jeremiah a marvelous and descriptive revelation of the future restoration of Israel and of His faithfulness to the Davidic covenant. *Thus saith the Lord; again there shall be heard in this place, which ye say shall be desolate the voice of joy, and the voice of gladness, the voice of the bridegroom, and the voice of the bride, the voice of them that shall say, praise the Lord of hosts; for the Lord is good; for his mercy endureth forever.*

The destruction which Jeremiah dreaded would be temporary, because, the Lord continued (vss. 14, 15):

Behold, the days come. that I will perform that good thing which I have promised unto the house of Israel and to the house of Judah. In those days, and at that time, will I cause the Branch of Righteousness to grow up unto David, and he shall execute judgment and righteousness in the land.

Then, in verse 20, God reaffirmed the inviolability of His covenant:

If ye can break my covenant of the day, and my covenant of the night, and that there should not be day and night in their season; then may also my covenant be broken with David my servant, that he should not have a son to reign upon his throne.

Chapter 36 looks in flashback to the year 605, and reconstructs an event which took place in the fourth year of king Jehoiakim. The Lord instructed Jeremiah, *"Take thee a roll of a book, and write therein all the words that I have spoken unto thee."* Obediently, Jeremiah called in Baruch, his scribe and dictated to him all of the prophecies he had received. However, the religious leaders had excommunicated Jeremiah and banned him from the temple. Since he could not go, he instructed Baruch to go to the temple on a fast day, when there would be many people present, and read to them from the dictated scroll. He hoped, when they heard God's words, that *"They will present their supplication before the Lord, and will return everyone from his evil way."* Verse 8 reports that Baruch followed Jeremiah's instructions, and in verse 9:

In the fifth year of Jehoiakim, in the ninth month, they proclaimed a fast before the Lord to all the people in Jerusalem, and to all the people that came from the cities of Judah unto Jerusalem. Then read Baruch in the book the words of Jeremiah in the house of the Lord.

Micaiah, one of those who heard it read, reported these things to the princes and leading officials of the city, repeating the words which Baruch had read from Jeremiah's scroll. The city officials sent for Baruch and commanded him to read the scroll to them. Jeremiah's messages put such fear in their hearts, that their response was, *"We will surely tell the king."* They questioned Baruch intensely about how Jeremiah had dictated these words and how he had written them all down. They kept the scroll, to give to the king, and told Baruch that he and Jeremiah should run away and hide themselves in fear of the king's response. When Jehoiakim heard the officials' report, he sent for the scroll and had it read to Him. As he listened, he cut off each section and cast it into his fireplace. Verse 24 says, *"Yet they were not afraid, nor rent their garments, neither the king, nor any of his servants that heard all these words."*

As Jeremiah continued to preach and encourage his listeners to surrender to the Chaldeans, the officials became increasingly angry. Chapter 38:4 says that they *begged* the king to have him put to death for treason. They reported that he was discouraging the men of war and *"Seeketh not the welfare of this people, but the hurt."* The king replied, *"He is in your hand."* So, they took Jeremiah by force and dropped him down into a deep cistern. The cisterns were dug down in the courtyards of the wealthy people. They were lined with a plaster-like coating so that when it rained they would hold water, and the coated walls prevented seepage. However, if they were not cleaned out regularly, dust would blow in and eventually turn to mud when the water evaporated.

The cistern which was chosen as Jeremiah's dungeon had evidently not been used for a while, because when they lowered Jeremiah down into it with ropes, he sank into the mud. An Ethiopian took pity on him and received permission from the king to rescue him. Jeremiah was stuck in the mud so securely, that it required thirty men to pull him out. Verse 11 says they sent down worn out clothes and rags which Jeremiah used for padding under his arms when he tied the ropes around his chest which were used to pull him up. After this, he was kept in the court of the guardhouse.

Soon after this terrible experience in the cistern, King Zedekiah sent for Jeremiah to hear his counsel from the Lord. Jeremiah objected, saying that he knew the advice which he gave would not be heeded and that he would be put to death for giving it. The king swore to protect his life, so Jeremiah went to the king and repeated what he had said so often, viz., the way to spare the city and the lives of its inhabitants was to surrender to the Chaldeans. It seems that Zedekiah understood what Jeremiah was saying, but he was powerless to act because of his advisers. He commanded Jeremiah not to let anyone know that they had talked together, and gave him an alibi to use if their meeting did become known. It seems that even King Zedekiah was afraid of his officials. Did he fear assassination and a *coup*?

Chapter 39 describes the invasion of the city and the capture of Zedekiah. They killed his sons before his eyes, blinded him and took
him to Babylon where he later died. Nebuchadnezzar had heard of Jeremiah's encouragement to the people to surrender to them and gave orders to the captain of the guard, saying, *"Take him, and look well to him, and do him no harm; but do unto him even as he shall say unto thee. "* (39:12). Chapter 40 then relates how the captain freed him from his chains and gave him his choice between Babylon or anywhere he wished. The captain said he would be well treated. Even with these options, Jeremiah chose to remain in Jerusalem. Nebuchadnezzar appointed Gedaliah as governor over Judah, but as we read in chapter 41, he was slain by a man named Ishmael, a political zealot, who led an uprising. The people who were left in Judah decided to flee to Egypt in an attempt to escape the Babylonians. In revenge, they took Jeremiah with them by force because he had counselled them against going. (42-44)

Chapter 46 is a flashback to a time prior to the battle of Carchemish in 605. It records the prophecy of what happened to the Egyptians when they armed themselves to fight against the Babylonians. The remainder of the book of Jeremiah contains various prophecies regarding all of the surrounding nations. Finally, chapter 52 is an Historical Appendix which details some events to around 560 B.C. Verse 31 says that in the thirty-seventh year of the exile of Jehoiachin (who went into exile in 597) the king of Babylon showed favor to him, brought him out of prison, and gave him a regular allowance and portion of food for the remainder of his life. The parallel passage is in II Kings 25:27-30. This concludes the message of Jeremiah. In its historical context, the time span is from the thirteenth year of Josiah to approximately 560 B.C. in 52:31.

LXXXIII. HAGGAI'S MESSAGE OF MOTIVATION

We have studied all of the prophets who prophesied about the invasion of the Assyrians (to the kingdom of Israel), the invasion of the Babylonians (to the nation of Judah), the exile into Babylon and the release from Babylon. In Haggai and Zechariah, we find information detailing life in Judah in the latter part of the sixth century B.C. The people had been back in the land after the release by Cyrus, for almost twenty years. The temple had not yet been rebuilt, and the city walls around Jerusalem would not be rebuilt for another seventy-five years, under Nehemiah's leading in 444 B.C.

Two prophets, Haggai and Zechariah, were active just after the return of Zerubbabel, as recorded in the book of Ezra, but they prophesied before the returns of Ezra and of Nehemiah. Haggai is the second shortest book in the Old Testament; only Obadiah is shorter. Haggai contains four messages which were preached during four months, in the year 520 B.C., which was the second year of Darius, King of Persia. Because Cyrus had given instructions to the exiles to return to their homeland and rebuild the temple, the message of Haggai is one of exhortation, in an attempt to motivate the people to begin work on the temple. We studied previously how the work had been stalled after the initial foundation was laid. Now Haggai is on the scene to give them God's will and promise, *"From this day forward will I bless thee."* The seventy years of prophesied desolation for the temple had at long last ended.

Haggai's first message, which he preached in 520 B.C., in the sixth month (September-October), was that it is now time to begin work on the house of the Lord. Its central theme is *"Consider your ways."* Because they had been disobedient in this regard, God had brought judgment on their crops, and on everything they had put aside, as savings for the future. God said,

Ye have sown much, and being in little; ye eat, but ye have not enough; ye drink, but ye are not filled with drink; ye clothe you, but there is none warm; and he that earneth wages earneth wages to put it into a bag with holes.

In verse 7, He commanded again, *"Consider your ways."* He had been withholding blessings from them, but now He would shower them down if they would obey Him. *"Go up to the mountain, and bring wood, and build the house, and I will take pleasure in it, and I will be glorified, saith the Lord."* (vs. 8) God was saying, "Stop putting yourselves and your own houses first. Stop cheating Me and start building My house." In verse 14, Haggai's preaching was that the Lord stirred up the spirit of Zerubbabel the governor, and of Joshua the high priest, and all the people; *"And they came and did work in the house of the Lord of hosts, their God."* {See Ezra 6:14, 15. The date was March 12, 515 B.C.}

Haggai's second message begins in chapter 2. It was delivered in the same year, on the 21st day of the seventh month. It was addressed to Zerubbabel and began by pointing out that the temple he was building departed from the splendor of the temple built by Solomon. *"Who is left among you that saw this house in her first glory? And how do ye see it now? Is it not in your eyes in comparison of it as nothing?"* But this comparison in verse 3 is intended only as a prelude to the promise in verse 9: *"The glory of this latter house shall be greater than of the former, saith the Lord of hosts: and in this place will I give peace, saith the Lord of hosts.* "Why will it be so glorious? Because this temple, enlarged and beautified by Herod, {John 2:20} will be the one in which Jesus Christ taught.

Haggai 2:10ff contains the third message. It was delivered on the 24th day of the ninth month of the same year. In this third sermon, Haggai described the infectious nature of sin. Using an analogy taken from the law, he showed the people that just because they were living in the holy land, and were participating in the offerings and sacrifices, this did not make them acceptable to God as long as they remained personally unclean through disobedience.

Thus saith the Lord of hosts; Ask now the priests concerning the law, saying, If one bear holy flesh in the skirt of his garment, and with his skirt do touch Bread, or pottage, or wine, or oil, or any meat, shall it be holy? And the priests answered and said, no. Then said Haggai, If one that is unclean by a dead body touch any of these, shall it be unclean? And the priests answered and said it shall be unclean. Then answered Haggai, and said, so is this people, and so is this nation before me, saith the Lord; and so is every work of their hands; and that which they offer there is unclean.

Haggai showed that a man whose life was defiled by neglect of his responsibilities to God could not sanctify himself by mere outward conformity to ritual. The analogy he made was that just as contact with a dead body produced ceremonial uncleanness, until it was purged by the proper rites, even so, worship and offerings from disobedient people were defiled in

God's sight until they were purified by total obedience. A disobedient person is defiled in the sight of God and consequently every work of his hands is also defiled. Limited obedience in the form of sacrifices cannot cleanse or make holy a person who is disobedient to God's commands. And contrariwise, disobedience affects everything he offers and makes it unclean. Sin infects everything!

These priests, who heard Haggai's message, were conforming to outward ritual but were not obedient in their *hearts* to the Law of God. This principle has its New Testament equivalent in John 14:21, where the Lord Jesus said,

> *"He that hath my commandments, and keepeth them, he it is that loveth me: and he that loveth me shall be loved of my Father, and I will love him, and will manifest myself to him."*

Religion, or the outward symbols and rituals of religion, will not substitute for an obedient heart (I Sam. 15:22).

Haggai's fourth message begins in verse 20 and was also delivered on the 24th day of the month. It concerned Zerubbabel.

> *Speak to Zerubbabel, governor of Judah, saying, I will shake the heavens and the earth; In that day, saith the Lord of hosts, will I take thee, 0 Zerubbabel, my servant, the son of Shaltiel, saith the Lord, and will make thee as a signet. For I have chosen thee, saith the Lord of hosts.*

During the time of the exile, the continuity had been broken between the exilic and post-exilic people. The earlier promises were to the *pre-exilic* descendants of David. Haggai, in his fourth sermon, linked Zerubbabel to the Davidic Covenant, showing that through Zerubbabel, the descendents of David would continue without interruption. This is verified in Matthew 1:12, in the genealogy of Joseph, the husband of Mary, the mother of Jesus. In verse 12, we see that the lineage of Joseph is traced back through Zerubbabel and Solomon to David. God strengthened Zerubbabel in those critical days of responsibility and re-confirmed the Davidic Covenant to the post-exilic community.

There are critics who attack this book. They believe that Haggai was reviving the doctrine of an ideal king and had mistakenly identified Zerubbabel as the long-awaited Messiah. These critics use chapter 2:2-23 as their proof of the Messianic character ascribed to Zerubbabel, the prince of David's house. Because, in his second discourse, Haggai had announced the shaking of the nations of the earth, and he repeats the announcement in his fourth discourse, as if to link the two events together. Haggai promised that the shaking of the thrones of the kingdoms would pave the way for the establishment of the kingdom of God under the rule of the Messianic king Zerubbabel. So, according to these critics, subsequent history would prove that Haggai was in error when he erroneously centered his Messianic hopes on this descendant of David, named Zerubbabel, who would establish the kingdom of God. This erroneous conclusion has no historical basis for proof. It is another critical theory that is superimposed on the text of Haggai. Haggai is the inspired author.

We know that this portion of his book is Messianic, because other Messianic passages are found in his prophecies, such as in 2:7; the Desire of all nations; that is, the Messiah. What then is the true meaning of the passage? I believe that Haggai gave a message of consolation and hope. In Haggai's message, the Lord promised to establish Zerubbabel, who, although only a temporary ruler approved by the Persians, was also a descendent of David and an ancestor of the true Messiah. So, the chosen line of David was reconfirmed in Zerubbabel and was to remain intact even though the kingdoms of the earth would disappear.

LXXXIV. ZECHARIAH: PROPHET OF APOCALYPSE

Two months after the messages of Haggai began, the prophet Zechariah began to preach in Jerusalem. In 1:1 he tells us that the word of the Lord came to him in the eighth month of the second year of Darius. This was 520 B.C. From this we know that he began to receive his visions and messages during the revitalization movement to rebuild the temple. The differences between these two prophets appear to be that while Haggai's job was primarily to motivate the people to the outward physical task of rebuilding the temple; Zechariah, on the other hand, took up the prophetic end of the ministry and tried to motivate the people to a complete spiritual change. The prophecy of Haggai was primarily focused on the local historical situation as it affected the post-exilic community in Judah.

Chapters 1-8 consist of prophetic visions and chapters 9-14 contain assorted prophecies of the future. There are four divisions in the book: *First*, the introductory address (a call to repentance) is in 1:1-6. *Second*, is a series of eight visions which are followed by a symbolic transaction. These were all given to Zechariah in one night and although they had reference to the historical situation, they were also eschatological, extending to the latter days. These eight visions, and the symbolic transaction, are recorded in 1:7-6:15. *Third* is a message delivered in the fourth year of Darius. This was two years later than his first message and was an answer to the question of a deputation of men from Bethel. This is in chapters 7 and 8. *Fourth*, is a prophecy that was delivered later. It looks beyond the prophet's time and is totally eschatological. It deals with the future of Israel, the future of the Gentile world powers, and the Messianic Kingdom. These prophecies are in chapters 9-14.

This final eschatological division is divided into two parts. *Part One*, in chapters 9-11, is the burden of the word of Yahweh. There are two burdens which deal with the same subject matter. These are: the future judgment of the Gentile world powers, and the deliverance of Israel. In *Part Two* of the eschatological division, comprised of chapters 12-14, there is more detailed information about the manner in which the events announced in 9-11 are to take place.

Zechariah gives the most specific Messianic prophecies in the Old Testament. The most important aspects of Messiah, as presented by Zechariah, are: Christ as the Branch (3:8); Messiah as God's Servant (3:8); Messiah as the Shepherd (9:16; 11:11); Messiah as the smitten Shepherd (13:7); Messiah's entry into Jerusalem on a colt (9:9); Messiah's betrayal for thirty pieces of silver (11:12, 13); Messiah's pierced hands and feet (12:10); Messiah's return to the Mount of Olives (14:3-8); Messiah will remove iniquity (chapter 3); Messiah will unite the priesthood and kingship in His own Person (6:9-13); Messiah-King will be a suffering Servant (chapter 9); Messiah-Shepherd will be rejected by Israel (chapter 11); the death of the Shepherd (13:7); The conversion of Israel (chapter 13); and finally, the prophecy of the destruction of Israel's enemies, the salvation of Jerusalem, and the reign of the Messiah over the world from Zion. It is evident that the central theme of Zechariah's prophecies is to show that the restoration of Zion, the destruction of all the Gentile nations-Israel's old historic enemies, and the universal reign of the Messiah, Jesus Christ, will come to pass in God's time. In fact, the prophecy of Zechariah is to the Old Testament what the book of The Revelation is to the New Testament. It can be called the Apocalypse of the Old Testament.

Chapter 7 begins with an event which took place in 518 B.C., in the fourth year of Darius. The leaders of Bethel had sent a delegation to inquire from the priests and prophets whether or not they should weep and fast in the fifth month as they had done during many years before. An examination of II Kings 25:8, will show that this was a man made feast and fast, to commemorate the destruction of the house of the Lord by Nebuchadnezzar. The word of the Lord came to Zechariah telling him that he should ask, *"When ye fasted and mourned in the fifth and seventh month, even those seventy years, did ye at all fast unto me ?"* This was a man made observance of their calamity, not something established by God.

In verses 9-10, God continued speaking through Zechariah, saying,

Thus speaketh the Lord of hosts, saying, Execute true judgment, and shew mercy and compassions every man to his brother. And oppress not the widow, nor the fatherless, the stranger, nor the poor, and let none of you imagine evil against his brother in your heart.

In verse 7, Zechariah said that these words had been proclaimed by the former prophets much earlier when Jerusalem was inhabited and surrounded by prosperous cities. What had those people done with this same message? Verse 11 says that they had refused to listen they had stopped up their ears, and made their hearts like flint. As a result, *"They cried and I would not hear, saith the Lord of hosts."* He scattered them and the land became desolate.

In this way, and with this solemn illustration, Zechariah reminded the people that God expects true worship from the heart which is demonstrated by one's dealings with his fellow man, not outward ritual.

In 8:14-17, Zechariah applied the message to his own generation:

For thus saith the Lord of hosts; As I thought to punish you, when your fathers provoked me to wrath and I repented not, so again have I thought in these days to do well unto Jerusalem and to the house of Judah: fear ye not. These are the things that ye shall do; speak ye every man the truth to his neighbour; execute the judgment of truth and peace in your gates: and let none of you imagine evil in your hearts against his neighbour, and love no false oath: for all these are things that I hate, saith the Lord.

We read here that God expected the same things from the new post- exilic community that He had expected from the previous generation which He had to drive from the land because of their disobedience.

From his vantage point in the late sixth century B.C., Zechariah looked down through the centuries beyond our time to the Second Advent of the Messiah. This is a marvelous passage of Scripture. Zechariah 14' beginning with verse 1:

Behold, the day of the Lord cometh, and thy spoil shall be divided in the midst of thee. For I will gather all nations against Jerusalem to battle; and the city shall be taken, and the houses rifled, and the women ravished, and half of the city shall go forth into captivity, and the residue of the people shall not be cut off from the city. Then shall the Lord go forth, and fight against those nations, as when he fought in the day of battle. And his feet shall stand in that day upon the mount of Olives, which is before Jerusalem on the east, and the mount of Olives shall cleave in the midst thereof toward the east and toward the west, and there shall be a very great valley; and half of the mountain shall remove toward the north, and half of it toward the south.

Continuing in verses 16 & 17:

And it shall come to pass, that every one that is left of all the nations which came against Jerusalem shall even go up from year to year to worship the King, the Lord of hosts, and to keep the feast of tabernacles. And it shall be that whoso will not come up of all the families of the earth unto Jerusalem to worship the King, the Lord of hosts, even upon them shall be no rain.

Verses 20 & 21:

In that day shall there be upon the bells of the horses, HOLINESS UNTO THE LORD; and the pots in the Lord's house shall be like the bowls before the altar. Yea, every pot in Jerusalem and in Judah shall be holiness unto the Lord of hosts: and all they that sacrifice shall come and take of them, and seethe therein: and in that day there shall be no more Canaanite in the house of the Lord of hosts.

LXXXV. MALACHI: A PRELUDE TO SILENCE

Malachi, as the final prophet in the post-exilic community, brings to a close the one thousand years of prophetic revelation, which began with Moses in the years 1446 to 1406 B.C. The name, Malachi, means *angel*, or *my messenger*. It does not appear anywhere else in the Old Testament.

There are two generally accepted dates for the book. Some scholars favor a date of about 458 and the others prefer a date of about 433, or possibly a little later. 433 or later is more probable, because of the close agreement between Malachi and Nehemiah, in regard to the abuses which Nehemiah sought to correct (priestly behavior, no payment of tithes, neglect of the temple service, mistreating the Sabbath, mixed marriages). These similarities seem to indicate a close proximity in time. Certainly, the appeal by Malachi to observe the Law of Moses pre-supposes that Ezra had already been there to restore the law as recorded in Nehemiah 8-10. The condemnation by Malachi, of the unworthy sacrifices and unfaithfulness that the people exhibited in not bringing in the tithes, indicates that they were expected to provide for the sanctuary and the priests.

Contrariwise, in the time of Ezra, the government met the expenses of the temple (Ezra 7:15-24), but later in Nehemiah's day (10:32ff), provision was made by the people for the support of the temple. So, while Malachi condemns them, he also lets us see he was probably prophesying in the time period following Nehemiah, who visited Babylon in 433 B.C. (Nehemiah 13:6) Therefore, to put Malachi in his proper historical setting, assuming that he was prophesying in approximately 430 B.C., the people had been back in the land of Judah for over a hundred years. The temple was completed about eighty-five years previously, and the wall had been built for at least ten to fifteen years. Therefore, in the time of Malachi, the people were enjoying religious and political freedom. Nevertheless, they had not returned to God with their whole hearts. This is the central message of the book of Malachi.

"I have loved you, saith the Lord. Yet ye say, wherein hast thou loved us?" With these words, Malachi established the format which he will use throughout the book. God makes an indictment; the people dispute it; then the Lord points out the truth of the statement. The

behavior he condemns grows out of lack of respect, or fear, of the Lord. *"A son honoureth his father and a servant his master: if then, I be a father, where is mine honour? And if I be a master, where is my fear?"* You have despised My name, God points out, because you show no reverence for the sacrifices and offerings you bring to My altar. The sacrificial animals they brought were the blind, the lame, the sick, and those that had little or no market value. *"Offer it now unto thy governor,"* God says with some sarcasm. *"Will he be pleased with thee, or accept thy person?"*(1:8) The people would never risk insulting their rulers by such offerings but they dared to bring them to the Lord. By their attitude they said, "The table of the Lord is contemptible." The table of God was something to be despised. It would appear that the priests were so ungodly, that they did not even care that the people brought such unsuitable sacrifices, and their unconcern was reflected in the attitude of the people. They were bored with the ritual and the sacrificial system. *"Ye said also, Behold what weariness is it! And ye have snuffed at it."* (1: 13) They turned up their noses! They brought in sheep they had stolen, and animals which were torn, lame, and sick.

Verse 14 condemns the two-faced hypocrite. He was the person who vowed a prize male animal from his flock, in such a way that everyone would know about his piety and praise his generosity. Then, secretly, he would substitute a sickly sheep as his actual offering. *"Should I accept this of your hand? I am a great King, saith the Lord of hosts, and my name is dreadful among the heathen."* Because the priests were involved in this hypocrisy and corruption, God also rebuked them. Reminding them that He had chosen the tribe of Levi for the special service which was their privilege, He said in vs. 5, *"My covenant was with him of life and peace; and I gave them to him for the fear wherewith he feared me, and was afraid before my name."* This illustration described their ancestor Aaron, the first high priest, because he saw God's fire go forth and kill his two disobedient sons. (Lev. 10:1-5)

In 2:6, God lists four necessary facets of the priesthood. 1: The law of truth was in his mouth. 2: Unrighteousness was not found on his lips. 3: He walked with Me in peace and righteousness. 4: He turned back many from iniquity. Verse 8 continues to condemn the priests. *"Ye are departed out of the way, ye have caused many to stumble at the law, ye have corrupted the covenant of Levi."* The indictment ends with 2:17: *Ye have wearied the Lord with your words. Yet ye say, wherein have we weaned him? When ye say, every one that doeth evil is good in the sight of the Lord, and he delighteth in them; or, where is the God of judgment?* Malachi accused them of tempting God because, until that time, they had been getting away with it. They did not remember that God often reserves His wrath for a future time.

Chapter 3 begins with:

Behold, I will send my messenger, and he shall prepare the way before me. But who may abide the day of his coming? He is like a refiner's fire and like fullers' soap. He shall sit as a refiner and purifier of silver: and he shall purify the sons of Levi. Then shall the offering of Judah and Jerusalem be pleasant unto the Lord.

Verse 6 concludes, *"For I am the Lord, I change not; therefore ye sons of Jacob are not consumed.* "God states here that because He does not change, {His Immutability} He will continue to honor the Davidic Covenant. He continues to plead with them. *"From the days of your fathers you have gone away from mine ordinances. Return unto me, and I will return unto you."* Still, in their gross lack of understanding they asked, *"Wherein shall we return?"* *"You have robbed Me"* God said. They asked, *"Wherein have we robbed thee?"* They had robbed Him of tithes and offerings and therefore,

"Ye are cursed with a curse. Bring ye all the tithes unto the storehouse and I will pour you out a blessing that there shall not be room enough to receive it.

"You have spoken arrogant words against Me," God said. And they asked, *"What have we spoken against thee?"* But they had been saying, *"It is vain to serve God: and what profit is it that we have kept his ordinances?"* Yet even in that unheeding and scornful generation, there were among them those *"that feared the Lord, and that thought upon his name."* God remembered them also and promised them His blessing (3:16-18).

Chapter 4 is eschatological. Malachi said a day is coming when all that do wickedly, shall be stubble and burned with fire. *"But unto you that fear my name shall the Sun of righteousness arise with healing in his wings; and ye shall go forth, and grow up as calves of the stall."* In that day, the wicked will be as ashes under the feet of the righteous. Verses 4-6 are the concluding admonitions of God through Malachi. *Remember ye the Law of Moses my servant, which I commanded unto him in Horeb for all Israel, with the statutes and judgments. Behold, I will send you Elijah the prophet before the coming of the great and dreadful day of the Lord: And he shall turn the heart of the fathers to the children, and the heart of the children to their fathers, lest I come and smite the earth with a curse.*

These were God's final words to His people, for four hundred years, until John the Baptist came proclaiming, *"Prepare ye the way of the Lord."*

After Malachi: 400 B.C. to 4 B.C.

At the conclusion of Malachi the inter-Testamental period began. Many historical events transpired during this four hundred year period, which are important to the Bible student. Philip of Macedon was assassinated in 336 B.C. and was succeeded by his son Alexander the Great. Alexander destroyed Thebes in 335 B.C. He campaigned against Persia and defeated Darius at Issus in 333 B.C. He conquered Tyre and Jerusalem in 332 and defeated Darius in 331. Alexander occupied Babylon, Susa, and Persepolis in 330 B.C. In 326, after extending his empire to the Indus river, he was forced by his generals to turn back. He died in Babylon in 323 B.C. and his empire was partitioned among his generals. The Hellenistic period of Greek art began in 320 and extended until about 30 B.C. Alexander the Great had founded the port of Alexandria in 332, and Jewish trading centers were established in Egypt and Cyrene. It was in Alexandria, around the middle of the third century B.C., that the Hebrew Scriptures were translated into Greek, which resulted in the version which is named the *Septuagint* {seventy}. The Seleucids of Syria ruled Palestine until about 314 B.C. The Colossus of Rhodes was completed in 275 B.C. and was destroyed by an earthquake in 224 B.C. The Roman silver coin called the *denarius* was minted in 268 B.C., and the first public combat of gladiators took place in Rome in 264 B.C.

Looking back on the long sweep of history which we have studied, there is probably no better way to summarize it than quoting from Psalm 78:1-7.

Give ear, 0 my people, to my law; incline your ears to the words of my mouth. I will open my mouth in a parable: I will utter dark sayings of old: Which we have heard and known, and our fathers have told us. We will not hide them from their children, shewing to the generation to come the praises of the Lord, and his strength, and his wonderful works that he hath done. For he established a testimony in Jacob, and appointed a law in Israel, which he commanded our fathers, that they should make them known to their children: That the generation to come might know them, even the children which should be born; who should arise and declare them to their children; That they might set their hope in God, and not forget the works of God, but keep his commandments.

Then follows a long resume of all the wonderful things the Lord had done for His people beginning with the time He defeated the Egyptians and divided the Red Sea. With these reminders is the tragic litany of their faithlessness and disobedience, even while being the recipients of His numerous and continual blessings. The Psalm ends with a reminder of the kings He had given them, through whom would be the Messiah, the greatest blessing He could give. In verses 70-72

He chose David also his servant, and took him from the sheepfolds: from following the ewes, great with young he brought him to feed Jacob his people, and Israel his inheritance. So he fed them according to the integrity of his heart, and guided them by the skillfulness of his hands.

I trust these insights have uncovered fresh avenues of study which will help in your study, your preaching, and your teaching.

Finis

Made in the USA
Columbia, SC
09 August 2023

21428704R00288